M000005553

FORGOTTEN
LEGACY

President William McKinley,   Congressman George Henry White,
1896   ca. 1897

FORGOTTEN LEGACY

William McKinley, George Henry White, and the Struggle for Black Equality

BENJAMIN R. JUSTESEN

LOUISIANA STATE UNIVERSITY PRESS

BATON ROUGE

Published by Louisiana State University Press
www.lsupress.org

Manufactured in the United States of America
First printing

Designer: Mandy McDonald Scallan
Typeface: Sentinel

Jacket photograph: President McKinley at Southern University, New Orleans, May 1901.
Courtesy Louisiana State Museum.
Frontispiece of William McKinley courtesy Courtney Art Studio; frontispiece of
George Henry White courtesy Odessa Spaulding.

· Library of Congress Cataloging-in-Publication Data

Names: Justesen, Benjamin R., 1949– author.
Title: Forgotten legacy : William McKinley, George Henry White, and the
 struggle for black equality / Benjamin R. Justesen.
Other titles: William McKinley, George Henry White, and the struggle for
 black equality
Description: Baton Rouge : Louisiana State University Press, [2020] |
 Includes bibliographical references and index.
Identifiers: LCCN 2020013978 (print) | LCCN 2020013979 (ebook) | ISBN
 978-0-8071-7385-5 (cloth) | ISBN 978-0-8071-7462-3 (pdf) | ISBN 978-0-8071-7463-0
 (epub)
Subjects: LCSH: McKinley, William, 1843–1901—Relations with African
 Americans. | McKinley, William, 1843–1901—Friends and associates. |
 White, George H. (George Henry), 1852–1918. | African
 Americans—Politics and government—19th century. | United States—Race
 relations—Political aspects—19th century. | African Americans—Legal
 status, laws, etc.—History—19th century. | African Americans—Civil
 Rights—History—19th century. | United States—Politics and
 government—1897–1901. | African American postmasters—History—19th
 century. | Postmasters—Selection and appointment—United
 States—History—19th century.
Classification: LCC E711.6 .J87 2020 (print) | LCC E711.6 (ebook) | DDC
 973.8/8—dc23
LC record available at https://lccn.loc.gov/2020013978
LC ebook record available at https://lccn.loc.gov/2020013979

To my beloved grandchildren
Sloane, Kaylen, and Dean Spencer

May you always learn more from history.

CONTENTS

1901

Illustrations follow page 156

ACKNOWLEDGMENTS

Much of any historian's research requires a constant struggle to ensure complete accuracy in citations and footnotes. Without the capable guidance of many reference librarians—particularly those in the Library of Congress reading rooms, and in the National Archives—I would not have discovered much of what I learned during the seven years I spent working on this manuscript. They are too numerous to name, but they are all greatly appreciated.

For Vince Spaulding, who never stopped encouraging me to write just one more book about George Henry White, I offer my sincere thanks for the decade of friendship and more we have shared.

For Rand Dotson and his staff at LSU Press, I offer my warmest appreciation for helping fashion my unwieldy manuscript into something far more presentable.

For my eagle-eyed copy editor, Susan Murray, I have only the highest praise. Your patience was extraordinary, and your advice most helpful.

For my dear wife, Margaret, who helped me get through the process in ways large and small, there are no words to express my gratitude.

I have dedicated this book to my three grandchildren, in the hope that they will take away something of permanent worth in reading the history I have attempted to record here.

NOTABLE AFRICAN AMERICAN FIGURES DURING THE MCKINLEY ERA

Adams, John Q.: journalist of Minnesota; publisher of the Appeal.

Anthony, Colin: North Carolina county commissioner, GOP leader; named postmaster of Scotland Neck, 1897, but rejected by the U.S. Senate, 1898.

Arnett, Bishop Benjamin W.: AME clergyman from Ohio; major adviser to McKinley; active in National Afro-American Council.

Baker, Frazier B.: South Carolina schoolteacher; U.S. postmaster in Lake City, South Carolina, 1897; murdered by lynch mob, 1898.

Bruce, Blanche K.: former U.S. senator from Mississippi; GOP leader; register of the Treasury, 1897.

Calloway, Thomas J.: educator, lawyer, and college president from Tennessee; U.S. special agent to Paris International Exposition, 1899.

Chase, W. Calvin: GOP leader; attorney from Washington, D.C.; publisher of Washington Bee.

Cheatham, Henry P.: former GOP congressman from North Carolina; recorder of deeds for the District of Columbia, 1897.

Cooper, Edward E.: Washington, D.C., publisher of Colored American.

Cox, Minnie M.: Mississippi schoolteacher and GOP leader; postmaster of Indianola, 1897.

Dancy, John C.: religious journalist from North Carolina; active Republican leader; collector of customs for Wilmington port, 1897.

Deas, Edmund H.: GOP leader; deputy internal revenue collector for South Carolina, 1897.

Fortune, T. Thomas: New York journalist; publisher of New York Age; officer in National Afro-American Council, 1898.

Green, John P.: lawyer; former GOP state senator from Ohio; U.S. postage stamp agent, 1897.

Hargett, Israel D.: North Carolina schoolteacher; postmaster of Rocky Mount, 1897.

Havis, Ferdinand: Arkansas businessman; GOP activist; named postmaster of Pine Bluff, 1898, but rejected by US Senate.

Howard, John: North Carolina schoolteacher; postmaster of Weldon, 1898.

Knox, George L.: Indiana GOP leader and journalist, publisher of Indianapolis Freeman.

Langston, John Mercer: former congressman from Virginia; GOP leader.

Lee, Joseph E.: lawyer and GOP leader from Jacksonville, Florida; deputy collector of customs and deputy internal revenue collector for Florida, 1898.

Loftin, Isaiah: Georgia schoolteacher; U.S. postmaster in Hogansville, Georgia, 1897; shot and wounded, 1897.

Lynch, John Roy: lawyer, former GOP congressman from Mississippi; paymaster in U.S. Army, 1898.

Lyons, Judson W.: lawyer, GOP national committeeman from Georgia; register of the Treasury, 1898.

Manly, Alexander: North Carolina journalist; editor until 1898 of Wilmington Daily Record; then editor of Washington (D.C.) Daily Record, 1899.

McGhee, Frederick L.: lawyer and Democratic leader from Minnesota; member of National Afro-American Council.

Murray, George W.: former congressman from South Carolina; businessman; and GOP leader.

Parker, James B.: journalist and constable from Georgia; prevented third shot by tackling William McKinley's assassin, Leon Czolgosz, at Pan-American Exposition in Buffalo, New York, 1901.

Pinchback, Pinckney B. S.: former Louisiana governor and businessman; GOP leader.

Pledger, William A.: attorney and journalist of Atlanta, Georgia; active member of National Afro-American Council.

Powell, William Frank: GOP leader and schoolteacher from New Jersey; U.S. minister to Haiti, 1897.

Rucker, Henry A.: GOP leader from Atlanta, Georgia; collector of internal revenue for Georgia, 1897.

Smalls, Robert: former congressman from South Carolina; GOP leader; collector of customs for Beaufort, 1897.

Smith, Harry C.: Ohio journalist and GOP state legislator; publisher of Cleveland Gazette.

Smith, Rev. Owen L. W.: AME Zion clergyman from North Carolina; U.S. minister to Liberia, 1898.

Vick, Samuel H.: North Carolina schoolteacher, businessman, GOP leader; postmaster of Wilson, 1898.

Walters, Bishop Alexander: AME Zion clergyman from New Jersey; first president of National Afro-American Council, 1898.

Washington, Booker T.: Alabama educator; head of Tuskegee Institute; adviser to McKinley.

Wells-Barnett, Ida B.: influential Illinois journalist; editor of Chicago Conservator; secretary and head of antilynching bureau for National Afro-American Council.

Wright, Richard R., Sr.: Georgia educator; active Republican; president of State College of Industry for Colored Youth, Savannah; named paymaster general in U.S. Army, 1898.

Young, James Hunter: North Carolina GOP leader; publisher of Raleigh Gazette; colonel in Third North Carolina regiment, Spanish-American War, 1898.

FORGOTTEN
LEGACY

INTRODUCTION

The President and His Prophet

At best, they were an unlikely pair: a dignified white midwestern governor known for political skills and fatherly demeanor, and a spellbinding black orator and teacher whose success as a prosecutor belied roots as a field hand in rural southern swamps. Only in the unpredictable world of American politics could two such strange bedfellows ever become acquainted as equals. In the turbulent post-Reconstruction era of U.S. history, that their paths crossed at all remains almost unthinkable a century later; that they came to know and trust each other against the hardening backdrop of Jim Crow–era segregation and political violence seems more the plot of a fictional novel than real history.

Almost inevitably, the little-known alliance between William McKinley and George Henry White failed at a critical time, doomed by political currents neither could control in a four-year relationship defying the usual rules of U.S. politics. Yet even as their alliance unraveled, they shared a bond transcending differences in background and status. In the year their paths first crossed, McKinley—called "the Major," for his wartime rank—was the Republican nominee for U.S. president, while the younger White was an upstart Republican candidate for Congress from a state McKinley strategists hoped to carry in the fall.

Over the next two years, their unparalleled relationship would deepen and mature as they worked with each other on a surreal joint mission: advancing the lot of America's most talented African Americans at a time when most blacks were being deprived of political rights and steadily squeezed out of citizenship. Before their relationship succumbed to intransigent political reality in 1900, McKinley and White would quietly manage, in plain sight, to appoint the largest number of black officeholders at one time in U.S. history to date and begin a modest rewrite of the rules governing racial segregation in the U.S. military.

1

In retrospect, McKinley's role as a sincere friend and benefactor of African Americans may be among the best-kept secrets of American political history. His views on race have been largely downplayed or overlooked by biographers, who refer sparingly to McKinley's actions on racial equality issues—mostly prepresidential, often reflecting only personal distaste for segregation. Writing in an era before racial justice was a popular theme, Margaret Leech says almost nothing to indicate more than minor sympathy on McKinley's part in her widely acclaimed 1959 biography, *In the Days of McKinley*.[1]

More recently, in the most generous assessment yet of McKinley's progressive nature and actions, Kevin Phillips gives a refreshingly revisionist analysis, dubbing him "Surprisingly Modern McKinley" for his quiet devotion to women's suffrage and equity for African Americans.[2] Yet even Phillips steps back from portraying McKinley more expansively: "Beyond the usual Republican administration's quota of federal jobs for blacks, McKinley did not do much. The contrary national tide was strong," he writes, although his successors Theodore Roosevelt and Woodrow Wilson fare far worse by comparison.[3] Still, Phillips portrays McKinley's racial policy more favorably than does Robert Merry, who describes McKinley's vaguely hypocritical and "patronizing attitude toward African Americans—lamenting their tragic fate, and cheering them on as they struggled against it" but offering little concrete assistance.[4]

The Major's friendship with Ohio legislator and religious leader Bishop Benjamin Arnett—called "the most powerful individual Negro at the White House" during McKinley's first term—is given no real importance by either biographer.[5] His closer relationship with former Mississippi congressman John Roy Lynch—a lawyer and savvy adviser whose opinion McKinley genuinely valued—is barely mentioned by Leech or Phillips, emerging only in Lynch's obscure memoir.[6] Almost inexplicably, McKinley's growing admiration for Booker T. Washington—whose Tuskegee Institute he visited with his cabinet during late 1898—seems lost compared to Washington's more active relationship with Theodore Roosevelt, in whose vigorous shadow McKinley is so often lost.

Even Bancroft Prize–winning historian Louis Harlan, Washington's biographer, relegates McKinley's Tuskegee visit to the level of campaign caricature, citing its "considerable symbolic significance" but slyly lumping it with "visits of the millionaires," playing up Washington's accommodationist plea for racial peace as based on second-class status for most blacks.[7] And among black historians who could well have given McKinley the benefit of the doubt for sincerity, Rayford Logan instead lambastes McKinley and his "callous disregard for the constitutional rights of Negroes," in a chapter titled "The Nadir under McKinley."[8] His grudging admission that McKinley deserved credit for "continuing the practice of appointing a few Negroes to federal positions in the South" seems almost an afterthought, buried under an avalanche of angry criticisms of McKinley's reticence on disfranchisement and failure to act on lynching.

Fleshing out McKinley's views on racial justice and advancement is therefore complicated. His parents, ardent abolitionists, bequeathed their son a passionate sympathy for victimized black slaves. His eventual belief that freed blacks deserved citizenship was undeniably catalyzed by his Civil War service. If there is no clear evidence he witnessed black soldiers in action, he certainly afterward espoused the cause of black suffrage, perhaps on personal principle: black soldiers who fought for their country were morally entitled to vote. The Major must have admired Ohio's black citizens' early contributions to war efforts in Cincinnati as the so-called Black Brigade, building fortifications defending against Confederate attack. After 1863, more than five thousand African American Ohioans fought as Union soldiers, first as the Twenty-Seventh Ohio Volunteer Infantry, recruits raised in 1863, then renamed the Fifth United States Colored Troops and 178th U.S. Colored Troops in 1864.[9]

McKinley's first public support for black suffrage came in 1867, during speeches in Rutherford Hayes's successful gubernatorial campaign, McKinley's first foray into politics. That year's controversial Ohio constitutional amendment favored black suffrage ahead of its national constitutional mandate; whether Hayes supported the unsuccessful amendment as fervently as his protégé is doubtful. After serving as Ohio governor, the dark-horse Republican presidential nominee in 1876 won election only by trading with southern electors offering winning electoral votes in exchange for ending Reconstruction.

Hayes, to his credit, steadfastly maintained his support for black southern voters, regularly opposing efforts to weaken federal laws but taking no extraordinary measures to protect against inevitable state restrictions. Curiously, Logan offers some faint praise for the Hayes position, if far less than for that of his protégé McKinley.[10]

McKinley's enthusiasm for progressive causes was not dampened by defeat in 1867. A longtime advocate of voting rights for women, he and his wife hosted Victoria Woodhull, presidential candidate of the Equal Rights Party in 1872 in Canton, Ohio. Much of the impetus for that event may have come from his wife's family, many of whom favored women's suffrage. Early attempts to give women full voting rights in Ohio failed, although women there won school board suffrage in 1894, and Ohio was later the fifth state to ratify the national amendment allowing full suffrage.

The two suffrage causes were not closely linked, and there is no evidence the McKinleys ever entertained black visitors or mixed socially in interracial circles. Yet this future president scorned the discrimination faced by black constituents, both in a brief term as a county prosecutor and later as a private attorney; after his election to Congress in 1876, he pointedly refused to stay in hotels that would not admit black patrons in Cincinnati and New Orleans.[11] By the 1880s, even as much of the South began revoking the political rights of black voters, McKinley's principled views on black suffrage were instead reinforced by alliance with Rep. William Kelley of Pennsylvania, a congressional supporter of black suffrage since Radical Reconstruction.

If he encountered only a few blacks personally during formative years—the 1860 census, when McKinley was seventeen, shows just 80 free blacks among Trumbull County's 30,000 residents—he would gradually encounter black citizens on an increasingly large scale in the years between military service and Congress. His wife's native Stark County, in which McKinley won his first elected office (county prosecutor) in 1869, and where he practiced law in the 1870s, was larger but marginally less white (0.5 percent nonwhite by 1880, compared to 2.4 percent statewide).

Even Ohio's largest cities had yet to attract significant black populations; by 1890, just before McKinley became governor, Franklin County—surrounding Columbus—was home to roughly 4,000 black residents, of more than 80,000 overall, second only to Cincinnati's Hamilton County (10,000 of 300,000). But by 1890, McKinley had spent more than a decade in Washington, D.C., where blacks accounted for one-fifth of the population. By the end of McKinley's first term as president, in 1900, the capital boasted the nation's largest-single urban concentration of black residents: 86,000, nearly one-third of its population.

As Ohio's governor from 1891 to 1895, McKinley quietly courted black votes, building a strong network of informal black advisers in a state where black legislators served in all but one General Assembly session after 1880—

as many as three members during McKinley's second term, a record outside the South.[12] Bishop Arnett, McKinley's close friend and trusted adviser, lost reelection in the 1880s for helping to abolish racially segregated schools in Ohio and rankling his predominantly white constituency. Out of office for a decade when McKinley became president, Arnett remained an imposing figure among Ohio's black voters, one on whom McKinley depended to secure black votes during the 1896 campaign: the first time U.S. black leaders could arguably claim that black votes had enabled a president's election—by cementing victories in Ohio and to the east, in New Jersey and Pennsylvania.

Although regarded as McKinley's most influential African American adviser, Arnett was just one of those on whom the president's small circle would now begin to call on for advice in matters of race. Booker T. Washington, not yet the gatekeeper of the Roosevelt era, was nevertheless a useful contact and second-tier adviser. Among black leaders in Washington, D.C., two Mississippians—John Roy Lynch and Blanche Bruce—became reliable sources of information and confidential conduits of information, often meeting directly with McKinley or with his trusted handler Mark Hanna. Both Lynch and Bruce served with McKinley in Congress, and Lynch's publicly expressed admiration for McKinley was politically beneficial.[13]

Lynch also admired the political skills of McKinley's trusted adviser.[14] From 1895 on, well before McKinley's election as president, Hanna carefully cultivated McKinley's back-channel ties to African Americans in an inspired but delicate dance, of which Hanna was a masterful choreographer. For most blacks, the experience since 1884 had been a long downward spiral. As their importance faded, fewer black Republicans could expect appointments, and as fewer blacks were appointed, fewer blacks felt loyal to the party of Lincoln.

By the mid-1890s, fewer blacks could vote in the South, where new obstacles had decimated their numbers in most states. Worse, Republican leaders were often powerless to reward those who still voted, since patronage—the award of federal offices to rank-and-file voters—was often limited unless one party controlled both houses of Congress. More than anyone else, Hanna seems to have understood and channeled anxieties felt by southern black leaders, building on that as he positioned his candidate on a path toward the White House. Masterful machinations by Hanna at Saint Louis, however, began two years earlier in Thomasville, Georgia, just before McKinley left Ohio's governorship.

&

As their personal friend for years, Hanna opened his Cleveland home to the McKinleys whenever possible, missing no opportunity to nudge McKinley forward politically. The wealthy businessman's winter home in Thomasville became a proving ground for candidate McKinley, who visited Georgia in mid-March 1895 as Hanna's guest, ostensibly for Mrs. McKinley's health. But the trip was hardly a vacation, for McKinley soon began receiving delegations of southern Republican leaders, including an all-important black component.[15]

"No color line was drawn. Negroes as well as white men were introduced to the amiable Mr. McKinley," journalist Herbert Croly wrote in a posthumous biography of Hanna.[16] It was hardly a surprise that black leaders—among the nation's most loyal Republicans—would make the pilgrimage; the novelty, as Eric Rauchway notes, was the presence of so many white Republican leaders in this Democratic stronghold.[17] From Thomasville, the governor journeyed east to Savannah to meet with fifty prominent black leaders, then to Jacksonville, Florida, where he held a controversial meeting in his hotel suite with seventy-five black leaders, led by Joseph Lee, secretary of Florida's Republican state committee.[18] During a visit to Washington, D.C., in April 1895, McKinley next met with his longtime friend John Roy Lynch, easily gaining Lynch's support.[19]

By the time Republicans met in Saint Louis fifteen months later, Hanna and McKinley had virtually assured a first-ballot victory over opponent Thomas Reed, in part by winning favorable votes from almost every African American convention delegate, almost one-tenth of the total. In 1896, the District of Columbia and at least twelve states—all but one in the South—sent one or more black delegates and alternates to the nominating convention; other states named black alternates on all-white delegations. Hanna, McKinley's campaign manager, was clearly "the power behind the throne" in 1896.[20] Determined to obtain a quick nomination, Hanna negotiated directly and indirectly with wavering delegates, including blacks favoring silver coinage, rather than the strict gold standard favored by most delegates, and he was comfortable courting support from both veterans and newcomers.

Although delegates are rarely identified by race in most convention records, analysis of official lists of delegates and alternates identified 74 of 924 voting delegates in 1896 as African American, nearly 8 percent. At least 59 alternates, from eleven midwestern and northeastern states and Arizona Territory, were also African Americans.[21] The practice was not new, merely resurgent: black delegates attended every Republican convention after 1864, almost all as southern delegates.

Perhaps the best-known black voting delegates in Saint Louis were ex-congressman Robert Smalls of South Carolina; former judge Mifflin Gibbs and businessman Ferd Havis of Arkansas; Georgia party chairman William Pledger; and Mississippi's national committeeman James Hill, each attending his fifth national convention. Other veteran power brokers in 1896 included Joseph Lee of Florida, Edmund Deas of South Carolina, and Perry Carson of Washington, D.C. (fourth convention); Madison Vance and ex-senator Henry Demas of Louisiana and Judson Lyons of Georgia (third appearances); and Henry Rucker and Monroe Morton of Georgia (second appearances).[22] Influential alternates included Ohio's ex-senator John Green, Dr. Samuel Courtney of Massachusetts, ex-congressman Thomas Miller, future state legislator Caleb Simms of New York, Indianapolis publisher George Knox, and veteran Louisiana activist James Lewis.[23]

There were first-timers, of course, and among the fresher faces in Saint Louis was that of North Carolina's George Henry White, newly minted Republican nominee for Congress in the "Black Second," North Carolina's Second District, who earned barely a mention in most convention coverage. Neither White nor Lyons was widely known outside his own state, yet both men were successful lawyers, clearly leaders deemed by both Hanna and Lodge to make a great difference for either candidate. White was named to the Committee on Rules and Order of Business as its only black member, a signal honor.[24]

If Hanna's courtship of veterans and newcomers was ridiculed in newspaper cartoons—such as the watermelon-cutting "Br'er Hanna" depicted on the front page of the *St. Louis Post-Dispatch* on June 15, 1896—he was facing a growing black insurgency, fueled by supporters of Tom Reed and Sen. Henry Cabot Lodge.[25] After conferring with black leaders from four states, Lodge declared that "colored Southern delegates have been badly treated by the McKinley managers. They were promised very great consideration, and given none."[26]

The predicted flood to Reed never materialized; Hanna worked overtime to soothe ruffled feelings and reassure a larger group of black leaders, including delegates—among three hundred meeting on June 15 in a local church—who sought inclusion of an antilynching plank in the party platform, among key demands.[27] The convention's antilynching plank swayed most black delegates, and McKinley won the nomination on the first ballot, sweeping past Reed and other opponents.

Still, Hanna alienated some blacks by helping to unseat the anti-McKinley Texas delegation—led by veteran Norris Cuney—and seating a pro-McKinley alternate slate with fewer black members. Other black delegates left Missouri unhappy with the party's new gold plank, as the *Raleigh (N.C.) News and Observer* speculated, but were philosophical in defeat. "All but five of us voted against the money plank in the platform," George White told that newspaper's correspondent on the train, "but when it came to the adoption of the platform we had to take it as a whole."[28]

Black leaders who had long supported successful Republican presidential nominees—from Garfield in 1880 to Harrison in 1888 and 1892—were hardly naïve in supporting McKinley in 1896. For ten of the past twelve years, America's black voters had already experienced life in a political wilderness, nationally; the chance to help reverse that tide in 1896 was irresistible, for practical and idealistic reasons. If motivated primarily by desires for patronage, they were also encouraged by cynical white party leaders offering psychological reinforcement, but little else.

The truth was that as the nineteenth century neared its end, black support was becoming far less important—or necessary—for Republicans to win nationally. Nowhere was the increasing marginalization of black votes better reflected than in dwindling numbers in Congress. Never large since Reconstruction, the number of elected black representatives had declined to just one in the Fifty-Third and Fifty-Fourth Congresses: South Carolina's two-term Rep. George Murray, defeated for reelection that fall.[29] Black state legislators, by contrast, were confined mostly to the Upper South and Midwest.[30]

His own symbolic importance was not lost on White. At forty-four, the mixed-race North Carolina native had risen in spectacular fashion from rural poverty: college graduate, teacher, accomplished lawyer, legislator, two-term elected prosecutor, and vigorous orator. His 1894 attempt to win the "Black Second" District's Republican nomination had pitted him against his brother-in-law Henry Cheatham, an ex-congressman awarded the nomination by national arbitrators after a convention deadlock but unable to win the general election. White reemerged in 1896 to vanquish Cheatham—making his fifth try at the nomination—to become the new national face of North Carolina's black-majority Republican Party.

White's résumé was distinctive and impressive. No black North Carolina predecessor in Congress had served in both houses of the state legislature or won election to any other state-level office; eight years as a district solicitor had burnished White's image as a serious contender. Selection as a traveling speaker in McKinley's fall campaign—both in North Carolina and beyond—was another important sign of favor by party elders. Such junkets quickly elevated White to the company of better-known black colleagues, such as John Roy Lynch, John Mercer Langston, and Blanche Bruce, as well as Ohio's ubiquitous John Green, who recalled traveling with White in "several campaigns." Speeches made by White made on McKinley's behalf are not listed but probably included Ohio, Tennessee, Virginia, and West Virginia.[31]

Thus White's political pedigree seemed almost tailor-made for success under McKinley. That they would become early allies—perhaps even personal friends—seemed preordained by party leaders, if not by divine providence. Yet their personal, political, and professional backgrounds had discernible differences beyond race. McKinley had grown up in a large family, with six full siblings. White had been born into a smaller family core—one known half brother, two half sisters—but was raised by his stepmother, who married his father when he was a toddler. White was a graduate of Howard University's Normal Department, whereas McKinley had studied at two different colleges without receiving a degree. McKinley had grown up in a comfortable middle-class midwestern environment; White came from a rural southern agricultural environment, laboring on his free working-class family's turpentine farm. McKinley was a field officer in the Civil War; White never served in the military.

As head of the nation's majority party, the Major was far better known nationally. Before becoming president, McKinley served six terms in Congress, including one term as chairman of the House Ways and Means Committee. He had most recently served twice as Ohio's governor and once as a county prosecutor. He had also lost reelection twice—once as prosecutor in 1869 and once to Congress in 1890, when Democrats gerrymandered him out of his district.

Although well known in eastern North Carolina, White was hardly recognized beyond its borders, except by black journalists and Republican strategists, and was only a celebrity—a household name in communities whose residents subscribed to any major black weekly newspapers—during his congressional campaign. At home, his legislative service and two terms as state prosecutor serving a six-county area had groomed him well. He had never lost a reelection bid, although he had once failed to win a state senate seat, and twice lost party nominations for offices he later won. An affluent lawyer, he had a flourishing private practice.

By appearance, the two men were noticeably different, although both were barrel-chested and tended toward stoutness. White was taller—a shade under six feet in height, compared to McKinley's five-foot, seven-inch stature—and heavier, weighing well in excess of McKinley's two hundred pounds. McKinley's fair complexion and blue-gray eyes revealed a pure Caucasian heritage, whereas White's far darker complexion, sometimes described as "bright copper," revealed racial admixtures (white, black, and Native American). McKinley was clean-shaven; White wore a moustache. Their obvious differences in background, national exposure, and physical appearance aside, the president and the congressman shared a surprising number of similarities, common characteristics likely to breed temperamental and emotional compatibility as they came to know each other in early 1897.

Both men had recently lost their fathers; McKinley's, for whom he was named, died in 1892; White's father died a year later. Both men were strongly devoted to female parents: White's stepmother and McKinley's mother, both still alive in early 1897. McKinley had lost both of his daughters before age four; White's youngest daughter had died early, although he still had two older daughters and a younger son. Their attractive wives offered unexpected similarities: both were well educated with work experience before marriage, Ida McKinley in her father's bank after attending a finishing school, and Cora Lena White as a schoolteacher after graduating from normal college. Both now struggled with significant health issues. Mrs. McKinley, an epileptic, was already a semi-invalid, although her illness was not public knowledge; her frequent public appearances were always attended by her doting husband. Cora Lena, seventeen years younger than Ida, had been frail since her last pregnancy; after an apparent nervous breakdown in 1898, she was a near-recluse during White's second term in Congress. She would die at age forty in early 1905, followed two years later by Mrs. McKinley.

Both president and congressman were active Masons and good speakers with strong, clear voices; both worked as teachers before practicing law. Successful lawyers before Congress, both dressed conservatively and impeccably, preferring to be photographed almost exclusively in vested suits. Both combined on-the-job training under established attorneys with law studies in a formal college setting and passed the state bar on their first attempt. Both were Protestants: McKinley was a Methodist; White, a Presbyterian. Both entered Republican politics at an early age, McKinley at twenty-six, White at twenty-seven.

Yet their most telling similarity—one that helped cement mutual trust—was unbridled idealism. Despite years of political trench warfare, both men embodied a stubborn devotion to honesty and personal integrity setting them apart from both average politicians and political bosses of the age. Both retained a certain childlike innocence—almost naïveté—in the face of political expediency, leaving them unprepared for the consequences of painful decisions forced by circumstance and competing agendas.

As optimists in a largely cynical world, they were victims of enduring disappointments that men of lesser character or a less sensitive nature might shrug off. That their friendship took root at all, perhaps, is more surprising than its inevitable collapse. Born of political opportunity rather than more lasting social or personal factors, this noble alliance had little chance of withstanding adversity. Despite their personal commitments to racial equity and justice, neither man could long withstand the political pressures raging around them, forcing them backward while they struggled to move forward.

This account of the two men's brief and complicated alliance, from hopeful beginning to bittersweet end, offers a cautionary tale of inevitable conflict between political hopes and reality. The charismatic president was ambushed by competing political battles on two fronts; the dynamic congressman gradually assumed the role of public conscience of his increasingly oppressed race. The chronicle of their years together in Washington from 1897 to 1901 provides unusual insights into their public politics and private dreams.

1897

1

WASHINGTON BEGINNINGS

The constituted authorities must be cheerfully and vigorously upheld. Lynchings must not be tolerated in a great and civilized country like the United States; courts, not mobs, must execute the penalties of the law.
—**President William McKinley**, March 4, 1897

Margaret Leech's bare-bones description of President McKinley's swearing-in on March 4, 1897, mentions only the Bible used by the new president, not its unusual origin: "Chief Justice Melville Fuller moved forward. The clerk held up the big gilt-edge Bible, and in a clear, solemn voice William McKinley repeated the oath."[1] Thoughtfully arranged by Benjamin Arnett, McKinley's close friend from Ohio, the impressive gift had been donated by bishops of the African Methodist Episcopal (AME) Church, including Arnett. "The Bible is a masterpiece of the bookmaker's art . . . the binding of the finest and most expensive gros-grain morocco, dark blue in color, padded . . . a fine line of gold around the outer edge."[2]

On this day, the AME bishops' King James Bible was marked at 2 Chronicles 1:10: "Give me now wisdom and knowledge, that I may go out and come in before this people; for who can judge this thy people, who is so great?"[3] The scripture offered a humble yet triumphant entrance for a new chief executive, whose convincing victory four months earlier—by nearly six hundred thousand popular votes over Nebraska's William Jennings Bryan—showed the largest margin since Ulysses Grant's 1872 reelection.

The weather itself was cooperative: chilly, brisk, and clear, with no sign of the snow marring previous inaugurations. The enthusiastic crowd included outgoing president Grover Cleveland, suffering from gout and hampered by a heavily bandaged foot. The day was remarkable in several ways: as the first inaugural ceremony recorded by a motion picture camera, the first to feature a glass-enclosed viewing stand for the traditional parade, the first to feature a congressional luncheon for both president and vice president, and the last inauguration not planned by the Joint Congressional Committee on Inaugural Ceremonies.

Throngs of onlookers were here to see the new president, a respected former congressman and, more recently, governor of Ohio. Technically old enough to have been father to the thirty-six-year-old Bryan, McKinley's "front-porch" campaign had sparked dubious rumors of possible ill health, but on this day, McKinley looked serene, thoughtful, and vigorous—a stark contrast to Cleveland. At fifty-four, McKinley was younger than fifteen of his twenty-three predecessors on assuming office. He had written the four-thousand-word inaugural address himself, mixing the platitudes he was fond of intoning and specific policies he intended to implement. If he did not mention Cuba, or recent unrest in that Spanish colony, he was determined to avoid exaggerating the urgency of dealing with Cuba, or alienating Cleveland, whose advice he sincerely welcomed on certain matters.

McKinley's plan to call the new Congress into special session immediately—rather than allowing it to open in December, more common in past inaugural years—was not a complete surprise but reflected a seasoned belief that waiting nine months to introduce legislation and make nominations served no one's purposes well, except perhaps those of outgoing Democrats:

> The condition of the public Treasury, as has been indicated, demands the immediate consideration of Congress. . . . I do not sympathize with the sentiment that Congress in session is dangerous to our general business interests. . . . It has always seemed to me that the postponement of the meeting of Congress until more than a year after it has been chosen deprived Congress too often of the inspiration of the popular will and the country of the corresponding benefits. . . .
>
> Again, whatever action Congress may take will be given a fair opportunity for trial before the people are called to pass judgment upon it. . . . *In view of these considerations, I shall deem it my duty as President to convene Congress in extraordinary session on Monday, the 15th day of March, 1897.*[4]

Perhaps most remarkable of those subjects to which McKinley did refer was his insistence on mentioning a controversial issue—violent lynchings by armed mobs—and the nation's court system as its only cure. A short phrase, buried halfway through the speech among traditional praise for American liberty and institutions, was one long sought and urged by Benjamin Arnett and other African American leaders: "The constituted authorities must be cheerfully and vigorously upheld. *Lynchings must not be tolerated in a great and civilized country like the United States; courts, not mobs, must execute the penalties of the law.* The preservation of public order, the right of discussion, the integrity of courts, and the orderly administration of justice must continue forever the rock of safety upon which our Government securely rests."[5]

The meaning of McKinley's phrase reflected an equally brief yet remarkable condemnation of such violence in the Republican Party's 1896 platform: "We proclaim our unqualified condemnation of the uncivilized and preposterous [barbarous] practice well known as lynching, and the killing of human beings suspected or charged with crime without process of law."[6] The importance of his language was not lost on any astute African American within McKinley's hearing, certainly not the one black congressman from the outgoing Congress—South Carolina's George Washington Murray—or his replacement as "leader of the black phalanx," George Henry White.

And while neither platform nor inaugural address promised special attention to African American economic betterment, other language in McKinley's inaugural address hinted at his hopes for those at the low end of the economic spectrum, with both universal education and universal opportunity awaiting those willing to work hardest:

Nor must we be unmindful of the need of improvement among our own citizens, but with the zeal of our forefathers encourage the spread of knowledge and free education. Illiteracy must be banished from the land if we shall attain that high destiny as the foremost of the enlightened nations of the world. . . .

Reforms in the civil service must go on. . . . As a member of Congress I voted and spoke in favor of the present law, and I shall attempt its enforcement in the spirit in which it was enacted. The purpose in view was to secure the most efficient service of the best men who would accept appointment under the Government, retaining faithful and devoted public servants in office.[7]

Politically knowledgeable black leaders knew the issues went hand in hand: an educated population was necessary to produce the next generation of leaders and the best workers in both races, within and outside government. And rewarding those who had already striven to advance themselves through education would inevitably inspire those watching and planning their own futures. Over the next four years, McKinley himself would regularly encourage black citizens to improve their educational status.

Calling the special session of Congress allowed newcomers like White to jump-start their legislative careers. Once sworn into office, he could present nominations far sooner than in normal circumstances and gain a national spotlight for early speeches: in short, it was a rare opportunity to make a quick difference, if he acted effectively. For the moment, an early session of Congress had one additional, less desirable effect upon the president's agenda. Almost overnight, McKinley was besieged by crowds of Republican office-seekers, in the company of newly installed congressmen and state party leaders. A surprising number of office-seekers were African Americans, energized by promises given them since 1895 by his campaign manager, Mark Hanna.

But the president's reference to lynching had a far more tangible effect on White's career. Within a year, the infamously brutal murder of a black U.S. postmaster by an armed South Carolina mob would change White, almost overnight, into a reluctant champion of the wavering cause—though not with the precise results he might have wanted. To understand the transformation more clearly, one need only recall another city, Saint Louis, and another momentous event involving all three men: McKinley, ex-governor of Ohio, not yet present but dominating the circus-like atmosphere; Mark Hanna, still grooming McKinley as his nominee for president; and White, making his first appearance at a national convention.

To win over Reed delegates for McKinley, Hanna had apparently promised federal appointments for many delegates, a fateful move later to haunt him in the Senate.[8] Many months later, as Louisiana prepared to disfranchise black voters, the state's "lily-white" Republicans became furious at McKinley's nomination of Henry Demas as naval officer at New Orleans, one nomination engineered as early as Saint Louis, with little chance of passing the next Senate. How many similar promises Hanna made is not known, but what is known is that half or more of Saint Louis's black delegates—and many black alternates— did receive appointments to federal office by the end of 1899.[9]

Like many of his predecessors, the new president planned to hold court in a six-room suite of offices on the second floor of the east wing of the White House. But like only a handful of his predecessors, McKinley quickly decided to stop conducting executive business in the large official office, when noise from the waiting room proved annoying and the privacy of conversations suspect. So McKinley moved instead into the cabinet room next door, where visitors had once waited for him, redesignating his own larger office as waiting room.

The substitute "chamber had a cheerless look, at once official and neglected. It might have been the directors' room in an old-fashioned and not very flourishing bank," in Leech's words. But it was well-lit and suited McKinley, "and there, throughout his administration he received his callers, dispatched his correspondence, and prepared his papers and addresses" while seated in a swivel armchair at the head of the cabinet table.[10] It was to this cabinet room that droves of office-seekers and their patrons began their treks over the first months of McKinley's administration.

Yet just getting there was a challenge. The old staircase was long and difficult, and there was still no elevator in that wing, as noted vocally by elderly callers. "It is often ludicrous to witness the puffing of distinguished statesmen before they reach the top," one observer wrote, "and the first thing they say when they reach the top is that an elevator ought to be put in."[11] Indeed, the White House was showing its age. According to Leech, the east wing "was in the last stage of decay. The tramp of generations of place seekers had weakened the floor beams until they were as shaky as those in the great parlour underneath" the executive suite. But elevator or not, by the hundreds they came, in time-honored tradition, each pressing forth candidates and candidacies for thousands of offices the new president was duty-bound to fill.

Thanks to late action by Grover Cleveland, who had built upon civil service reforms begun during his first term, perhaps eighty thousand federal offices—more than half—were no longer subject to patronage. Even so, the contest for offices that remained became fiercer than ever; in Leech's words, "the sudden contraction of the prizes severely intensified the rapacity of the competition," especially for such plum posts as domestic postmasters and consuls abroad.[12] And while not a majority of the applicants, African American supporters of

McKinley were every bit as eager as their white counterparts, and no less persistent. Whether accompanied by white party leaders from Georgia, Louisiana, and the two Carolinas—where their votes had made McKinley's losses more competitive—or in large single-race groups, the stream of African American office-seekers provoked regular comment in local newspapers, particularly the *Washington Evening Star*'s column "The White House," a popular front-page source of political news and gossip.[13]

One early report noted the president's gracious and warm attitude toward visitors of both races, a marked difference from the distaste shown by the previous president. "President McKinley seems to be glad to see the people, and enjoys the evidences of their regard for him," wrote the *Evening Star* on March 8, 1897. McKinley's "evident pleasure" led one caller to speculate effusively that "he seems to be fond of the people."[14] Such pleasure waned as his enthusiasm faltered in the wake of the physical exhaustion caused by incessant demands from Republicans—especially from Georgia. "The Georgia delegation wanted everything in sight, more than they were entitled to," one Atlanta newspaper quoted McKinley as confiding to a less than discreet House member.[15]

Georgia's longtime party chairman William Pledger, among the South's most influential African Americans, anxiously sought a consul's post in the Caribbean, preferably Kingston, Jamaica. Pledger and white party boss Col. Alfred Buck, presumptive U.S. minister to Japan, made their wishes clearly and repeatedly known to the White House. Among the "large number of colored men among the White House visitors" noted by the *Evening Star* on April 17 were three Saint Louis delegates—Thomas Dent, Henry Rucker, and Judson Lyons—and Augusta publisher Alford Wimberly. The quartet, "piloted" to the president by Buck, ostensibly pushed for consular appointments for Dent and Pledger, although the *Evening Star* gently reminded readers that Lyons—the state's national committeeman—sought Augusta's postmastership.[16]

Other African American visitors that day included Chicago's Cyrus Adams, seeking to become U.S. minister to Bolivia, and two candidates for federal auditor's positions: Richard Toomey of Greeneville, Tennessee, and James Shepard of Durham, North Carolina. Adams and Toomey came with respective congressmen, whereas Shepard was escorted as part of a much larger delegation led by Sen. Jeter Pritchard, paving the way for a compromise slate of North Carolina appointees—former representative Henry Cheatham, now the leading candidate for District of Columbia recorder of deeds, and religious journalist John Dancy, contending for either that job or Treasury register.

With Pritchard, Cheatham, and Dancy on this day was the state's freshman congressman, George White, the only African American member of the new House. "The matter was gone over with the President, and Senator Pritchard believes everything is now fixed," said the *Evening Star.* "The North Carolina men confidently claim that they are entitled to more consideration than the republicans in any other state because of the showing they made in the last election."[17]

It was not White's first visit to the executive mansion. He had appeared there nearly three weeks earlier, accompanying visiting black legislator Lee Person. On March 31, White had made history simply by entering the White House: a rare honor, as an incoming freshman representative invited to the White House to present nominations—in this case, for a Canadian consulship for a Pritchard designee—or to shake the new president's hand during their first month together in office. It capped a memorable week for White, who had given his maiden House speech one day earlier.[18]

White and McKinley did not yet know each other very well, and precisely how the two men interacted during and after their initial meeting is not clear. But it is likely that they took each other's measure carefully and decided that they could trust each other. One can imagine a familial relationship beginning to develop—like that of father and son, almost, or kindly uncle and impetuous nephew—between these two men, ten years apart in age, from different worlds. If McKinley had not heard White's maiden speech in person, he may well have read brief newspaper reports of it.[19]

In that speech, White introduced himself as "the sole representative on this floor of 9,000,000 of the population of these United States, 90 percent of whom are laborers," and the importance of the tariff for which the special session had been called:

> I desire not only to add a word in behalf of the articles mentioned by my colleague [Romulus Linney] ... but wish especially to emphasize a word in behalf of the people of eastern North Carolina on that part of this bill which includes lumber. Under the Wilson bill the contracts which had been entered into by the mill men had in many instances to be forfeited; the mills that had been running day and night ... were shut down. ...

These men, the heads of families, were forced to see their loved ones pinched with want, with no way for them to earn a dollar. This bill, because of this lumber schedule, commends itself especially to the Southern people who have to labor to get bread and meat for their families.[20]

He rejected Democratic arguments that the proposed tariff would do serious harm to free trade, slyly segueing into a more serious issue: "I have been amused, Mr. Chairman, by my Democratic friends, though not surprised, because I have heard that old yarn before in their advocacy of 'free trade,'" White said. "Why, they have from time to time advocated 'free whisky' also; and in the last campaign their shibboleth was 'free silver.' In fact, the Southern element of the Democratic party has advocated 'free' everything except free ballots and free negroes."[21] White's mildly barbed joke drew cheers and repeated laughter from fellow Republicans and gallery watchers, and perhaps a chuckle from McKinley himself, who presumably had been briefed on White's rhetorical skills, both in the courtroom and beyond. His closing remarks, however, carried a more somber reflection, etched in rhetorical acid, on southern Democrats who resented his mere presence on this floor:

Well, I am a Southerner to the manner born and reared . . . but when Democratic members on the other side of this House drag into this great Congress . . . the expressions of the Southern plantations in regard to "the darky and the heels of a mule," then I think the imputation is a correct one. . . . [I]t comes with bad grace from the gentleman [Stanyarne Wilson] to talk of misrepresentation of the Southern people when he considers the fact that 130,000 voters in his State are not allowed to vote at all.

I want to say to him that while I know little of South Carolina as it now is—I used to know something of it when it was a State in the Union, with the privileges of sister States of the Union—yet I do know something of the sentiment in . . . North Carolina, and many other States, and . . . there is a growing sentiment prevailing . . . that the industries and labor of America shall be protected against the pauperism and the cheap labor of foreign countries, Democratic thunder to the contrary notwithstanding.[22]

His brief speech drew thunderous applause from Republican colleagues, stony silence from Democrats. South Carolina had stripped the vote from nearly all African American voters at its 1895 constitutional convention; other southern states were poised for similar action. For the moment, only North Carolina seemed immune to a building wave of disfranchisement. And if the "Democratic thunder" White heard remained only a metaphor for now, ominous threats of future repression—increasingly political, not purely economic—could not be ignored. He would speak of it as often as he saw fit and occasionally use it to predict future events.

He was already beginning to relish his dual roles, one as race representative—expected of him, as the only black congressman—and another as prophet, which fewer might have expected. Over the next four years, he would often return to this prophet's role, seeking to impart his conflicting visions of what the future could be—a fair, equitable environment for black Americans, marked by peaceful political participation and prosperity, or a darker, more violently repressive landscape scarred by lynchings and the encroachment of second-class citizenship under Jim Crow rules. Either could be true, but only one would be.

What he did not realize—as no prophet ever truly understands until it happens—was whether his words would be believed and taken to heart or scorned by those who dismissed him as a troublemaker. Would he become a revered predictor or be dismissed as another Cassandra?

Both White and Jeter Pritchard, of course, were now concerned with North Carolina's image in the president's eyes—considering the less savory spectacle presented simultaneously by Georgia Republicans—and both men doubtless preferred careful compromises not hindering other important appointments sought for white Tar Heel Republicans. If Georgia's persistence bordered on political gall, North Carolina's frequent requests for presidential audiences were tolerated far more graciously, for strategic political reasons. North Carolina's importance to president and party needed little exaggeration: Republicans controlled that state for the first time in a generation, having won both the governorship and state legislature in the 1896 fusion campaign with the Populists.

Pritchard and his Populist counterpart Marion Butler were the only U.S. senators from the South not elected as Democrats. Butler's metamorphosis into a Populist leader, from the state legislature to the Senate, depended on ties to his former party, with whom his present party still danced a delicate minuet: married to national Democrats in support of William Jennings Bryan, while going steady with local Republicans for statewide races. He harbored clear hopes of achieving national prominence by negotiating with national Republican leaders during the McKinley era, sharing leadership of the state's eclectic congressional delegation in 1897: three Republicans, five Populists, and, almost incredibly, just one Democrat, down from eight in 1893.[23]

Although McKinley had not carried a single southern state, he had done fairly well regionally. North Carolina voters gave McKinley his second-largest bloc of southern votes—more than 155,000, behind Texas—and more than the 140,000 votes polled in Alabama, Arkansas, Florida, Louisiana, Mississippi, and South Carolina combined. Moreover, North Carolina came closest of any southern state to favoring McKinley—just under 47 percent of the presidential tally, ahead of Tennessee and Virginia (each 46 percent) and far above Texas (under 31 percent). Pritchard, eager to make his state's case with McKinley, made his first visit to the White House on March 9—among at least eight senators that day—and returned at least five more times in March, alone or with others.[24] Pritchard quickly became a close friend and adviser to the president, despite declining an appointment to McKinley's cabinet.[25]

Georgia, by comparison, managed just 37 percent for McKinley: hardly compelling, if still the best GOP showing in state history. Its claims were predicated on an optimistically upward trend and prospects for McKinley's reelection, and pure chutzpah. With no Republican congressmen to plead, William Pledger, Judson Lyons, and Alfred Buck could only exaggerate their importance, however annoying such persistence might be to the president and his advisers. With White still little known outside his native state, his position upon arrival in Washington was nonetheless at once stronger than that of any of his three Tar Heel predecessors. All had served under Republican presidents with patronage hopes for constituents, but neither John Hyman, James O'Hara, nor Henry Cheatham had ever served alongside a Republican senator—a critical boost for nominations at the White House. Moreover, none had ever served while the GOP controlled either the state's legislature or governorship; during White's first term, the party controlled both.

All three predecessors served either as delegates or alternate delegates to party national nominating conventions, but only after their elections. Only White had won the honor of selection as a statewide delegate before entering Congress. Neither Hyman, Cheatham, nor O'Hara could help nominate the president under whom they served, or otherwise to distinguish themselves at an early convention. White had done both; in addition to voting for McKinley, he had served on the Committee on Rules and Order of Business.[26]

In the spring of 1897, just how much of a role he could play in helping settle the vexing question of which North Carolinians received top national posts was undefined. White was content, wisely, to leave such decisions to Senator Pritchard and other state leaders; his own interests lay in the dozens of appointments he planned for offices within his district, primarily postmasters. If consulted at all during negotiations for other offices, he may well have assumed a backstage part in complicated negotiations involving two contenders: Cheatham, his long-estranged brother-in-law, and Dancy, his onetime Howard classmate, both seeking high office.

The four posts generally accorded African Americans included register of the U.S. Treasury, District of Columbia recorder of deeds, and U.S. ministers to Haiti and Liberia. Republican presidents since Grant had appointed African Americans to all four. Democrat Cleveland had appointed just two black Democrats. Charles Taylor held two of the positions—minister to Liberia and then recorder of deeds in his second administration, after the Senate declined Taylor's controversial nomination as minister to Bolivia.[27] The *Evening Star* totted up nineteen register applicants, including six African Americans, and insiders believed the other three top positions would also go to black men. The president was reported to have told a white applicant in early April that "he would give this [Treasury] place to one of the colored applicants" for reasons of historical inertia: "Once a position was given the colored republicans, they afterward concluded that the office should be theirs for all time."[28]

According to the columnist, "the leading colored applicants are J. C. Napier of Tennessee, ex-Representative Cheatham of North Carolina, B. K. Bruce of Mississippi and young [Henry] Arnett of Georgia, a son of Bishop Arnett." But an important caveat involved North Carolina's favorite sons, Cheatham and Dancy: "There is an impression, whether well founded or not is uncertain, that North Carolina will get the treasury place or the recordership. The state, however, would hardly be given both places."[29] That is, should Cheatham get the treasury post, Dancy would not become recorder—and if Dancy became recorder, Cheatham would be left out.

As party leaders weighed choices, White may well have proved instrumental in helping fashion the final compromise. All three men had begun their careers as college-educated schoolteachers and knew each other well: Dancy was elected register of deeds in Edgecombe County and held an important, lucrative federal position under Harrison—collector of customs at Wilmington's port—for four years, while Cheatham was in Congress. Cheatham served as Vance County register of deeds before Congress and was a trained lawyer, though he had never practiced. Both seemed eminently qualified for the recorder's position.

The timing for mediation certainly appealed to White, whose political and personal feud with Cheatham needed quick resolution. It dated to 1894's deadlocked race for the congressional nomination, which poisoned the political atmosphere for months. Both men claimed to have won the nomination at a district convention, with disputed votes; neither was willing to concede. Just weeks before the 1894 election, the national Republican congressional committee interceded to choose a formal nominee: Cheatham, who, as the better-known ex-congressman, was perhaps the logical choice. White angrily refused to campaign for Cheatham, who lost the general election to incumbent Democrat Frederick Woodard in a landslide and understandably blamed White. Their estrangement was both personal and political; their feud played only a small role in the final vote, for White's assistance could not have changed the outcome significantly.[30]

Next time out, White easily won the nomination over Cheatham and then defeated the same incumbent, Woodard. In 1896, Cheatham's federal career appeared over. But once elected, White could afford to be magnanimous by urging Cheatham's appointment, as well as encouraging Dancy to accept a lesser post. Cora Lena White and Louisa Cheatham, devoted sisters, may well have favored the arrangement, always hoping to restore family peace and enable them to live near each other in Washington, D.C. Persuading Dancy to accept a consolation prize—his former post in Wilmington, among the highest-paying federal positions available in North Carolina—required equally tactful personal mediation, and White was a logical choice. The sooner the situation was resolved, the sooner other important issues could be addressed.

On May 11, McKinley nominated Cheatham as recorder of deeds, provoking a front-page story in the *Evening Star,* alongside a rare illustrated likeness.[31] A minor flap had already erupted in the press after the president requested incumbent Charles Taylor's resignation to facilitate his own nominee as recorder of deeds.[32] After Taylor grudgingly agreed, Cheatham was confirmed by the Senate in less than a week. No decision was announced for register, or on Dancy's expected appointment as collector of customs; the four-year term of the incumbent collector ran until February 15, 1898, delaying Dancy's nomination.[33] But when it came, Dancy was confirmed by the Senate almost immediately.

For White, Cheatham's selection and the rapprochement between the brothers-in-law was helpful, if anticlimactic. Since early April, following his first White House visit, he had submitted nominations for "Black Second" postmasterships; by July, when the special session of Congress ended, he proposed more than a dozen black postmasters, mostly in small post offices in predominantly black communities. Thanks to Senator Pritchard and a benevolent president, the steady flow of nominations continued for much of the next year—at least two dozen by February 1898, the largest number ever recorded in North Carolina during so short a period.[34]

For his part, the new president appeared to comply enthusiastically with any request White's office sent forward. By the summer of 1897, the black-owned *Raleigh (N.C.) Gazette* credited White with twenty-three black nominees for Second District postmasterships alone.[35] The *Gazette*'s precise total cannot be confirmed, but the unmistakable trend it portrayed can be clearly documented. The first thirteen appointees known to be African Americans, all announced between April and July 1897, covered five Black Second counties: Bertie, Halifax, Northampton, Warren, and Wayne.

White's choices ranged in age from twenty-six to forty-four years, including just one postmaster with experience under President Harrison: ex-legislator James Pittman, forty-four, resuming the position at Tillery first offered by Cheatham (April 9). New Bertie County postmasters included schoolteacher Daniel Baker at Lewiston and three young farmers: Lewis Bond (Windsor), Freeman Ryan (Quitsna), and James Cherry (Drew), all in their mid-twenties. Halifax County appointees included farmer Edward Cheek, thirty-eight

(Halifax), who named a son after Pritchard; Halifax housewife Alice Burt, thirty-four (Ita), his first female appointee; and Henry Mayo, a thirty-six-year-old butcher (Littleton).[36]

Two appointments were made April 14, for Northampton County farmer James Martin, thirty (Severn), and Warren County farmer James Wortham, thirty-one (Ridgeway). In Wayne County, thirty-five-year-old farmer Allen Smith was appointed May 27 at Mount Olive. On July 21, White nominated Brasier Langford, a fifty-two-year-old Northampton farmer, at Potecasi. Six days later, after the special session of Congress was adjourned, White's nominee at Rocky Mount, Edgecombe schoolteacher Israel Hargett, thirty-one, received a temporary commission as postmaster; his formal nomination came in January 1898, after Congress reconvened.[37]

Hargett's nomination presented a special case, the only one of this first group of nominees requiring Senate confirmation. In most cases, confirmation was a result of the postmaster's salary; salaries for only six post offices in the Second District exceeded $1,000, and Rocky Mount's $1,600 salary made it quite attractive.[38] Most other postmasters received smaller salaries or were allowed to keep revenue from postage sold, simply taking office after being appointed and having local bonds posted for them.

Mindful of public sensitivities, White had so far been careful to select only literate blacks as nominees, from a variety of backgrounds and occupations, including both youthful applicants and mature individuals. Most were farmers, many with previous public service, from county commissioner to state legislator; several were experienced postmasters. Almost all were married with children, which was seen as evidence of social stability and civic responsibility. Yet the sheer number of appointments by White, and the wider political atmosphere in which they occurred, reinforced their eventually negative impact.

Political frustration among Democrats was a major factor in the remapping of political strategies in the Tar Heel State. Furious at their new impotence after the 1894 and 1896 elections, Democrats struggled to regroup for the critical 1898 elections. White's actions stirred grumbling but little anxiety within his district, yet echoes reverberated loudly outside. The few black appointments by Governor Russell were already being trumpeted unfavorably by Democratic newspapers, although most Republicans tended to ignore ominous early echoes of "Negro domination" or dismiss them as sour grapes.

However feeble that cry, it gained momentum with each new appointment, particularly in the Raleigh and Wilmington newspapers. Even black editors recognized both the new depth of partisan feelings and White's emerging national status as lightning rod. In the words of Young's *Raleigh Gazette*, "His efforts, as Congressman, to give the Negro recognition in government patronage, are being severely criticized by the Democratic party for securing places for his own people."[39]

If localized backlash was reported to the president, he would have dismissed it as irrelevant. Yet how much of McKinley's acquiescence to White's first round of nominees was due to political pragmatism and how much to an intangible desire for racial equity in a predominantly black district will never be known, for McKinley never spoke publicly of his commitment to black officeholding, even though his personal beliefs leaned toward fairness.[40] What is undeniable is McKinley's actual track record: at least ten times more black nominees to federal office in one year than his successor, Roosevelt, offered in his first term, and more than any previous president had ever offered.[41]

Among his successful black appointees was New Jersey educator William Powell, named U.S. minister to Haiti in mid-1897. Favored by New Jersey's junior senator, William Sewell, Powell was active in Republican politics in Camden, teaching in both that city's black and white school systems, after working in the Treasury Department as an auditor's clerk under Ulysses S. Grant. Before 1897, he reportedly declined appointment offers under Arthur—consul in Cap Haïtien, Haiti, in 1881—and as minister to Haiti under Harrison in 1891. Trained as a pharmacist in New York City, Powell had studied at Lincoln University, after service in the Union navy.

How Sewell persuaded Powell to leave Camden is not known, but he was probably assisted by Vice President Garret Hobart, a veteran New Jersey legislator well acquainted with Powell's record, whose strong working relationship with McKinley soon earned him the unusual informal title "assistant president." Perhaps as an added inducement, McKinley also agreed to upgrade the position to envoy extraordinaire and minister plenipotentiary, as well as chargé d'affaires to Santo Domingo. Since Grant, presidents had offered posts in both Port-au-Prince and Santo Domingo to distinguished black appointees such as John Langston and Frederick Douglass.[42]

Powell was just one of many black diplomatic and consular appointees. The sheer breadth of McKinley's appointments would soon astonish some observers, coming as they did in almost every governmental department, numbering nearly twice as many as those extended by Harrison. And with advice from White and Pritchard, North Carolina's black appointees emerged as the largest group from any single state, a clear mark of political influence, with no limits to what might still come.

On the lighter side, one black journalist not desiring a consular appointment was perfectly willing to pretend he did. The *Washington Bee*'s whimsical editor, the socialite and lawyer W. Calvin Chase, poked gentle fun at office-seekers of either race—some of whom were there at the same time—on a late June Saturday, when the *Evening Star*'s watcher asked Chase what he and his friends sought. "I want to be minister to Dahomey," Chase insisted, all but winking at his fellow journalist.[43] It was a harmless joke—the Kingdom of Dahomey was a French protectorate, with no resident diplomats—and Will Marion Cook's legendary play still years away from performance. But there was a deeper edge to his irony.

Chase was an early admirer of the president's measured approach to appointments of African Americans to consular and diplomatic posts, often defending McKinley and upbraiding critics who chafed at the slow pace. But he was also quick to pick public quarrels with anyone taking credit for McKinley's choices, especially Bishop Arnett, who claimed no appointments "of a colored man to Presidential office will be made without my indorsement. All papers of colored applicants are referred to me." Nonsense, chided Chase, who derided the "gall and impudence" of Arnett, a "self-constituted leader" with no more influence over presidential decisions than Hawaii's late King Kalakaua.[44]

2

CHARTING THE COURSE

The Negroes of the South are not in the deplorable condition that they are
painted by men who come North presumably in aid of institutions
among Negroes, but in fact for their own aggrandizement.
—**George H. White,** Brooklyn, September 22, 1897

George White took no small pride in the advancement of qualified members
of his race and fervently believed every man or woman, regardless of race,
ought to receive "an even chance in the race of life."[1] But in exchange, he expected appropriate behavior by those being offered such opportunities. A strict
teacher and relentless prosecutor, he was well aware how many whites in the
South viewed blacks as both inferior and incapable of sustained high-level
performance.

From the day he entered Congress, White was delighted to accept speaking
engagements whenever possible, and he favored institutions of higher learning—particularly at commencements—to preach an encouraging yet no-non-
sense gospel of hard work and tenacity: work hard, behave properly, and prepare to make your race proud. He doubtless delivered prepared remarks along
similar lines at Scotia Seminary in Concord, North Carolina, in late May 1897,
when his daughter Della graduated. He next delivered a commencement address on June 1 to teaching graduates at his alma mater, Howard University, encouraging them to "do all their power to elevate themselves and others, to have
an aim and stick to it, and to live a life of which they would not be ashamed." In
September 1897, he was keynote speaker at Educational Day at North Carolina's Edenton Fair, before attending Emancipation Day in Brooklyn, New York.[2]

A social conservative, White regularly emphasized proper behavior, hard
work, and abstinence from alcohol in speeches to black audiences. If he did
not yet spell out public views on what he constituted unacceptable behavior
in House speeches, White was simply biding his time. His longest public statements on race-related issues—largely on economic and labor issues affecting

black southerners but also covering related social matters—would come as his congressional term neared its end, in detailed testimony before the Industrial Commission on Agriculture and Agricultural Labor in early 1900. (By prior agreement, all testimony avoided extended references to or comments on political matters.) Close friends and House colleagues, after hearing him speak for three years, were hardly surprised by his traditionalist views on critical issues, particularly on education—long championed as the only way black southerners could raise themselves up from centuries of slavery and repression—or the importance of hard work, thrift, and determination, on which he aligned with Booker T. Washington.

Yet some listeners might have been shocked by his frank willingness to criticize inappropriate behavior by blacks, particularly regarding alcohol use. In his testimony, White blamed many, but not all, failures by his race on weakness for alcohol. "I think it is the curse of our race—one of the greatest curses of the colored man," he told the Industrial Commission, as an aside. "His propensity for drinking whisky . . . is one of the curses of his race."[3] Although not a strict teetotaler, White was a devout Presbyterian, and at most a moderate social drinker, limiting his intake to occasional brandy after meals. This problematic weakness for alcohol among fellow blacks was a recent development, he believed, one not widespread during slavery.

White believed, furthermore, that freedmen cultivated this taste for alcohol by imitating white behavior. Such imitation may have been necessary for them to gain advancement—a goal expected to take many years—but was a perilous path indeed. "You can hardly blame him, or expect him with an emancipation of 35 years to get out of what has been taught him for two centuries," he told the Industrial Commission. "He is very much a copyist, a plagiarist, very adjustable . . . a great imitator, and, unfortunately for him, he has imitated his white brother in these vices as well as his good qualities."[4]

Imitating white behavior also carried a subtler danger: unrealistic expectations for blacks. White did not believe equality of the two races was a practical goal in the United States: "Perfect equality of the two races, either in education, industry, or politics, is next to the impossible. Even though the colored man should be admitted to equality, the white man's superior civilization from long years in advance of him, and his supremacy, wealth, and superior education, would tend to keep the colored man his inferior."[5] Moreover, he saw political equality, even though guaranteed by the Constitution, as increasingly elusive in southern states: "Up to a year or two ago our condition was decidedly on the upper trend. The best feeling that I have known anywhere in the Southland existed between the whites and colored in our State."

"Politics, though, has made things a little bad for us. . . . [W]e have a bad state of affairs and the way looks dark for the future," he said.[6] That "dark" future was not confined to southern life. On the separate issue of "race envy," or "passing for white," he had no sympathy for northern blacks ashamed of their skin color. Of mixed racial ancestry himself—black, white, and Native American—he was proud of his heritage and brusquely chided northern audiences for their futile preoccupation with trying to become "white."

One example came after a public ceremony in Brooklyn on September 22, 1897—marking the anniversary of Lincoln's advance announcement of his Emancipation Proclamation—at which White "reviewed briefly the history of the negro from the time he was brought to America to his emancipation" in only positive terms, saying that it was right that colored people should assemble on September 22, celebrating with appropriate services their anniversary or emancipation from "the most cruel, bitter and abominable slavery known in ancient or modern history." He enumerated the struggles of blacks in bondage, recalled their patience and long sufferings, and declared God heard their prayers and raised up Lincoln to emancipate them.[7]

Later that day, he changed gears markedly in addressing businessmen and professionals at Siloam Presbyterian Church. Unlike many in this audience, White claimed he was "proud that he was a Negro and there were thousands of colored men in the South just as proud as he. They were acquiring property, investing money in business and making history for the race."[8] For those listeners "who did not patronize their own professional men and thereby keep money in the coffers of the race," he had nothing but scorn.

"The tendency among the most of them was to get away from the Negro race, that instead of saving money and investing it along lines that would be beneficial to the race they were extravagant and invested in patent hair straighteners or complexion compounds to make themselves white," he thundered. He excoriated those misrepresenting conditions among southern blacks, insisting that "the Negroes of the South are not in the deplorable condition that they are painted by men who come North presumably in aid of institutions among Negroes, but in fact for their own aggrandizement."[9]

Such remarks did not endear White to some African American leaders, especially independents and northern Democrats who viewed him as a rural upstart with little knowledge of urban life and struggles, and who were already moving away from the GOP. But the sentiments served only to reinforce his reputation for plain-spokenness and a distinct following within upper Republican ranks, including Reps. George Southwick of New York, Charles Sprague of Massachusetts, and Alfred Harmer of Pennsylvania, and future Speaker David Henderson of Iowa, all of whom White came to know during his first term, and Vice President Hobart, whom White genuinely admired.

The congressman seemed poised for national stardom—perhaps even a cabinet post in McKinley's second term—unless southern tides of disfranchisement spread to North Carolina and swept him from office. For the moment, White was on the rise, gaining confidence in his new dual roles: "leader of the black phalanx" in the House and the nation's highest-ranking elected African American. In October 1897, he accompanied yet another North Carolina applicant to the White House, former legislator Charles Cook, who was seeking reappointment as U.S. district attorney in the state's east, his former post for four years under President Harrison.

"Mr. Cook has the indorsement of Representative White and Senator Pritchard for district attorney of the eastern district of North Carolina," wrote the *Washington Evening Star*. "The office is being temporarily filled and the North Carolinians interested would like to see the appointment made."[10] A Warrenton lawyer, Cook was a rare white Republican to represent Warren County in the General Assembly, winning elections to the state senate in 1886 and 1894, and state house in 1896. The appointment went instead to Greenville attorney Claude Bernard, but Cook remained active in Republican politics, soon becoming an associate justice on the North Carolina Supreme Court before moving to Oklahoma.[11]

During the congressional recess, White offered more nominations for postmaster, following up his first dozen from the special session with another dozen between August and November 1897, including five more African American women.[12] Female postmasters were fairly commonplace in North Carolina, but as in the nation at large, they had previously been white postmasters' widows—witness Mary Daniels, longtime Wilson postmaster and mother of Josephus Daniels. Since 1865, North Carolina had seen just two African American postmistresses: Cora Davis at Halifax (1889–1890) and Mary Ann Baker, at Dudley from 1891 to 1893, whom White reappointed.

Mrs. Baker and her female colleagues joined White's male nominees at Rich Square, Macon, Brinkleyville, Essex, and South Gaston.[13] The only controversial male nominee would be Colin Anthony, a saloonkeeper and Halifax County commissioner named at Scotland Neck in September 1897, the only post requiring Senate confirmation.

In many small U.S. towns or rural areas, postmasters operated out of homes or small stores, forcing white customers in black-managed post offices to visit unfamiliar residential areas. And although most counties in North Carolina's "black belt" had elected various black men to local and county offices for decades without incident, white newspapers began periodically in 1897 to voice displeasure at the spectacle of white women dealing with black postmasters. The race of postmasters thus raised a more delicate issue than had that of elected registers of deeds, magistrates, county commissioners, or justices of the peace.

Not all of White's nominees were black; significant offices at Kinston, Goldsboro, and Tarboro, also subject to Senate confirmation, went to white Republicans, including ex- congressman Joseph Martin, reappointed at Tarboro; John Dobson at Goldsboro; and Ada Hunter, reappointed at Kinston. Meanwhile, dozens of smaller post offices were served by white postmasters either named by him or allowed to continue, generally loyal Republicans whose presence provoked no opposition.[14]

Nor was White alone in proposing black postmasters for the state; he may have interceded for two outside the Second District—ex-legislator Clinton Battle in Battleboro, Nash County, appointed in 1897 by Populist William Strowd of the Fourth District—and may have served as reference for one postmistress in Bladen County, Mary Guion, appointed at Tar Heel by Populist Rep. John Fowler. By the early spring of 1898, the state's running total would exceed thirty-four black postmasters.[15]

Although North Carolina had the nation's only black congressman, Republican leaders in states with substantial black populations also proposed black postmasters. In 1897, roughly two dozen black postmasters were appointed or reappointed in eight other southern states—Alabama, Arkansas, Florida, Georgia, Louisiana, Mississippi, South Carolina, and Virginia—followed by at least a dozen more in four states in 1898 and 1899. Some longtime Republican postmasters—Joshua Wilson of Florence, South Carolina, who served intermittently for three decades after 1876, and Mississippians Thomas

Keys of Ocean Springs (1889–1911) and Thomas Richardson of Port Gibson (1870–1911)—were influential party officials and perennial convention delegates during long tenures. Respected Georgian Charles Jackson of Darien, reappointed in 1897, served roughly a decade with little controversy.

But elsewhere, reappointments of two black postmasters—Minnie Cox of Indianola, Mississippi, and Frazier Baker of Lake City, South Carolina—were destined to figure in angry national scandals because of their race, forcing the Post Office Department to close their post offices. Under Theodore Roosevelt, Mrs. Cox later resigned after a protracted national standoff between the White House and southern Democrats. Baker, a schoolteacher serving Effingham briefly from 1892 to 1893, was appointed in July 1897 to Lake City; by early 1898, he became a tragic symbol of armed resistance to perceived federal overreach.

In the early fall of 1897, neither Baker nor Mrs. Cox was of concern to the McKinley administration. Far more troublesome were the cases of two black Georgia appointees—one requiring confirmation—who presented knotty political headaches for the new president, the first signs of trouble in his honeymoon period. Attorney Judson Lyons and schoolteacher Isaiah Loftin, friends and strong supporters of McKinley, would soon cross paths unexpectedly in Washington, as both their futures hung in the balance.

Lyons's two-year journey from national Republican committeeman and convention delegate in 1896 to national officeholder in 1898 was based on decades of party loyalty. At age twenty-two, he became an alternate delegate to the 1876 Republican national convention and full delegate in 1880. After graduating from Howard's Law Department, he returned to Augusta to practice law and resumed his role in state party politics, becoming Georgia's national committeeman in 1896. Among McKinley's strongest supporters in Georgia, Lyons was widely touted for high office—including foreign postings as consul or higher—but preferred to remain in the United States, preferably in Augusta.

His possible nomination as Augusta's postmaster surfaced just after McKinley's inauguration. Although it was a seemingly natural reward for long service, it sparked vehement Democratic opposition, due in part to its $3,100 salary, among the largest of any federal appointee in Georgia. Lyons was personally popular and highly qualified but lacked strong support from white Democrats for the postmastership. Most supported certain black Republicans for other federal appointments in Georgia, but few were willing to force a black postmaster on predominantly white Augusta. Moreover, many Augusta leaders had already publicly endorsed him for a foreign posting.

For both family and practical reasons, Lyons wanted to remain in Augusta, where he earned as much from practicing law as most federal jobs paid. Yet he was willing to accept Augusta's postmastership, even after being publicly linked by the *Washington Evening Star* to a violent attack on Loftin, the black postmaster at Hogansville. Lyons insisted he did not "fear any violence in case of receiving the appointment" in Augusta, but there were obstacles, among them personal opposition to Lyons as postmaster by Postmaster General James Gary of Maryland.[16]

The protracted controversy soon forced Lyons to withdraw his candidacy before the Senate could vote when it reconvened in December. McKinley admired Lyons and genuinely wanted to give him an important position. Quite distressed, he next offered Lyons a high-ranking position in the Post Office Department—reportedly a superintendent's post, less lucrative but more visible nationwide, possibly even the U.S. stamp agent's job given to Ohio's ex-senator John Green. Lyons was not interested; private distaste for Postmaster General Gary—linked to the South's nascent "lily-white" movement—seemed a likely reason.

Lyons's name continued in public mentions for Treasury register but was again passed over.[17] McKinley's selection of Bruce as register—a position he had held under Presidents Garfield and Arthur in the 1880s—was announced in December, as Congress opened its regular session.[18] (Despite press attention, Bruce did not expect the post; McKinley had initially opposed reappointments for previous officeholders, at least to former offices, but Bruce dutifully accepted the president's change of heart.)

But while the Lyons situation simmered in Augusta, on Georgia's eastern border with South Carolina, a different crisis burst into national headlines in the small western village of Hogansville in late 1897. Over the next several weeks, conflicting reports in the *Washington Evening Star, New York Times, Chicago Tribune,* and *Atlanta Journal* contradicted each other, often daily, in a classic case of one-upsmanship by newspapers scoring headlines. Isaiah Loftin, a Clark University–educated schoolteacher, was not the first black postmaster to serve Hogansville; Harrison appointee John Clopton had resigned under community pressure in 1890.

J. W. Hardaway, the man he replaced, objected strenuously to Loftin, as did many white citizens. Hardaway refused to step aside, running a "shadow" post office that received and delivered most local mail through third parties. No one would rent Loftin a building downtown, forcing him to open a new outpost in a predominantly black neighborhood, far removed from the railroad station. Postal revenues fell to under one dollar per week, not even 5 percent of previous sales, Loftin told a Chicago journalist.[19]

Loftin reportedly worked closely with Col. Alfred Buck in organizing black voters' support for McKinley in 1896. But during his first month at work, Loftin was shot several times one evening outside the post office. He could not identify his assailant, who was never apprehended, and his wounds were not life-threatening, despite early reports to the contrary; his wife ran the post office until his return. There was a troubling family history: Loftin's brother Augustus had been shot to death earlier in another unsolved incident, after becoming deputy collector of internal revenue. Some observers blamed both shootings on white supremacists; others linked Loftin's shooting to a personal feud.[20]

The Hogansville shooting sent temporary shock waves through the nation; months later, many readers were still convinced Loftin had died, as erroneously reported initially. Yet even as he returned to work, the postal boycott continued, despite Postmaster General Gary's action to shut down Hardaway's "shadow" operation. By the end of September, the Post Office Department reportedly declared a temporary moratorium on appointing black postmasters in southern states, or so claimed the *New York Times*.[21] But as an unidentified aide told the *Chicago Tribune*, McKinley was determined to appoint postmasters of his choosing, no matter how angry it made local residents.[22]

"From now on, the matter is to be a contest in which the government is one of the contending parties," the aide said. "The people of Hogansville may refuse to have their mail handled by a negro, but in that case they will have no mail at all. *President McKinley has accepted the responsibility of seeing that his appointment is honored, and the whole power of the government will be behind him to enforce it.*" And he had no intention of discontinuing appointments for black postmasters, so said his aide. "There have not been many colored postmasters appointed in the South. . . . [T]he percentage is remarkably small . . . it falls between twenty-five and 100, and when one remembers that several hundred postmasters are appointed in a day it dwindles to comparative insignificance." But McKinley was "convinced that an attack has been made on the authority of the federal government, which amounts almost, if not quite, to treason," and violence like that against Loftin "must be met and punished."[23]

The Post Office Department officially played down the story, claiming it was "inclined to regard the incident ... as closed" and admitting that "the matter was exaggerated from the beginning." Unnamed officials told the *New York Times* on September 28 that Loftin returned to duty and "is not being made the subject of further annoyance."[24] He visited Washington, D.C., in early October, although precise reasons were never given. "Neither the President nor any Georgia republican leaders has seen Isaac [*sic*] Loftin, the Hogansville postmaster, who is reported to have come to talk to administration officials about the recent shooting affair," wrote the *Evening Star* on October 4, dismissing rumors that "Loftin has resigned as postmaster and will be given a position in Washington."[25]

Colonel Buck, by now in Tokyo, could provide no useful leverage for Loftin; if the postmaster met with any postal officials, there is no record of it. The *New York Times* attributed the resignation rumors to "a suggestion made by Loftin's wife, who is also assistant postmaster. . . . [She] expressed fear for both her husband and herself. She had begged her husband to resign but he had declined." Loftin's friend Lyons, also in Washington, said he was confident Loftin would stay in his job—after offering similar counsel, no doubt, to Loftin.[26]

Not all black postmasters provoked such strong reactions in Georgia as either Lyons or Loftin. Opposition was muted to the July appointment of Monroe Morton—another 1896 convention delegate—as postmaster in the university town of Athens, which had had a black postmaster, Madison Davis, under Harrison. No one objected strenuously to the wealthy Morton, a real estate owner with coal and lumber interests, as postmaster. In South Atlanta, merchant Ellic Simon was widely respected in his small community, while the reappointment of Charles Jackson provoked hardly a ripple on the surface of otherwise placid Darien.

Any moratorium on black southern postmasters such as that proclaimed by the *New York Times* was short-lived at best, perhaps nonexistent. McKinley himself approved a temporary commission on September 17, two days after Loftin's shooting, for White's nominee at Scotland Neck, Colin Anthony, whose

confirmation hearing sparked a bruising political brawl in the Senate. Unde-
terred by Loftin's shooting, White proceeded to nominate at least eleven more
black postmasters across the Second District by March, six in January alone.[27]

Like their colleagues across the Second District, these new nominees
were respectable and uncontroversial: a sawmill operator, three farmers, two
merchant-grocers.[28] All served predominantly black communities in counties
with black-majority populations: Aurelian Springs, Kelford, Panacea Springs,
Powellsville, Princeville. However important these early postmasters were to
White, however, they were simply a footnote to the larger mosaic being formed
by McKinley.

As detailed in the *New York Times* on October 27, President McKinley's record
of appointments and promotions of black officeholders during his first seven
months in office was impressive. He had recorded a total of 179 "appointments
of colored persons to Government posts" between March 4 and October 15,
according to official records, for positions representing "salaries of $129,390 a
year," with salary averaging just over $700.[29]

Thus far, this list included only two high-level appointments for blacks—
U.S. minister to Haiti, William Powell (State Department), and Cheatham, the
District of Columbia's recorder of deeds (Interior Department). Except for
those two jobs, most appointments cited here were almost certainly low-level
positions at the U.S. Government Printing Office (53), and a scattering of low-
and midlevel slots at the Treasury Department (72), including its Customs
Service and Internal Revenue Service. The remaining low-level and midlevel
appointments were scattered between the Departments of State (4), Interior
(18), Agriculture (10), Navy (8), and Post Office (14). In addition, 125 promotions were awarded black workers during the period that ended October 4,
with annual salaries totaling $85,740.[30]

Those numbers dwarfed comparative totals for the same period during
Harrison's first year, when fewer than one hundred black officeholders were
appointed, carrying salaries totaling just $75,690; 20 Harrison promotions
carried salaries of $17,830.[31] In 1889, Congress had not been in special session,
accounting for some of the difference, but clearly McKinley outperformed
his last Republican predecessor. As to how many of the 1897 appointments

and promotions required input or advice from White, there is no record—but presumably only nonpostmaster appointments involving North Carolina residents, and only then as part of a larger circle of Republican leaders. In national matters of important racial consequence, McKinley's prime confidant and adviser appeared to be Bishop Arnett, called "the most powerful individual Negro at the White House" during the period.[32]

A close McKinley associate for a decade, the ex-legislator limited his interests primarily to Ohio patronage and the "top four." Only selecting fellow Ohioan John Green as U.S. postage stamp agent—highest-ranking black in the Post Office Department—would likely have stirred Arnett's reaction greatly; his other primary concern seems to have been securing political plums for his sons.[33] Mark Hanna and Cleveland barber George Myers were other likely resources, along with Blanche Bruce, all of whom could be expected to give sound advice and make sensible recommendations. A year later, Alabama educator Booker T. Washington joined the second tier of McKinley advisers, although Washington's political instincts were already recognized by other party leaders.

In some cases, McKinley was forced to find jobs for appointees whose suitability he may have doubted, such as Henry Demas of Louisiana; his appointment as naval officer for New Orleans, later blocked, set off immediate warning bells. In other cases, perfectly suitable nominees were opposed for reasons beyond his control, such as Ferdinand Havis of Arkansas, the wealthy black Republican McKinley selected as Pine Bluff postmaster. It was, of course, part of the patronage game, and McKinley gamely soldiered on, attempting to satisfy as many of the competing interests in both parties as he could.

But in other instances, the president's African American appointees were uncontroversial, such as those involving consulships at less desirable and less competitive foreign postings. All but one of those consuls were either trained lawyers or physicians; some were initially recess appointments in late July 1897, later confirmed by the Senate, including former judge Mifflin Gibbs of Arkansas, for Tamatave; attorney John Ruffin of Tennessee, for Asuncion; and Dr. George Jackson of Connecticut, for Cognac. Early McKinley consuls also included Dr. Henry Furniss of Indiana (Bahia); Dr. Lemuel Livingston (Cap-Haïtien); ordained minister Mahlon Van Horne of Rhode Island (Saint Thomas); Dr. John Williams of North Carolina (Freetown); and law professor Richard Greener, confirmed first as consul to Bombay, then transferred to Vladivostok.[34]

They would be joined as U.S. diplomats abroad in early 1898 by a well-regarded AME Zion clergyman from North Carolina, Owen Lun West Smith, easily confirmed by the Senate as new U.S. minister to Liberia. Ministers Smith and Powell completed the "big four" scorecard for McKinley, and both served on into the second McKinley administration and that of Theodore Roosevelt. White scored a resounding victory in December 1897 by convincing the president to appoint Smith, one of his constituents, as minister to Liberia. White's visit to the White House with recommendation in hand provoked a particularly telling observation by the *Washington Evening Star:* "Mr. White has been quietly urging the qualifications of Mr. [Owen] Smith for some time, and the President at last decided to give the appointment to the colored congressman's friend. The decision shows the standing of Mr. White at the Executive mansion."[35]

A dark horse for this appointment, Smith had once been informally conscripted into the Confederate army as a servant, escaping to join invading Union forces in 1865 before his fourteenth birthday. He studied law at the University of South Carolina in the mid-1870s, then taught school and became a Reconstruction-era magistrate. The forty-six-year-old held a doctorate in divinity from North Carolina's Livingstone College. A clergyman in the AME Zion denomination since 1881, Reverend Smith had lately served a congregation in Wilson, among the larger county seats in White's district.[36]

That White was able to persuade the president to appoint his constituent was no small feat for the novice; the minister's post was eyed eagerly by many ambitious black Republicans with influential friends. Smith's qualifications and White's sound judgment proved a happy coincidence; the highest post White had managed to gain so far was limited to postmasters in North Carolina's "Black Second."

With characteristic prudence, the president continued vetting his tentative choice; after White's morning visit, the president discussed Smith's selection separately with Bishops Arnett and James Handy and other black church leaders, who "made no opposition" to Smith's appointment.[37]

⁊♥

As his first calendar year in office neared an end, McKinley may have paused to give thanks for accomplishments and the acclaim given his first annual message in early December. But the year also brought him profound grief. Despite the pressures of office and his wife's poor health, he had journeyed back and forth between Canton and Washington to attend his mother's bedside after her November stroke while preparing his annual message, and, two days after that speech, to attend her funeral. The gracious and sprightly woman, eighty-eight at the time, captured the nation's hearts while attending her son's inauguration in March. Four of nine children survived to mourn, including the president's younger brother Abner and older sisters Helen and Sarah Elizabeth.

His annual message, not surprisingly, had been devoted to the increasingly complex foreign situation involving Spain and its unruly Caribbean colony Cuba, in revolt for the past three years. It was "the most important problem with which this Government is now called upon to deal pertaining to its foreign relations," although McKinley gave no hint that he envisioned war between the nations as the outcome. The Spanish response to Cuba's insurrection thus far had been brutal, bordering on genocide—the president called it "extermination"—and he insisted that Spain's new government must act more equitably and humanely.

McKinley firmly instructed his new minister to Spain "to impress upon that Government the sincere wish of the United States to lend its aid toward the ending of the war in Cuba by reaching a peaceful and lasting result, just and honorable alike to Spain and to the Cuban people." The Sagasta government responded "in the direction of a better understanding," so the president claimed. "It appreciates the friendly purposes of this Government. It admits that our country is deeply affected by the war in Cuba and that its desires for peace are just.... [T]he present Spanish government is bound by every consideration to a change of policy that should satisfy the United States and pacify Cuba within a reasonable time."[38]

McKinley then announced what many Americans were delighted to hear: "To this end Spain has decided to put into effect the political reforms heretofore advocated by the present premier, without halting for any consideration in the path which in its judgment leads to peace. The military operations ... will continue, but will be humane and conducted with all regard for private rights, being accompanied by political action leading to the autonomy of Cuba while guarding Spanish sovereignty."[39] Within two months of his speech, everything would change in a flash, setting the stage for a military confrontation McKinley tried in vain to prevent.

Meanwhile, the nation's only African American congressman continued to labor behind the scenes as he prepared for the second session of his first Congress. Appointed to the House Agricultural Committee on July 24, just before the special session adjourned, White played an active role on that committee during the regular session. But so far, White's first duty had been to his constituents, including those whose nominations went to the White House. Such postmasterships presented a delicate issue for White, whose reputation for political integrity and stubborn independence was already well known; his dilemma was deciding whom to choose and how to determine competence and merit.

White's natural instinct was to select potential appointees on the basis of reputation from the pool of available talent, with political suitability a second or third criterion. Not yet fully accustomed to seeking outside advice, he was nonetheless learning his limits. In 1896, White had depended on assistance for the first time—from influential power broker James Young—to win the congressional nomination, although he balked at corrupt practices such as "selling offices" to get ahead.[40]

In the spring of 1897, White had displayed a sensible willingness to compromise on taking unpleasant advice against certain types of appointments. In April, shortly after taking office, he considered but decided against nominating a black candidate for appointment to West Point, after newspaper accounts of a possible nomination provoked public outcry and implied an unwelcome backlash.[41] By the winter of 1897, he was gaining confidence and seemed willing to take more risks, as evidenced by his nominee at Scotland Neck. The former county commissioner had many influential friends in both races, but in the turbulent world of local politics, it was often the presence of a few powerful enemies that mattered more—enemies whose power White may well have dismissed or underestimated.

Before it ended, the Anthony nomination consumed far more political capital than expected, provoked an unwelcome battle between his state's two senators, left White chastened and bruised on the sidelines—and set an ominous example for other appointees, including some already in office. The practical education of George White in politics—in a new and somewhat unfamiliar national arena, a potential minefield—was about to begin.

1898

3

FIRST TESTS OF FIRE

*Will the American Congress sit supinely by and declare its inability to interfere . . .
while our organic law, the Constitution of the United States, is being openly violated?*
—**George H. White,** U.S. House, January 11, 1898

Blizzards blanketing New York and other northeastern cities at the end of January 1898 did not reach as far south as Washington, D.C., but capital city temperatures—8 degrees above zero on February 1—kept most lawmakers, officials, and citizens safely inside.[1] Only heat generated by growing concern over civil unrest in Cuba and possible evacuation of U.S. citizens from that island kept many observers warm. Before the month was over, that fleeting sense of calm and peace would vanish in two unrelated, fiery explosions—one ninety miles offshore from Florida, the other within four hundred miles of the U.S. Capitol.

Each disaster carried its own unsettling long-term consequences for the nation by changing history in unexpected ways—especially for African Americans, still seeking continued leadership on race-related issues by a friendly Republican administration. The two events placed the first subtle strains on the relationship developing between George White and President McKinley, propelling White into an unaccustomed role of spokesman on two complex racial issues defying easy answers: an increased presence for black soldiers in the segregated national army and protecting innocent victims from rampant racial violence. Unlike the simpler appointments of postmasters, local in nature, these new issues carried more political significance nationally and, for the first time, exposed presidential vulnerability to political pressures McKinley had so far dismissed, deflected, or delegated.

Although the president still depended on Mark Hanna's advice, their relationship underwent a critical change after Hanna's election to the U.S. Senate in March 1897; he could no longer serve as McKinley's chief adviser. Mindful of new offices and separate duties, both men sought to maintain a correct distance, avoiding perceptions of McKinley favoritism, although friends and critics alike helped perpetuate the continuing myth of Hanna's dominance. Uniquely positioned as chairman of the National Republican Committee, Senator Hanna certainly played a major role in patronage appointments, yet the president now preferred to choose many appointees on his own—among factors contributing to a new, uncertain equilibrium.[2]

The events also interrupted a string of successful moves by White, whose growing popularity in the House and within the GOP had so far strengthened his personal political position and inspired a stronger sense of confidence in the first-term congressman. But hidden dangers awaited White, now venturing into uncharted territory and neglecting to cultivate useful allies on complicated issues. With his first lengthy speech in the House on January 11, he denounced the growing disfranchisement of black southern voters. Certain southern congressional districts, notably in Mississippi and South Carolina, he said, had reduced their voting basis to a tiny fraction of that in "the North, East, West, and some few of the Southern States from 5,000 to 11,000," compared with "an aggregate vote cast anywhere from 30,000 to 50,000."[3]

"How long, Mr. Chairman, will this increased representation, brought about by the disfranchisement of certain American citizens, be permitted to go on unrebuked?" White asked. "Will the American Congress sit supinely by and declare its inability to interfere . . . while our organic law, the Constitution of the United States, is being openly violated?" His ringing question came in a statement ostensibly devoted to reforming the civil service law, but that included a wide range of comments on the hypocrisy of extending this inconsistent record to other nations—the former kingdom of Hawaii, where Americans had tacitly condoned the queen's overthrow, or Spanish Cuba, where aid once promised "to Cuban sufferers" by the GOP platform of 1896 was conveniently forgotten.[4]

For more than two centuries, the United States willingly tolerated slavery by ignoring "the specific letter in our declaration of rights that all men are born free and equal, endowed with certain inalienable rights, among which are life, liberty, and the pursuit of happiness," White asserted. Only a "fratricidal war of four years' duration" had managed to end the "festering cancer" of "this living lie," recurring in a new battle over the meaning of the due-process clause in the Fourteenth Amendment as the South disfranchised former slaves.

White's question predicted two possible outcomes: positive action ending disfranchisement, and the alternative of no action at all. His January 11 remarks starkly warned fellow congressmen of the hypocrisy of preaching democracy to foreign citizens without insisting on it at home. Remembering that his speech was required to adhere to the issue at hand, however, he ended by returning to the issue of so-called civil service reform, prompting the second prophecy made in his brief tenure: "I think the time has come for us to call a halt [to the civil service extension], and if we have not the manliness to stand up and destroy this measure before it ruins our body politic, the electors of these United States will on the eighth day of November next rise in their might and in their wrath, and send men here who will do their bidding. Mark the prediction, and be governed accordingly."[5]

White's speech was warmly received by the Republican majority, who offered "loud and prolonged applause." Southern Democrats were less likely to appreciate the barely concealed threat of reduced House representation for their states if disfranchisement efforts continued. Whether the House would be emboldened to act on White's call for ending disfranchisement—or punish states who pursued it—remained to be seen. And whether voters might find his argument against civil service "reform" compelling enough to hold Congress responsible for failing to block it was less clear.

Whatever the outcome on either front, White's persistent references to disfranchisement of black voters would continue throughout his congressional career, both on and off the House floor. Whether he warned his colleagues of his plans in advance is not clear, but his implied call for congressional reprisals against South Carolina and Mississippi certainly reflected growing sentiment in Republican quarters to halt spreading disfranchisement. In the weeks to come, he addressed more immediate issues raised by February events—first in Cuba, then in South Carolina. And it was here that he took his first unilateral steps, after consulting only his own conscience.

Much has been written about the fate of the USS *Maine,* which exploded in Havana harbor under mysterious circumstances on February 15, killing hundreds of U.S. sailors and leading to war with Spain. Far less has been written in recent years about the murderous fire a week later in Lake City, South Carolina, claiming just two lives. Yet for very different reasons, both events touched the soul of African America's troubled citizenry and quickly intertwined rallying cries for action.

The *Maine's* destruction offered black men an opportunity to dispel lingering perceptions by white America of their lack of patriotism, by volunteering to fight a foreign enemy. The Lake City murders offered a far less pleasant reminder of the lynching scourge sweeping the country and prompted calls both for protection by the federal government—against white vigilantes—and for more direct action, arming black families to protect themselves against violence. In both instances, White staked out strong positions, only to find himself with fewer allies than expected or needed.

Like his predecessor, McKinley faced a delicate diplomatic situation over Cuba, with the same unpredictable consul general at the Havana helm: Fitzhugh Lee of Virginia, a onetime Confederate general appointed by Cleveland and retained by McKinley, despite blunt warnings. Determined to maintain neutrality on the Cuban question, Cleveland kept U.S. warships away from the island to avoid provocation, but he inadvertently complicated matters by appointing Lee as Havana's highest-ranking U.S. diplomat. The headstrong Lee rankled the island's elite with barely concealed zeal for the independence movement.

Annoyed by Lee's stubbornness, Cleveland advised his successor to recall and replace him. But so far, McKinley had declined, and Lee continued to favor Cuban independence. So to promote an amicable air of "business as usual," McKinley reversed Cleveland's moratorium on military port calls. After Lee urgently requested contingency plans for the possible evacuation of Americans if local violence endangered them, McKinley stationed the *Maine* in Key West under Lee's direct control. Whatever reservations the new Sagasta government had about McKinley's arrangement, it soon agreed to a military exchange program. Spain's first vessel, the *Vizcaya*, was scheduled to arrive in New York harbor by late February.

Unexpected events, however, speeded up the American timetable. An angry mob attacked Havana newspaper offices in mid-January 1898, targeting those favoring the limited autonomy offered by Spain. With little notice to Lee, McKinley sent the *Maine* and 350 sailors to Havana as a precaution; by January 26, the *Maine* had moored itself off Havana for a brief visit, at a buoy specified by Spanish authorities. Soon it was shuttling U.S. officers into the city for rounds of parties and dinners, bringing back Spanish and Cuban dignitaries for ship visits. Lee changed his mind about wanting the *Maine* so close, yet was nonetheless impressed at its appearance. In a letter to Assistant

Secretary of State William Day, Lee called it "a beautiful sight and one long to be remembered."[6]

The *Maine* would be long remembered—but, sadly, not much longer for its physical beauty.

❧

Among the *Maine*'s crew members were the U.S. Navy's championship baseball team, including its only black member, star pitcher William Lambert, left-handed fireman second class, among thirty black sailors aboard the *Maine*. Described by one teammate as "a master of speed, curves and control," Lambert was an engine stoker among the African American crew—firemen, oilers, and coal passers—assigned to the *Maine* engine room. His team had recently won the navy's championship in Key West, defeating the USS *Marblehead* team by a lopsided 18 to 3.[7]

A relatively new vessel incorporating coal-fired steam boilers, the *Maine* was well equipped for war, with tons of explosive powder ready to fire its guns. Most black sailors aboard the *Maine* were mess attendants and landsmen. But there were five black petty officers, with another three of seaman rank—signifying considerable sailing experience—and one ordinary sailor.[8] The American navy had long depended upon a healthy contingent of black personnel aboard U.S. ships, enjoying a rare degree of social equality there—unlike the army situation, in which black soldiers were confined to segregated units and rarely assigned beyond isolated western outposts. If few black sailors held deck ratings, and most worked in menial tasks in the mess or engine room, the racial environment aboard ship and at shore stations still remained peaceful, even friendly.[9]

Those black sailors given shore passes would have found a reasonably congenial setting in Cuba's capital, at least on one level. Slavery had been abolished a decade earlier in Cuba, and racial relations between its African and Afro-Cuban mulatto minorities—together numbering perhaps a third of the population—and white-majority Spanish immigrants and creoles were far less tense than at home. Yet relaxation of old traditions had been complicated by recent economic woes and the current uprising; the so-called "Cuban liberating army" was largely manned by black and mulatto rebels, and Spain had sent more than two hundred thousand soldiers since 1895 to beat them back.[10]

The Sagasta government's compromise solution—autonomy without in-dependence for Cuba or Puerto Rico—was hobbled by a strategic miscalcula-tion: selecting the conservative diplomat Enrique Dupuy de Lôme as Spain's minister to the United States. What he perceived as American arrogance to-ward Spain angered Dupuy de Lôme, who thoroughly disliked both McKinley and U.S. policy. To a Spanish acquaintance, the minister indiscreetly expressed his private opinions of McKinley. When that letter ended up in the New York press, as the *Maine* lay off Havana, public uproar forced the minister's recall in mid-February.[11]

The diplomat's indiscretion damaged Spain's already precarious image in the U.S. mind, even as the *Maine* continued its goodwill mission. No decision had yet been announced on how long the *Maine* might stay in Cuba, although the secretary of the navy announced a related move in early February. The U.S. cruiser *Montgomery* was scheduled to visit other Cuban ports, though not Havana, and then remain in the Caribbean indefinitely.[12] The *Maine*'s original brief visit to Havana was into its third week on February 15, when a sudden se-ries of explosions tore through the *Maine*'s hull and sank the vessel in a matter of minutes, shortly after 9:00 PM.

More than 260 sailors died in that blast or drowned as the *Maine* sank, including William Lambert and twenty-one more black sailors in the dead-liest U.S. naval incident since the end of the Civil War. Injured survivors were evacuated to Key West, where another eight sailors died of wounds and were buried. In Washington, a suddenly beleaguered McKinley ordered a full investigation into the *Maine*'s sinking, as did the Sagasta government. Alle-gations swirled that a Spanish mine had triggered the first explosion, despite no evidence that mines were in Havana harbor. The Sagasta inquiry quickly concluded that the explosions were all internal, but few Americans believed that. The media frenzy for war against Spain was well under way when the U.S. investigation contradicted the Spanish conclusion in mid-March, instead blaming an underwater mine for the explosion—despite eyewitness accounts making that cause unlikely.[13]

"Remember the *Maine!*" quickly became the phrase on American lips. But nowhere, perhaps, was patriotic sentiment stronger than in black commu-nities, which quickly took up the cause of war as a sadly providential way to show their commitment to the nation—and to mourn the loss of black sailors. Before war was finally declared, the drumbeat among black leaders to summon recruits to the cause—fueled by casualty lists published in black newspapers—was deafening.[14]

The precise timing of any declaration of war against Spain was still uncertain, yet war clouds clearly loomed on the horizon, and both Congress and the War Department were deeply involved in contingency planning. On March 9, Congress appropriated $50 million to beef up the woefully inadequate U.S. military, pending outcome of the Naval Court of Inquiry into the *Maine;* that decision, announced ten days later, blamed a mine for the explosion.[15] Public opinion, already inflamed, now all but guaranteed war between the United States and Spain.

In the U.S. Army as then constituted, only a small number of black soldiers—two enlisted, all-black regiments each in infantry and cavalry, among forty regiments overall—were eligible to participate. Determined to ensure that any military buildup included increased participation by black soldiers, on March 7 White proposed creating a fifth all-black artillery regiment—a controversial issue still on the back burner when the war ended.[16]

On the evening of February 21, however, war with Spain remained only a possible nightmare as Lake City postmaster Frazier Baker's family retired for the evening. Before dawn broke, the family would become casualties in a far more insidious war, one pitting black citizens against whites and the federal government against its own people—in this case, a determined band of masked marauders evoking eerie images of the long-dormant Ku Klux Klan.

Vigilantes were intent on reclaiming Lake City's independence from perceived overreach by the president in appointing an outsider to handle their mail. But in the eyes of outsiders, the appointment was a trivial act blown out of all proportion to reality—and the vigilantes, cold-blooded murderers.

ॐ

Not long after arriving in Lake City in the late summer of 1897, Baker had gained a potent taste of the community's antagonism toward outsiders. A boycott against his first post office, in a local black minister's parsonage, had driven many white patrons to conduct postal business in nearby towns.[17] His skin color was hardly the only reason for ostracism; above-average intelligence and education made him suspicious to typical white customers. Perhaps most damning was his apparent effrontery in taking the small town's only federal office from a white man, exacerbating political subcurrents. Worst of all, he was not local, and subject to no one's control in Lake City.

A quiet, unassuming father of six, Baker seemed in retrospect a surprise choice, with no discernible political connections beyond friendship with Edmund Deas and one year of postal experience in Effingham under Harrison.[18] After being quietly replaced by Cleveland in 1893, Baker had resumed duties as schoolmaster and farmer. If few Republicans in South Carolina were surprised when Baker's name resurfaced in 1897, after McKinley's inauguration, his inexplicable choice for Lake City baffled observers and its citizens alike.

Other towns and cities across the largely Democratic state had come to terms with Republican postmasters—even black Republican postmasters, as in Florence—but Lake City showed far less patience. Located twenty miles south of Florence, it was a small agricultural community of four hundred residents—a virtual white island that did not reflect surrounding Williamsburg County's African American majority. And unlike the county's political complexion, where overwhelmingly Republican sympathies still simmered quietly, Lake City was proudly Democratic.

Like his Georgia counterpart at Hogansville, Baker was literate and seemingly qualified—more so than the average U.S. postmaster—but in terms of community acceptance and support, he was the wrong man for the job. Loftin, at least, had been a resident of Hogansville. Baker was from Effingham, fifteen miles away—in his case, another insult by an arrogant outsider. However gracious and polite he may have been, he might as well have come from another planet: singularly out of place, as a Republican from another county, appointed by a Republican president in Washington, at the behest of a black Republican power broker from Darlington.

By December 1897, unhappy Lake City citizens—half the town's residents—petitioned the Post Office Department to remove Baker. Their petition cited six major reasons, five involving "impoliteness to ladies" and allegations of improper business conduct. Newness to Lake City was sixth. "He [Baker] was not a resident of the county when he applied for this office," the citizens complained, "and had resided here only a few days when he received his commissions."[19]

Lake City's post office, established in 1856, had recently been run by popular businessman Charles Kelley, who "conducted its [postal] affairs to the satisfaction of all" for seven years, or so thought editor Marion Clark of the

Lake City Times. Kelley's replacement had since become a major source of local friction, Clark told a Charleston journalist in early 1898, although public objections failed to dislodge Baker. "We have little courtesy shown us and the service is as poor as can be," said Clark. "We have four mail trains a day that stop at the depot, and before this negro [Baker] was appointed we had three daily mails. Now we have one. There have been no changes of schedule, but I presume he found it took too much of his time to attend to three mails."[20]

Clark knew better. Shortly after Baker arrived, Lake City did endure a reduction in daily mail deliveries, but only after Baker and assistant James Braveboy reported being shot at while retrieving mailbags in December 1897, leading Postmaster General Gary to halt nighttime exchanges or drops of mail for security reasons. Mail deliveries outside daylight hours were taken by train to Scranton, three miles away, and redelivered to Lake City by messenger only after daylight.[21] But the petition to the fourth assistant postmaster general was printed for all to see. "The charges can be substantiated and all we want is an investigation," Clark claimed.[22] His subsequent interview took place "while the Lake City postoffice trouble was supposed to be at its height," though the *newspaper* delayed printing it.[23]

Perhaps the newspaper felt concern for Baker's well-being or hoped the "Lake City trouble" would blow over; with luck, he would simply resign. In the meantime, Edmund Deas remained Baker's most ardent supporter, among his few real friends in the political world. The Darlington Republican, recently reappointed as South Carolina's deputy collector of internal revenue, praised the new postmaster's courage, counseling Baker to stand firm against local intimidation. If he did so, Baker's name would surely "go down the corridors of time as one of the bravest and most patriotic men of his race."[24]

Deas was hopelessly optimistic; Baker was increasingly fearful for his own safety. He and Braveboy had escaped injury when, a month before his family's arrival, Baker's first post office—the vacant parsonage—burned under suspicious circumstances. After the January fire, Baker received assistance from postal inspector H. T. B. Moye, of the Chattanooga, Tennessee, district office, who later described a five-day visit to Lake City.

Moye "was there when the [second] office was opened and gave Baker instructions on how to put up the mail," he testified in 1899. "On January 14, 1898, I went to Lake City and remained there until the morning of January 19. I located the [second] office." Local citizens were courteous but unwilling to help him.[25] "We did not locate it nearer the centre of the town because we could not get a building.... Mrs. Rogers refused to let the office go in her building. Dr. Williams had no place for us." Former postmaster Kelley, now Lake City's intendant, or mayor-equivalent, "refused to let me rent a building that he had."[26]

Local residents feared arson if they complied. Inspector Moye had one option: a one-room former schoolhouse, outside town limits, next door to a church. The frame structure measured thirty feet by fourteen feet, with a rear fireplace for heat and cooking. Partitioning the building would accommodate both a dwindling postal business and residence. The building faced the Atlantic Coast Line railroad tracks, expediting handling of delivery mailbags, although the depot lay a half mile away.

About three hundred square feet of living space could hold a large family, but with few creature comforts—open clay fireplace, four windows for ventilation and light, and an internal doorway from office to living quarters, with an outdoor well and pump for water. Flanked by trees and thick undergrowth, the building's only door opened onto the street. It had one glaring physical disadvantage: only one way in or out.

Undoubtedly lonely and eager to bolster his image as a local citizen, Baker moved his wife, Lavinia, and six children down from Effingham in early February. He created a cozy, temporary living area in the rear for Lavinia and toddler Julia; oldest daughter, Rosa; and four younger siblings, who arrived with furniture and belongings about February 7. For two weeks, son Lincoln Douglas, eleven, shared chores with sixteen-year-old Rosa and fourteen-year-old Cora; younger sisters Sarah, seven, and Millie, five, cared for Julia while their mother helped sort mail.[27]

On February 21, as afternoon drew into evening, a few customers came in and collected their daily mail. After 4:00 PM, Lavinia Baker went into the living quarters to prepare the evening meal, using buckets of well water. The Lake City post office closed, and the Bakers sat down for their evening meal before retiring. The furor over the sinking of the *Maine* in faraway Havana was still commanding the front pages of U.S. newspapers; consul Fitzhugh Lee demanded divers in Havana to retrieve bodies and effects from the harbor.[28]

Baker was armed, his wife later testified—but even with a gun in his house, he did not feel safe. Nine days earlier, he had written to Edmund Deas, describing his situation. His February 13 reply from Washington addressed Baker as "Dear Friend," bolstering his waning resolve to stay on:

Yours of the 12th inst. duly received. I was exceedingly glad to hear from you. You have certainly made a great fight and taken a manly stand. . . . You will certainly go down the corridors of time as one of the noblemen of our day and time. Excuse brevity as I am sick. The colored men of Williamsburg . . . will stand up for their manhood under a brave leader. Your example is worthy of emulation. I am glad the people are standing by you and that there has been formed an inseparable alliance with them. Truly your old friend and warm admirer, E. H. Deas.[29]

The letter was small comfort. Baker's renewed plea for protection—addressed to superiors at the Post Office Department in Washington—went out in the town's last outgoing mail delivery, picked up at midday February 21 by the southbound train. But it arrived in Washington too late to save him.

The details of the grisly murders of Baker and his daughter and the wounding of his wife and other children are well described elsewhere, particularly by contemporary newspaper accounts and more recently by historian Terence Finnegan.[30] By the time Inspector Moye arrived two days later to investigate, Baker's smoldering body had been taken away and buried. After searching the site, Moye testified he found "several artifacts . . . mail sack clasps, shells, mail sack locks. All the articles were burned and blackened. The lock indicated that the mail bag was locked. A watch, which evidently had been sent through the mail . . . had been stopped at exactly 12:49 o'clock."[31]

Much of the federal government was closed Tuesday, February 22, for George Washington's birthday, but a day later, the city buzzed with official reactions to the murders. The president was deeply disturbed by the news; the Baker murders were discussed briefly at the February 23 cabinet meeting, and Postmaster General Gary was directed to undertake a full investigation.[32] The grisly news spread quickly in newspapers from Charleston to New York. "Murder in South Carolina," blared a *New York Times* headline on February 23, followed by "The Outrage at Lake City" a day later, announcing the postmaster general's first rewards: three hundred dollars each for the arrest and conviction of those responsible for burning the post office and killing Frazier Baker.[33]

Around the country, condemnation of the murders was nearly universal. Politicians were at a near loss for words, for once. Democratic Rep. William Elliott, whose district included Williamsburg County and who had defeated the state's last black congressman, in 1896, was dumbfounded. "My God, it can't be true," he reportedly gasped, telling the *Charleston News & Courier*, "Such hot-headed action does not represent the feeling in South Carolina, I'm sure." South Carolina's junior senator, John McLaurin—elevated from the U.S. House eight months earlier—visited Postmaster General Gary personally February 24 to express "his horror at the crime" and urged Gary's department to use "every means at its command to discover the perpetrators of the crime." McLaurin offered to do everything in his power to assist.[34]

For once, there was no immediate comment from McLaurin's firebrand colleague "Pitchfork Ben" Tillman, whose white-supremacist sentiments were well known. Strangely, Edmund Deas, who had counseled Baker just days earlier to remain in Lake City, now reportedly blamed the McKinley administration for "cowardly" behavior. The *News & Courier* writer described Deas, in Washington on business, as "greatly stirred up over the summary killing of two of his race . . . and is disposed to put the blame on the Administration, which he accuses of having been very cowardly in the matter."[35] It was the inverse image of a common South Carolina view—that McKinley invited these horrible events by taunting whites with black appointments.

There was as yet no way to identify Baker's killers—and specific charges against members of the lynch mob, if and when apprehended, remained dependent on competing laws of South Carolina and the United States. Federal law covered only burning the post office and destruction of the mail, not the deaths of Baker and his daughter. Murder charges, conversely, could only be brought by the State of South Carolina, and few expected lynch mob members to be tried for murder, much less convicted or given a death penalty. Still, rewards were posted in Washington and Columbia for apprehension and conviction of those responsible for Baker's death. South Carolina governor William Ellerbe offered five hundred dollars for information, if with little explanation. Postmaster General Gary now offered two separate rewards: three hundred dollars for information on the fire, five hundred dollars more for information on Baker's death. But he also closed the Lake City post office indefinitely—the community's severest possible penalty.

The postmaster general and the governor were a study in political and personal contrasts. James Gary was uncomfortable with appointments of black southern postmasters, having once warned McKinley he might as well concede Maryland back to Democrats in 1900 if he pushed Judson Lyons in Augusta.[36] At sixty-five, Gary also lacked the physical vigor for a controversial case, and he soon resigned, citing poor health. The far younger Ellerbe, in his second year as governor, was already a seasoned politician; just thirty-five, he had served twice as state controller before succeeding Governor Tillman. From a prominent upcountry family, Ellerbe symbolized a moderate center in the state's fractious Democratic Party, between Tillman's bellicose wing and the conservative older establishment. In 1896, Ellerbe handily won his first term as the so-called "representative of conciliation" in the governor's race.

Considered by many the state's most popular politician, Ellerbe now faced a difficult reelection campaign, with five fellow Democrats running. Despite ideological differences, however, Tillman had great respect for Ellerbe and refused to oppose him.[37] Yet by offering a reward for Baker's killers, Ellerbe defied Tillman allies among the party's white-supremacist wing and could hardly expect to gain any votes on the right.

By early March, South Carolina's attorney general, William Barber, commenced his own investigation. But federal officials had already dispatched South Carolina's U.S. district attorney, Abial Lathrop, to Lake City to begin their investigation, just after postal investigators arrived. There visitors found a stunned local population, roundly insisting that no one in their town was responsible—that the lynchers had been strangers and outsiders—yet nervously determined to defend themselves against rumored attacks by black vigilantes from as far away as Chicago.

Williamsburg County officials began their inquest into Baker's death on February 24 but quickly adjourned until February 26. Even then, after hearing testimony from seven witnesses, the coroner's jury decision was suspended "to await new developments," amid raging rumors that blacks from adjacent towns planned to burn Lake City down.[38] Predictably, the rumors were baseless. But the contagious fear that claimed Baker's life—an all-consuming fear of outsiders—seemed rooted among townspeople.

For the McKinley administration, dogged by drumbeats for war from William Randolph Hearst's *New York World,* the Lake City murders were a reminder of the stubborn persistence of important domestic events. Even as strident stories of the *Maine* tragedy filled the nation's daily newspapers, relegating Baker's death—when mentioned at all—to inside pages, McKinley did not forget his promise for a thorough investigation. However distracted he may have been by Cuba, McKinley asked the first cabinet meeting in March to devote an hour to hearing the postmaster general's report.[39]

The text of Gary's report was not released publicly but was surely replete with graphic details of the horror, the reading of which was distasteful for the courtly Baltimore industrialist. It was becoming a sad habit, of sorts; just a week after Baker's death, Gary reported to the cabinet the murder of a second southern U.S. postmaster—this one white, at Ada, Georgia.[40] After the March 4 meeting, Gary did issue a press statement on the incident, the most comprehensive version of the story published so far, ending with a direct appeal to the nation:

> It is needless for me to add that the Administration . . . fully appreci-
> ate[s] the enormity of the crime which has been committed, not only
> against this unoffending man and his family, but against the Govern-
> ment, as represented by the Postmaster. . . . I assure you that the Post
> Office Department, in cooperation with the Department of Justice, will
> do everything in its power to apprehend and convict the men who com-
> mitted this terrible outrage. Both of the departments mentioned are
> using every means in their power to the end that justice may be meted
> out to the criminals.[41]

Like most Americans of either race, Gary was shocked by the crime's brutality, and he agreed wholeheartedly with editorial views in his hometown *Baltimore Sun* condemning the "atrocious act of a mob." But like its reader Gary, the *Sun* expressed a nagging caveat, simultaneously chiding the administration for "forcing colored men into positions of responsibility in the South without regard to the preferences or protests of the majority of the people."[42] Delivering the report was Gary's last official cabinet task. Within a month, he left the administration, in a secondary ripple from the Baker murders—his decision perhaps expedited by reading aloud the murder's graphic details.

Outside the cabinet, not everyone was content to wait and see what actions the administration chose. A week after the murders, concurrent resolutions were introduced in both House and Senate calling for the appointment of a six-member joint fact-finding committee to pursue an investigation.[43] The resolutions were referred to committees in both houses, where the proposal soon disappeared from view. Another congressional ripple from the murders—this one more ominous, both for immediate reactions and its lack of success—occurred when George White proposed offering financial assistance to the Baker family.

White suggested one thousand dollars—more than a year's salary for many U.S. postmasters, yet hardly excessive—but objections by Georgia's Rep. Charles Bartlett precluded discussion of the matter. The wording of House Resolution 171 was brief and indisputable:

Joint resolution for the relief of Mrs. [Frazier B.] Baker.

Whereas on or about the 21st of February last, 100 armed men or more fired upon and killed the postmaster at Lake City, S.C., and killing one of the family and wounding several others, and burning all they had; and

Whereas the said family is now suffering even for means for medical treatment and for other necessities of life:

Be it resolved by the Senate and the House of Representatives of the United States of America in Congress assembled, That the sum of $1,000 is hereby appropriated out of any money in the Treasury of the United States not otherwise appropriated, to be immediately available, for the relief of the said family.[44]

White's resolution was read aloud, then referred to the Committee on Post-Office and Post-Roads, where it languished; a committee report was issued in May 1898 but no further action taken.[45] White later told Chicago journalist Ida Wells-Barnett that he initially planned to ask for fifty thousand dollars but lowered it to one thousand dollars to ensure acceptance.[46]

But his action had one unexpected consequence: a rift with Wells-Barnett, in Washington to take up her familiar cause of lynching, demanding that White withdraw his resolution in favor of one proposed by Illinois senators. Despite nursing a five-month-old son, Wells-Barnett began an energetic campaign on Mrs. Baker's behalf. White refused to withdraw his resolution, and the ensuing standoff between the two stubborn leaders became an open secret on Capitol Hill, yet another unexpected ripple emanating from the original events.[47]

Accompanied to the White House on March 21 by junior Illinois senator William Mason—and seven Chicago-area congressmen, plus many local residents—Wells-Barnett presented McKinley with a four-page typewritten plea, seeking monetary compensation and a federal lynching ban. Wells-Barnett prevailed upon Illinois's senior senator, Shelby Cullom, for a letter of introduction. "To our appeals for justice the stereotyped reply has been that the government could not interfere in a state matter," she wrote. But she insisted that "Postmaster Baker's case was a federal matter. . . . He died at his post of duty in defense of his country's honor, as truly as did ever a soldier on the field of battle. We refuse to believe this country, so powerful to defend its citizens abroad, is unable to protect its citizens at home.[48]

"President McKinley received us very courteously, listened to my plea, accepted the resolutions which had been sent by the citizens of Chicago, and told me to report back home that they had already placed some of the finest of their secret service agents" in South Carolina, Wells-Barnett wrote in her memoir. If not widely noted in Washington, her meeting received front-page treatment in midwestern newspapers like the *Indianapolis News*, which listed all her congressional delegation and "a set of resolutions adopted at a mass meeting in Chicago."[49]

To White she argued—perhaps a bit too shrilly—that Senator Mason should take the lead, reasoning that any sum requested by a black congressman would be too high for southern segregationists. "My reply to him was that he did not know the South as well as I had hoped for; for if he did, he would know that they would object to the compensation of five dollars not because of the amount, but because of the principle of the thing." Mason's concurrent Senate resolution was identical to White's, in all but the sum sought, ten thousand dollars.[50]

Chicago Rep. William Lorimer—who sat on the Post-Office and Post-Roads Committee—was prepared to offer a substitute House bill for that same amount but could only do so if White's bill were reported out of committee and disposed of first. For five weeks, Wells-Barnett pursued her cause on Capitol Hill, "trying to get connections and Mr. White's cooperation," but White refused to back down, enduring the Chicago crusader's scorn for the next two decades. Wells-Barnett was notoriously persistent; in this case, she was also almost certainly correct, but White had no patience with her tactics.

White's refusal to negotiate with Wells-Barnett subtly showed the darker side of his political stubbornness, recalling his angry break with Cheatham during their 1894 contest over the Second District Republican nomination. But rejecting Wells-Barnett's suggestion was a different and riskier matter, demonstrating that a characteristically pragmatic White sometimes ignored practical considerations, even when it guaranteed success for the goal.

In Congress for barely twelve months before proposing the resolution, White remained a novice in navigating the complicated waters of House politics. But he knew he had other options: he could easily have recruited House cosponsors for his resolution in advance of introduction—Reps. Henry Bingham of Pennsylvania and Lorimer himself would have been inspired alternatives, or any of twenty southern Republican colleagues.[51] To ensure quick passage, he might have taken the draft to friendly colleagues—Representatives Southwick, Sprague, or Harmer—for assistance, although bringing on cosponsors meant sacrificing sole responsibility for the resolution and its wording. In the end, he did neither; his first major effort as a freshman legislator suffered badly, and a useful alliance with Wells-Barnett was sidetracked.

Both White's House proposal and the concurrent Senate resolution foundered, quickly lost in the war fever sweeping Washington weeks later. Even Lorimer's promised resolution in the Fifty-Sixth Congress, after the 1898 elections, came to nothing. In the end, Baker's widow and children received no government compensation at all.

4

SELECTING BACKUPS AND RECRUITING VOLUNTEERS

The President assured Mr. White of his sympathy with the movement for a larger recognition of the Negro soldiers, and expressed admiration for the valor and capacity of the colored comrades.
—The *Colored American*, May 14, 1898

For any president responsible for nominating prospective officeholders, particularly nominees requiring Senate confirmation, a list of replacements is always useful. In some cases, the confirmation process fails, compelling the president— or a congressman—to select another nominee. Sometimes a nominee withdraws before confirmation or, more rarely, dies or resigns after taking office.

For both President McKinley and George White, that standard practice of picking backups and replacements would come into play by the spring of 1898. One occasion for McKinley came at a moment of great sadness, but high political theater as well, in mid-March 1898, just weeks before the Congress declared war on Spain. Political activities in Washington ground to a sudden halt in homage to a fallen political giant, former senator Blanche Bruce, recently confirmed as register of the U.S. Treasury, arguably the best-known surviving Reconstruction-era black leader.[1]

Those who had either known Bruce well or might wish to bask in his reflected fame now paid respects at the "people's church," the enormous red-brick Metropolitan AME edifice on Northwest Washington's M Street. Thousands of well-wishers thronged through for a last glimpse of the only African American man so far to serve a full Senate term—an ex-slave turned plantation owner and millionaire, still in high office two decades after Reconstruction.

McKinley was genuinely fond of Bruce and personally saddened by his death—two sentiments well evoked by the "unusual richness and beauty" of the White House floral tribute, in the *Washington Evening Star*'s description:

"The card of President McKinley was attached to a large and exquisite wreath of white roses, lilies of the valley, white carnations, calla lilies and rare orchids sprayed with feathery asparagus and lily leaves. A broad white satin ribbon was tied over two crossed leaves of palm attached to the wreath."[2]

The *Evening Star*'s lengthy report on Bruce's funeral left no doubt of his importance—or of the respect he commanded within the nation's black community, evidenced by the distinguished honorary pallbearers selected by his widow to follow the casket out of the church. More than two dozen political figures, representing either southern, northern, or midwestern roots, had come together to bury Bruce, and to jostle each other, gently yet with subtle purpose, for position. Their ranks embodied the past, present, and future of black Republican political achievement: an ex-governor (P. B. S. Pinchback), two ex-congressmen (Lynch and Cheatham), and the nation's only current black congressman (White), along with McKinley favorites from Ohio days (John Green and Campbell Maxwell). Also on hand were younger men to whom the torch might yet pass—William Pledger, Robert Terrell, and Ralph Waldo Tyler—and even one sentimental crowd favorite, Lewis Douglass, Civil War veteran and son of Frederick Douglass.[3]

Some among them hoped even to succeed Bruce as register of the U.S. Treasury, placing his signature on the nation's currency, a symbolic position in the executive branch—but arguably the highest appointive federal office yet held by a black man. Bruce himself held the office twice, accepting it again in December 1897 to defuse a brewing political quarrel among office-seekers, despite failing health, in his last political favor for a new president. Yet in dying so quickly, Bruce unwittingly reopened the political battle to a new, more aggressive generation, with little warning.

Bruce's death came just four months after that of another black Republican lion—Virginia's John Mercer Langston, diplomat and ex-congressman—and only three years after Douglass's passing. It was clearly time for the mantle to be passed to someone, almost certainly younger. But to whom? For those in whose eyes Bruce represented an old, tired wave of slave-born leaders, younger pallbearers represented a new breed, nearly all born or educated outside the South, "many of whom had helped 'bear the burden' in the heat of many days for Maj. McKinley" in 1896.[4]

Among them were "younger, abler, and truer" men whom Ohio journalist Harry Smith strongly preferred to Bruce. Smith's affections did not apply to fellow Ohioan John Green—a frequent target of Smith's ridicule, and nearer Bruce's age than Smith's thirty-five—but his sobriquet probably extended to Ohio lawyer Maxwell, about to be appointed in his mid-forties as the first U.S. consul general in Santo Domingo, perhaps even to Ralph Tyler, thirty-seven, rising Ohio journalist and protégé of Cleveland sage George Myers.

Almost certainly, Smith's favor applied to attorney Robert Terrell, thirty-nine, Harvard University graduate and popular local principal. Even Georgia's political firebrand William Pledger was only forty-five. All were eager, all available.[5] Yet McKinley likely paid little mind to Smith's agenda, or even to the expectation of more carping from Cleveland's gadfly. With or without advice, McKinley had apparently selected his new nominee well before Bruce's death, and he publicly announced that name the next day, after his funeral. Acting with almost unseemly haste—just five days into the sad vacancy—but for the most prudent of political reasons, McKinley sought to avoid giving critics any opportunity to build momentum for their preferences.

With Bruce gone, the chief executive had little practical choice but to move on, and quickly. McKinley chose someone he trusted and clearly preferred—and had named publicly for another job, blocked then by intransigence among white leaders in both parties. His next register was not among Bruce's pallbearers; McKinley's choice was another slave-born man—a full generation younger, a rising star at home and in Washington. The new register pointedly signaled the transcendence, on one level, of perseverance over actual power, and the attention still paid by the president to Georgia's symbolically important black Republicans.

At this critical stage, with war on the horizon, perhaps only Judson Lyons could have taken Bruce's place without provoking unrest within the African American ranks. Lyons had come of age at a time when talent, ambition, and education trumped all else, elevating freedmen's children from poverty to middle-class status in one generation. From humble slave origins in Burke County, he had risen to regional renown in Augusta, as a student at Augusta Institute, which was moved and renamed Atlanta Baptist Seminary and was still producing distinguished leaders a century later as Morehouse College.

In his first career, Lyons briefly taught school before pursuing the higher calling of politics and public service. A national convention delegate in 1892 and 1896, he had received another signal honor in 1896: state committeeman of the Republican National Committee, a rare African American member.[6] Now law partners with Henry Porter, Lyons was personally respected by his peers of both races; white Augusta's attorneys, in fact, provided Lyons with glowing, nonspecific endorsements, expecting that office to be in Washington or abroad—not as the city's postmaster.[7] Only intervention by the lone southerner in McKinley's cabinet persuaded McKinley to drop the Lyons nomination in 1897. "I believe Lyons is a good negro," Postmaster General Gary reportedly told one Georgia congressman. "Perhaps he deserves this place, but I also know well enough the temper and feelings of the Southern people not to inflict upon them unnecessarily."[8]

In opposing the Augusta appointment, Gary counseled McKinley to wait "with the idea of giving him [Lyons] something better." A year later, the controversial Marylander watched Lyons's sudden reemergence to claim "something better." Gary was now leaving the cabinet, and few dared oppose Lyons's selection now for a "top four" position—anointing a new power to be contended with, strengthening Georgia Republicans' voice nationally.

Gary's departure ushered in a new era for the Post Office Department, with an able successor, Philadelphia newspaper publisher Charles Emory Smith, former U.S. minister to Russia. After his appointment in April 1898, Smith oversaw the continuing investigation into the Baker murders—and almost immediately endured an embarrassingly messy confirmation hearing for Colin Anthony, White's postmaster nominee, still languishing as a recess appointee.

During the twelve months now ended, McKinley had appointed thousands of U.S. postmasters, most requiring a formal nomination to Congress and significant paperwork for clerical aides. Most postmasters now served four-year terms, meaning almost all offices last filled under the Cleveland administration in 1893–94 were occupied; McKinley's remaining postmaster appointments included mostly new vacancies. Decreasing workload was welcomed but carried a subtle consequence; declining numbers allowed closer scrutiny of appointments before the Senate for confirmation in an election year.

Of postmasters nominated and approved since March 1897—the majority in bulk by voice vote, after consideration by the Post-Office and Post-Roads Committee—only a small percentage, fewer than eighty, had been black. Most served small, predominantly black county seats or other towns or rural villages in a dozen states, almost all in North or South Carolina; only a few served smaller cities with majority-white populations.

Perhaps a dozen more black postmasters would be nominated by the end of the Fifty-Fifth Congress, making Senate confirmation especially meaningful for black postmasters, including Samuel Vick in Wilson. Their situation was complicated by growing resistance from southern Democratic senators and white supremacists in Georgia and other states—witness the difficulty associated with Lyons's failed nomination in majority-white Augusta, followed by Isaiah Loftin's shooting in Hogansville in 1897 and Frazier Baker's murder in Lake City in 1898.[9]

Vick expected to win approval easily, but he and two more controversial black nominees—Colin Anthony and Arkansan Ferd Havis—encountered problematic challenges of different sorts in their confirmation quests. For White, who had successfully nominated three dozen black postmasters in his district alone in his first year in office, the outcomes of the Vick and Anthony nominations would be mixed: one would win but then almost lose, in a parliamentary battle related not to fitness but to the disastrous outcome of another's loss. When the smoke cleared, White's string of successes was interrupted and almost halted; just four more nominations of blacks lay ahead in his second year, and only three nominees actually took office.

For McKinley, the Havis nomination presented political challenges unlike those in other southern states. A rich and influential African American businessman in Pine Bluff and delegate to five national nominating conventions who boasted strong support from the Arkansas party's central committee, Havis was an ally of McKinley's U.S. minister to Mexico, Powell Clayton, a powerful ex-governor and ex-senator—the last of his party to hold either office in that heavily Democratic state. But only a few black postmasters had served Arkansas, and none had been appointed since 1891, under the Harrison administration.[10] By 1892, blacks lost the right to vote in Arkansas; the state's last black legislators left office in 1893, two decades after Havis's single term in the state House.[11]

Still, appointments of black Arkansas Republicans to federal office were not without recent precedent. Two well-known blacks received posts after McKinley took office: John Bush, receiver of public monies at Little Rock, and Jacob Donohoo, deputy collector of internal revenue for the eastern district. Bush's Senate confirmation occurred without incident; Donohoo's position had not required a vote, but both men had unblemished reputations. Clayton's recommendation for Havis downplayed a checkered past—links to gambling, suspected immorality, and a grand jury investigation into alleged double reimbursement for a voucher during a ten-year term as elected circuit clerk.[12]

Havis's hometown newspaper strongly opposed his selection, even though many white businessmen supported the three-term city alderman. More surprisingly, Pine Bluff's black community was divided. Yet the longtime former chairman of the Jefferson County GOP, vice president of the Arkansas party, and onetime Senate nominee remained a charismatic figure; the state central committee's unanimous vote ignored four white candidates, persuading McKinley to present Havis to the Senate on February 15.

According to the *Daily Arkansas Gazette*'s account, situations in Washington and Little Rock differed significantly. Senior senator James Jones assured state committee chairman Henry Cooper that Havis would be confirmed. But Democratic senator James Berry actively opposed him, with help from influential Arkansas Democrats, and the game suddenly changed; "Havis had no one at Washington to represent him and refute the charges brought against him."[13] After closed deliberations, the Committee on Post-Offices and Post-Roads reported his name out, unfavorably, March 23; a week later, the full Senate rejected the nomination by voice vote, along with that of a second unfortunate, though far less controversial, acting postmaster in Tucson, Arizona.[14] It was an embarrassing outcome for the White House and, worse, a poor omen for the future, one shortly reinforced by another negative outcome.

Unlike Havis, Colin Anthony had few political marks against him; the Halifax County commissioner and former register of deeds had made a solid political name in the heady days of Halifax's post-Reconstruction era. He won election in 1896 as the county commission's only Republican, a "swing" vote for Populist control of that body, and good relationships with Populists augured success as postmaster.[15] White Republicans initially supported him. Populist state senator Edward Clark wrote a complimentary letter in early April to Sen. Marion Butler, describing Anthony as a "manly well behaved colored man."[16]

But white Democrats, gearing up for a rancorous election in 1898, had little good to say; Anthony's annual salary of one thousand dollars galvanized white opposition, more so than either the actual size or importance of postal operations.[17] Since the beginning of Reconstruction, white residents of small towns had preferred to restrict large federal salaries to white appointees. Raising salary was one way to require Senate confirmation for Scotland Neck's postmastership; otherwise, the town's 1,300 residents had little claim to importance.

On September 17, 1897, Anthony succeeded Richard Smith, whose four-year term expired, as acting postmaster; his recess appointment lasted until a reconvened Senate could consider his nomination. But as confirmation approached, Butler ignored opinions of Populists and Republicans, instead channeling less flattering descriptions floated by Democrats and predecessor Smith. By taking up the opposition cause, Butler rashly provoked an open in-state break with Sen. Jeter Pritchard—another case mirroring the Jones-Berry dispute in Arkansas.

Anthony joined a number of black Halifax postmasters proposed by White, including those at Essex, Halifax, Littleton, and Tillery. He seemed an inspired choice, but local Democrats launched a furious letter-writing campaign to Butler, on the Senate Post-Office and Post-Roads Committee, the only person to whom Halifax attorney W. A. Dunn could turn.[18] Dunn and others provided a barrage of dubious antitestimonials, suggesting grounds for Anthony's rejection based on moral turpitude, principally his saloon and rumors of his having fathered two children outside wedlock. Defeated years earlier by White for district solicitor, Dunn sought now to embarrass him as congressman. "If the Administration deliberately sought to insult our people, it could not better succeed than by making these appointments," Dunn told Butler. "If it was the purpose to create race prejudice and set back the Negro it could not better succeed than by placing him where he is regarded as an insult to our people."[19]

Charges of personal immorality rarely arose against white nominees. Anthony was happily married with two daughters and had enthusiastic endorsements by state senator Edward Clark and R. J. Lewis, the well-regarded former Halifax sheriff, who knew no man of either race with "a more enviable reputation than Mr. Anthony." But the mudslinging worked. Guilt by association gradually transformed Anthony from upstanding businessman into depraved despoiler of the body civic, and Populist supporters melted away. The simple truth was that "the people here do not want a colored P.M.," one local Populist told Butler—not even "a good man" like Anthony.[20]

By the time the Senate committee reported out the nomination April 20, the once-safe appointment, with a solid Republican majority waiting to approve the president's choice, foundered on shoals of partisan animosity. The vote became a showdown between feuding Tar Heel senators. Just thirty-eight senators—not a quorum—appeared on May 23 to vote, and Pritchard could summon up only sixteen other Republicans for Anthony. Meanwhile, Butler's winning coalition included a Populist colleague from Nebraska, plus sixteen Democrats—most southerners—and four Republicans, including three renegade Silverites. (Perhaps anticipating the slim margin, sixteen senators—half Republicans, half Democrats—announced pairings for and against the nomination; had they all turned up, the outcome would still have been negative, though by a quorum.)[21]

In a curious denouement, the North Carolina senators now engaged in a parliamentary duel. Pritchard sought desperately to revisit the vote, first requesting and then postponing reconsideration, eventually conceding defeat only when outmaneuvered by the wily Butler, taking a significant hostage: Wilson's Samuel Vick. One day after Anthony's defeat, Vick was approved by voice vote as part of a group. But three days after Vick's approval, while Pritchard scoured the Senate for votes to reconsider as part of a quorum, Butler moved to ask the White House to return the resolution containing Vick's appointment; the White House had to comply.[22]

The important county seat of Wilson was a Democratic stronghold in the "Black Second," far more important politically and symbolically than Scotland Neck. Vick, a respected schoolteacher and successful businessman, had previously served five years as postmaster. Pritchard simply could not afford to save Anthony by sacrificing Vick—or worse, to lose both. By the time Butler withdrew his threat in early June, the Anthony case seemed closed; when a final vote came up, he was quietly defeated.

Down but not out, White devised a back-door solution by proposing another black appointee at Scotland Neck—this time, after the Senate's summer adjournment. The new postmaster was Thomas Shields, a thirty-four-year-old schoolmaster whose temporary commission extended well into 1899. Anthony's prosperous father-in-law secured Shields's bond; Shields took office on July 11, and he immediately hired Anthony as his assistant.[23]

But the damage from Scotland Neck was done. Whatever slim hopes White might have held out for future political cooperation with Butler—or at least, for keeping him neutral on noncontroversial black appointments—vanished. Worse, White's waning political capital with Pritchard appeared to be dissipating rapidly, perhaps irretrievably. Within two years, they were arch-enemies in different party wings: one seeking to uphold Lincoln's legacy, the other playing down the southern GOP image as dominated by black politicians and fair-weather white allies.

≥♥

However privately bruised White was by the Anthony affair, he shrugged it off publicly. His remarks at a banquet honoring Judson Lyons in mid-May addressed the subject of "The American Congress," to thunderous applause from Washingtonians. Days later, he was commencement speaker at Alabama's Tuskegee Institute, his first known contact with Booker T. Washington, and was reportedly received "with great enthusiasm." No details survive for that speech or for his more topical speech that same week in Atlanta, on "The Negro and the Present National Crisis" before a large Douglass Lyceum audience at Big Bethel Church, but at least one Atlanta newspaper praised White for "his forceful manner."[24]

White's Tuskegee speech was surely moderate in tone, aimed at inspiring new graduates with a veteran educator's restraint. But his forceful remarks in Atlanta almost certainly referred to a subject much closer to his politician's heart: increasing movements toward disfranchisement of black southern voters by controversial methods like literacy tests, or the dubious practice of exempting illiterate white voters on the basis of ancestry: the so-called "grandfather clause." Although that movement had yet to reach Georgia or North Carolina, recent successes in Mississippi, Louisiana, and South Carolina troubled him deeply.

This wave of disfranchisement was the subject of White's last long speech during this Congress. On April 22, he regaled the House with accounts of voter suppression in Mississippi, where fewer than 46,000 voters elected all seven congressmen in 1896. That represented roughly the votes cast in some single U.S. districts—more than 37,500 votes in White's district in 1896—and only about 4 percent of Mississippi's total population in the last census. Compare that to roughly 20 percent in most nonsouthern states "under ordinary election rules throughout the country, at an average."[25]

Most of those not voting in Mississippi had not avoided the polls in protest, he explained; most blacks had instead been turned away by the 1890 Mississippi constitution. "There ought to have been 229,252 votes cast in that election," White declared. "Somewhere in the neighborhood—notwithstanding the Presidential election there pending . . . of 150,000 voters that we may presume . . . had a right to cast their votes in that election . . . 150,000 votes of black men were suppressed and not allowed to vote because they were Negroes."[26] Disfranchisement was painfully personal, he added. "There is no one thing so dear to the heart of the colored man as his right to American citizenship, and yet he is not permitted to exercise that right." As his race's national spokesman, White felt this more deeply than most, "[for] I am easily the leader of one thing, and that is the leader of the black phalanx on this floor."[27]

The Congress faced a clear moral choice here, particularly as it considered exporting American-style democracy to Spanish Cuba, whose freedom the United States now sought through war. "The question, Mr. Speaker, that ought to concern the United States Congress at this time, in my opinion, is as to whether or not there is a republican form of government in the State of Mississippi, the State of South Carolina, the State of Louisiana, and other Southern States when you take up this record and examine the votes cast." The essential question was clear: "whether the United States will sit supinely by and see that these matters are relegated to the States themselves, and that these gentlemen can come here and occupy seats by the suppression of the vote of their district, simply because they are of a different complexion, of a different race or different politics, without any investigation being made or protest entered."[28]

Here there was a darker subtext, one more relevant since war had been declared in defense of democracy: "The lifeblood of the Union is thus being sapped; little by little it may be, but surely sapped, and one day or the other it will not be a Cuban question that confronts us," White now predicted. "It will not be a question of standing by and putting down the Spaniards, but it will be a question as to whether or not the Federal Constitution in this great Republic of ours shall be perpetuated or not." His sedate prophecy from January was now cast in stark, urgent relief, and he would never return to studied, cautionary language.[29]

And as for congressmen who dared to defend their states' new practices while openly disparaging black residents, the gentleman from North Carolina had only disdain: "Still, gentlemen come here and speak about the 'negro' and the 'darky,' and talk of him in dialect and old plantation language. It seems to me that such language, coming from the plantations in Mississippi and elsewhere, had better be uttered at home and not brought here in this dignified body. They come, however, and claim that there are 'fair elections' in all these cases where such a disparity in the votes is shown."[30]

White's speech arose circuitously, almost stealthily. His remarks were authorized only as comments upon a marginally related issue, as the House debated which of two Democratic Tennessee contenders to seat. There, black voters still retained superficial claims on representation, and could still vote—if they paid the new poll tax. White preferred neither contestant, wishing for a Republican in the race instead, but promised, grudgingly, to vote for "the lesser of two evils." Both sides appealed to a mysterious "higher law" entitling them to credit for a few disputed votes cast by blacks—and that "higher law" enabled him to slide effortlessly into his longer discussion.[31]

Days earlier, White had rushed back by train from North Carolina to cast his vote for war against Spain. He missed that deadline, arriving hours after the late-night vote, which he explained briefly April 19; "I now desire to say that if I had been here present, I should have voted in the affirmative."[32] His vote would have made no difference—the war declaration passed both houses of Congress comfortably, after parliamentary maneuvers—but as hostilities approached, White was determined to strengthen his bargaining position on adding black military units into the army.

His travel was forced by a seemingly minor incident: criticism by the *Raleigh Morning Post* of questionable use of congressional franking privileges. As White explained to his hometown *Tarboro Southerner*, it was absurd: his secretary inadvertently mailed copies of a "commendatory article as to myself" to White's friends in free franked envelopes, not properly stamped. But White was taking no chances. His original explanation to the *Morning Post* was edited and distorted by that paper into "garbaged extracts," he said. The friendlier Tarboro *Southerner* agreed to publish his letter as printed, as a courtesy. He delivered it by hand just before that newspaper's weekly deadline, only to learn the House was acting on war resolutions in his absence.[33]

What seemed a pointless overreaction to others—politically inexpedient, at best—was of utmost importance to White, who treasured his reputation for integrity and honesty and whose sensitivity to criticism was arguably his greatest personal flaw. The more attention he called to it, the worse it sounded. But in White's mind, even a matter so inconsequential as missing stamps could not be ignored in his reelection campaign. What he could not yet foresee, however, was a storm gathering on the horizon, one in which his very words would be used against him, like ricocheting bullets, after he addressed the Republican state convention.

ॐ

Before White could turn attention to his campaign, he needed to complete congressional duties for the Fifty-Fifth Congress, including promoting his March proposal—for an all-black artillery army unit—and continuing to appoint black Second District postmasters. Nominations of John Howard for postmaster at Weldon (May 2) and Samuel Vick at Wilson (May 4) generated no public opposition; both were confirmed after Senator Butler reported them out favorably May 24.

After Weldon's postmaster died in November 1897, Howard was named to succeed him in early 1898. He was described locally as "honest, reliable, inoffensive and respected by the white people of the town; if Weldon must have a colored postmaster, John Howard is the most acceptable man that could have been put in such an important position."[34] Previous Weldon postmasters had been appointed without confirmation, which became necessary only after Weldon moved up in class on April 1. The regionally important Wilson post office had long required confirmation, which Vick had easily passed in 1889.[35] Both confirmations came the same day the Senate rejected Anthony; Vick's confirmation grew controversial, in fact, only during Butler's subsequent hijacking.[36]

But even as turbulence simmered over Anthony's nomination, White turned his attention to war with Spain and the expected role for black soldiers. Assisted by the Lyceum of Washington's Second Baptist Church, White took up a new cause: expanding black presence in military ranks, particularly in creating the nation's first all-black artillery regiment. On April 25, he introduced Lyceum resolutions in the House, asking that "colored men be given an equal chance with all other American citizens to prove their fighting qualities in the coming conflict with Spain, and that both in the Army and in the Navy no discrimination be allowed or tolerated on account of race or color." The resolutions went to the House Committee on Military Affairs.[37]

The next day, White led delegates to the White House to deliver a letter signed by thirty black leaders. Most Republican politicians, officeholders, and conservative ministers and bishops—except for outlier Henry Turner—supported the war wholeheartedly, as expressed by this letter, which "touched the President deeply," wrote one Washington newspaper. After briefly tracing the chronology of black military service since the Revolutionary War, the letter ended with this ringing appeal:

The colored American is no less loyal and patriotic today than he was when he fought for his country's independence and for his own freedom. . . . His sympathy goes out to the oppressed everywhere and especially to the brave people of Cuba, who . . . are subjected to the intolerable and despotic rule of a foreign power. To support you in your determination to extend liberty on this continent and to maintain the honor and dignity of our country we tender you the moral and physical support of 9,000,000 colored Americans.[38]

The letter was hand-delivered by White's prominent friends: P. B. S. Pinchback and high-ranking McKinley appointees Lyons and Cheatham. Other signers included McKinley's close adviser Bishop Arnett of Ohio, three ex-congressmen, a son of late abolitionist leader Frederick Douglass, and the ubiquitous Lt. Henry Flipper.[39] Cheatham himself called on the president weeks later, wrote the *Washington Bee,* to seek approval of mustering in "a regiment of black immunes" from North Carolina"—yellow fever survivors, judged immune to recurrence of the disease.[40]

Such appeals were guaranteed to resonate with McKinley, a proud Civil War veteran still known as "the Major," who well remembered the bravery of the black Union soldiers he had once served alongside. This chief executive had already appointed roughly as many African American men to federal office as all his predecessors together. McKinley's decision to allow black soldiers to serve in this highest patriotic role was certainly expected, at least by black leaders, who saw the war as "an opportunity to change their downtrodden position" and by "gallant service," perhaps even "reawaken the conscience of the nation."[41]

Two weeks later, White again journeyed to the Executive Mansion to confer with McKinley, in a meeting not recorded by mainstream newspapers, but that did draw the rapt attention of the *Colored American:*

His latest signal service was rendered Wednesday [May 11]. Mr. White called upon President McKinley, and after a logical statement of the matter had been presented, the President assured Mr. White of his sympathy with the movement for a larger recognition of the Negro soldiers, and expressed admiration for the valor and capacity of the colored comrades, knowing their worth from actual contact in the field.

He stated that at least five regiments would be made up of colored men, and that they would be commanded by their own efforts. This is a long step in the right direction, and Mr. White is entitled to great credit for so promptly devoting his strength to spiking the guns of the obstructive daily press.[42]

Much headier war news dominated local newspaper pages that week, including two far-reaching stories: one detailing five sailors' tragic deaths after a gun battle with the Spanish navy in Cardenas, Cuba, another the resignation of Assistant Navy Secretary Theodore Roosevelt to join the army as a combatant. Both stories held broad regional and national implications. No one could yet guess how Roosevelt's enlistment in the war effort would soon catapult him into the governorship of New York and beyond. The death of Ensign Worth Bagley of North Carolina, among the war's first casualties, was a personal blow to his widowed mother and famous brother-in-law, Josephus Daniels, publisher of the *Raleigh News and Observer* and vigorous campaigner for war against Spain.[43]

Of less concern to the public, but almost certainly of great interest to White and the nation's black leadership, was a small article in that Wednesday's *Washington Evening Star* regarding possible reinstatement of ex–army officer Henry Flipper, as presumed colonel of a new all-black volunteer cavalry regiment. The 1877 West Point graduate had recently begun lobbying Congress to authorize that volunteer cavalry regiment, supplementing the army's existing all-black cavalry regiments and infantry regiments, awaiting reassignment to Cuba's invasion.

Flipper publicly denied any personal interest in returning to service that same week, but others insisted. As a new army lieutenant posted to Fort Davis, Texas, he was court-martialed in June 1882, convicted of conduct unbecoming an officer, and dismissed from the military. He had long maintained his innocence on all charges; bills to restore his rank and give him a new command had now been introduced in both House and Senate.[44] His fluency in Spanish and engineering experience made Flipper an immediate asset to the military, whose ranks included hundreds of black soldiers but just one active black officer.[45]

Despite a continuing wave of interest by black leaders, the Flipper bills never left their respective committees. Nor did White's hopes to create an all-black artillery regiment achieve fruition; for technical reasons, he could not offer an explicit amendment allowing black soldiers to serve as artillerymen before the war started, and he dropped his efforts after war was declared.[46] Yet White continued to believe black soldiers were "capable and worthy of any place in our Army," and anything less than equal rights was "very unjust discrimination" by their "comrades in arms." The "black phalanx is ready to be mustered in, one-half million strong," he declared.

During this speech, a soon-to-be-familiar phrase surfaced in White's public pronouncements. He would never demand special privileges for black citizens, only "a man's chance, a man's protection; in fact, all the privileges of an American citizen. We will be content with nothing less." Moreover,

> We appeal to American patriots to remove all statutory barriers prescribed against us. You have two hundred fifty years the start of us; and if you are honest, if you are fair, if you are not cowards, and of course you are not, you certainly will be willing to accord to us at this late day all the rights of American citizenship enjoyed by you. *An even chance in the race of life is all that we ask;* and then if we cannot reach the goal, the devil take the hindmost one![47]

White's March 7 speech, like most given during his tenure in Congress, drew "loud and prolonged applause," said the *Congressional Record.* That his proposal failed was more the result of a political disinclination to expand the army's permanent size than of any real animus against more black soldiers. As many as ten thousand black soldiers eventually volunteered during the Spanish-American War, most in new black regiments raised by five states— Alabama, Illinois, Kansas, North Carolina, and Virginia—and black companies in state volunteer regiments contributed by Indiana, Massachusetts, and Ohio. Another four regiments of black "immunes" were authorized by Congress, along with six regiments of white immunes.[48]

Black volunteers envisioned and encouraged by White, Pinchback, and other important black leaders nonetheless encountered certain hurdles not facing the more numerous white volunteers. Some obstacles were structural, born of steadily increasing institutional discrimination and quasi-legal racial segregation enveloping the nation in 1898; some were political, born of battles in

Congress and southern legislatures bent on disfranchising African American voters, while others were either internal to the race or ideological. Not all black Americans even favored a war that sought, however nobly, to liberate persons of color abroad while U.S. citizens faced increasing oppression at home. Anti-imperialists like Rev. Henry Turner of Georgia argued that a "Jim Crow" empire would extend U.S. racial oppression abroad, not improve living standards for Cubans or Filipinos.[49] For now, at least, Turner's voice represented a small minority of blacks.

Yet certain other problems, bureaucratic and political, remained to be acknowledged—and resolved—before McKinley could make the decision. For one, the controversial question of commissioning black officers to lead black soldiers—favored by many black leaders but far fewer whites, and by almost no one at the War Department—and logistical difficulties created by stationing large numbers of black soldiers in the segregated South during transport to Cuba. For another, there was no guarantee creating new federal regiments of black soldiers would pass Congress, where Republicans held a majority but could not block southern senators' filibusters. The army was not yet up to fighting a large ground war without thousands of volunteers to be trained quickly and transported; delaying training by wrangling over racial issues was not feasible to McKinley.

The president had been loath to go to war at all, preferring the continuation of lagging diplomatic negotiations with Spain. But having been forced into the war, McKinley was determined to prosecute it as efficiently as possible. So he sidestepped the issue of creating new black regiments of regulars, preferring to make the best possible use of existing all-black regular federal regiments: the Ninth and Tenth Cavalry and the Twenty-Fourth and Twenty-Fifth Infantry.[50]

Most of the Twenty-Fifth left its Montana posting for the Dry Tortugas—a small group of islands off the Florida coast, near Cuba—in March 1898, weeks before war began, but a disorganized War Department delayed the Twenty-Fifth's transfer orders until mid-April. By the time the Twenty-Fifth departed Missouri on April 10, it was divided temporarily between two new destinations: Key West and Georgia's Chickamauga Park. Most Twenty-Fifth soldiers arrived in Georgia two weeks later, along with the Ninth Cavalry; by May 3, both joined the Twenty-Fourth (out of New Orleans) in Florida camps around Tampa, remaining there for a month, while the Tenth Cavalry went to Lakeland. All four left for Cuba in late June, all led by white officers.[51]

Despite the *Colored American*'s confidence, whether the president actually promised five black regiments of black soldiers—with black officers—to White is far less clear, and likely just wishful thinking. War fever produced a wide range of questionable journalistic charges in all directions. At the White House, White defended his race against editorial attacks by the *Washington Post,* which criticized reportedly rowdy behavior by black soldiers transported to Florida in segregated "Jim Crow" train cars. Black leaders were infuriated by blatant discrimination against soldiers in Florida and Alabama and the white press's hypocritical tone.[52]

Indeed, second-class treatment of black soldiers at temporary stations in Georgia and Florida angered many soldiers, accustomed as most were to freewheeling frontier life at western outposts. Ninth Cavalry chaplain George Prioleau was dismayed at Tampa merchants' refusals to serve black customers at white-only counters, wondering aloud to the *Cleveland Gazette* whether "America [is] any better than Spain. . . . You talk about freedom, liberty, etc. Why sir, the negro of this country is freeman and yet a slave." Soldiers stationed temporarily near Lakeland and in Alabama faced mistreatment by merchants and citizens on the street. A large-scale riot a month later in Tampa, sparked by alleged mistreatment of a black child by drunken white soldiers, seriously wounded twenty-seven black soldiers and three white soldiers, all hospitalized in Atlanta for treatment.[53]

The complex, often-volatile racial situation across the South and most of the nation prevented many potential black soldiers from joining volunteer ranks at state levels. New York governor Frank Black explicitly refused to accept black volunteers to meet his state's quota under the first presidential call, citing traditional segregation by race of his state's militia. Likewise, governors of Texas and most other states ignored blacks' willingness to serve. Only three states—Alabama, Massachusetts, and Ohio—accepted any black volunteers under the first call; L Company, a black unit inside the white Sixth Massachusetts, eventually became the only black volunteers to see combat action outside Cuba. Alabama planned to mobilize its existing black battalion, while Ohio activated its militia's Ninth Regiment, led by Maj. Charles Young, the regular army's only black command-rank officer.[54]

For the four black regular regiments in the segregated U.S. Army, gearing up for war efforts was complicated enough. After most Twenty-Fifth soldiers arrived at Chickamauga, regimental chaplain Capt. Theophilus Steward recounted both his first Sunday service (April 24) and the reception afforded his regiment and the Ninth Cavalry, telling the *Cleveland Gazette:* "The prejudice toward the colored soldier was very great when we came here, but sentiment seems to be modifying very rapidly.... White men of the South are ready to fight side by side with the Negro, so [long as] they do not get too close together.... [T]hrongs of people and ... newspapermen from all over the country" were observing the camp. Still, Steward's outlook was positive: "I believe this war will very greatly help the American colored man of the South, and result in the further clearing of the national atmosphere."[55]

Steward's fellow chaplain, Captain Prioleau, assessed the mood among southern observers more darkly, noting that "enthusiastically given" welcomes had been commonplace during the journey from southwest Nebraska. "At places where we stopped the people assembled by the thousands ... the heavens would resound with their hearty cheers," Prioleau told the *Gazette.* But that changed in Nashville, Tennessee, where thousands of onlookers were held back from approaching the railroad cars after midnight, and "from there until we reached Chattanooga there was not a cheer given us."[56]

"The prejudice against the Negro soldier and the Negro was great," Prioleau wrote, but it paled beside what lay ahead for soldiers leaving for the Gulf Coast and Tampa. There, "the Negro is not allowed to purchase over the same counter in some stores that the white man purchases over. The Southerners have made their laws and the Negroes know and obey them," a depressing reminder of slavery, to Prioleau.[57] In part because of malaria he contracted there, he could not accompany his troops farther than Port Tampa—only one white chaplain served as spiritual adviser to black troops in Cuba—and thus missed seeing black soldiers "help to free Cuba" before being mustered out to return home, facing the very different domestic "battle of American prejudice."

Other black arrivals at Chickamauga noticed similar prejudice, but at least one took a less pessimistic view. John Lewis of the Tenth Cavalry, en route from Montana, watched a strange phenomenon at his first Kentucky stop— black and white greeters on different sides of the road in Hopkinsville—but recounted a far warmer greeting in Nashville than Prioleau's, perhaps because of the time of day. But from there on, no more cheers greeted black soldiers, Lewis said, particularly in Chattanooga, scene of a boisterous and ominously violent incident days earlier.

"At Chattanooga our pleasure was entirely cut off," Lewis wrote the *Illinois Record.* "Several days before the 9 th went in [Negro soldiers from the Twenty-Fifth] broke up the Jim Crow car and took several shots at some whites who insulted them, and the officers were afraid that serious trouble would arise." Lewis was enthusiastic about Camp Thomas—"one round of pleasure"—despite another ominous incident: the killing of a white southerner by a white soldier, angered at criticism of his black companions and expectations that he, as a white man, must agree.[58] "You would be surprised . . . [at] the friendly feeling that exists between the colored and white soldiers. . . . Many a resort had to close on account of refusing them [the Negro soldiers] certain privileges," Lewis wrote. *Record* readers in Illinois's capital, "where very little prejudice exists," should be aware of the bond between soldiers transcending skin color.[59]

Among thousands of soldiers at Chickamauga, at any given moment there were hundreds of African Americans, both regulars and volunteers. Most were destined for onward transport to staging camps around Tampa, although their presence was never unnoticed by residents of the immediate area around the rural park, or of the urbanized area around Chattanooga, nine miles north. Of the three state volunteer regiments, only Alabama's Third had to endure the onerous effects of southern segregation and racial discrimination, but they were already familiar with the increasing reach of "Jim Crow" laws into daily lives.

If black current army soldiers were restive during their stay in Jim Crow's South, they were still ready to fight in Cuba. But how many more federal regiments would join the four regular army regiments had not yet been decided. Ranks were bolstered, theoretically, by ten so-called "immune" regiments awaiting creation by Congress, up to four as "colored immunes." The *New York Times* noted in June that between eight thousand and ten thousand black volunteers—"and more negro officers than ever before in the service of the United States"—were anticipated shortly.

More than ninety thousand black troops had once served in the Union army, said the *Times,* but all under white officers, and the War Department "was worried somewhat by the problem of providing officers for these organizations." Army experts "regard the officering of negro regiments with negroes as an experiment which may or may not turn out well," troubling military planners. "Most of [the recruits] are illiterate and they know nothing about military tactics, but with good officers and careful training, they ought to fight well," one white recruiter told the *Times.*[60] But "there is some doubt whether colored soldiers will follow one of their own race as well as they would a white officer," the article concluded.[61]

ह๒

The birth of immune regiments stemmed from one of the more ironic political episodes in U.S. military history. Ex–Confederate general Joseph Wheeler, now an Alabama congressman, believed the regular army could not provide sufficient engineers for the Cuban campaign. Wheeler's bill (H.R. 10069, introduced April 23) authorized the War Department to recruit three thousand men for "special purposes"; he could not foresee his proposal metamorphosing into a larger recruiting tool for black soldiers. Wheeler, set for appointment as major general of new volunteers, watched as the House committee on military affairs raised the force to thirteen thousand men, apparently combining Wheeler's force with Secretary of War Russell Alger's request for a brand-new force of men immune to yellow fever.[62]

When the full House failed to act on Wheeler's bill, the Senate version spelled out two different groups: three thousand engineers and ten thousand volunteers with "immunity from diseases incident to tropical climes." Sen. Redfield Proctor's bill (S.R. 4266) eventually passed both houses easily, replacing Wheeler's bill despite critics' fears that the regular army "would dominate the volunteers by monopolizing most of the officer positions" and that McKinley held far too much power over appointments. A lesser practical reservation involved army capability to determine immunity from tropical maladies like yellow fever.[63]

It was widely believed—and true enough, as it turned out—that survivors of yellow fever were immune from future bouts. No vaccine existed against yellow fever, so the argument for using immunes quickly swayed enough support in Congress for passage. African American leaders suspected all ten immune regiments would consist of southern black men, as part of a "secret" War Department plan, so black leaders visited the War Department in mid-May to press their case.

"A delegation of colored men consisting of Hon. Judson Lyons, ex-Gov. P. B. S. Pinchback, Col. James Lewis, and Capt. Thomas S. Kelly, called on the Secretary of War Tuesday morning [May 17, 1898] to advocate the enlistment of colored regiments into the service of the United States, which was made possible by the passage of the 'immune bill,'" the *Washington Bee* reported. Secretary Alger repeated the promise given White by the president— that "the department [intended] to give five or possibly six regiments to the colored people."[64]

The ever-whimsical *Bee* editor W. Calvin Chase pushed immune plans, even if he was less enthusiastic than most about the war. He desired to nurture the fading political fortunes of Henry Demas, who had reportedly raised a black brigade of 1,500 "immunes" ready to fight. After being rejected in March by the U.S. Senate's Commerce Committee (for alleged unfitness) as naval officer at New Orleans's port, Demas had little chance, but Chase happily promoted him as a potential officer in immune regiments, regardless.[65]

By now federal immune regiments were authorized on paper, including the Seventh, Eighth, Ninth, and Tenth Volunteer Infantry regiments, to be recruited from African American men in the South and Ohio Valley. About thirty black regular enlisted men awaited commissions in immune regiments, but only up to a certain rank; only white officers could hold a rank higher than lieutenant. The only regiments in which black officers might rise as high as colonel would be black state volunteer regiments, organizing in Alabama, North Carolina, Illinois, Kansas, and Virginia under the president's May call for seventy-five thousand more volunteers.[66]

The states had unique reasons for mustering up black regiments for the army. Republican governors in North Carolina and Illinois wanted to repay political debts by recruiting African American voters. North Carolina's GOP membership was still more than 50 percent black as disfranchisement loomed, with its first Republican governor in twenty years, Daniel Russell, who taunted a virulent Democratic explosion of white-supremacist sentiments. Appointing protégé James Young as colonel of the state's regiment became a hot-button campaign issue in November.[67]

In Illinois, Gov. John Tanner wanted to become his state's militia commander in Cuba, a suggestion the War Department rebuffed. His state's small black population was centered mostly in Chicago and other cities; the idea of an Illinois regiment was more symbolic than strategic but bolstered Tanner's image among black voters. Kansas had a larger proportion of black residents but a smaller population, and Populist Gov. John Leedy sought to "bolster his declining political fortunes by courting black voters." Desperate for traction in a reelection year, Leedy "by-passed the regular militia organizations" to muster in volunteers. His efforts failed, and Leedy lost to a Republican.[68]

But despite political and demographic differences, the three governors agreed on one matter: black officers for black regiments, from colonel down.[69] Not so in Virginia, whose Democratic governor—an ex–Confederate soldier—

faced a delicate political situation, one defused with pragmatic diplomacy. Gov. James Tyler firmly believed the state's black militia units deserved to serve as federal volunteers, if only under white officers, but angry black state militiamen refused to serve without black officers. Tyler's compromise allowed almost all unit officers to be black, except for "two white men who served as commanding officer with the rank of Lieutenant Colonel, and a surgeon with the rank of Captain."[70]

Alabama's situation was different. The state's militia already included a small African American unit—the First Battalion, Colored, headquartered in Mobile with black officers—and Democratic Gov. Joseph Johnston was willing to allow black volunteers in the state's volunteer ranks, just not with black officers. Up for reelection in 1898, Johnston "seems to have desired . . . to appeal to Negroes by allowing them to demonstrate their patriotism in a way that would not offend the racial sensibilities of whites," many preferring black Alabamians to join a separate, all-southern regiment (never formed). Alabama's new black regiment became the only one without black officers, although Johnston's explanation—a federal ban on black commissioned officers above lieutenant—did not satisfy black critics.[71]

Members of a Birmingham volunteer unit elected their own officers, conditioning their availability on Johnston's willingness to commission them. Johnston claimed he wanted to but the federal ban blocked him. (Eager to fill the state's quota, he could not afford to alienate potential black volunteers, and stretched the truth—the ban was soon lifted, a decision Johnston ignored.) At any rate, Birmingham volunteers agreed, reluctantly, to serve under Johnston's white officers. Even Mobile's leading newspaper expressed editorial sympathy for black volunteers: "They are quite right in standing by their old and faithful officers, and their action does them honor."[72]

With the second volunteer call, the Third Alabama grew to regimental status to satisfy a larger quota; more than one thousand black volunteers served, briefly, in the unit. Ironically, state recruiters now competed with federal recruiters seeking Alabamians as black immunes.

Almost all black volunteers, whether state or federal, spent time in Georgia, for one simple reason: its number of training camps. In addition to the huge

Camp Thomas, more than two dozen of varying sizes emerged in Georgia, due to its proximity to Florida. But Georgia, for its own reasons, chose to raise only white state regiments, so many of its three regiments ended up in training camps with black volunteers. While awaiting onward orders for Puerto Rico, the Georgia First Infantry was posted in mid-September to Camp Poland, just outside Knoxville. Still full of adrenaline from participating in the earlier massive "Sham Battle" training exercise at Chickamauga, Georgia, troops were called "terrors of the camp."[73]

Eager for action, boisterous First Georgians decided on their own to stage a smaller "sham" battle—ambushing the unsuspecting, all-black Third North Carolina Infantry, freshly arrived at Camp Poland, among few army regiments with a black commander, Col. James Young. On September 18, their first full day in camp, Colonel Young's black volunteers hit the field for practice drills, only to encounter surprise fire from First Georgia men. Both sides traded fire in the surreal battle of Camp Poland without serious casualties, but the violent, hour-long prank—duly reported to army superiors by Colonel Young—created alarm and dismay among observers. The incident led to house arrest for the First Georgia, as well as the precautionary decision to place Second Ohio soldiers as "chaperones" in nearby woods, after hotheaded Georgians repeated threats to "get" the Third North Carolina's men.[74]

Yet as fate would have it, it was the last unfriendly fire facing men involved in Camp Poland's incident. First Georgia men were boarding their Savannah ship when peace was declared. The Third North Carolina was transferred to Camp Haskell, outside Macon, along with the Seventh and Tenth immunes and the Sixth Virginia—easily the most notorious among black volunteers, for its widely reported "mutiny" against appointing replacement white officers. Anonymous letters to Virginia's *Richmond Planet* from two Sixth Virginia soldiers detailed both the mutiny and a continuing series of race-related incidents witnessed during postings in Virginia, Tennessee, and Georgia. "Ham" had once reported the "Battle of Camp Poland," and now both he and "Black Man" provided insightful, sometimes amusing glimpses of wartime life at Camp Haskell, while chronicling deadly racial violence outside.[75]

At first eyed as a curiosity by Macon's white population—"the idea of 4000 Negro troops in line was something they had never dreamed of before"—black soldiers soon found white laundries closed to them and streetcar lines segregated. After white patrons complained bitterly about riding in cars with black soldiers, the trolley line attached black-only trailers behind most cars—a far cry from Knoxville's reception. "This state [Georgia] has created a very unfavorable impression in my mind," Ham wrote after the war.[76]

The Macon war, however, continued as long as Camp Haskell operated. At least three soldiers refused to leave main cars for "Jim Crow" trailers, and were summarily shot for impertinence by armed conductors, according to Georgia newspapers. Ham reported the trolley-car death of fellow Virginian Elijah Turner in a *Planet* letter, angrily describing Macon as "this pest hole of the South" and longing to be mustered out. The conductor who killed Turner was released by a jury finding his actions "justifiable homicide," and Ham reported two more black soldiers—North Carolinians—were "shot and killed in a street fight in the town. . . . Hasn't a week passed since [arriving] that some of Uncle Sam's black boys in blue haven't been 'justifiably homicided,' at least this is the only word that seems to strike the minds of all juries who try cases for 'killing nigger soldiers,'" he wrote.[77]

Because the war ended so quickly, the Third Alabama never left Alabama, and like all others, mustered out of service in early 1899, despite protests by influential white leaders.[78] North Carolina and Virginia regiments mustered out simultaneously, after being stationed only at southern transshipment points. Few black volunteers saw any type of military service abroad. Company L of the Sixth Massachusetts arrived in Puerto Rico for a brief conflict, and only the Eighth Illinois and Twenty-Third Kansas actually entered Cuba, sent to Santiago Province for peacekeeping and cleanup in August, after hostilities ceased.[79]

And what of the black immunes, the only new federal units authorized by Congress? Just one entered Cuba: Louisiana's Ninth Infantry. Their first task was to guard a Spanish prisoner camp near San Juan Hill, where, ironically, immunity to yellow fever offered little protection from equally deadly malaria. A large number contracted it, and some died; those who recovered now wrongly believed themselves immune to that disease, but unlike yellow fever, malaria was chronic.[80]

The few black soldiers facing actual combat in Cuba—the Ninth and Tenth Cavalry and Twenty-Fifth Infantry—were all regular army units, with white officers. And while their courageous fighting in July 1898 earned praise from nearly all quarters—producing five Medals of Honor for the Tenth Cavalry— the sustained wave of national goodwill which many African American leaders expected to arise from black war participation quickly receded.[81]

5

POLITICAL STORMS BEGIN

These brave black men ... vindicated their own title to liberty on that field, and, with our other brave soldiers, gave the priceless gift of liberty to another suffering race.
—**William McKinley,** Springfield, October 15, 1898

No trustworthy transcript exists for George White's address at the Republican state convention in Raleigh on July 20, 1898, but two dueling newspaper accounts—neither flattering, one far less so than the other—recounted a long, thundering speech by the state's only black congressman, on summer leave from Washington. In a campaign soon dominated by shrill headlines of "Negro domination" of state government and compounded into tragedy after a strategic misstep by a black Wilmington editor, charges growing out of his speech seem comparatively mild and inoffensive, in retrospect.

But in this emerging era of Jim Crow segregation, White was now painted by detractors as loudly demanding social equality for black citizens—pursuing a goal of racial integration of all social institutions. This was pure partisan fantasy, and as far as one could go from past utterances by the pragmatic White, who always carefully distinguished political equality—which he demanded and idealized—from social equality, which was unlikely and counterproductive for the foreseeable future. But in this hyperbolic world of yellow journalism, popularized by William Randolph Hearst's sensational wartime practices, there were few limits to what could be printed without regard for accuracy or consequences. The nation's only black congressman was suddenly fair game.

The *Raleigh Morning Post,* no friend of White's since unleashing the franking scandal, now described the speaker as "proud of his Southern blood" and well aware of the complicated racial situation his own party faced. His speech was characterized as "vile and rampant," although his words—even as paraphrased—seemed simply frank:

No white man dare enter my house unless invited there, and I dare not enter any white man's house unless invited there. The laws of the land do not regulate social equality. Man regulates the social problem for himself. There's nothing to this social equality plea ... a scheme to get in on. For 240 years the Negro has been enslaved, working for the white man, working to make him rich.

The Democrats are going to say that I am a Negro office holder. Yes, and there are going to be more just like me. The constitution gives me the right to vote and this gives me the right to hold office. I am going to be in the fight and work for the principles you have adopted. I am going to uphold William McKinley, Jeter C. Pritchard, and Daniel L. Russell.[1]

There was much truth here: White remained a fervent supporter of McKinley, for whom he had energetically campaigned in 1896, and was still allied with Pritchard; his feelings for Russell were correct, if less warm. But the *Morning Post*'s anti-Republican agenda was barely concealed by its generally fair coverage of the rest of the convention. North Carolina's newspapers were divided into opposing trumpets, blaring across partisan lines of the state, since fusionist Republicans and Populists overthrew Democrats in the 1894 legislative elections and claimed the governorship in 1896.

Still, the *Morning Post* version of White's speech was far milder than the take-no-prisoners tone of the *Raleigh News and Observer*—words unmistakably editorialized by Josephus Daniels's increasingly venomous blue pencil—in "The Negro White Speaks":

Congressman White was then called upon to speak. He denounced with bitterness the Democratic position and defended the placing of power in the hands of the Negroes, and heaped his abuse upon those who wanted to keep the government in the hands of the intelligence of the country.

"I have noticed," he said, "men who did not like the name Republican, who stopped at the half-way house, calling themselves Liberals, or something like it, but they all wind up finally as straight-out Republicans. ...

"You dare not enter my door to enjoy social equality unless I invite you there. We are not afraid of social equality."[2]

That this quotation contradicted every public sentiment ever expressed by White on the subject of racial segregation—a social practice he disliked but had long ago accepted as beyond his ability to change—did not bother the *News and Observer,* which instead sharpened its knife by twisting White's every word into cartoonish defiance of all racial conventions:

> "I am not the only Negro who holds office. There are others. There are plenty more being made to order to hold offices. We are the modestest people in the world, and don't hold as many offices as we will. I invite the issue. If you will come into my district, we have a joint debate.
>
> I am going to hold up the hands of Jeter C. Pritchard, Daniel L. Russell, and William McKinley. We imitate white men. You steal and so do we. You commit crimes and so do we."
>
> He praised Daniel L. Russell for putting Negroes in command of regiments, and putting negroes in high positions. He sat down amid thunders of applause.[3]

But the *News and Observer* was not finished assessing White's performance, characterized as a belligerent appeal to the "lowest plane upon which any man, white or black, ever talked to the people about. It showed the low tone of the convention and the unworthy mind of the Congressman. The hurrahing and cheering was such as was heard twenty years ago in the days before the taxes of white men gave them schools." One anonymous black critic provided dubious reinforcement: "I was ashamed of my race, that when it has a chance to put a man in high positions, selects a man who will make so mean a speech." This was standard operating procedure, because "negroes always put their worst representatives forward."[4]

Almost before the ink dried on the *News and Observer* pages, the editor of the Democratic *Wilmington Morning Star* took up Daniels's drumbeat, calling out white supremacists under the headline "There Will Be More." Three days after the convention, William Bernard, a respected Civil War veteran and unhappy witness to Republican domination of municipal government, cast dire predictions in the clearest possible terms:

> That is what White, the negro congressman from the First district, said in his speech before the late Republican convention (so-called) at Ra-

leigh . . . the coarsest, most vulgar, shameful, malicious speech made. . . . This malicious windbag was not speaking for himself simply, but was speaking as a representative of his race, a representative in the broadest sense, for they sent him to the Congress of the United States, and that he is regarded as their representative is proven by the storm of colored applause that greeted his utterances.

And there will be "more of them." They have got a taste of office, it has whetted their appetites for more, and they will not be satisfied with small offices, either. They are beginning to realize their power and will work it for all it is worth. They . . . have secured more recognition from the present administration than they ever before received and this has encouraged their aggressiveness. . . .

There are now more Negroes in office in North Carolina than in any other state in the Union, and unless Democracy triumphs in the next election, there will be, as White defiantly declared in that speech, more of them, and a good many more. They haven't yet made a fair start. *It remains for the white men of North Carolina to say whether this negro's impudent, audacious threat is to be verified.*[5]

During the next three months, as the General Assembly elections approached, the theme repeated in both newspapers, echoed by the *Charlotte Observer* and most of the state's one-hundred-plus Democratic newspapers. Repeated attacks on White gained shrillness, especially after he stated, with exquisite accuracy, in September at Jackson that black voters had a majority in many counties "and could elect a negro to every office" if they chose but had not done so. The *Morning Star,* the *New Bern Journal,* and the *Kinston Free Press* immediately engaged in a sensational contest, attempting to see who could name the most offices held by blacks in eastern counties. Kinston claimed the prize, running its list under an insultingly eye-catching headline: "Nigger! Nigger! Nigger!"[6]

White was by now accustomed to occasional one-sided and exaggerated coverage of his speeches. His reelection to Congress was almost a foregone conclusion as long as registered Republicans held a comfortable majority in the "Black Second," although he planned a vigorous campaign. Meanwhile, his rapidly rising star in the national GOP was reflected by lavish praise from Rep. George Southwick of New York. "His fellow Republicans in the House regard him as a most capable and worthy man . . . sturdy of frame and limb, sturdy of voice, sturdy of Republicanism," Southwick wrote black journalist "Grit" Bruce. "With depth of mind, breadth of experience and charm of manner he combines an instinct of humor well developed which attracts the sympathy and support of all his colleagues, except those to whom color is an insuperable barrier."[7]

That Southwick and others considered White "a credit to the colored race and to the American people [and] one of the most prominent Republicans in the House" made no difference to Josephus Daniels, who never cared for White personally, nor that White was a member of the executive committee of the National Republican League, as North Carolina's member at the national convention a week earlier in Omaha, Nebraska.[8] Daniels soon transformed him into a black lightning rod in a dustup for fall elections—an object of scorn and derision, not admiration, an aggressive apostle of offensive social equality for America's black citizens.

During his first year in Washington, White encountered instances of racial discrimination in social establishments, as the capital's increasingly segregated environment—still very much a southern-style environment, despite its increasingly affluent black population—made life a frustrating experience for well-educated, cosmopolitan blacks, routinely restricted to certain neighborhoods, whose children attended segregated public schools. Whatever personal reservations he held about racial segregation, White had publicly preferred so far to champion only political equality for black citizens, not equal social status.

As the only black congressman—at least an honorary member of Washington's black social elite—White may have personally experienced little actual discrimination based on his race. He did not mention it in speeches, nor do contemporary newspaper accounts of public appearances indicate any effort to force the issue. His well-publicized status and regular admission to McKinley's White House—whether alone or accompanied by white and black visitors—helped give him unofficial immunity against routine discrimination and indignities faced by all but the city's wealthiest black residents and visitors; historian Willard Gatewood describes it as "Capital of the Colored Aristocracy."[9]

The closed circle of Washington's black upper class tended to confine social lives to those with similar lifestyles, incomes, educational backgrounds, and status. Exemplified by Mary Terrell, the refined and educated wife of an up-and-coming lawyer, the black elite "belonged to a few select clubs, attended two or three high-status churches, vacationed together, and were often related by marriage if not by blood."[10] Those with lighter complexions sometimes escaped discrimination altogether, even if dark-skinned blacks of high social standing—poet and writer Paul Laurence Dunbar, for one—were chastised by whites for consorting publicly with lighter-skinned companions.[11] According to journalist Richard Thompson's 1895 notes characterizing the social stratosphere of Washington's black elite, the "colored aristocrats" rarely ventured outside familiar settings, preferring to entertain each other in fashionable homes rather than attend public balls.[12] By 1898, their relative insulation was slowly crumbling, as Jim Crow discrimination spread to Washington, barring even wealthy black patrons from "public restaurants, hotel, theatres, and other public places."[13]

Any illusions White harbored about the lack of southern-style segregation and discrimination elsewhere were laid to rest by an unhappy incident in Chicago that summer. En route to Omaha's National Republican League convention, he changed trains in Chicago, where he and art student Robert Thomas were refused service by a State Street restaurant, said the *Illinois Record,* claiming they contemplated suing the restaurant's "prejudiced proprietor" for five hundred dollars in damages.[14] In its reprint, the *Colored American* called the incident "a strange showing for big-hearted, free and magnanimous Chicago to send out to the country. The gentlemen must have blundered unwittingly into a cheap hash-house ... about the only kind that are afflicted with color phobia in the Windy City."[15] The threatened lawsuit was never filed, but the insult loomed large in White's memory—preparing him for uglier public insults to come.

White returned to North Carolina to campaign for what had once seemed an easy reelection bid. Renominated without opposition in the spring, he faced two hometown opponents for Congress: Populist nominee James Lloyd and W. E. Fountain, ex-mayor of Tarboro, campaigning as an independent Populist in disguise as the candidate of Democrats unable to find a nominee. But the campaign was soon beset by a statewide wave of racial hysteria unleashed, in part, by a rash editorial by a black Wilmington newspaper editor.

As the state's largest black-majority city, Wilmington was home to slightly more than twenty thousand citizens, of whom just over half were black in 1898. The county seat of New Hanover and the state's largest port, Wilmington was important both economically and politically to both parties. It boasted a long, proud history, a prosperous black middle class, and reasonably amicable post-war race relations. Its nominal Republican majority of voters—mostly black—made it a GOP stronghold; the county had regularly elected Republicans to both legislative houses since 1868, including John Howe, one of the county's two North Carolina House members.[16] It was also home to ex-congressman and current Republican governor Daniel Russell.[17]

Never located in George White's "Black Second" district, New Hanover had last elected a Republican congressman in 1878: Russell, who served one term. But White was well-known there, having maintained a Wilmington law office since 1895 and often represented clients in U.S. federal court. He was also a familiar face in the city's black community; he spoke there on January 1, 1891, at Emancipation Day, and received a hero's parade after his 1896 election to Congress.[18] Federal customs collector John Dancy was among influential African American leaders in Wilmington; James Young had lived there before moving to Raleigh in the 1890s. Alex Manly, graduate of Hampton Institute and editor of the black *Wilmington Daily Record,* moved there in the 1880s as a house painter before entering journalism in 1894.[19]

But the political atmosphere in Wilmington was anything but serene; the complicated history of Wilmington's municipal government featured three competing boards of aldermen and three mayors in the spring of 1897.[20] Feud-ing between wings of the county's nominal-majority GOP caused political chaos. Until March 1897, after the General Assembly amended the charter to allow Governor Russell to appoint supplemental members, Democrats dom-inated the city board, under a complex electoral map essentially diluting the majority of black voters.

In the fall of 1898, three black members sat on the city council: Andrew Walker, John Norwood, and Elijah Green. Walker and Green, elected in 1896, continued onto the new board in 1897; Norwood, a former county school board member, was one of five Russell appointees.[21] The state supreme court affirmed the constitutionality of the amended city charter in November 1897, certifying

Russell's board and ending the standoff between claimants. Current aldermen included six Republicans—four appointed by Russell—and four Democrats, including one Russellite, but relations between the majority and three elected Democrats remained frosty.[22] Alderman Silas Wright, chosen as mayor in March 1897, was succeeded on the board by an appointed white Republican.

Manly's Republican-leaning *Daily Record* had so far enjoyed broad support from black readers and white Wilmington advertisers. His editorial tone was even-handed until the infamous August 1898 editorial, responding to a rabidly intemperate speech by outspoken lynching proponent Rebecca Latimer Felton of Georgia, only now reprinted by the *Wilmington Morning Star*.[23] Mrs. Felton, wife of a prominent ex-congressman, made stark assertions:

> When there is not enough religion in the pulpit to organize a crusade against sin; nor justice in the courthouse to promptly punish crime; nor manhood enough in the nation to put a sheltering arm about innocence and virtue—if it needs lynching to protect woman's dearest possession from ravening human beasts—then I say lynch; a thousand times a week if necessary.
>
> ... And I say, with due respect to all who listen to me, that as long as your politics takes the colored man into your embraces on election day to control the vote; and so long as politicians use liquor to befuddle his understanding and make him think he is a man and brother when they propose to defeat the opposition by honey-snuggling him at the polls. And so long as he is made familiar with their dirty tricks in politics, so long will lynchings prevail, because the causes of it grow and increase.[24]

Just why the *Morning Star* reprinted Mrs. Felton's speech when racial feelings were running high in Wilmington can only be guessed at. Most observers would have recognized a calculated move to galvanize Democratic voters in Wilmington, to vote out Republican officeholders, recapture the state legislature, and undo city charter amendments. In the end, the *Record*'s fervent response—heartfelt, if ill-timed and shortsighted—to Mrs. Felton's defense of lynchings unleashed disastrous overreactions. The author accused her and other whites of hypocritically looking the other way when roles were reversed:

> Our experience among poor white people in the country teaches us

that the women of that race are not any more particular in the matter of clandestine meetings with colored men than are the white men with colored women. Meetings of this kind go on for some time until the woman's infatuation or the man's boldness bring attention to them and the man is lynched for rape. Every Negro lynched is called a "big, burly, black brute," when in fact many of those . . . had white men for their fathers. . . .

Tell your men that it is no worse for a black man to be intimate with a white woman than it is for a white man to be intimate with a colored woman. You set yourselves down as a lot of carping hypocrites in that you cry aloud for the virtue of your women while you seek to destroy the morality of ours. Don't think ever that your women will remain pure while you are debauching ours. You sow the seed—the harvest will come in due time.[25]

The *Daily Record*'s message—more balanced than Mrs. Felton's angry call for lynchings—was still defensive and inflammatory, and as any reader could predict, as dangerous as shouting "Fire!" in a crowded theater. The editorial had two immediate effects. First, it placed black Wilmington leaders in an awkward position: to defend Manly meant calling more attention to an uncomfortable issue, inevitably antagonizing the white-supremacy movement. Many black Republicans, including city executive committeemen, therefore disavowed it, and him, immediately. Manly's motives were suspect; it was widely rumored that Manly had not written the editorial, while others fantasized that Democrats had paid him to run it.[26]

The second effect forced a marginally profitable newspaper—in daily publication for a year—into near-bankruptcy overnight. Advertising by white businesses fell off precipitously; within days, his downtown landlord forced him to vacate the premises, after ominous gatherings by whites outside, and move to a less convenient location.[27] Death threats abounded; by October, Sen. "Pitchfork Ben" Tillman of South Carolina was reportedly calling publicly for Manly's lynching.[28]

More insidious was emergence of the White Government Union (WGU), Democratic brainchild of ex-congressman Furnifold Simmons and legislative candidate Francis Winston. More than eight hundred WGU branches formed across North Carolina, part of Simmons's well-oiled plan to mobilize white "men who could speak, men who could write, and men who could ride" in the white-supremacists' campaign to regain Democratic legislative control. Meteoric growth of WGU clubs was catalyzed by Red Shirts, imported from South Carolina, whose firearms and distinctive apparel—red shirts of "calico, flannel, or silk, according to the taste of the owner"—began intimidating black voters on horseback weeks before the election. Their rallies often shared the same speakers as public WGU meetings, indicating crossover appeal and, likely, shared membership.[29]

It was against this unsettling backdrop that the apostle of accommodationism, Booker T. Washington, appeared in early September 1898 on a speaking tour. Washington's advance man, Frank Saffold, described the situation in clear terms: "Just now Wilmington (that is the colored & white people) is agog and excited because of the statement made by a negro editor here regarding white women . . . and how this is going to affect your reception on the parts of the whites I don't know. A lynching, they tell me, is an impossibility at this seaport—the whites therefore are making much political capital out of it and the Wilmington *Messenger* is exceedingly bitter."[30]

Still, Saffold saw the speech as "an opportunity for you to—if you care to, bring about a fine feeling between the races. Many have referred to your Atlanta speech as being just the thing to help defeat the force of these Democratic denunciations of the whole race."[31] However nervous Washington was about the circumstances, he and his wife made successful separate appearances, one speech drawing more than one thousand listeners. No text survives for that speech, but the *Morning Star* said Washington "begged his audience to rid their minds of the expectation of sky-rocket oratory, and went on to refer to the problems confronting the colored race. . . . The burden of his speech was the necessity of the industrial education of the Negro."[32]

Although well acquainted with Washington from his Tuskegee commencement speech months earlier, White attended neither speech, at St. Stephen's AME Church or St. Luke's AME Zion Church. Imminent plans to meet the president in Washington may have prompted White not to attend, for fear of politicizing the visit. Still confident that Republicans could carry North Carolina—and perhaps add a seat in Congress—White soon assured McKinley, along with journalists outside his office, that he "regret[ted] the unholy war that Democrats are making on the color line" in North Carolina.[33]

"The strife and ill-feeling which have been stirred up have never existed before and will hurt my people and State," he told the *Washington Evening Star* afterward. The charge of "negro domination is bugaboo" and would not succeed. "There has never been negro domination in any county in the state," he recalled telling the president. The *Raleigh Morning Post* quickly reprinted the article, calling his statements "remarkable" but making no further comment.[34]

Preoccupied with demands of his own campaign, White returned to North Carolina rather than attend the organizational meeting later in September in Rochester, New York, of a new nationwide civil rights organization formed by T. Thomas Fortune of the *New York Age* and AME Zion Bishop Alexander Walters, among others. White enthusiastically supported the nonpartisan group's aims, and signed Walters's call for the National Afro-American Council, a reinvigorated version of Fortune's defunct National Afro-American League, in response to Frazier Baker's lynching and other racial violence.[35]

The group's inaugural meeting was announced in late August to coincide with the dedication of a new statue honoring Frederick Douglass, but it drew only a few attendees from outside New York—among them John Dancy, Ida Wells-Barnett, and ex–minister to Liberia John Smythe. Walters was elected president of the new Council; Dancy, first vice president; and Wells-Barnett, secretary. Among urgent guiding principles were opposition to lynching, to the convict lease system, and to so-called "separate car laws." (Smythe, much too conservative for Fortune, was denied membership, after Fortune threatened to resign.)[36]

Back home, White's busy campaign schedule included stump speeches across the sprawling Second District; he named five large towns as speech sites, and doubtless spoke in rural villages as well. Republican strategists likely summoned White to other states to energize black votes in other congressional elections, as in 1896. The *Colored American* listed seven black Republican nominees for Congress in Alabama, Mississippi, Missouri, South Carolina, Tennessee, and Virginia, describing 1898 as a "great campaign" for black candidates.[37]

White campaigned energetically over the next two months, with mixed results. He interspersed speeches with family outings—including a much-publicized circus visit in Tarboro October 8, when his entourage allegedly refused to vacate the whites-only seating section and was nearly ejected. The story appeared in the *Greenville Reflector,* then in the *Raleigh News and Observer*—including a follow-up article with eyewitness affidavits—and sought to embarrass White, who stoically endured bad publicity without comment. Another account of a train incident when 150 Lenoir County "Rough Riders" reportedly prevented White from disembarking at Kinston for a speech appeared only in the *Wilmington Messenger,* described as a "fake" by the hometown *Free Press* ("The Messenger has been imposed upon by a liar"). White was silent, waiting two years to deny both incidents by letter to the *Free Press.*[38]

Only inaccurate reporting of actual speeches annoyed White enough to provoke timely responses. In an October 7 letter to the *Raleigh Morning Post,* White denied published reports concerning his speech in Rich Square, which allegedly advised "negroes to get their guns and ammunition ready" and be prepared to "demand their rights" at polls. The owner of the vacant lot where he spoke reportedly ordered White to leave after hearing him, but his version was far different: "I counseled the people to be forbearing, law-abiding, and to avoid everything that might lead to disorder, riot or bloodshed. . . . I made the same speech there that I made in Kinston, Windsor, Goldsboro, Wilson, Tarboro and other points . . . pleasantly noticed by the honest Democratic editors of this district."[39]

His public complaint did nothing to stem the tide of anti-White articles in Democratic newspapers, nor did it affect the steady stream of vitriolic cartoons in the *Raleigh News and Observer,* courting white voters by vilifying Governor Russell and black Republicans. One week before the election, both messages coalesced to ratchet up the tone in startling fashion by involving—for the first time—family members in a sensational fake scandal. A boxed, front-page article, boldfaced in oversized type, appeared on the *News and Observer's* front page on November 1. Its title was guaranteed to shock readers, especially those who knew it contained no truth: "Negro Women Active: Congressman White's Wife Gets Rifles and His Daughter Asks Negro Women Not to Work for White People."

The article appeared, not coincidentally, beneath a cartoon titled "Under Which Flag?," drawn by cartoonist Norman Jennett, juxtaposing a courtly white southern gentleman and a grinning obese, cigar-smoking black man around a ballot box and two flags: "Negro Rule" and "White Rule."[40] The cartoon's coded inference was clear: voting for any black candidate was a vote for "scandals, incompetency, corruption, and white women insulted," whereas voting for white candidates meant "good government, prosperity, peace, and protection to white women." Votes for George White encouraged unseemly, dangerous behavior by his misguided wife and daughter.

The story's only true statements: White represented the Second District, and his wife and his unnamed daughter (Della, a schoolteacher) lived in Tarboro. The allegation against Della was "learned on good authority," according to the unnamed writer, but the rest, as everyone in Tarboro knew, was pure fiction, with no source listed.[41]

Preoccupied during October with his own ten-day swing for midwestern Republicans, the president knew nothing of the alarming developments in White's campaign. But McKinley remained eager to energize voter turnout among Republicans, especially African Americans in urban centers outside the South. Addressing a mid-October crowd of forty thousand from the steps of the Old State House at Springfield, Illinois, he took pains to praise black soldiers for recent efforts during the war with Spain, noting Lincoln's devotion to the cause of emancipation, and the patriotism of black citizens since 1865: "[Lincoln] saved the Union. He liberated a race—a race which he once said ought to be free because there might come a time when these black men could help keep the jewel of liberty within the family of freedom. If any vindication of that act or of that prophecy were needed, it was found when these brave black men ascended the hill of San Juan in Cuba and charged the enemy at El Caney."[42]

America's black soldiers "vindicated their own title to liberty on that field, and, with our other brave soldiers, gave the priceless gift of liberty to another suffering race." Black soldiers helped save countless Cuban lives and were soon to wage a similar battle for democracy in America's newest colony, the Philippines. By continuing to support Lincoln's party at the polls in 1898, he might have added, they could continue that valiant fight during an equally perilous postwar crisis. "We went to war [against Spain], not because we wanted to, but because humanity demanded it. And having gone to war for humanity's sake, we must accept no settlement that will not take into account the interests of humanity."[43]

The president referred to the complicated process of negotiating a peace treaty with the Spanish, with hostilities over. But securing permanent domestic peace and equality for America's returning black soldiers—an issue not raised, if surely envisioned—would be no less difficult, whatever the election outcome. A curious incident involving a Virginia postmaster's appointment, publicized in mid-October, highlighted political hostilities facing black Americans.

Rev. James Twyman, a respected African American Republican in Franklin County, had quietly been appointed in August to run the Junta post office, suggested by Virginia's newest U.S. marshal, Morgan Treat. Such appointments were recommended by national committeeman George Bowden, an ex-congressman who delegated this task to Treat; why Twyman was selected is unknown, but Treat did sound out Franklin GOP leaders beforehand, if neither Bowden nor anyone outside Franklin seemed to know his race.[44]

Still, there was ample recent precedent. Twyman was McKinley's second black appointee in Virginia, after Robert Cauthorn at Dunnsville in 1897. John Jackson, selected in 1891, still served Alanthus; William Johnson had recently completed four years at Baynesville. All three served without incident. Since 1885, Junta's post office had so far had just one white postmaster, William Angel.[45] Yet despite the county's predominantly white population, little local opposition greeted Twyman.

Only after the appointment became public knowledge in Richmond did his race became a hot-button issue in the marginally Democratic Fifth District congressional race. Republicans poked fun at segregationist Democrats for opposing Twyman, claiming Democratic congressmen had written letters seeking to retain local black officials. According to the *Washington Evening Star*'s front-page account, "the affair has its amusing side, and the discussion of it is giving the public an insight into political methods only known to the initiated."[46] Twyman soon resigned, replaced by a young, white, and presumably Democratic postmistress, Tula Finch; the incumbent Democrat, after eking out a narrow victory against a much stronger Republican in 1896, won overwhelming reelection to Congress.

But while Twyman's controversy played out, McKinley was treated to an electrifying Chicago address by Booker T. Washington.[47] The educator was among Peace Jubilee speakers personally invited by the University of Chicago president to address an overflow crowd at the city's gigantic auditorium. Discussing black soldiers who had fought in Cuba, Washington said this: "When you have gotten the full story of the heroic conduct of the Negro in the Spanish-American War—heard it from the lips of Northern soldier and Southern soldier, from ex-abolitionists and ex-masters—then decide for yourself whether a race that is thus willing to die for its country should not be given the highest opportunity to live in its country." But he would not forget the man who had made this patriotic display possible, and was listening intently: "In this presence, and on this auspicious occasion, I want to present the deep gratitude of nearly ten millions of my people to our wise, patient and brave Chief Executive for the generous manner in which my race has been recognized during this conflict. A recognition that has done more to blot our sectional and racial lines than any event since the dawn of freedom."[48] He promised to make McKinley's future efforts to end prejudice and discrimination against black citizens as effortless as possible: "We of the black race shall not leave you unaided. We shall make the task easier for you by acquiring property, habits of thrift, economy, intelligence and character, by each making of himself of individual worth in his community. . . . You know us; you are not afraid of us. When the crucial test comes, you are not ashamed of us. We have never betrayed or deceived you."[49]

Washington chose his words carefully, for his audience was national—not just the president and cabinet—all digesting his words appreciatively. He was an unashamed admirer of McKinley, whom he recently invited to visit Tuskegee. He was ambitious, not just for himself, and determined to reinforce positive tendencies within both government and philanthropic circles. Washington still needed to convince many of his strategy's effectiveness, but there were skeptics—in regions South, North, and beyond—who distrusted black ability and viewed black achievement with suspicion. Some within his own race saw him as an Uncle Tom, offering insincere obeisance in exchange for favoritism, and did not wish to see him succeed.

On Tuesday, November 8, White narrowly won reelection to Congress from the Second District, receiving 49.5 percent of ballots in a three-way race. Although he carried only four of the district's nine counties, he won those by lopsided margins, losing his home county of Edgecombe by just fourteen votes to Tarboro's longtime mayor; margins in four other counties were unusually close.[50] He was, however, one of the state's few outright Republican winners, along with his colleague Romulus Linney; Richmond Pearson was initially defeated, according to results revisited by the U.S. House, but was seated after contesting his loss.[51]

GOP control of the House was cut significantly; nationwide, Republicans lost nearly two dozen seats, and the shrinking role played by southern Republicans in Congress was worrisome. Just five Republicans were initially elected from southern states in 1898—two each in North Carolina and Tennessee, one in Texas—compared to more than a dozen in 1896.[52] McKinley still hoped to carry North Carolina and other southern states in 1900, but year-end results were not heartening for that cause.

How closely the president or Republican leaders outside the state followed the North Carolina campaign is not clear. Jeter Pritchard, the only Republican southerner in the Senate and a powerful ally, probably provided the White House with status reports, but strained relationships between state and national party leaders were plagued by infighting, and the state party's gradual split into quarrelsome factions, further clouded by collapse of Populist fusion. Tar Heel Republicans would struggle to maintain a united front for McKinley's 1900 reelection effort.

Governor Daniel Russell, an increasingly unpopular leader barred from reelection in 1900, was rendered impotent by a Democratic General Assembly landslide. His once-potent supermajority of Republicans and Populists vanished in both houses; among supporters, just five black Republicans won—four in the House (from Craven, Northampton, Vance, and Warren Counties) and one senator (Warren County), fewer than half the seats won by black nominees in 1896.[53]

Intimidation of black voters by Red Shirts appeared to depress black turnout across the east, particularly in New Hanover, where official results were dramatically ominous. In a county with a sizable Republican majority, once easily carried by McKinley, several Republican candidates withdrew from their races rather than risk reprisals. Only a handful of Republican votes were even tallied by officials, including that cast by the state's governor; no Republican won a single county office.

None of this boded well for either the Republicans of New Hanover County or for their party in general. But for both groups, the worst was yet to come.

6

WILMINGTON FALLS AND A
NEW COUNCIL RISES

The time has now come, in the evolution of sentiment and feeling under the
providence of God, when, in the spirit of fraternity, we should share
with you in the care of the graves of the Confederate soldiers.
—**William McKinley**, Atlanta, December 14, 1898

Press reports of a racial massacre at Wilmington on November 10, 1898, filled
state and national newspapers for days after the city's municipal government
was overthrown in an armed coup d'état—the only such event in U.S. history.
Between seven and thirty black citizens and one white man died during twenty-four hours of armed hostility; hundreds of black citizens fled to nearby
swamps and forests after armed white men took over the city. A mob eventually forced resignations by the mayor and board of aldermen and the permanent expulsion of Republicans of both races, including the chief of police, a
former deputy sheriff, and a U.S. District Court justice of the peace.

Local newspaper editor Alex Manly, whose August editorial had become
a rallying cry for white supremacy, and his brother Frank escaped without
injury, although their newspaper office and printing press were burned.[1] Both
soon resettled in Washington, D.C., where they opened a newspaper; Alex appeared at rallies in New York City and New Jersey, before becoming White's
private secretary. Other exiles pleaded their cases in Washington: Robert
Bunting, former justice of the peace, and ex-chief John Melton claimed they
"dare[d] not return to their homes in Wilmington" lest they be "shot on sight."[2]

No national leaders were more concerned about the violence than McKinley and Secretary of War Russell Alger, who met in urgent session on November
11 to discuss the situation.[3] The president was warned of violence in two urgent telegrams from ex-congressman Thomas Settle, one warning the riot was
under way at Wilmington and "one hundred armed men have just left Fayette-

ville on a special train for Wilmington; situation serious," another describing Governor Russell as "apparently inactive. I hope you will wire him at once."[4]

Sen. Jeter Pritchard received status reports on Wilmington events from William Chadbourn and was alarmed; Chadbourn warned him in October that "riot, arson, and bloodshed" loomed unless the GOP ticket withdrew from the election. A Fusionist rally on October 29—featuring Russell, Pritchard, Marion Butler, and congressional candidate Oliver Dockery—was canceled, for fear of inflaming the situation and provoking violence.[5]

Coup leader Alfred Waddell, ex-congressman and the next Democratic mayor, boldly threatened in October to "choke the current of the Cape Fear River with carcasses"—presumably Republicans and blacks—if necessary to seize control of Wilmington.[6] Russell, who had defeated Waddell for Congress in 1878, received death threats if he appeared in Wilmington, although he still voted there November 8—among the few Republican ballots tallied.[7] He avoided capture on the train home only by hiding in the mail-baggage car at Hamlet, where angry Red Shirts waited; in Raleigh, chanting marchers menaced the executive mansion.[8]

Russell had tried to ward off violence by authorizing a state judge to issue bench warrants in Richmond County "against parties who broke up meetings, assaulted candidates and whipped Negroes." Two weeks before the election, his executive proclamation enjoined "all ill-disposed" persons to "desist from all unlawful practices and all turbulent conduct." Reports circulated in October—never validated—that McKinley's cabinet had already discussed the situation, but there was a large caveat: federal intervention required proof that state forces were incapable of preserving the peace.[9]

In truth, McKinley had few practical options. According to news reports, one cabinet member declared the president had authority under Section 5299 of the federal Revised Statutes, which dealt with "Insurrection." Enacted in 1870, the section covered situations in which "insurrection, domestic violence, unlawful combinations or conspiracies in any state so obstructs or hinders the execution of the laws thereof," empowering the president "to take such measures, by the employment of the militia, or the land and naval forces of the United States, . . . for the suppression of such insurrection, domestic violence, or combinations."[10]

Black journalist John Adams of Minnesota wired McKinley with the same suggestion—to intervene under Section 5299, "that order may be preserved and the threatened bloodshed averted"[11]—but no precedent existed. Statutory powers dating from the military Reconstruction era applied to outlawed Ku Klux Klan activities but were never used. In 1898, perpetrators brazenly defied the rule of law by wrapping themselves in invisible white-supremacist rhetoric, a public and more insidious foe.

Pending a report from Attorney General John Griggs, McKinley and cabinet members "unanimously condemned . . . the Wilmington massacre" and "greatly deplored the situation." One member "unhesitatingly stated that the white people had gone too far." In practical terms, the president arguably could take whatever action was suitable and necessary, but without Russell's specific request, would likely do so only "if there is any further progress in the rioting or killing."[12] Direct intervention by federal soldiers to restore order was almost unprecedented in U.S. history, and dangerous in the fragile political situation enveloping North Carolina.

Another option—Governor Russell calling U.S. volunteer soldiers into action—was a complicated process, Alger stated. First, volunteers must be mustered out for conversion to state authority: "Up to this hour no word has been officially received from the State. No consent for any troops to be ordered out has been given. None can be. If the Governor orders out any troops, they must be State troops, and not under any conditions can he order any United States volunteers until they have been finally mustered out of the service, when they cease to be United States troops, and are again under the command of the Governor."[13]

Here, fate was all but tying McKinley's hands. Russell called out state militia in Wilmington—under the command of his close friend Walker Taylor—and summoned reinforcements from Clinton, Kinston, and Maxton. A few arrests were made, of unruly blacks, but there was no violence for troops to quell; sullen mobs evaded capture by dispersing to reassemble elsewhere.[14] The governor, stymied, refused to intervene in the new political order. He retained power to appoint up to five city aldermen, but reality confounded his capability; no Republicans would accept appointments, and the new Democratic legislature would revoke his power as soon as it convened. Exhausted and friendless, Russell and his wife fled to Asheville for a long vacation.[15]

Failing Russell's clear signal—or renewed violence—McKinley had no appetite for provoking a domestic war. Almost inexplicably, however, he failed to mention the violence in his annual message to Congress in December. Other political factors influenced him; his message dealt primarily with the aftermath of the Spanish-American War and other foreign affairs issues. He planned a major southern trip in mid-December, to attend the Atlanta Peace Jubilee, address the Georgia legislature, and visit black colleges in Georgia and Alabama; stirring up racial unpleasantries beforehand was not beneficial. Rumors circulated, never confirmed, that advisers of both races discouraged him from speaking out on Wilmington's violence.[16]

White and James Dudley, president of North Carolina's public Agricultural and Mechanical College for the Colored Race, hoped to expand McKinley's itinerary en route to Atlanta. In separate letters, each coaxed McKinley to make a symbolic appearance in Greensboro, while changing trains. White's official letter to McKinley, dated December 12, the day his entourage departed, read as follows:

My dear sir:—

I have just received a communication from Prof. Jas. B. Dudley, President of the A & M College for the Colored Race, at Greensboro, N.C., in which he extends you an invitation . . . to visit the above named institution while you are in the South. . . .

The A & M College at Greensboro is the only Institution for Colored that receives any National support . . . a credit to our State . . . indeed a fine school. The citizens throughout the State would greatly appreciate a visit from you to this Institution either as you go South or on your return. I most sincerely hope you may see your way clear to stop over there if only for an hour or so between trains. With best wishes, I have the honor to remain, Your obedient servant, Geo. H. White[17]

There was no formal reply, making it unclear when the White House received the letter; regardless, White simply reinforced Dudley's existing invitation, recounting efforts supporting McKinley as a delegate in 1896 and seeking to cash in a political chit: "I hope you can grant this only and first personal favor I have ever asked you," Dudley wrote. He mildly inflated his role, claiming to have "organized[d] a successful revolt against the present Governor of this State and other Republican leaders . . . to cast the vote for you at St. Louis, as Senator Hanna and Bishop Arnett will readily verify." McKinley's secretary promised to raise the matter with McKinley at an appropriate time, but "plans for the President's proposed Southern trip have not as yet been fully matured."[18]

When he dashed off his own note, White had just returned from speaking in Massachusetts and Canada. But was his letter part of a carefully designed joint strategy with Dudley? Possibly so, as both men avoided mentioning Wilmington. Five years later, Dudley recalled that he had visited Wilmington that month "to see after my family in the disturbed conditions of affairs there." In his 1903 letter to Booker T. Washington, Dudley recalled an alarming memory: "I met about one thousand soldiers who were drumming four Negroes from the city."[19]

As the event faded off national front pages, White's mind swirled with hopes of convincing McKinley to lead popular opinion against the Wilmington violence. His impassioned December 1 speech to listeners at Boston's Charles Street AME Church would have unsettled Republican congressional leaders—perhaps even McKinley—for implied threats against political parties unresponsive to black Americans' needs. "That most of the ills that, as a race, we in the South complain of grow out of our unflinching support of the republican party," White said, "none will deny who has sufficient knowledge about the matter to advance an opinion." Moreover,

A neutral ground politically, or affiliation with the bourbon democracy of the south, would have averted many horrors through which we have come.... To affiliate with a party in which we have no faith is to don the toga of a hypocrite. To continue affiliation with the Republican party is to invite a continuation of crime and dastardly deeds. Must we look to that party for protection and redress of our wrongs?

It is quite clear that we cannot hope for redress from state officials, even though our lives are placed in jeopardy to put them in office. We have a Republican president and an overwhelming majority in the U.S. house. . . . [But] when we call upon the government to protect us it throws up its hands in holy horror and reminds us that its own brave, patriotic and long-suffering black citizens are without remedy under the stars and stripes.[20]

Southern black citizens had three options: to remain politically active in the South, "and take our chances on being annihilated"; to give up all civil and political rights, "thus virtually becoming slaves" again; or to move elsewhere "and thus remove excuse for the false howl of 'negro domination' or mob violence to which we have often been subjected." White preferred systematic emigration, reaching this conclusion with a heavy heart, for he loved North Carolina and often spoke of "the friendly relations existing between the two races there."

> But in the last contest the negro was made the butt of a false howl by political leaders out of a job, and the lower and baser element of the ignorant whites was appealed to and inflamed.... Law and order were set at defiance ... cowardly assassins from the border sections of South Carolina came into our state ... the 'red shirters,' with their shotgun policy.
>
> ... Friends and business relations have been torn asunder, property destroyed, men and women shot down like dogs by a bloodthirsty mob under the pretense of law; American citizens were intimidated and forced away from the ballot box and the right of franchise denied them ... ballot boxes were stuffed and the holding of an election made a miserable farce and a mockery. Honorable citizens, both black and white ... are now exiles in other states.[21]

White's most detailed description so far of Wilmington's violence showed clear frustration with Americans' willingness to "wink" at the situation: "The world hears but one side of these horrible stories. It is given to the public that the Negro always is the aggressor and always causes the trouble, harmless and defenseless as he is. Thus the mind of the nation is prepared to receive him as a savage brute, incapable of civilization and refinement." Though even white church leaders declined to condemn the violence, he remained optimistic that "justice, like murder, will out in the end. God and the right must someday prevail."[22]

White's speech distinguished him unfavorably from the "quiet work of Tuskegee" in racial advancement, opined the *Boston Transcript*. White argued that black citizens should refuse "even for policy's sake, [to] put their hands upon their mouths and their mouths in the dust under the political repression with which they are visited," wrote the *Transcript* editor, a risky strategy unlikely to work as well as Washington's.[23]

White told much the same story in a "thrilling" ninety-minute speech to a Halifax audience days later and was treated like a visiting head of state, "the first time ever a colored man was known to dine in the Government House as a guest."[24] This appearance—a favor to African American acquaintance Rev. Francis Robinson—was not widely reported in the U.S. press. In the U.S. capital, *Washington Post* readers heard a more sedate version of events by Register Lyons, whose "Black Side of the Race Issue" column consumed three newsprint columns in White's absence.[25]

But White's biting response to a published letter from South Carolina's junior senator—one with whom he had served briefly in the House—must have alarmed Republican leaders.[26] John McLaurin's guest column in Sunday's *Washington Post* on November 27 mixed strong defenses of white supremacy with subliminal warnings for McKinley, couched in praise for presidential inaction: "It has been fortunate for the Carolinas, for the South, and for the country at large, that the recent demand for federal bayonets to sustain negro domination was not carried out. President McKinley is a good man. He is better and stronger than some of his advisors."[27]

McLaurin strongly defended Wilmington's armed mob and denounced "negro domination" in language that "astonished" White, "especially that portion . . . which refers to the State of North Carolina. I was born and reared in North Carolina . . . and believe that I know the situation of affairs there as well as any man in the State," White told the *Post*.[28]

"I state without hesitation that the cry of Negro domination in the State is a myth and wholly without foundation," and his numbers, though somewhat dated, proved it:

> The two places in the State where the great excuse for the recent disturbances and murders were committed [are] New Hanover and Craven Counties. . . . In New Hanover . . . the Clerk of the Superior Court, Criminal, and United States Court and their deputies [and] seven out of ten aldermen are white men; . . . the Mayor . . . the Chief of Police and . . . the Deputy United States Marshal and the bailiffs of the court are white men; yet this is . . . the county in the State that has been pronounced as under negro regime.
>
> . . . [U]p to the last campaign the most cordial feeling existed between the whites and the blacks in my State. . . . [T]he recent troubles

may be attributed to the inflammatory speeches of Senators Tillman and McLaurin, and the introduction of the red-shirt desperadoes of South Carolina and their shotgun policy along the borders of our State.[29]

For any Republican congressman to challenge McLaurin or Tillman, or both, to a verbal duel was a strategy none but the most reckless Republican would advise at this delicate moment. Both had terrible tempers and were censured after a famous 1902 fistfight on the Senate floor, propelling McLaurin's retirement.[30] McKinley's advisers must have read White's statement, on the same page as Sen. Jeter Pritchard's comments—made during a North Carolina interview—decrying trends toward a "lily-white" Republican Party in the South.[31] But if the president read either *Post* article before departing, he did not comment.

McKinley left December 12 for his southern tour and was warmly received by state leaders in Georgia and Alabama. After addressing state legislatures at Atlanta and Montgomery, where he spoke at the old Confederate capitol building, his itinerary included stops in Tuskegee and Savannah, regaling appreciative audiences at black educational institutions: one led by Washington, the other by McKinley's wartime U.S. Army paymaster, Richard Wright.

The president's various speeches were part of a well-conceived public relations strategy aimed at reassuring southerners of their honored place as U.S. citizens, and of his warm personal regard for them, with carefully tweaked messages tailored to specific situations. No trace of partisanship emerges in newspaper accounts, and only hints of painful Civil War memories, military occupation following Confederate surrender, or abortive federal Reconstruction. At Montgomery, he glossed over Alabama's wartime recalcitrance, rewriting history subtly to suit his message: "We are glad you did not go out [of the Union], and you are glad you stayed in. Alabama, like all the States of the Union North and South, has been loyal to the flag and steadfastly devoted to the American Nation and to American honor," even after noting Montgomery's historic status as "first capital of the Confederate states." The president preferred oblique appreciation—an enemy soldier extending olive branches to conquered subjects—for being "warmly and enthusiastically welcomed as a President of a common country."[32]

At Tuskegee, he endorsed Washington's "worthy reputation as one of the great leaders of his race, widely known and much respected at home and abroad" and the "unique educational experiment, which has attracted the attention and won the support even of conservative philanthropists in all sections of the country." Tuskegee, much like Hampton, "is to-day of inestimable value in sowing the seeds of good citizenship.... The practical here is associated with the academic, which encourages both learning and industry. Here you learn to master yourselves."[33]

McKinley's visit to Savannah's Georgia Agricultural and Mechanical College invoked much the same theme. "'Keep on' is the word I would leave with you to-day. Keep on in moving upward, but remember that in acquiring knowledge there is one thing that is as important as that, and that is character. Nothing in the whole wide world is worth so much, will last so long, and serve its possessor as well as good character," the president told Wright's pupils. He admonished white leaders to remember that both races deserved the same public education: "There is not a foot of ground beneath the Stars and Stripes where every boy and girl, white or black, cannot have an education to fit them for the battle of life."[34]

The president also repeated his Springfield remarks: "At San Juan Hill and at El Caney ... the heroism of the black regiments which fought side by side with the white troops on those historic fields" could not be forgotten. "Mr. Lincoln was right when, speaking of the black men, he said that the time might come when they would help to preserve and extend freedom.... [Y]ou have been among those who have given liberty in Cuba to an oppressed people."[35]

Yet for all his inclusive words and sincere homilies, one short sentence in McKinley's address to Georgia legislators symbolized his southern swing and plagued his relationship with African Americans. *Atlanta Constitution* editor Clark Howell had long pressed federal authorities to assume partial responsibility for the perpetual care of Georgia's Confederate graves and those elsewhere. In a rush of generosity and patriotic inclusiveness, McKinley agreed, drawing wild cheers of approval: "The time has now come, in the evolution of sentiment and feeling under the providence of God, when, in the spirit of fraternity, we should share with you in the care of the graves of the Confederate soldiers."[36]

That spirit of generosity—underlain by a carefully modulated appeal to southern Senate holdouts to approve his peace treaty with Spain—was sadly lost on purist T. Thomas Fortune, who was seething at McKinley's silence on racial violence. This latest move was further evidence of presidential cowardice, thought Fortune; his reportedly inebriated speech in Washington, D.C., in mid-December voiced angry vitriol at which most listeners could only shake their heads and cringe.

"I came down here to fight the president. He has gone back on us," Fortune bellowed. "I want the man whom I fought for to fight for me, and if he don't I feel like stabbing him."[37] It was dangerous language to use about a president—even one with disappointed black supporters—and neutral observer "Grit" Bruce called the speech full of "rash and ill-judged utterances" that were "unfortunate."[38]

A suddenly tense relationship between the White House and a minority of black leaders was complicated by emergence of the National Afro-American Council (NAAC) as a major nonpartisan player in the political arena. Although the NAAC was avowedly neutral—avoiding all partisan political activities—it was bound to be drawn into controversial issues affecting black citizens, more than once falling off its neutral fence by trading strategic inclusiveness for partisan extremism.

Bishop Alexander Walters, the NAAC president, penned incisive comments on the situation in a *Washington Bee* column before the Council's special session. Almost as disappointed as Fortune at McKinley's lack of action, Walters was generally pessimistic. Under the title "What Must We Do to Be Saved?," Walters gently chided the president, who had "abandoned us to our fate," but pleaded with Council members to act thoughtfully. Black citizens must act "not as an angry mob, but as sober, loyal and thoughtful citizens, and consult together as to what is the best to do at this crisis."[39]

Not coincidentally, his *Bee* column appeared alongside a reprinted *Evening Star* account of Fortune's torrid speech—demonstrating Chase's malicious delight in fomenting nervousness among black leaders. A *New York Tribune* journalist, Mrs. J. M. Holland, reported Chase's alarming duplicity in the debacle to Booker T. Washington and anyone else who might listen: *Evening Star* editor Crosby Stuart Noyes, even McKinley's secretary, John Addison Porter. Washington quietly sent Holland's letter to his protégé Fortune, who predictably blasted her ("she takes more interest in my affairs than she should, and I have already warned her about it") and other critics. Washington decided against attending Council sessions, perhaps unwilling to endure verbal crossfire between Fortune and the president or anyone else.[40]

When the NAAC convened, Walters was more assertive about its plan. "I cannot understand some of our so-called friends who advise us to be quiet and let the white man have his way," read his annual address. "Shall we remain silent when the President of the United States, who could not have been elected without our votes, is utterly silent in his last message to Congress concerning the outrages in North and South Carolina, and other parts of the country?" he added. "Shall we not speak out when innocent men and women of our race are burned at the stake, hung to the limbs of trees, and shot down like dogs?"[41]

Most other speakers echoed Walters. John Green's unfortunate choice of words provoked raucous debate, inflaming high feelings among attendees and goading Fortune into angry demands. Green defended McKinley's message to Congress—"No man has been more zealous of the rights of the negro than President McKinley," both before and since becoming president—by placing responsibility on "advice of some of the most prominent men of the colored race" for McKinley's failure to mention racial violence. Fortune demanded Green name these "black Judases," after which Green disappeared to confer with Fortune and Bishop Abraham Grant, the next speaker. Fortune later reported, to loud guffaws, that Green "did not know the names of the men who had advised President McKinley."[42]

Green's assigned topic was "Protection of American Citizens." But his efforts collapsed into a pointlessly humiliating episode that might have been avoided had he not been a last-minute substitute for the more pragmatic White, who apparently neglected to brief his friend Green fully on what to say—and what not to say. (White reemerged to guide a Council delegation, delivering a written address on New Year's Eve at the White House.)

Still to speak, however, was one defender of the president's southern trip, Henry Cheatham, foreseeing a promising future of new hope:

> He met the Southern people, not as an enemy, but as a friend. He had been denounced by some hot-headed Southern white men because he was a friend to the Negro, and because he had appointed negroes to post-office and internal revenue positions in the South. But how did he act when he went down among these people? Did he go to stir up strife? He went and carried in his hands the olive test of peace and good will.

He was the President of the whole country, not the North nor the South, or the East or the West, not the blacks nor the whites, but the President of the United States and the friend of all.[43]

Almost alone among black leaders in defending McKinley's Atlanta remarks, Cheatham even sent a congratulatory telegram mentioning "your great speech . . . timely and productive of great friendly results in the South of the future."[44] Cheatham's rosier view of McKinley's agenda was sincere, if less than persuasive to critics.

The Council's address to the nation was a "rather mild affair," a committee effort, not the hard-hitting, energetic appeal for racial justice many expected. It only mildly criticized McKinley by implication, expressing "regret" that he "saw fit to treat with silence this vital matter in his recent message to Congress" yet hoped he "will use his good offices to adjust the matter in the Carolinas to the satisfaction of all fair-minded men and to the honor and glory of the nation."[45] But by the time the NAAC presented this address, the annual White House New Year reception resembled a group rally by other black citizens for the same cause.

Rep. John Dalzell's Pittsburgh delegation, five black clergymen and a layman, presented a memorial December 29 that "severely criticized conditions in the South and alleged brutal lynching of colored men without cause, for no other reason than their color," demanding appropriate legislation to prevent injustice.[46] When the NAAC entourage arrived December 31, an Iowa delegation ahead of them presented its memorial "signed by the colored people of that State in relation to the recent race trouble in the South."[47]

Council delegates included Walters and two dozen others, shepherded by White. Among them were ex-congressmen Cheatham and George Washington Murray, ex-governor P. B. S. Pinchback, Bishop Arnett, and appointee-advisers Lyons and Dancy.[48] "The finest aggregation of colored men ever brought together for a visit of this company . . . embodied the very best religious, intellectual, political commercial, and industrial forces of the race," read Edward Cooper's glowing *Colored American* account. Originally set at fifteen members, the delegation ballooned to at least twenty-two—although Fortune, who was named, protested loudly to the *Washington Post* that he "had not crossed the threshold."[49]

Their fifteen-minute interview with McKinley was "quite satisfactory," its "largely confidential" contents informally embargoed "until the President feels that it is expedient to speak." Cooper asserted that "Mr. McKinley can be depended upon to do the right thing, when his judgment tells him the right time has come. A good purpose may be defeated by hasty and ill-considered action. Give the President a chance to think—and a rest."[50]

Yet what form would his strategy take in the new year? No one knew. For White, McKinley's stalwart defender on the House floor and energetic campaigner outside, any chance to exert meaningful influence on that strategy was slowly slipping away.

1899

ENTERING A CRITICAL PHASE

I will sit here only two years longer, should I live, and I am going to try mighty hard to live that long. . . . How long will you sit in your seats here and see the principles that underlie the foundation of this Government sapped away little by little?
—**George H. White**, U.S. House, January 26, 1899

The Fifty-Fifth Congress was midway through its final session in January 1899 when George White went home to deal with North Carolina's racial situation. The new Democratic-controlled legislature was debating possible measures with outsized effect on black citizens, and White was worried. With no assurances from President McKinley or party leaders about possible federal action to resolve or reverse Wilmington's coup d'état, he felt the need to galvanize black leadership into a united front for unilateral action: pushing systematic emigration by blacks to western and northern states.

No widespread support existed for emigration, still controversial in North Carolina—tried in 1889–90 with inconclusive results—roundly unpopular among white businessmen for depleting cheap black labor. White came to favor controlled emigration only after Wilmington's violence, but he soon publicly pressed his case in Boston. He hoped for a receptive audience among black leaders at the Council of Colored Men of the State, which he helped organize and lead.[1]

That council's elected leaders—White, John Dancy, and Raleigh attorney Edward Johnson—urged members to approach Democratic legislators with a simple request: not to worsen a tense situation by recommending a state constitutional amendment aimed at disfranchising black voters. The trio knew they had little leverage, but not all members agreed that emigration threats would prevail against the new regime's arsenal. Instead of endorsing White's proposal, the group effectively stymied any possible momentum for it.

The planning meeting was soon beset by disagreements. At least two of more than fifty leaders at Raleigh's black Presbyterian church—Dr. Lawson

Scruggs and Rev. Richmond Leak—left the meeting in protest rather than agree in advance to vote for "whatever resolution the caucus should agree upon."[2] According to the *Charlotte Observer*, the group was split: "An effort was made by White and some others to have a resolution adopted advising the negroes to emigrate in case the Democrats 'made their stay in North Carolina intolerable,' and agreeing that each would aid the others in so emigrating. . . . [T]he convention agreed to strike out this part of the resolutions . . . [by] 42 to 37."[3]

Thomas Fuller, the 1899 Senate's only black member, stayed—determined to ensure "nothing rash was done."[4] Black House colleagues William Coates (Northampton), Moses Peace (Vance), Isaac Smith (Craven), and John Wright (Warren) did not attend. But Smith had already set the stage for a fight, if the council favored emigration. The wealthy black New Bern businessman won election in November by openly courting Democrats. In his January 5 letter to the *Raleigh News and Observer*, a day after the General Assembly convened, he publicized a "certain circular letter addressed to the colored people of the state," encouraging them "to emigrate to parts out of the state." The unidentified "leading name on the circular"—presumably, George White—"has an axe to grind, for the reason that I do not believe he has the slightest nor the remotest idea of leaving the state," Smith wrote.[5]

The true purpose behind the memorial, Smith argued, was "to dictate to the present Legislature what kind of laws to pass for the colored people who of their own good sense should decline to emigrate, but rather remain in their beloved Carolina." There was no reason to distrust Democratic leadership—"the wisest and most brainy of any since the Civil War"—and black citizens should not "let anybody keep you at unrest by telling you this Legislature is going to disfranchise you."[6]

Smith and White were political adversaries, for good reason. Seen as a "closet Democrat" in his first elected office, the truculent Smith soon achieved dubious distinction: expulsion from the Republican Party—unanimously ordered by the GOP legislative caucus—for cooperating too closely with Democrats. Smith left public life to resume his successful business career, still "begging his white friends not to charge to Negroes the mistakes and misrule of Governor Russell."[7]

The group's memorial was submitted to the General Assembly by Fuller and others, its moderate tone less assertive and less likely to influence legislators than White preferred. "The memorial and address are conservative,"

wrote the *News and Observer.* "Those members who were for passing a sensational and radical address were set down upon by the cooler heads, who were
largely in the majority."[8] Fuller, a Warrenton minister and schoolteacher, told
the newspaper that "he had attended the Council and used his best endeavors
to see that nothing rash was done."[9]

Among leaders who did attend, the best known were White, Dancy, and
Edward Johnson, future clerk to the U.S. attorney for eastern North Carolina.[10]
All became officers of the permanent council—Johnson a vice president, Dancy
secretary—but the group's continuing role is uncertain, and its memorial disappeared into committee files.[11] A separate address to black citizens cautioned
readers "not to be hasty in seeking any changes in their present surroundings
and plans, but to quietly and industriously fulfill all contracts with landlords . . .
and where necessary enter into new ones for the current year."[12]

The council's action had little effect on fast-building Jim Crow momentum
in state politics. The dreaded constitutional amendment passed the General
Assembly in February, for submission to voters in 1900. Back in Washington,
White delivered his first major House speech in months. Ostensibly favoring
a bill to extend military funding for another thirty days, White quickly shifted
gears into a thoughtful review of the circumstances facing his race, among his
career's most moving speeches.

He styled himself "the only representative on this floor of 10,000,000 people, from a racial standpoint. . . . They have no else to speak for them, from a
race point of view, except myself." His time left in the House was short—"I will
sit here only two years longer, should I live, and I am going to try mighty hard
to live that long"—yet the problem he cited "not only touches my people, but in
my humble judgment it reaches out and ramifies and affects every citizen. . . .
How long will you sit in your seats here and see the principles that underlie the
foundation of this Government sapped away little by little?"[13]

His penchant for predictions was sharper and more focused on positive
outcomes, as he next told House colleagues:

Now, gentlemen, what are you going to do with this problem . . . ? I believe the time is coming very soon when the color of a man's skin, so far
as business relations are concerned, as far as citizenship is concerned,
will cut no figure at all. A man will be regarded as a man whether
wrapped in a white or a black skin.

I believe the time will come when we will have no riots in the South on account of color, when civilization will so develop all over this nation that there will be no more lynchings and barbarity and mobocracy, now so prevalent in some portions of this country.[14]

White was convinced a future beckoned with black citizens treated as political equals—sooner rather than later, he hoped: "I believe the time will come—yes, soon—when the condition that prevails to-day in Boston . . . where all are recognized, both black and white, will prevail in South Carolina, North Carolina, Louisiana, and Mississippi. We cannot live on the dead ashes of the past. Slavery and its institutions, racial distinctions and wrongs will come to an end."[15]

Numerically, America's black citizens were underrepresented: they deserved at least one-eighth of the House—fifty-one members—yet had just one; a black Supreme Court justice, a place in the cabinet, thirteen senators. But when? "Our ratio of representation is poor. We are taunted with being uppish; we are told to be still; to keep quiet," White repeated. "How long must we keep quiet?" The time had come to act decisively rather than simply hope for the best, White warned:

We have kept quiet while hundreds and thousands of our race have been strung up by the neck unjustly by mobs of murderers. If a man commits a crime he will never find an apologist in me because his face is black. He ought to be punished, but he ought to be punished according to the law as administered in a court of justice. But we keep quiet; do not say it, do not talk about it.

How long must we keep quiet, constantly sitting down and seeing our rights one by one taken away from us? As slaves it was to be expected . . . we were docile and easily managed; but as citizens we want and have a right to expect all that the law guarantees to us.[16]

American's black citizens were making slow, steady progress, against unfair public expectations: "Public sentiment may be against us because we have not done better, but we are making progress. . . . We do not ask for domination. We ask and expect a chance in legislation, and we will be content with nothing else. . . . It is well to stop and consider; you cannot always keep a free man down. When he is once made free, it will be difficult to ever enslave him again, either physically or intellectually." If no one wanted actual slavery again, he said, "there is a slavery that is even worse than manual slavery—the slavery of the mind, the beclouded intellect." Here Congress must act, to "help lift the curtain of darkness, the curtain of ignorance, the curtain of vice that you helped to nail and foist upon us . . . that we may leave the miserable valley of vice and degradation and climb to the top of the mount where we can breathe God's pure air as American citizens."[17]

White offered Congress a moral imperative to ponder as it mulled establishing governments for newly acquired overseas possessions: Cuba, Puerto Rico, Hawaii, and the Philippines. Only if the United States first saw fit to "recognize your citizens at home, recognize those at your door, give them the encouragement, give them the rights that they are justly entitled to," could the nation hold its example up elsewhere. All men would "rejoice with you in that we have done God's service and done that which will elevate us in the eyes of the world."[18]

With this speech, White revealed a subtle yet unmistakable change in philosophy of the nation's emerging racial paradigm, particularly in the South. He had always believed in the essential fairness of the U.S. political system, having grown up in a state where blacks had participated in electoral processes since 1868—weathering challenges, but always with clear optimism, convinced that fairness could triumph over prejudice and intransigence without federal intervention. Recent events proved that such optimism was shortsighted—that it might be time for a new type of Reconstruction, forced upon the Democratic-controlled South by courts and a Republican Congress.

In what would become common parlance a century later, White's consciousness had been raised by the dreadful effects of white-supremacist campaigns and Wilmington's violence. The issues about which he often spoke and wrote during his second House term were disfranchisement and lynching, his new guiding lights—signaling distinct changes in his attitude toward his party. He remained the president's faithful supporter, campaigning for him in 1900 and urging black voters to do likewise—if with lowered expectations—and help push the GOP forward on issues the party of Lincoln and McKinley might prefer to avoid.

Unlike a growing minority of black colleagues, White was clearly not ready to abandon the Republicans—certainly not prepared to embrace Democrats, making inroads among black voters in northern and midwestern cities. Yet he was prepared to embrace and preach the merits of independence at the polls and carefully conceived, effects-driven political leverage.

In thoughtful speeches delivered that spring to Washington's Second Baptist Lyceum, White refined his new message carefully. First, as he reminded his all-black, mostly Republican audience, he planned to remain a Republican, but he had limits: he "would stand by that party as long as it stood by him, and no longer." He refused to wear "a Republican collar."[19]

But he also refused to abandon McKinley. He understood dissatisfaction among blacks with the administration's record so far, which "has not lived up to the expectations of its Negro friends and adherents, but nothing is to be gained by denouncing and abusing President McKinley." Only careful productive action would work, not "fiery speeches, volcanic resolutions, with long-drawn out preambles" unless "backed up by intelligent, well directed and continued action along definite and systematic lines."

> The Negro must find and adopt the happy medium between these extremes, and pursue a course, which . . . will command the respect of all fair-minded people. What is the use . . . to sit down and rail at the Administration . . . ? Why indiscriminately denounce the white people, and inaugurate a crusade of blood when we are so hopelessly outnumbered 7 or 8 to one. . . .
>
> Let us as men make our appeal for fair play. . . . Then if the full measure of our desserts is not accorded us, the Negro must turn to such resources as he can command for the enforcement of his natural rights—for relief from the conditions that make possible such horrible crimes as those perpetrated at Palmetto, Ga., Wilmington, N.C., and Texarkana.[20]

White's recommended course required organization, money raised by the race itself, and steady emigration "from the terror-ridden sections of the South" to "liberal states of the North and West. Conditions will be better for those who go, and since the Negro labor of the South is an indispensable factor . . . better wages and wider latitude would be given those who remain." After just a few years, he theorized, strategically relocated black voters would gain "a balance of power in a sufficient number of states to practically decide who shall occupy the presidential chair ... [to] make and unmake parties, and demand all that is justly his."[21]

A month later, White returned to the Lyceum to promote the NAAC as principal speaker for a seminar. Both speaker and speech were drenched with Richard Thompson's flowery language in the *Colored American:* "For nearly an hour this giant leader held his hearers spellbound by an address that was scholarly, forceful and convincing, and delivered with a dramatic intensity that showed the man's whole nature to be stirred by the outrages and indignities to his race, which he so graphically and eloquently depicted." Moreover,

> Possibly at no time in the history of our freedom has the effort been made to mould public sentiment against us and our progress so strongly as is now being done. . . . . A race of people with the patience, forbearance ... which has characterized us during the past 285 years will not [back] down at the bidding of any man ... and it would be well that all the bloody host of lynchers and assassins all over this country should learn this now.
>
> As slaves we were true to our rulers—true in every trust imposed in us. While the white father and son went forth to battle against us ... to perpetuate our bonds, the strong, brawny arms of the black man produced the food to sustain the wives, children and aged parents of the confederate soldier, and kept inviolable the virtue and care of those intrusted to his keeping.[22]

White recited statistics showing the hypocrisy behind charges that southern blacks were lynched only for rape and so-called protection of the home; hundreds had been wantonly murdered for trivial or nonexistent offenses. Quoting Rabbi Joseph Silverman and Col. Robert Ingersoll on lynching, plus Washington's pleas for blacks "to rise above themselves, above race, above party; above everything that hampers the sympathetic and friendly relation of the element here thrown together by a decree of God," White astutely characterized current trends: "But with all this mobocracy, God still lives and his heralds of the cross cry aloud in the North, in the East, and in the West, against these inhuman atrocities. Nor is the Press silent, but people all over the country ... see the results of the growing evil and with one accord will join hands in wiping it out of existence. The lance must be placed at this festering sore which tends to sap out the life blood, before the putrifying cancer destroys our body politic."[23]

Only effective organization would help blacks win. Black Americans wanted "no special favors, but wished to be measured by the same standard of merit that was applied to the white man, and to be permitted to enjoy the fruits of his labor and talent," White said. "What the colored man needs most now is diversity of trades and professions and callings of every character . . . to place himself after a trade or profession has been acquired."[24]

White offered unorthodox advice to Howard's law students, warning upper-classmen there in March not to enter the trap of government service. "When I graduated here I was offered a position as messenger in one of the [federal] Departments, but I refused to accept; . . . I knew it was far better to go out into life and carve out my own destiny without the aid or assistance of Uncle Sam," he noted. Classmates taking such jobs "are here today, still paying rent and cannot get away if they wanted to."[25]

After graduating with a teaching degree, he studied independently and became a lawyer two years after leaving Howard, prospering as a New Bern attorney. "The Southland offers many opportunities for the young man of to-day. . . . It is there where the lawyer can work out his future destiny. The people need your talents, your services and your ability," he declared, adding:

> Be moulders of public sentiment, have a mind of your own; be original thinkers with opinions of your own . . . have the courage of your convictions to maintain them until they are dislodged by others. . . . What the world needs to day is efficient young men and women . . . who have an object in view, a purpose to accomplish. . . . I do not accept the one theory of industrial education as advanced by Booker T. Washington, as the panacea of all our ills . . . [but] he is doing a great work and is filling a long-felt want.[26]

He offered subtle, ironic criticisms of his profession, toward which his listeners now headed: "While the average man throughout the country looks upon lawyers as liars, and it has become almost a common belief that they are unscrupulous and untrustworthy," he said, "I never found anything in the profession that prevented a successful lawyer from being an honest, dignified, truthful, Christian gentleman."[27] But as White returned to Congress, he found little opportunity to prod fellow Republicans into action. The Fifty-Fifth Congress was adjourning, with party numbers reduced in the Fifty-Sixth, making Republicans less likely to agree on penalties for southern states disfranchising blacks. And with his eyes on the likely rematch against William Jennings Bryan, who carried every Deep South state in 1896, McKinley seemed intent on cultivating, not antagonizing, southern Democrats.

Members of the NAAC were determined to exert moral leadership on key issues of disfranchisement and lynching, leaving White little choice but to get in front on both issues. He still hoped to nudge McKinley proactively on lynching; the recent upsurge in vigilante actions by southern mobs alarmed White, who later tallied 166 lynchings—all but ten involving black southerners—during the sixteen-month period ending in April 1899.[28] Not to lead the charge risked allowing Bishop Walters and twin firebrands T. Thomas Fortune and Ida Wells-Barnett to erode support for McKinley, whom White still saw as the best hope of black Americans. But as 1899 began, news from the southern front was increasingly bleak.

The spring of 1899 brought depressing news of continuing hostility by white mobs toward black offenders, particularly in Georgia. In mid-March, Palmetto vigilantes slaughtered six blacks charged with arson, before trial. In Newnan in April, black farmer Sam Hose killed his white employer in self-defense but was falsely charged with raping his employer's wife; both Hose and a black minister defending him were lynched by mobs.[29] As widely reported, Hose was mutilated and publicly burned; Elijah Strickland's execution was noted only by black newspapers. The name Sam Hose soon became a rallying cry for White and antilynching activists.

The best-publicized case involved the federal trial of Frazier Baker's killers in Charleston, where federal prosecutors prepared to try thirteen Lake City men for conspiracy in the 1898 deaths of Baker and his daughter.[30] The two-week trial drew national headlines and was chronicled in great detail by the *Charleston News & Courier*. A compelling scenario, it was the first such trial in the South, with an intriguing cast. From the one-armed Confederate veteran on the bench and a star witness for the prosecution recruited from among white defendants—derided as a "hit man" by defense lawyers—to testimony by the pitiable black widow, her grieving children, and neighbors of both races, the characters and setting of the trial might well have been lifted from a lurid popular novel. Historian Terence Finnegan, who researched the trial for his 2013 treatise on southern lynching, provides graphic detail about the case.[31]

Behind the scenes, U.S. Attorney General John Griggs worked diligently with prosecutor Abial Lathrop. During initial investigations, Lathrop complained how an atmosphere of terrorism made it extremely difficult to convince potential witnesses to come forward, prompting the use of a witness protection scheme.[32] "I am glad to inform you that this Department ... has spared no expense and devoted all possible time to ferret out the evidence that would secure the conviction of the guilty parties," Griggs wrote Booker T. Washington as the trial began. "I have employed as special counsel for the United States, one of the ablest lawyers in Charleston. . . . The special inspectors and detectives have worked night and day to secure the evidence. If the prosecution fails, it will only be because the jury will not convict in the face of clear evidence."[33]

The trial was delayed until four defendants, all Spanish-American War veterans, returned from Cuba. That it ended in a hung jury and mistrial was almost predictable—and yet still shocking, after momentum seemed until the last to be building toward an earthshaking guilty verdict. Predictable, perhaps, except for an ironclad case built by federal investigators and prosecutors, or the judge's refreshing impartiality.[34] Predictable, except for fervent backstage support from the U.S. attorney general and president. Predictable, except for unshakable testimony by eyewitnesses—fearing for their lives while testifying openly against men they believed were monsters.

Simply reading the charges aloud required more than an hour. A forty-eight-page federal indictment document listed twenty-four separate charges under four sections of the Revised U.S. Statutes (Sections 5.506, 5.509, 5.513, and 5.466). Because traditional crimes of murder and attempted murder on nonfederal lands were state crimes, the deaths of Baker and his daughter and his family's wounding were technically not the issue here. The legal case, more complex, required proof of the existence of an actual conspiracy leading to the murders and attempted murders. But the penalty could not be execution; Congress had recently eliminated capital punishment for all federal crimes, save treason.

In the dock were Joseph Newham, Early Lee, Marion Clark, and ten other defendants. (Newham and Lee turned state's evidence, received immunity, and were never tried; Clark and two others were acquitted.) The defendants, ranging in age from nineteen to forty-three, had lived in Lake City or environs; most were farmers, clerks, or merchants. All but four were apprehended and charged in the summer of 1898, and free on bail since.[35]

The others—Corporal Clark, Sergeant Charles Joyner, and Privates Oscar Kelly and Edwin Rodgers—joined the Second South Carolina Infantry in the spring of 1898. Joyner, Kelly, and Rodgers returned a year later from Cuba for final discharge. Clark, former editor of the *Lake City Times*, was discharged earlier.[36]

The grand jury returned true bills of indictment after hearing the legal theory of conspiracy, which U.S. District Judge William Brawley explained:

A conspiracy is an unlawful agreement or combination of two or more persons to do an unlawful act or to accomplish an unlawful purpose.... Nothing can be more dangerous to the peace of society than a combination of men engaged in a lawless enterprise where those restraints which commonly control the individual ... are broken down and men in a body are led on to the commission of act from which, as individuals, they would shrink with horror.

For this reason, the law denounces the conspiracy itself, apart from any acts done in pursuance of it. The heinousness of any crime committed in the course of it is merely a matter of aggravation.... [I]f there is proof that two or more persons have combined for an illegal purpose, any act done by one in pursuance of the original concerted plan, and in the carrying out of the common object, and any declaration made by one during the prosecution of this enterprise, is evidence against all.[37]

The crimes themselves were terrible, the judge continued: "A more heinous crime has rarely darkened the history of this State. It would be an everlasting reproach to our Government and to our civilization if those charged with the administration of the law failed to bring to trial the perpetrators of this crime." Despite community sentiments against Baker, there was "no excuse for the horrible offenses charged in this indictment."[38]

A Civil War veteran who had lost an arm in battle, Brawley was a respected solicitor, state legislator, and Democratic congressman before Cleveland selected him for the bench in 1894. Considered fair-minded and objective,

Brawley was a stickler for details and an efficient administrator, determined to try the case expeditiously—another session of District Court waited a week later at the other end of the state. Yet unexpected obstacles interfered: a special assistant prosecutor was detained at the Supreme Court, and Attorney General Griggs telegraphed to plead for continuance. One juror fell ill, briefly; testimony delivered without him had to be repeated when he returned. The case required two full weeks to try.

Brawley's private political sentiments were barely noticeable, although his charge to the grand jury hinted at private distaste for the politics propelling Baker's untimely end. Despite his unchallenged right to serve, "it is probably true, that Frazier B. Baker was very obnoxious to the community that he was appointed to serve," Brawley said.[39] Unnamed Republicans had "aroused the popular fury to such an extent" and bore some "moral responsibility" for the crime to which Baker's selection inexorably led, Brawley admitted, yet he was unsympathetic, personally or legally, to abhorrent mob actions. "Whatever reason may have existed for the feeling of the community on this subject, there were other and legal ways in which that feeling might manifest itself, and other and legal remedies for such complaints," he said; there could be no "extenuation of this dreadful crime. No consideration of that kind can furnish palliation or excuse for the horrible offenses."[40]

The all-white jury came from all over South Carolina rather than from Charleston's original "five-mile box"; black voters in the pool were not selected. All jurors were promptly sequestered in a local hotel for protection, after their names appeared in Charleston's newspaper.[41] The prosecution included both public and private players: U.S. District Attorney Lathrop and his assistant Benjamin Hagood, joined by private counsel J. P. K. Bryan and William Barber, ex–attorney general. For the defense, the debonair William Jervey was lead counsel, joined by W. T. Bass and future congressman George Legaré.

Easily the saga's most complex player, Newham had been spirited away from Lake City on trumped-up charges of illegal liquor sales, then sent back twice as an "undercover" operative by inventive federal agents, under coaching of the "viper whispering in his ear" (as the defense characterized Early Lee, who never testified). Newham held a temporary job—ironically, a mailbag repairman—in Washington, D.C., until the trial.[42]

Dozens of witnesses included Baker's African American neighbors, who identified up to four mob members they knew personally, and other area residents. The U.S. postal inspector who immediately investigated the scene—as well as a previous fire—described the graphic results. Other white witnesses recalled their refusal to join the lynchers after being recruited by defendants. During the trial, Newham identified Epps, Godwin, Joyner, Lee, McKnight, Rogers, Stokes, Ward, and Webster as mob participants and attack planners. But Clark, Kelly, and Rodgers were not involved, he swore, and charges against them foundered.

Defense lawyers ridiculed the state's key witness—a liar, turncoat, and would-be contract killer, not even present at the lynching—and challenged the case's strength. Airtight alibis emerged for eight main defendants. Strangers from elsewhere must have committed this awful deed, not these law-abiding defendants.

Baker's widow and three children testified to the events and their injuries. Saddest of all was Lavinia Baker, "a small woman, very black, and [who] wore deep mourning," who recalled her dreadful ordeal in clear, convincing terms but recognized neither her attackers nor their race. After the building was set afire, shots pierced the walls, she testified. Her husband threw buckets of water on burning walls and began to pray; son Lincoln, wounded by early gunshots, was unable to help. Holding Julia in her arms, she was paralyzed with fear, until her husband grabbed her and yelled, "Come on, we might as well die running as standing." As he opened the front door, he was shot dead and fell backward onto her. Lavinia and two children were shot and wounded inside the house but escaped, without further injuries, through a gauntlet of armed horsemen.[43]

In the end, the jury could not agree on a verdict, despite twenty hours of deliberation, and reported a hopeless deadlock—reportedly, either 6 to 6 or 7 to 5 for acquittal—to the judge, who wept at the apparent miscarriage of justice.[44] Brawley surely sensed the shift in momentum toward the real possibility of a hung jury—or perhaps outright acquittal, but the prosecution's once-invincible case had imploded. One major witness's testimony was disallowed, another's reputation all but discredited. Three defendants were exonerated, forcing Brawley to instruct jurors to acquit them for lack of evidence.

Jurors "looked pale and tired when the men filed slowly into the Court yesterday [Saturday] morning.... [T]he long stay in the jury room had wearied them and they were glad to go away, but they were not willing to change an opinion which would mean a verdict."[45] In the judge's words, they were not to blame—society at large was accountable: "I am one of those persons disposed to believe that this world is growing better . . . but sometimes I doubt whether we in South Carolina are improving or not. . . . Sometimes I feel that the moral fibre of the people is growing weaker instead of stronger, and that there is a growing deterioration in both races." The crimes here were barbaric: "We look on our own race and what do we see? Whoever heard of a lynching forty years ago, or of mob violence to redress grievances, or the execution of people without a trial? Who ever heard of the humble house of a man being burned and his children butchered? All of these things indicate that the law is no longer being respected by communities and people; the law has lost its sanction. And what does that mean? It means anarchy, the disintegration of society."[46]

Specters of race and white supremacy were no excuse for monstrous behavior. "The white people in South Carolina cannot escape its responsibility. The white people have the government in their hands, and if they cannot enforce the law they confess their impotence," the judge continued. He did not blame the jury for failing to reach a verdict, fighting back tears in consoling them: "Gentlemen, the Court regrets that you have not been able to reach a conclusion and verdict. A great deal of time and labor has been expended, but this Court has no word of comment or censure. . . . If you cannot agree, you cannot agree, and no man's conduct in a great matter like this can be judged by another."[47]

Comforted by the knowledge that at least five jurors had voted to convict the remaining defendants, Brawley fully expected to be asked to preside at a fall retrial. (Finnegan says the jury reportedly voted 11–1 to convict one defendant.)[48] But as the Justice Department delayed its decision indefinitely, witnesses began disappearing from Lake City, some in apparent fear for their lives. Most defendants remained in Lake City, but at least four left South Carolina. Lathrop had worked tirelessly to bring the case to trial, but being replaced as district attorney in 1901 ended his involvement in any retrial; he retired from public office and moved upstate. Colleagues and opponents remained active in South Carolina politics and the law. In 1902, defense attorney Legaré won Brawley's old seat in Congress; Brawley retired in 1911, still haunted by the case.[49]

Three months later, Lavinia Baker and her children went to live in Massachusetts, spirited away under sympathetic care of Bostonian Lillian Jewett. Just after the trial, Jewett began soliciting funds for their welfare, taking them to public rallies across New England in 1899.[50] William Lloyd Garrison II, son of the late abolitionist, raised funds to purchase a Boston home for them.

Jewett, who clashed with other supporters in both states, left the cause after Garrison's intervention.[51]

But Jewett publicly blamed the McKinley administration for not seeking to retry the defendants, and many African American leaders agreed with her sentiments, sharing her disappointment and frustration. The Justice Department concluded that no better result would ever be reached, particularly after key witnesses dispersed. By April 1900, the Post Office Department came to a similar conclusion, quietly reopening the Lake City post office under a new postmaster.

Little is known about Della Carter's background, except that she was white, literate, and married with four children.[52] But perhaps most remarkable about Mrs. Carter was that she was named at all, for she had no post office to serve. Since 1898, the Lake City post office had been closed indefinitely, and its mail redirected to Scranton, three miles north. As one observer noted: "The Post Office Department...forbade the mail agent on the train to receive letters. The little drop door to the mail car was always locked before reaching Lake City."[53]

Reopening Lake City's post office signaled a return to normalcy, of sorts, for South Carolinians. But among McKinley critics, the trial's outcome and uncertainty over a retrial exacerbated growing disenchantment with him. Less than a month after the trial, Fortune angrily blasted the president as "a man of jelly, who would turn us all loose to the mob and not say a word. He may not mean to do so, but he is vacillating, uncertain...and a man of putty and jelly, influenced by others."[54] Fortune blamed McKinley for rising southern violence against blacks, as "the one man in Washington who has done more to breed disquiet and create these outrageous acts than anyone else" by tacitly encouraging armed mobs.

It was a nearly surreal moment, even for Fortune; the Afro-American Conference had no ties to the NAAC but met at New York City's Zion Church, home to the Council's president. Sober for once, Fortune sensibly did not repeat his December threat to "stab" McKinley, even to grimly cynical clerics. Committed to social justice goals and activist outlooks, the bishops were dismayed and indignant at the growing violence in the South, where so many blacks still lived; Fortune, like Walters, appeared to find this audience more receptive than a year earlier.

The trend disturbed black Republican officeholders, and as the NAAC's next annual meeting approached, White and others were drawn to Chicago to gauge the mood and feelings of members and defuse defections from the president's camp. If pessimism and disenchantment with McKinley's leadership among African American leaders were not overwhelming, how quickly the mood took hold was shocking. One year earlier, McKinley had ridden a national wave of popularity for successfully prosecuting the war against Spain and, among blacks, for welcoming thousands of black war volunteers into the military. Federal appointments for hundreds of African Americans, including ninety postmasters across thirteen states, had not gone unnoticed during the fall campaign, when Judson Lyons penned a laudatory paean to McKinley listing about sixty notable black men and women in high-profile positions and lesser jobs.[55] In "Appointments Which Afro-Americans Have Received from President McKinley," Lyons reminded black leaders that as a group, black federal workers earned salaries totaling "considerably over seven million dollars per annum"—far more than under the Grant administration—from service at the Post Office, Interior, and State Departments, in the Army, Navy, and War Departments, and lesser bureaus. McKinley had "commissioned in one day between 75 and 80 colored officers in the Army."[56]

Yet by early 1899, most volunteers were being mustered out, with unanticipated repercussions; no longer were temporary black officers needed. Resentment was rising against the military and the commander in chief; the war's brevity disappointed black volunteers who expected longer tours of duty. White's inability to convince Congress to create an additional permanent army artillery regiment still rankled.

Those black soldiers with overseas tours extended after the war had mixed reactions to their experiences. As recounted by historian Willard Gatewood, some preferred to stay in Cuba forever; Dr. W. C. Warmsley, a black physician with Louisiana's immunes, claimed to "hope and trust that the educated colored men of America will come over here. . . . A doctor would make a fortune soon in any of the Cuban towns on this end of the island," he wrote from Santiago in May 1899.[57] Even army regulars like cavalryman John Lewis (H Troop, Tenth Cavalry) dreaded returning to Texas and "receiving such treatment as we have generally received in the South"; the U.S. "color line" had no effect in Cuba, where economic opportunity was superior, he wrote in December 1899.[58]

Comparatively few black soldiers benefited from continuing hostilities in the Philippines, where a rebellion against U.S. "liberators" soon broke out. After July 1899, companies from the army's permanent four black regiments were sent to help crush the rebellion, followed by two newly created volunteer regiments recruited that fall, who arrived in 1900 and remained until 1902, led by black officers selected from soldiers distinguishing themselves in Cuba or state volunteers with "impressive service records." But adjustment problems abounded; some black soldiers viewed Filipino rebels' passionate cause—independence—as antithetical to their mission and questioned the morality of U.S. annexation. Filipinos would be treated, they feared, like most U.S. blacks, as second-class citizens.[59]

Whether McKinley might have blunted growing dissatisfaction over his record among blacks by positive action is questionable. Annexation of the Philippines in February—by the closest of margins, a tie broken by Vice President Hobart, and achieved by last-minute maneuvering to South Carolina's John McLaurin—did not reassure those who fervently believed in the Filipinos' rights to self-determination, or long-term prospects for autonomy or democracy. The president made no conciliatory speeches restoring confidence in his desire to help black U.S. citizens, meeting only sporadically with black advisers or appointees.

White, meanwhile, spent much time between sessions away from Washington. Still disappointed over McKinley's failure to visit Greensboro, he made only one recorded visit to the White House, with NAAC members, before the Fifty-Sixth Congress convened in December.[60] But hopes of reengaging the president during the new Congress were never far from mind, simply prioritized behind more demanding matters.

On a personal level, both men were increasingly concerned with their wives' health. Determined to attend state dinners and public events despite occasional seizures of epilepsy, Ida McKinley's nervous condition deteriorated in early 1899, prompting a discreet ten-day vacation with her husband at Virginia's Hot Springs. Among apparent reasons, according to Leech: her brother, George Saxton, was murdered in 1898, and the lurid trial of his jilted lover, a beautiful divorcée whose marriage George had broken up, ended in April with acquittal. Mrs. McKinley long feigned obliviousness to the scandal, but as her husband reported to his nephew John Barber in April, she "has not been very well for the last ten days," with the Canton trial under way.[61]

He consoled Barber over the illness of his mother, Mary Saxton Barber, hoping she was "standing the great strain through which she is now passing"—an oblique reference to the trial. In May, Ida McKinley suffered a severe epileptic attack while visiting friends in western Massachusetts and "sank into a hysterical depression such as she had not known for ten years or more."[62] Vacations at Lake Champlain, New York, and Canton did little to help.

For White, circumstances were eerily similar. Cora Lena White's health was never strong after her last child's birth in 1893, and she was ill with a debilitating and mysterious illness, eventually diagnosed as chronic neurasthenia. Nearly a complete invalid, she moved to Washington, D.C., after White's reelection in a campaign involving scurrilous personal attacks on her and his stepdaughter Della.[63] A nervous collapse or breakdown may have resulted from intense unfavorable publicity, and her illness eventually compelled serious surgery in 1901. Like Mrs. McKinley's epilepsy, symptoms were exacerbated by nervous stress; its wide variety of physical and mental symptoms seems related to what is now called chronic fatigue syndrome.

White later recalled taking her on a recuperative trip in 1899 along the southern New Jersey coast, in the resort county of Cape May, whose healthy climate and serene seaside environment appeared conducive to restoring health. "My wife's health has been wrecked on account of the maliciousness of the attacks made upon me," he told the *New York Times* in August 1900. "She is now ill in New Jersey, and I am afraid she will be an invalid for a long time."[64]

The Whites soon began treating New Jersey as their second home, particularly after the George H. White Land and Development Company began its new town north of Cape May City. Later named Whitesboro, it was envisioned as a refuge for southern blacks fleeing Jim Crow–era restrictions. Among investors was the famous writer Paul Laurence Dunbar, who owned Cape May property and recommended it as early as 1899.[65]

Cora Lena could obtain expert medical care in Washington and was cheered by the affectionate company of her older sister Louisa Cheatham and her beloved nephews and niece. Their children were close in age, spent much time together, and were educated in the capital's racially segregated public schools. But Louisa's sudden illness—described as "catarrh of the stomach [gastritis] complicated by acute indigestion"—and death in September 1899 depressed Cora Lena, now a virtual recluse.[66]

Their wives' health was not the only sad issue concerning both men. Both were disturbed by the deterioration of Vice President Hobart, whose heart condition was so severe that he withdrew from public life and returned to New Jersey for rest. No longer could the McKinleys enjoy restorative visits with the Hobarts, whose "Cream White House" on Lafayette Square provided a much-needed and frequent respite from pressures of daily Executive Mansion life. Jennie Hobart, trusted friend and companion to Mrs. McKinley on joint vacations, was sorely missed by the ailing first lady. Deprived of his two closest advisers—Hobart, the wise and prudent "assistant president" who shouldered much of the presidency's burden, and his alter ego Mark Hanna, now preoccupied with Senate duties—McKinley was increasingly alone during a difficult transition.

With Congress closed until December, the president had only sporadic contact with other party leaders on several pressing issues, including the thorny dilemma over replacing Secretary of War Russell Alger, who refused to resign, despite pressure from almost everyone. McKinley, who could not bring himself to fire Alger, turned in frustration to Hobart to handle the disagreeable task. Alger and his wife planned a July vacation at the Hobart seaside home near Long Branch, New Jersey. During that visit, the ever-dutiful Hobart adroitly convinced Alger to step aside, drawing warm praise in the national press for "crystal insight" and "velvet tact."[67] Opening the way for the more talented Elihu Root, however, was Hobart's last major task.

Nor was White present as the Alger drama played out, having launched speaking tours in New York and Canada, where he was warmly received. After delivering lectures "to large audiences of colored and white people" in two Canadian cities, White said he found "no discrimination against the Negro" in Canada, but little evidence of better economic conditions for his race. He discouraged talk of emigration to "Africa or some other congenial country" as "all bosh. It is wholly impracticable. [America] is the black man's home. Here he must live and die and work out his own destiny."[68]

꒰꒱

White's favored scheme to redress the geographic imbalance of blacks by controlled emigration was still not resonating widely. The sheer logistics of such a scheme mitigated against large-scale adoption; 80 percent of black citizens remained in southern states, most with minimal education and few nonagricultural skills. A steady pace of small groups on a controlled basis would require decades for a dent in southern numbers; in 1900, about 7 million black citizens of 8.8 million nationwide still lived in eleven Old Confederacy states.[69]

White's southern strategy differed from that advocated by other Republicans, watching their last strong regional political foothold slipping away as Democrats reinforced nearly monolithic control of state governments. Since Reconstruction, only North Carolina's GOP had controlled both legislature and governor's office, and only by fusion with Populists. The future for fusionists was grim, witnessed by the 1898 election, and in the rest of the South even bleaker. Republicans had won no statewide office in any other southern state since Reconstruction; state legislative numbers, including black Republicans, were steadily declining. Only three other southern states elected black Republican legislators after 1895—Georgia, South Carolina, and Texas—and no black Republican save White had gone to Congress since.

The southern GOP faced its worst dilemma in two decades. One answer was effectively splitting into separate parties—a lily-white party led by white Republicans, and "black-and-tan" parties in South Carolina and Georgia. Intraparty squabbles in some states had already forced national conventions to choose between factional slates, as in 1896, when a pro-McKinley delegation replaced veteran Cuney's group—the first time in twenty years he was not a Texas delegate. Almost all southern delegations in 1896 included at least a few blacks, but overall, the number of black delegates soon dwindled from seventy-three to forty in 1900.

Politics aside, Georgia was a perfect example of a state where emigration was both difficult to implement and economically disruptive. More than 1 million blacks lived in Georgia in 1900, up 20 percent from 1890, representing one-seventh of all southern blacks. Most black Georgians still lived in rural areas, only 10 percent in Savannah, Augusta, Macon, and Atlanta. Despite party preponderance, black Republicans had little influence on state elections but carried strong influence in Washington—and heartily voiced oversized opinions.

Most strongly supported McKinley in 1896, and were impressed by the number of Republicans of both races he initially selected for Georgia patronage posts. In 1897, black Georgians reportedly "regarded McKinley as the best friend they ever had," citing early appointments for "more Negroes to responsible positions in Georgia than all earlier presidents combined."[70] McKinley's notable attention to Georgia's political needs included significant black appointees—Henry Rucker, John Deveaux, Christopher Wimbish, and Jackson McHenry among them—although his largess did not extend as far down the patronage list as many hoped.[71]

Only four black Georgia postmasters were appointed—all in 1897 (at Athens, Darien, Hogansville, and South Atlanta)—compared to more than five hundred white postmasters from all three parties, recommended by the Democratic congressional delegation. The president's notorious inability to appoint Judson Lyons in Augusta still distressed black Republicans. Worse, during his Georgia tour, many blacks were vocally unhappy over their exclusion from the reception committees in cities McKinley visited.[72]

As the 1900 election campaign neared, sentiments among black Georgians were shifting measurably against the president. The political idealism of McKinley's first year gave way to cold political reality; he needed strong political support from southern Democrats. As early as December 1898, just after he visited Atlanta and Savannah, black Republicans of Georgia's Second District met in Albany to condemn McKinley's appointments of white Democrats and Populists to federal office—an obvious attempt by a Republican president to curry political favor with leaders of other parties, including Georgia's governor, congressmen, and senators.[73]

As the year ended, the haunting sentiments of one black career soldier abroad reflected growing disenchantment with a country he loved but to which he could not bear to return—at least to the South, his likely next posting. John Lewis, on garrison duty in Manzanillo, Cuba, was transferring home after just eight months; he hoped to remain in Cuba until 1900 and dreaded the return. "I am tired of being in the South and receiving such treatment as we have generally received in the South," Corporal Lewis wrote the *Wisconsin Weekly Advocate* in December. Lewis wanted to be stationed up North, but his Tenth Cavalry was destined for Texas. "Thank God my time is not long to remain [in Texas] and when I soldier again my regiment or troop will never be stationed in the South."[74]

"I cannot risk all and receive no credit and [have] about all my rights taken from me because I am black," he asserted glumly. Service in Huntsville en route to Cuba made him pessimistic about future American race relations. The time was coming, Lewis feared, that American Negroes "will call a halt and strike back, and if our general government doesn't protect you, protect yourself.... It is only a question of time when it will come, if the South is not more just to the American blacks."[75]

For Lewis, the disappointment was personal. Eighteen months earlier, he had written much more hopefully from Florida, begging black volunteers "to be an honor to [their] race" in the war with Spain: "I hope that you, dear sir, will appeal to the young colored men of this country in defence of a common cause. It is the time every patriotic young colored man should come to the front and defend its honor and show that we are true American citizens; that we can protect our homes and government."[76] Even witnessing Lakeland's racial turmoil did not weaken Lewis's faith in the United States' ability to rectify injustice.

But his mind changed, after weeks in Alabama and months in Cuba watching U.S. soldiers and government representatives struggle to impose "the color line." The military's stubborn failure to commission black officers for black soldiers undermined his confidence in his country's systemic fairness. The specter of such a race war—however far-fetched—was an ill omen indeed for the nation, its president, and the party that had once promised much to black members but was now on the verge of discarding them.

8

STOPS AND STARTS ON THE ROAD
TO RACIAL PEACE

Lynchings must not be tolerated in a great and civilized country like the United States. Courts, not mobs, must execute the penalties of the laws.
—**William McKinley**, December 5, 1899

As George White prepared for the Fifty-Sixth Congress to convene, a plan for combating the growing nationwide upsurge in lynchings was taking shape in his mind. Like most observers, he was profoundly disappointed by Charleston's April mistrial and eagerly awaited a fall retrial. But his summer speaking tour across Canada and the northern United States energized his quest for other alternatives, particularly passing a federal law to punish lynch mobs. Under no illusions about the difficulty of passing such a law, he enlisted bright legal minds, such as the well-regarded black attorney Edward Brown of Boston, and the enterprising black scholar Daniel Murray, assistant librarian of Congress.

Other consultants included Attorney General John Griggs, who had worked so diligently with prosecutor Abial Lathrop on the Lake City case, and other Department of Justice attorneys. White's final proposal received strong backing from civil rights crusader Albert Pillsbury of Boston, graduate of Harvard Law and former attorney general of Massachusetts, an especially fervent backer of civil rights causes. The bill's origins dated back to the August meeting in Chicago of the National Afro-American Council (NAAC) and its express goals of prodding both McKinley and the Republican Party on many issues, particularly lynching. Led by Ida Wells-Barnett, chair of the NAAC antilynching bureau, a move to force passage of a national antilynching law was the most pressing issue in shoring up McKinley's support among black Americans. As the meeting ended its first day, the *New York Times* trumpeted the group's shocking plan on lynching: "to make it a crime against the United States Government."[1]

That was only the beginning. The NAAC resolution text was shriller: "We are heartily grieved that the president of the United States and those in authority have not from time to time used their high station to voice the best conscience of the nation in regard to mob violence," it read in part. "It is not right that American citizens should be despoiled of life and liberty while the nation looks silently on." Demanding passage of "such national and constitutional legislation as shall at least secure as great protection from mob violence to Americans as is today afforded citizens of foreign countries resident here," it described lynching as "an offense against civilization which demands punishment, and we believe that it lies in the power of congress to enact such repressive legislation."[2]

White's unofficial role at the meeting was to gauge the depth of anti-McKinley sentiment among NAAC delegates—and, if possible, head off any moves to embarrass or criticize the chief executive—but he faced an uphill battle when Bishop Walters encouraged delegates' fervor. More palatable wording that omitted language assigning personal responsibility to McKinley for inaction on lynching was voted down after "violent debates and much personal feeling"; sponsor Theophile Allain, a transplanted Chicago Republican, bemoaned the absence of McKinley surrogates to defuse tension. (His appointees Lyons, Cheatham, and Green each declined to appear in Chicago, as had Bishop Arnett.)[3]

The *Chicago Tribune* noted the Council actions and generally approved most other resolutions as "within bounds." But the *Tribune* chided the group for its "unfair" decision to censure the president, however indirectly: "It is certain that the President views with grief and horror the lynching outrages" in the South, but his hands were tied in most cases ("in ninety-nine cases out of a hundred the offenses are against State not federal laws"). The NAAC was ignoring his action in the Lake City murders and blaming him because "he could not secure a conviction from a South Carolina jury."[4] A federal antilynching law was pointless; the NAAC had no political leverage.

Though unable to derail the unfriendly resolution, White made the best of a delicate situation by agreeing to become the second of nine NAAC vice presidents—after Rev. Elias Morris of Arkansas, ahead of five other clergymen and two journalists—and accepting a lead role in drafting antilynching legislation he was expected to introduce in the House that winter.[5] Constructing such a bill required careful attention to constitutional issues of law, particularly if the contemplated law involved federal penalties for murder, currently reserved almost exclusively to the states. The last such proposal for legislation, advanced the decade before by Benjamin Harrison, had suggested certain measures in response to the notorious mob executions of Italian immigrants acquitted of murder in New Orleans in March 1891. Harrison's proposal was only part of a solution, as he suggested in his December annual message to Congress, for "Federal officers and courts have no power in such cases to intervene, either for the protection of a foreign citizen or for the punishment of his slayers."[6]

Nor had Congress yet seen fit "to make offenses against the treaty rights of foreigners domiciled in the United States cognizable in the Federal courts." That being the case, Harrison believed it entirely logical "that the officers of the State charged with police and judicial powers in such cases must in the consideration of international questions growing out of such incidents be regarded in such sense as Federal agents as to make this Government answerable for their acts in cases where it would be answerable if the United States had used its constitutional power to define and punish crime against treaty rights."[7] His proposal, submitted to Congress in 1892 but never enacted, was limited to lynchings of foreign nationals on U.S. soil, ignoring separate issues raised by domestic lynchings. Harrison used executive powers to pay a twenty-four-thousand-dollar bounty to the Italian government, provoking strong congressional reaction.[8]

On its face, White's new strategy seemed straightforward: to make murder by lynch mob punishable in federal courts, with appropriate penalties similar to those for treason, and to create a federal police authority for the purpose of investigating lynching deaths and charging and apprehending alleged participants in lynch mobs. The latter agency should create uniformity in investigations rather than trusting the separate states to follow through. But logistical and constitutional problems existed. Among final acts in early 1897, the Fifty-Fourth Congress had effectively abolished the death penalty for most federal crimes, retaining it as a discretionary penalty for treason and four other offenses, but not for murders committed in states and subject to state prosecution.[9]

By tradition, murder and other offenses for which state penalties already existed were not covered by federal law, under which murder trials covered only acts committed in the District of Columbia, on military reservations, and on Indian reservations. Expanding federal coverage of murder prosecutions into nonfederal lands, or the nation at large, was not likely to be approved by

Congress so soon after the 1897 act, the wording of which the Supreme Court upheld in 1899.[10] A related constitutional hurdle was more ominous. Establishing a centralized federal police force in peacetime, even one with strictly limited powers, was an idea not yet acceptable to most American lawmakers—it was all too reminiscent of Reconstruction's military forces and likely to provoke southern senators who opposed expansion of federal power over state authority.

White and his advisers were aware of the obstacles to passing such a federal law but were determined to push the issue as far as it would go, hoping to shame lukewarm Republicans—perhaps even McKinley—into proactive stands. White was also determined to stay one step ahead of his critic Wells-Barnett, crusading chair of the NAAC bureau on lynching, after their tense encounter over Lavinia Baker's compensation a year earlier. The Republican Party was on record with strong antilynching language in its 1896 platform: "We proclaim our unqualified condemnation of the uncivilized and preposterous [barbarous] practice well known as lynching, and the killing of human beings suspected or charged with crime without process of law."[11] McKinley had acted decisively to prevent at least one lynching as Ohio's governor, and he denounced lynchings in his 1897 annual message, having long opposed the practice on both moral and legal grounds.

If almost all members of Congress publicly opposed lynching, most Democrats and many Republicans in both houses appeared convinced that states must be the primary actors in controlling lynchings; changing a majority's mind otherwise might be difficult. Ironically, individual states had recently passed legislation punishing public officials who allowed mobs to kidnap and execute individuals. In 1897 alone, Kentucky, Tennessee, and Texas criminalized acts of mob violence and lynching, although prosecutions under new laws were rare, and Texas soon repealed its law.[12] White was convinced the president would endorse his legislation, or so he told others before introducing his bill; when and how the president made his feelings known, however, was never specified, although he did address lynching in his annual message.

◈

Shortly after the Council's annual meeting, McKinley made an unprecedented historic move: appointing more than seventy black officers in new volunteer regiments headed for the Philippines. The astonishing move fulfilled wartime promises to reward black soldiers, as he selected new captains, first lieutenants, and second lieutenants for the Forty-Eighth and Forty-Ninth Regiments of Infantry, U.S. Volunteers.[13] Including veterans of four regular black regiments, the four immune regiments, and every state volunteer regiment, the newly minted officers served under white colonels, lieutenant colonels, and majors—but were now the highest-ranking black officers in the nation's army.[14]

McKinley's nine-state presidential campaign tour that fall—a run-up to the 1900 reelection campaign—took the president and cabinet members as far west as the Dakotas for appearances and speeches, beginning October 5, just after an extravagant tribute to America's conquering hero of the Philippines, Admiral George Dewey. The adulation accorded Dewey during his triumphant return, including a Washington parade rivaling an inauguration, was vaguely unsettling for McKinley's campaign advisers—Dewey was boomed as a presidential candidate—but the president artfully co-opted the hero by receiving him graciously, agreeing to his suggested naval reinforcements in the Philippines, then leaving on his own well-publicized visit. But even besieged by last-minute preparations, McKinley found time for a nearly daylong political consultation on October 2 with Mark Hanna and Henry Payne, members of the Republican National Committee, on party planning matters—ostensibly to discuss politics in Ohio and Wisconsin. Payne, widely regarded as Hanna's successor as chair, was always careful to nurture relations with the party's leader.[15]

On a decidedly more inclusive scale, McKinley also agreed to host a much larger NAAC delegation presenting that group's newly passed annual resolutions on issues affecting African Americans—specifically, lynching, mob violence, and disfranchisement. Led by sociologist Jesse Lawson, the fifteen members were introduced to McKinley by his own high-ranking black appointees, Lyons and Cheatham. Notables included White and P. B. S. Pinchback—two of the nation's best-known political figures, if of different generations, and the only NAAC officers attending—along with NAAC Executive Committee member William Pledger of Georgia. Other familiar faces included Athens postmaster Monroe Morton; exiled Wilmington publisher Alex Manly; Henry Arnett, son of Bishop Arnett; and local journalists Edward Cooper and Richard Thompson. Noticeably absent was Bishop Walters, along with the more militant voice of Ida Wells-Barnett, NAAC secretary and antilynching bureau chair.[16]

Widely circulated in August, the resolutions were at once both shrill and conciliatory in tone, reflecting the conflicting factions at the Council's Chicago session. On lynching, the Council sharply characterized its widespread use as "an offense against civilization which demands punishment, and we believe that it lies in the power of congress to enact such repressive legislation as shall prevent justice in America from becoming a byword and a mockery," then upbraided white leaders for inaction: "*Resolved,* That we are heartily grieved that the president of the United States and those in authority have not from time to time used their high station to voice the best conscience of the nation in regard to mob violence and the fair treatment of justly deserving men. It is not right that American citizens should be despoiled of life and liberty while the nation looks silently on."[17]

But on this day, Lawson prudently offered context for the resolutions, affording an opportunity for McKinley and other leaders to redeem this shameful heritage. In his own remarks to the president, Lawson demanded equal treatment for both races, when most whites faced no threat of mob violence, while blacks regularly faced mob executions for pettier crimes: "We condemn, unsparingly, every act or outrage committed by our people against anybody whomsoever, and we pledge ourselves as far as our power lies, to bring before the bar of justice every perpetrator of such acts," the address promised. But "members of our race are made the special victims of mob violence. . . . The whole machinery of government is in the hands of the white people, and why they need to go outside the regular channels of justice to punish crime is what civilization cannot understand."[18]

According to historian Shawn Leigh Alexander, Lawson and colleagues had personally prevailed upon the White House for this important visit, perhaps recognizing their last opportunity before the president's annual message to drive home the urgency of their message.[19] The NAAC plainly sought to make amends for far more radical language voiced by many members in Chicago in August. "Whether in military or civil life, we ask that the same treatment be accorded us that is given to other American citizens," Lawson declared. But clearly downplaying the more critical August tone of many NAAC members, he moved to "commend" the president "for his actions on other issues," particularly "the advance steps you have taken in the organization of the two colored regiments for the volunteer service."[20]

The Lawson group did not speak to the Council's desire for concerted action on disfranchisement, still forming in its legislation bureau. Walters would, however, raise that issue in his own speech the following week before the Boston NAAC chapter. He quoted liberally from John P. Love's recent essay "The Disfranchisement of the Negro," an occasional paper published by the American Negro Academy, with stirring arguments against the practice; Walters's use of Love's reasoning clearly reinforced the Council's determination to keep the issue alive.[21]

Walters ordered one thousand copies of the thirty-eight-page pamphlet for listeners, few of whom faced the same onerous difficulties in voting; Massachusetts's constitution required only simple literacy in the English language of voters—ability to read the constitution and write their name—while Mississippi required would-be voters to "give 'a reasonable interpretation' of the constitution to the satisfaction of a registration officer." As Love pointed out, "compared with the Mississippi provision, that of Massachusetts is as modest and simple as the average Mississippi school house." To ensure equal access and preparation, Massachusetts also spent four times as much as Mississippi on educating schoolchildren of either race.[22]

"The nation cannot put up with many more of these instruments of disfranchisement. It cannot endure the present ones very much longer," Love concluded, after an exhaustive study of the southern treatment of black voters since Reconstruction and the substance of recent attempts to restrict or eliminate black suffrage. "The question is ceasing to become one merely of interest to the Negro; it is rapidly becoming one of national moment. It is becoming a contest between democracy and oligarchy, in which the stability and integrity of republican institutions are involved. . . . The government cannot long continue half republican in form and half oligarchic."[23]

McKinley heard none of this reasoning by Walters, though the president was well aware of arguments being advanced by Edgar Crumpacker and other party leaders that southerners bent on disfranchising black voters were corrupting democracy—and if the South could not be dissuaded, it should be punished through reduced representation in Congress. For the moment, lynching and the need for national action to combat it were far more visible issues on the agendas of black supporters of McKinley, opponent of mob violence and defender of justice for all accused persons. But would he provide the same determined effort in the upcoming push for such national legislation as White now sought?

McKinley had been well aware of lingering dissatisfaction among Council members on both issues just weeks before in Chicago, during his midwestern tour. He delivered nearly one hundred speeches during his two-week swing, at stops in Illinois, Indiana, Iowa, Michigan, Minnesota, North Dakota, Ohio, South Dakota, and Wisconsin, and subject matter varied by location—mostly national issues, such as expansion, the economy, trade, American sovereignty, Philippine democracy, and a strong merchant marine. At a Minneapolis banquet, he waxed poetic about the topical need for a larger, global unity—"the hope of world peace inspired by the recent convening of the powers at the Hague Conference."[24]

Disappointingly, he never mentioned lynching in those recorded speeches but was still careful to remember the Republican faithful, including those at his Chicago stop, where interim encouragement to black citizens came with a brief, gratifying speech at Quinn Chapel AME Church, among the city's oldest black congregations:

My Friends, It gives me great pleasure to meet with you on this memorial day. The noblest sentiment of the human heart, after love of God, is love of country, and that includes love of home, the corner-stone of its strength and safety. Your race has demonstrated its patriotism by its sacrifices, its love of the flag by dying for it. That is the greatest test of fidelity and loyalty.

The nation has appreciated the valor and patriotism of the black men of the United States. They not only fought in Cuba, but in the Philippines, and they are still carrying the flag as the symbol of liberty and hope to an oppressed people.[25]

More than three thousand well-wishers greeted McKinley at Quinn Chapel, thoughtfully arranged by Bishop Arnett and fellow clerics. "It was the greatest day in the history of the church, to which belong some of the leaders of Chicago's colored population," wrote the *Chicago Tribune*, "and someday their children's children will point to the place in the pulpit where the President of the United States once stood." The president joined in singing "My Country, 'Tis of Thee" as he entered the towering church, where his audience featured influential Chicago politicians like Theophile Allain and Col. John Marshall and uniformed soldiers of the Eighth Illinois, veterans of Cuba.[26]

After the president returned to Washington, his African American supporters could only await his annual message for signs of their much-desired reward. But before the president's annual message was delivered, and before the new Congress could convene, the antilynching measure lost its strongest potential Senate ally, a man without whose encouragement and tacit approval no such measure could withstand southern Democratic resistance.

ॐ

Vice President Hobart, having departed Washington in June, during the congressional recess, was resting in New Jersey under doctor's care. By September, Hobart's health was declining rapidly, and he had rarely left his Paterson home except for seaside resort visits since then. Despite his relative youth, Hobart's heart was already so weak from angina that during his final weeks he could no longer lie flat in bed; he began sleeping in a chair and finally withdrew from all social and political activities in late October. Three weeks later, the popular vice president was dead at fifty-five.[27]

The national press followed Hobart's decline with regular optimistic updates through spring and summer. Rumors he would withdraw as McKinley's next running mate were quickly scotched by spokesmen, although McKinley and a close circle of friends were well aware of Hobart's severe heart condition, after an apparent attack of influenza weakened him during a spring vacation in Georgia. His last known political action was to persuade Secretary of War Russell Alger to resign, although he continued meeting with associates and political allies almost to the day he died.

Certainly among the last to confer with Hobart during his final illness was his much-favored protégé John Griggs, whose appointment as attorney general Hobart had personally recommended to McKinley a year earlier, and who was now assisting the nation's only African American congressman in drafting antilynching legislation McKinley reportedly promised to support. The two had been quite close since Hobart had backed Griggs for governor in the mid-1880s, and Griggs depended on his mentor's counsel in major decisions. There is no public indication of Hobart's position on the antilynching bill language being drafted by White and his advisers in the fall of 1899—or what role a healthy Hobart might have taken in a Senate campaign for the bill in the Fifty-Sixth Congress—but two things are certain: Griggs would never have pushed antilynching legislation if either the president or vice president had disapproved, and such a controversial bill could not succeed in either house of Congress, or even be reported out of the Judiciary committees, without enthusiastic backing by the GOP leadership. Badly disappointed by the failure of meticulous efforts in the trial of the accused lynchers of Lake City's postmaster, Griggs was personally committed to changes in federal law envisioned by White's bill, but he was likely to take positive, assertive action only after assurance of support from senior leaders.

In the Senate, Hobart's attentive and remarkably prudent leadership as presiding officer during the Fifty-Fifth Congress had surprised many observers in 1897 and 1898. Hobart used his vast business experience and principles to run the Senate like a well-oiled machine, if always carefully maintaining a backstage presence on policy substance. He quickly became a close adviser and confidant, on matters both official and personal, to McKinley and was labeled "assistant president" for his unusually supportive role. The president frequently visited the Hobarts' rented residence just across Lafayette Square for extended conversations, often accompanied by Ida McKinley. During their first two years in Washington, Jennie Hobart had become Ida McKinley's closest friend and surrogate sibling, tending to her health and comfort both at public receptions and on joint vacations taken by the two couples.[28] Another frequent visitor to Hobart's residence had been Sen. Mark Hanna, the president's virtual alter ego, who depended on Hobart's generous support for his own legislative career.

The party's reduced majority in the House and sometimes-precarious balance in the Senate made united leadership essential on delicate issues such as a new federal ban on lynching. Only Hobart's tie-breaking vote had salvaged the president's Philippines peace treaty in February and prevented a controversial move toward that nation's immediate independence. Without Hobart's presence, the role to be played by other party leaders in the Senate on the issue was suddenly uncertain—with Senate opposition by southern Democrats sure to emerge, perhaps even a filibuster.

The first hurdle facing White's bill lay in the House, and it was there that Republican strategists faced even more uncertainty. The new Speaker was expected to be David Henderson of Iowa, an admirer of White, after Speaker Thomas Reed resigned his seat in Congress before the Fifty-Sixth Congress convened. Second in command as Republican conference chairman was Joseph Cannon of Illinois, a future Speaker. But the Republican House majority suffered noticeably in 1898 elections, holding a margin of fewer than twenty seats over Democrats and assorted factions, and Henderson's extreme partisanship promised rocky relations with southern Democrats on many issues.

All that lay weeks in the future, however, as McKinley, his cabinet, Supreme Court justices, and a bipartisan stream of congressional friends traveled to New York by train and then to Paterson for Hobart's sad funeral in the last week of November. It was a command performance for the Senate—all sitting senators were invited, although some were unable to return to Washington in time—and a representative delegation of House members appointed by incoming Speaker Henderson, including White.[29] A staunch admirer of the vice president, White had campaigned energetically for the McKinley-Hobart ticket in 1896, at the request of national party strategists, and would not miss such an opportunity to show party allegiance on this tragic occasion.

Hobart was the sixth U.S. vice president to die in office and the third in less than a quarter century.[30] Yet in just two years in office, he had quickly become the most active and well-respected vice president in U.S. history. McKinley was described as heartbroken at the loss of his close friend and trusted adviser; the caravan of railroad cars from Washington to Paterson for his funeral was astounding in its length and the prominence of its passengers.[31] Two separate trains actually brought Washington dignitaries to Paterson's Broadway Station: the first bearing McKinley and cabinet members, a second arriving ten minutes later with scores of senators, congressmen, and U.S. Supreme Court justices.[32]

Upon arriving at the Hobarts' Paterson home, McKinley told Jennie Hobart and the family, "No one outside of this home feels this loss more deeply than I do."[33] A future without Hobart's steadying influence was almost unimaginable for the McKinleys, who had long depended on his friendship and sound financial advice. Such a future was equally bleak for Senate colleagues, including Hanna and New Jersey's William Sewell, among Hobart's closest friends, and Attorney General John Griggs.

Hobart's role as president of the Senate would be assumed for a year, at least, by president pro-tem William Frye of Maine, in the Senate for two decades, a dependable colleague but hardly a Hobart-style activist. Republican conference chairman William Allison of Iowa, a pragmatic conservative, was capable of designing compromises with Democrats as needed but not known for strong feelings on lynching. How much practical assistance could be provided to the cause by Ohio's senators Hanna and Joseph Foraker was uncertain—and it was not at all clear who might be willing to do battle with Democratic caucus chairman James Jones of Mississippi, a formidable opponent, and firebrand South Carolinians Benjamin Tillman and John McLaurin.

Lacking a mainstream spokesman, the antilynching crusade's unofficial trumpet during the new Congress fell to the columns of the *Colored American* newspaper, which regularly mentioned the bill and White's role in promoting it in both news articles and editorials as the new congressional session opened in December. In "Mr. White's Bill," an editorial printed December 9, Edward Cooper detailed the plan of action: the language, still being refined, must "accord with the Constitution and command the support of all who are honestly seeking a remedy," especially McKinley, who "has promised his aid to Mr. White's measure," while White, Daniel Murray, John Griggs, and others continued joint labors.[34]

A week later, Cooper invited black Democrat Fred McGhee of Minnesota to offer his views on the subject, which were not terribly sympathetic to McKinley, whom he viewed as committed only to political preservation, but more thoughtfully deferential to White, "noble representative of a noble and loyal people, [who] stands ready to present the measure." McKinley should do it himself, McGhee sneered ungraciously.[35] On January 6, Cooper added: "When a state is unable, for any reason whatsoever, to control its mobs and secure to every individual the privilege of an impartial trial . . . the strong arm of the government should have the right to be exerted." The proposal's constitutionality was beside the point: "If there is no law to provide for this, there should be one," and "White . . . will insist that [his bill] be discussed upon its merits."[36]

For the record, McKinley's sentiments on the subjects of lynchings and mob violence had already been clearly and convincingly stated in his third annual message to Congress, offered the first week of December. After appropriate tribute to American ideals—"the love of law and the sense of obedience and submission to the lawfully constituted judicial tribunals . . . the guaranties of life, liberty, and of civil rights should be faithfully upheld, the right of trial by jury respected and defended. The rule of the courts should assure the public of the prompt trial of those charged with criminal offenses, and upon conviction the punishment should be commensurate with the enormity of the crime"—the president demanded "the severest penalties" for American vigilantes who "constitute themselves judges and executioners": "What I said in my inaugural address of March 4, 1897, I now repeat: The constituted authorities must be cheerfully and vigorously upheld. *Lynchings must not be tolerated in a great and civilized country like the United States. Courts, not mobs, must execute the penalties of the laws.* The preservation of public order, the right of discussion, the integrity of courts, and the orderly administration of justice must continue forever the rock of safety upon which our Government securely rests."[37]

Earlier in this same message, McKinley mentioned continued lynchings of foreign citizens; at least five more Sicilian immigrants had recently been executed by a Louisiana mob, and that thorny subject continued to plague the U.S. government's official relationship with Italy and its king. He therefore renewed Harrison's call for legislation on the subject of protecting foreigners from lynching with his own plea: "The recurrence of these distressing manifestations of blind mob fury directed at dependents or natives of a foreign country suggests that the contingency has arisen for action by Congress in the direction of conferring upon the Federal courts jurisdiction in this class of international cases where the ultimate responsibility of the Federal Government may be involved."[38]

Lynchings of foreigners were clearly a related political issue, but they were not covered in White's bill, which dealt only with mob violence against American citizens. In his annual message, McKinley appeared to be calling for separate action on both issues. However the president might feel about specific merits of White's more controversial domestic lynching bill, it was clearly now time, in his opinion, for a stronger national stand on the larger subject of lynching. But before his bill could be introduced, White encountered new demands on his time, including responsibilities related to a coveted seat on the District of Columbia committee: a rare honor for a black congressman, one certain to reinforce his standing in the House hierarchy.

White's second assignment added to continuing duties on the Agriculture Committee and cemented useful relationships with two northern Republicans on the District committee, Alfred Harmer and Charles Sprague. White's appointment was announced by Speaker David Henderson on December 18, just after his own election. Days before releasing his committee choices, Henderson had been described by the *Colored American* as "a warm admirer of Congressman George H. White and characterizes the North Carolinian as one of the brainiest representatives of the Negro race that he has ever met." Among the most senior members of the House, Henderson had known almost all black leaders since Frederick Douglass and was "wholly devoid of anything as soulless as race prejudice." He "has been the friend of every measure brought forward that seemed likely to broaden the Negro's opportunities educationally, politically, and industrially."[39]

If anyone could be expected to assist White's antilynching bill, Speaker Henderson seemed the perfect choice. But no clear path lay to success on the antilynching bill, only lukewarm support nationally for punitive measures directed primarily at the South, where most lynchings tended to occur. The nation itself was wearying of the seemingly intractable problem of race in the South, whose state leaders stubbornly resisted advice from any person or institution outside the region and marginalized homegrown hints of progressive thought or resistance to inexorable encroachment of Jim Crow–style segregation.

Even the South's minority Republicans were privately frustrated by dealing with relentless demands from the party's black membership for patronage, coupled with insistent calls for solutions to race-related problems; North Carolina's Sen. Jeter Pritchard, reasonably progressive on racial issues—especially when compared to the reactionary stances of the state's elected Democrats—kept a lower profile on this issue, while nervously assessing the GOP's regional "lily-white" movement.

Only carefully timed intervention by the president in mid-December prevented what would have been a disastrous reduction in the size of southern delegations to the next Republican national convention. The night before the National Committee's annual meeting, McKinley met with Wisconsin committeeman Henry Payne, who proposed redrawing traditional allocations based on state population into a more realistic formula rewarding states where the party was successful, under a resolution he planned to offer the full committee. McKinley strongly disapproved of the plan, for two reasons: Payne's plan would deliberately antagonize southern Republicans in an important election year, and worse, it would signal to black voters elsewhere—in Ohio, Kentucky, and Indiana—that southern black votes were being written off.[40]

By accepting disfranchisement of most black southern voters as a fait ac-
compli, the national party risked legitimizing an odious practice and symbolically transforming the party's southern wing publicly into the nearly all-white
organization a minority of white Republicans preferred. McKinley had no wish
to anger Payne—his solution was both practical and long overdue—but he saw
no recourse except to scotch the plan as the 1900 reelection campaign neared.
His Ohio allies at this meeting, especially Maj. Charles Dick and Gov.-elect
George Nash, vigorously opposed Payne's resolution, citing dangers to usually
reliable black turnouts in Ohio and other nonsouthern states, and on McKinley's behalf, pressured Payne to forego his resolution.

Payne passionately defended his reform plan but was outnumbered and
finally agreed to drop his resolution. How much the southern minority of national committeemen—roughly one-fourth of the total—knew about Payne's
resolution is not clear, but few southern Republican leaders would have acqui-
esced to reduced representation. Judson Lyons of Georgia, delegate to the 1896
nominating convention and certain to repeat in 1900, would strongly oppose it.

Reactions by other black 1896 delegates hoping to return to Philadelphia's
convention might have been equally combative; competition was keen enough
without the prospect of fewer seats to distribute. All doubtless agreed with
McKinley's sidelining a potentially divisive disruption of tradition. Among
veteran black delegates with national recognition were Mississippi's James
Hill, former national committeeman; Alabama's Herschel Cashin; Florida's
Joseph Lee; Georgia's Henry Rucker; South Carolina's Edmund Deas, ex-congressman Robert Smalls, and William Crum; Charles Ferguson of Texas; and
North Carolina's George White.[41]

White's political antennae were usually sensitive to such developments,
although he may have been too distracted by other pressing personal demands
on his time to pay much attention to the Payne plan or its implications for the
1900 convention and beyond. As Christmas came and went, a sudden decline
in Cora Lena's health—on the verge of a near-fatal coma, soon to require life-
saving surgery—necessitated the urgent services of her mother, Mary Ann
Cherry, as temporary nurse and nanny for his younger children; Mrs. Cherry
was assisted by George White's oldest daughter Della, now living in Washington and soon to become a Census Bureau clerk.

Despite personal complications, he drew strength from crowds during
his Ohio campaign appearances for the Republican state ticket in Octo-

ber. His busy ten-day schedule took him to Springfield and ten other cities, where he discussed North Carolina's upcoming literacy amendment and defended the administration against unfair expectations in dealing with lynching: "There is a great deal of talk about the proposed interference of the federal authorities in lynchings, but how are the authorities to know when a lynching is to occur? In those states, the authorities do know, and yet they do nothing, and throughout the South all these administrations are Democratic," he told the *Ohio State Journal*. "There is some feeling in my section on the lynching outrages, but we understand where to place the blame."[42]

After returning home, White continued seeking intellectual and political feedback from social gatherings with a broad circle of influential black leaders, drawn from both nonpartisan ranks of the NAAC and McKinley appointees, as well as counsel from national GOP leaders. He would need all the support he could garner in the year ahead, destined to be the busiest and most momentous of his life.

President McKinley's inauguration, March 1897.
(Library of Congress)

President McKinley and his cabinet, 1897.
(Library of Congress)

Vice President Garret Hobart, ca. 1898.
(Library of Congress)

President McKinley and Booker T. Washington,
Tuskegee Institute, December 1898.
(Library of Congress)

Baseball team of the USS *Maine,* ca. 1898.
(Library of Congress)

Widow and children of murdered postmaster Frazier
Baker, 1899. (J. E. Purdy & Co., Library of Congress)

President McKinley at Southern University, New Orleans, May 1901.
(John Norris Teunisson Photograph Collection, Louisiana State Museum)

President McKinley at the Pan-American Exposition, Buffalo, New York, September 1901. (Library of Congress)

Assassination of President McKinley at Buffalo, New York, 1901. (Library of Congress)

1900

9

PREPARING FOR THE FIGHT
OF THE CENTURY

The world is notified that those whom the Constitution of these United States,
by the Fourteenth and Fifteenth amendments, has enfranchised are to
be reduced once more to the condition of goods and chattels.
—**George H. White**, U.S. House, February 5, 1900

As the nineteenth century entered its last full year, the pace of George White's personal and professional lives grew increasingly frantic. His wife's frail health had deteriorated into a precarious state; after undergoing surgery, she required constant attention by nurses and family members. In Congress, he juggled duties on two demanding committees, while preparing a major address before the Bethel Literary and Historical Association, proofing final text of an important national magazine article on disfranchisement, and preparing to testify before the Industrial Commission on Agriculture and Agricultural Labor in mid-February—the longest single statement he ever gave. All this came while he tweaked the final wording of his long-awaited bill to ban lynching, grimly determined to make the bill both comprehensive and specific, as its uncertain constitutionality provoked private and public quarrels.

Those closest to him recognized the interlocking strain of such conflicting pressures, "enough to break down three ordinary men," in Edward Cooper's only mildly exaggerated characterization. The *Colored American* characterized White as "preparing to make the fight of his life on behalf of the people he represents—the 10,000,000 Negroes of the United States" with his antilynching bill. But Cooper worried aloud that his friend needed constant support from others; he "must be careful of his health, for much depends upon his vigor and ability to bring to bear his best thought and action." Therefore "friends of the race should come to his rescue and relieve him as far as possible," he wrote, issuing a command to all to "Share this responsibility with him, for he is fighting the people's battle, and all will share in the result."[1]

Under such circumstances, it was hardly surprising that White should seek occasional solace from friendly faces and conversation as distraction from more pressing matters. He had closed out 1899 with a lavish luncheon at Gray's Hotel, entertaining visiting members of the National Afro-American Council (NAAC) Executive Committee and a small group of congenial out-of-town guests: Fred McGhee, T. Thomas Fortune, and Bishop Cicero Harris. In addition to Council president Bishop Walters, NAAC leaders included Edward Brown and Daniel Murray—White's cohorts in drafting the antilynching bill—plus Alex Manly and stalwarts P. B. S. Pinchback and Judson Lyons.[2] Primary subjects of the day were the NAAC's continuing work "and the best means of enlarging its scope and work," and consideration of Indiana representative Edgar Crumpacker's proposed amendment to reduce representation in Congress of southern states disfranchising black citizens, strongly favored by Pinchback, among others.[3]

It was his second festive evening in a month, just weeks after an informal Thanksgiving-style gathering at his new home near Dupont Circle, at which "Mr. White proved himself an ideal host, and left nothing undone that seemed likely to enhance the pleasure of the evening." Holiday musical selections were performed by "a coterie of young people," including daughter Mamie, son George Jr., and niece Mamie Cheatham.[4] Guests included such local luminaries as brother-in-law Henry Cheatham, Judson Lyons, postal official John Green, journalist Richard Thompson, law student Samuel Lacy, Major Charles Douglass, and Lewis Douglass.[5]

As always, conversations at both meals provided the main course for White, whose interactions with politically astute friends and colleagues were ample fodder for public ventures, beginning with a well-attended presentation January 2, 1900, at the Bethel Literary and Historical Association. A favored speaking venue in the District, the Bethel Association's three-speech seminar on "The Negro in Politics" assigned White the topic of "His Present Political Status." Pinchback addressed the political past, while attorney Robert Terrell tackled the political future. Their audience was local, not national, and there is no text of their remarks.[6] But White's presentation undoubtedly contained at least some of the information about which he mused publicly in an upcoming article for the *Independent,* an influential New York periodical edited by H. C. Bowen.[7]

"The Injustice to the Colored Voter," published in the *Independent*'s January 18 issue, represented White's first address to a national audience, a measured counterpoint to that issue's article by Sen. Hernando Money (D-Mississippi). White's essay compared the current situation faced by black southern voters— in Louisiana, Mississippi, and South Carolina, where fewer than eighty-eight thousand voters elected twenty members of Congress in 1898—to the possible future of voters in his own home state.[8] In "Shall Illiteracy Rule?," meanwhile, Money brazenly defended southern disfranchisement efforts by declaring "Suffrage is not a natural right" and lamented the "great mistake to give the Negro the ballot too early."[9]

Money admitted that Mississippi's racially imbalanced population—nearly 200,000 more blacks than whites—was the underlying political factor. But he also claimed his own state's new literacy requirement, modeled on that of Massachusetts—which he deemed "more liberal" because it did not require prospective voters to write—simply attempted to ensure that only reasonably educated voters participated in elections. To allow illiterate voters "absolutely incapable of self-government" to control elections was unwise. "An ignorant vote in Mississippi is felt in New York or Massachusetts. It is felt everywhere. It may determine a national election," Money declared, pointing out that Crumpacker's amendment would affect not only the South but also states like Massachusetts with literacy restrictions.[10]

Such arguments were irrelevant to White, who dismissed them as "frauds." In North Carolina, blacks accounted for less than one-third of the population, with no chance of electing statewide officers alone. (Although a clear majority of the state's Republicans—perhaps two-thirds of statewide membership in 1896—were black, a black majority of voters existed only in White's district.) In the most recent election there, more than thirty-five thousand votes had been cast, under the South's least restrictive system, or "eight thousand more votes . . . than in seven districts in Mississippi, and almost seven thousand more than in seven districts in South Carolina." Reasons for the significant difference lay in recent disfranchisement of black voters in both states.

And the disfranchisement wave across the South might soon spread. "My own state would be reduced to the level" of representation in Mississippi and South Carolina "should the [North Carolina] constitutional amendment be adopted" and upheld by courts, White pointed out. In any fair election, the amendment would be defeated by a coalition of white and black Republicans and "sensible Populists," but he expressed concern that Democrats controlling the legislature would not permit it in August 1900. "Under the new election law, with absolute Democratic control, a fair vote is impossible," he wrote, citing election results in Halifax County, where a Republican majority of 2,100 registered voters carried not a single office—losing to minority Democrats by an implausible 2,500 votes: "a reversal of 4,500 in a single election."[11]

The troublesome wording of North Carolina's amendment incorporated Louisiana's detested "grandfather clause," allowing exceptions to literacy requirements for any voter with an ancestor able to vote in 1867—conveniently, a year before blacks regained the right to vote in 1868. Only a few of North Carolina's black voters—White estimated roughly 5,000—could expect to prove eligibility, primarily those who had moved from states where they or their ancestors had been allowed to vote before 1867.[12] All other black registrants would first have to prove, to the satisfaction of white Democrats, that they could read and write, an unlikely prospect in a state now bent on preventing most black Republicans from voting in elections after 1902.

Paradoxically, many black leaders had already publicly endorsed literacy requirements—so long as they applied equally to both races. As early as December 1898, the NAAC accepted "legitimate restriction of the suffrage" so long as "restrictions shall apply to all citizens of all states. We are willing to accept an educational or property qualification, or both."[13] But it was always clear to NAAC leaders that new state constitutions in Mississippi, South Carolina, and Louisiana aimed squarely at disfranchising only black voters, not all illiterate voters—at least, not white Democrats. Louisiana's "grandfather clause" seemed tailor-made to engineer unfair discrimination against blacks, specifically, and Republicans generally; illiterate white Democrats were certain of exemption, whereas any illiterate Republican of either race would face strong scrutiny.

Under current circumstances, only the passage of Crumpacker's amendment would remedy the immediate situation characterized by "these frauds in the South" and serve to prevent rule by "dishonesty and rascality."[14] However strongly White favored Crumpacker's amendment, his role in its success was limited to that of cheerleader. Southern Republicans were a dying breed in Congress in 1900, holding only eight of ninety House seats in eleven states of the Old Confederacy.[15] The battle over Crumpacker's amendment would be won or lost by Republicans in the Northeast and Midwest, where no consensus yet existed.

As White prepared to introduce his antilynching bill, the NAAC quietly prepared offstage to raise funds to test the Louisiana disfranchisement law, in a case expected to be heard on appeal first by the Louisiana Supreme Court, then by federal courts.[16] Both objectives had been high on the NAAC priority list since 1898, along with Crumpacker's amendment. White was increasingly invested in the first two efforts and later became one of five attorneys preparing the brief for *State ex rel. Ryanes v. Gleason,* as the case was known; he and fellow NAAC leader Fred McGhee helped represent that plaintiff, the illiterate New Orleans voter David Ryanes.

But for now, opposition to both his bill and Crumpacker's amendment was beginning to coalesce, as southern Democrats prepared to defy federal interference in treatment of black citizens. Emboldened and invigorated by the Supreme Court's nearly unanimous 1896 ruling in *Plessy v. Ferguson,* which had essentially condoned the Jim Crow–era social structure of "separate but equal" segregation, the Old South was girding up to roll back the most enduring legacy of Reconstruction and postwar amendments to the Constitution. As southern resistance leaders readied for battle, the public face of the movement was embodied by Josephus Daniels and his *Raleigh News and Observer,* backbone of the white-supremacy movement catalyzing the Wilmington racial massacre and coup d'état, and whose front pages had portrayed White's family members as little better than domestic terrorists.

For more than a year, the *News and Observer* had all but ignored White, but that silence was about to erupt into a new and ferocious series of editorial attacks aimed squarely at the "nation's only nigger congressman."[17]

❧

For McKinley, the year 1900 opened with an impressive show of continuing popularity, at least three thousand well-wishers crowded into the White House for the New Year's Day reception.[18] The president and first lady were joined in the receiving line by his cabinet, led by Secretary of State John Hay—now next in line of succession, following Vice President Hobart's death—and Mrs. Hay. Despite snowy sidewalks and long lines, the nation's highest leaders greeted scores of foreign dignitaries, including five ambassadors, a dozen ministers, many members of Congress, military personnel, and selected members of the general public.

On this day the president was more concerned with pressing foreign developments than with domestic issues as he prepared for the year's first cabinet meeting. High on the list of topics at that meeting were continuing talks with European nations regarding the "open door" commercial status of China, led by Secretary Hay, who reported that all European nations except Italy had so far agreed to joint proposals; this spared McKinley from the unpleasant necessity of temporarily seizing sections of Chinese territory to protect U.S. commercial interests. A second, less publicized venture involved the president's separate meeting with Admiral John Walker, head of the U.S. Isthmian Canal Commission, whose members were leaving on a fact-finding mission to examine proposed routes in Nicaragua and Colombia's Panama province.[19]

McKinley also awaited an important report on recommendations for policy options in dealing with the newly acquired Philippine Islands, undertaken a year earlier by the separate Schurman Commission, headed by Cornell University's president. Released just two weeks into the New Year, that report recommended creating a transitional civilian government: an appointive colonial governor, a mixed legislative assembly with both elected and appointed members, and administrative subdivisions with provincial governors. In late January, McKinley began implementing their recommendations by selecting Ohio's William Howard Taft, now a federal judge, as the first U.S. governor.[20]

Of less long-term significance to foreign policy, perhaps, were ongoing preparations for a foreign venture made by a third special commissioner, Thomas Calloway. Yet Calloway's mission bore special personal interest for McKinley, who had helped select the young attorney and ex–college president in late 1899, and helped push special funding through Congress in near-record time. In January 1900, Calloway and rising scholar W. E. B. Du Bois were spearheading the collection of data and photographs for a special exhibit on achievements by black Americans at the upcoming International Universal Exposition at Paris. That same week, Calloway and two colleagues were touring Atlanta, New Orleans, and Tuskegee seeking materials for the April fair.[21]

The *Negro Exhibit,* as it is generally known, paid tribute to "the economic and social progress accomplished by the negro race in the United States since its emancipation." Primarily the brainchild of Calloway, who brought Du Bois on board immediately, it included a stunning series of photographs and other materials chronicling both economic achievements by black Americans since emancipation from slavery and by black academic institutions, particularly Tuskegee Institute.[22]

Calloway, thirty-three, had already been president of Alabama's Alcorn Agriculture and Mechanical College and, more recently, vice principal at Tuskegee. A trained lawyer, he had the rare ability to bridge almost effortlessly philosophical divides within African American ranks, such as that now developing between Du Bois and Washington. Calloway's October 1899 letter to dozens of leading African Americans—politicians, educators, activists, and Bishop Arnett—galvanized the movement to create the *Negro Exhibit* in Paris, and not surprisingly, inspired his selection as exhibit architect.[23]

He later recounted serendipitous circumstances that quickly propelled him into the public eye after his letter: "In the meantime President McKinley had become interested. Mr. Booker T. Washington made a personal visit to the President on behalf of the movement and he was seconded by Messrs. Lyons, Cheatham, and White. The result was that the President became deeply interested and after a consultation between the President and the Commissioner General, I was told that the exhibit had been arranged for and I had been selected to carry out the plans."[24] Not commissioned until November 15, Calloway faced a myriad of pressing logistical problems, including pressures of money and time; just five months remained to put together the exhibit, transport it to Paris, and set it up there. White intervened, Calloway recalled, and "introduced in Congress a bill appropriating fifteen thousand dollars for the Negro Exhibit... indorsed by President McKinley, Commissioner General Peck, every member of the Appropriations Committee... and passed without a single objectional vote in either House of Congress."[25]

White's H.R. 4745 was introduced in mid-December, shortly after the Fifty-Sixth Congress opened, and was immediately referred to the Committee on Appropriations, which reported it out favorably.[26] Calloway's annual salary was set at $2,400; he brought his exhibit in under budget and on time, rare for any government-funded project. It promised to be a star feature of the Paris fair—and even if the president could not to travel to Paris to review it, McKinley still anticipated seeing it re-created in the United States.

White's timely assistance reinforced his already glowing image as a hard worker in the eyes of the president, his party, and the minds of many African American colleagues. Among his efforts on the Paris exhibit was White's letter to the White House in mid-January regarding Calloway's appointment, according to John Addison Porter. The letter's contents are not available but were duly noted as evidence of cooperation on an issue dear to the president.[27]

Whether the president felt as deeply about White's simultaneous legislative effort cannot be gleaned from public comments. White's long-awaited antilynching bill, H.R. 6963, "A Bill for the Protection of All Citizens of the United States, against Mob Violence, and the Penalty for Breaking Such Laws," was introduced at about the same time, accompanied by the first of many supporting petitions. One was signed by "2,413 citizens of Massachusetts, urging legislation making lynching and mob violence a crime against the United States . . . and for the creation of a central detective bureau at Washington . . . to collect and transmit information of the movements of such lawless bodies."[28]

White spent weeks drafting this bill, with capable assistance from Attorney General John Griggs and ex–attorney general Albert Pillsbury of Massachusetts, among others.[29] But the proposal to create a central police force, much like the future Federal Bureau of Investigation, to investigate and apprehend lynch mob members was not well received universally and was dropped from the final language. When the House convened in December 1899, White perhaps hoped to draw cosponsors from among fellow House members for the bill, which he introduced in January, but none appeared.

Despite strong support from some Republican quarters for the revamped bill, southern Democrats were far less eager to hear about the bill after its official introduction. White's first attempt to speak on his bill's merits—by having the heading of the petition read aloud—was blocked for parliamentary reasons by Rep. James Richardson (D-Tenn.), an ambitious Democrat who had lost the race for Speaker weeks earlier. He now complained that the petition "ought to take the regular course of all other petitions and memorials," which was technically correct, and Speaker Henderson could find no grounds to grant an exception.[30]

White entered Pillsbury's long supportive letter into the record but did not mention Griggs's advice, rendered far less publicly and generally noted only by black newspapers.[31] Nor did he mention the expert assistance of others, including Boston lawyer Edward Brown or librarian Daniel Murray. Griggs, of course, had been named attorney general at the suggestion of Vice President Hobart and would almost certainly not have helped White without encouragement—tacit or otherwise—from Hobart and McKinley, who reportedly "had promised his aid to Mr. White's measure."[32]

Almost two weeks passed before another opportunity surfaced for a brief comment from the House floor about lynching, during a spirited debate between two other House members, Republican Romulus Linney and a Texas Democrat. The Texan claimed most lynchings resulted from assaults upon white women by black men, and Linney fired back a stinging retort: "There you have it, Mr. Chairman. You cannot discuss any subject with a Southern Democrat, no matter what it is, that he does not holler 'Nigger'!" White's spontaneous interjection—granted by request, as the only House member of the race—seemed unrehearsed, his briefest floor comment during two terms, fewer than fifty words.[33]

But even in its brevity, White's comment echoed hot-button comments of the *Wilmington Record* editorial eighteen months earlier—the much-reprinted statement still blamed for unleashing that city's deadly wave of racial violence—and was guaranteed to spark a ferocious torrent of abuse from his old nemesis Josephus Daniels. White was once again a marked man, this time apparently with no holds barred.

"It is bad enough that North Carolina should have the nation's only nigger congressman," Daniels editorialized in "The Colored Member," published in February. "It is sufficiently humiliating to the white people of the Second district; a sad enough commentary upon the political conditions that have obtained in this state." White's recent comment on lynching particularly infuriated Daniels, who sputtered venomously about the "blatant mouthing of a mere negro . . . beneath contempt" who "must be made an impossibility for the future."[34]

White presented a convenient scapegoat for the ever-belligerent Daniels, who within a week charged both White and Linney of tampering with the *Congressional Record* by softening White's actual language. According to the *Record*'s official version, White said this: "I have examined that question, and I am prepared to state that not more than 15 percent of the lynchings are traceable to that crime, and there are many more outrages against colored women by white men than there are by colored men against white women."[35] The first Associated Press report of his speech contained a somewhat different version: "I have investigated the lynchings in the South and find that less than 15 percent of them are due to the crime of rape. And I desire to announce here that if it were not for the assaults of white men upon black women, there would be less of the other class."[36]

Debate over White's language soon descended into surreality when an AP reporter insisted to the *News and Observer* that new evidence—original stenographic notes—indicated a much longer version, different from either previously reported: "I have investigated the facts in regards to these lynchings for the past two and a half years, and I say that less than 75 percent of the lynchings which have occurred in the United States were chargeable to the cause stated; and that if there were not outrages and assaults committed—not upon white women by black men, but by white men against black women, there would be less of the other class."[37]

Such improbable discrepancies in language aside, several factors were in play here, including Daniels's known political distaste for Linney and simmering anger at White's proposal to make lynching a federal crime. For some time, Daniels had publicly opposed lynching as both illegal and imprudent, but elevating it to the level of a federal crime was unthinkable to any southerner schooled in historical battles over states' rights versus federal laws. Daniels wasted no time in denouncing it.

When White rose on the floor of the House to speak February 5, it was to hoist this red flag even higher, describing the *News and Observer* as a "vile, slanderous publication" that typified the abuse that "the poor colored man in the Southland has to undergo from a certain class." After having the House clerk read "The Colored Member" aloud, White asked the House to judge for itself whether "my character and my conduct for the last three years on this floor . . . has conformed to the description given by this fellow who edits the News and Observer and pollutes the country with such literature."[38]

Daniels had grievously misrepresented his original January 31 statement, providing an account "slanderous and wholly untrue." His statement was exactly what he told the Bethel Literary and Historical seminar weeks earlier: "less than 15 percent of the lynchings in this country were for assaults committed upon women, not in the South, but in the United States": "I did not justify the commission of assaults by black men upon white women on the grounds that white men did the same in regard to black men. . . . I repudiate as much as any man can anyone, whether he be a white brute or a black brute, who commits an assault upon any woman, whether a white woman or a black woman. I think such a man ought to be hung—hung by the neck until dead. But it ought to be done by the courts, not by an infuriated mob such as the writer of that article would incite."[39]

For years, White had endured gratuitous insults from Daniels and his white-supremacist corps of journalists and politicians bent on redeeming North Carolina from the waning clutches of Republican-Populist fusion and the imaginary scourge of "negro domination." He had so far refrained from anything more than a carefully timed stump speech during the heat of a campaign. Yet with state voters due to vote on a constitutional amendment on disfranchisement in six months, White knew this Daniels salvo was more than a simple personal attack. Daniels's editorial amounted to an open declaration of war on him and his race by those who would steal his good name and political justice in his state, and White could no longer restrain his anger. He could not watch the wave of political repression seeking to engulf both him and his race.

"Mr. Speaker, this article is but an evidence of what we have got to contend with—an absolute perversion and slanderous misrepresentation of the truth—preparing for the election to be held in August," he thundered. Let there be no mistake about the intended outcome of that election, he now predicted, with chilling clarity: "The world is notified that those whom the constitution of these United States, by the Fourteenth and Fifteenth amendments, has enfranchised are to be reduced once more to the condition of goods and chattels," at the hands of "such men as the one who edits the News and Observer."[40]

It was the most ominous prophecy to date by the South's only African American congressman, who held few illusions about the darkening political future in his home state. If he still bravely hoped for defeat of the August referendum, White sensed the increasing fury of winds blowing against him. Daniels and his legion of white supremacists could well marshal the same intimidating tactics used to such advantage in November 1898, when black voter turnout sank to its lowest levels in thirty years; unless Fusionist whites somehow reunited in a solid front of opposition, the dreaded amendment might well pass, however narrowly. Still, the long and enthusiastic applause that White's House speech received—doubtless led by Romulus Linney, among the few southern Republicans left—must have bolstered his spirits. Those cheers might well have been heard in nearby Senate chambers, where Republican Sen. Jeter Pritchard mulled his declining political fortunes at the hands of North Carolina's new Democratic legislative majority; his own term ended in 1903.

Pritchard's lengthy, occasionally barbed January 22 speech contained the most detailed description of issues affecting past and future party registrations in North Carolina ever given in the Senate, provoking heated exchanges with other southern senators—particularly South Carolina's Benjamin Tillman and Mississippi's Hernando Money—as he condemned the constitutional amendment on suffrage awaiting North Carolina voters. He specifically addressed critical remarks days earlier by Alabama's John Morgan on Pritchard's resolution—asking the Senate to condemn the amendment—but held many listeners in thrall with broader charges of a patently unconstitutional Democratic attempt to reduce Republican votes across the South by depriving black citizens of the vote.

White citizens outnumbered black citizens in North Carolina by two to one, making "the cry of Negro domination" a ridiculous fantasy that "is ludicrous to the extreme," Pritchard all but shouted: "No intelligent citizen can be induced to believe that two white North Carolinians are in any danger of being dominated by one negro." Only twelve of ninety-seven counties, by his count of the 1890 census, had populations with black majorities, "and not one of them has been dominated or controlled by the colored people."[41] The senator made short shrift of Democrats' true intentions with the amendment:

> It was conceived and enacted by the self-constituted leaders whose chief desire was to secure their own preferment regardless of the effect that it might have upon the good citizens of that section. I regard the proposed amendment as an attempt to legalize the fraudulent methods and practices of the Democratic party that have obtained in the conduct and control of elections in the past. . . . The Republican party cannot afford to fold its hands and permit the Democratic party to again secure political ascendancy in the nation by resorting to such unrepublican and unconstitutional methods.[42]

Whether Pritchard's speech provoked more than a temporary ripple in the Senate's long-running reflections over the constitutionality of southern disfranchisement by the region's ascendant Democrats is sheer speculation. As the only Republican senator from a near-solid Democratic South, his speech received extensive coverage in both local and national newspapers, even if it proved unable to change the Senate's collective mind.[43]

Populist Marion Butler, preparing to deliver his own Senate speech a day later on the "proposed suffrage amendment"—a week after a courtesy meeting with McKinley—made only a brief comment during Pritchard's speech. Butler may have been more devoted to private musings about his less promising future, regardless of White's impetuous comments; his term ended in 1901.[44] But White's speech was certainly worthy of discussion by the Republican Congressional Campaign Committee, meeting in Washington to begin planning the 1900 election by reelecting Wisconsin's Rep. Joseph Babcock as chair.[45] Within days, it may have reached Thomas Calloway and W. E. B. Du Bois, still in the South gathering exhibit materials for the Paris International Universal Exposition, even though long-term implications for them and their race were less clear.

Its echoes may even have reached the White House just blocks away, as McKinley continued to consider strategic plans for his renomination in Philadelphia that summer and his fall reelection campaign.

The president's February 1 meeting with Senator Butler was unremarkable—its subject not listed in public accounts—but a second meeting that month with defeated congressional candidate Oliver Dockery, during which Butler's name arose, must have mystified the chief executive. The leader of North Carolina's imploding Populist Party had once helped lead fusion efforts with Republicans in North Carolina, albeit grudgingly, and had more than once cooperated with Pritchard and other Republicans on certain issues. But since fusion's unraveling, Butler's availability had become less consistent, as witnessed by his open feud with Pritchard in May 1898. Yet he still retained a staunch following among the state's more optimistic—perhaps, more fanciful—Republicans like Dockery, still pursuing a long-shot House contest against incumbent Democrat John Bellamy.

Neither candidate Dockery's unusual meeting with McKinley nor his suggestion that Butler might yet play a key role in a revived fusion ticket in North Carolina in 1900 made practical sense. Dockery, an ex–Confederate officer and two-term Reconstruction congressman from the Sixth District, had not held elective office since his 1870 defeat. But the well-regarded lawyer stayed in the public eye as a Republican leader, running unsuccessfully for governor in 1888. He had been Harrison's U.S. consul general in Rio de Janeiro. His quest to return to Congress in 1898 failed badly, though he was still convinced the House would seat him by displacing Bellamy.

But Dockery's fantastic plans for Butler—casting him as fusion candidate for governor on a revitalized Republican-Populist ticket, alongside a reliable Republican candidate for lieutenant governor to succeed Butler, after Republicans won back the General Assembly and reelected him to the Senate—seem almost comically unrealistic.[46] Dockery sincerely believed North Carolinians would reject the heavy-handed disfranchisement amendment and reverse the Democrats' stolen election of 1898, thereby avenging the disappearance of a score of Wilmington's "best colored men" after that election. Like White, he held an idealistic view of the state's overall electorate and their positive attitude toward black voters.

It was all very serious business for Dockery, who cast the state's upcoming election as "a life or death struggle" for Republicans. The 1898 election had been a wake-up call for democracy, he theorized. "Nearly all the counties of my district—known as the shoestring—lie along the South Carolina border," he told the president February 20. "These counties were invaded by red shirt riders from South Carolina, sent over by Senator Tillman, and thousands of republican voters were kept away from the polls by rank intimidation." And if the amendment should be adopted, "there will no longer be a republican party in North Carolina. The democratic party will be established forever."[47]

It is unlikely that Butler's future plans came up during his own next visit with the president four days later, on behalf of a North Carolina candidate for appointment to the Philippine Commission.[48] No, this was the aging Dockery's swan song, his final appearance in the public spotlight; his hope to make one last appearance in Congress was soon dashed by a House committee on elections. For McKinley, it was another bitter reminder of the legacy of Wilmington's coup d'état—recalling his inability to rescue that beleaguered city, Republican officeholders, or doomed black citizens—and of the increasingly sad state of political affairs in once-promising North Carolina. And it recalled, more subtly, White's persistent but unsuccessful attempts to force the president's hand on federal intervention.

For now, the emerging battle between White and political enemies in North Carolina was not widely covered in Washington. The *Evening Star* mentioned White's February 5 remarks only briefly in daily legislative coverage, describing his speech simply as "a question of personal privilege to reply to an editorial denouncing his course in Congress which was printed in the *News and Observer*."[49]

Hundreds of miles to the South, the *News and Observer*'s publisher sat at his Raleigh desk studying the debate, each day poring over the *Congressional Record*—still the official transcript, however suspect its authenticity—for further clues and taking delight in dispatches from friendlier journalists in the capital. Daniels might well have read the *Evening Star*'s faintly pejorative mention of his beloved newspaper, amid faintest echoes of the thunderous din generated when the ex-prosecutor denounced him. If so, he may have smiled grimly, perhaps even muttering a mild oath: *By George, if it's war you want, then it's war you will get.*

Three days after his angry response to Daniels's attack, White took a brief break from congressional duties to testify before the Industrial Commission on the labor and economic status of North Carolina's black population. The commission, established by McKinley in 1898, was mandated to investigate railroad pricing policy, industrial concentration, and the impact of immigration on labor markets, among many subjects; its four major areas of investigation were agriculture, manufacturing and general business, transportation, and mining; it was completely nonpartisan, and discussion of political issues was strictly prohibited. White's testimony was a key component of its report on agriculture and agricultural labor.[50]

The Industrial Commission was unique and controversial, having been vetoed by President Cleveland before final approval by McKinley. Its nineteen members included five U.S. senators and five House members—selected primarily from the membership of each house's labor committee—and nine citizens selected by McKinley, mostly businessmen, with three representatives of organized labor, as noted by early commission member Simon North's 1899 article. North expected the subject of black southern laborers—and implications of their emigration to other regions of the country—to be particularly important: "The presence of great masses of colored labor in the South presents another phase of the problem which is certain to grow more troublesome and more insistent as time passes. It is a body of labor which accepts lower wages than white labor, and is constantly pushing itself into new fields of competition with white labor. The negro problem, in its political phase, is the perplexity of this generation: its industrial phase is to become the perplexity of the next."[51]

Witnesses included both volunteers and experts selected with great care;

White was the only member of Congress on the list of some ninety witnesses to testify before the agriculture subcommittee, and one of only a handful of blacks to appear, even though issues applicable to African Americans were discussed by at least forty witnesses.[52] As an influential member of the House agriculture committee, White's appearance was anticipated and closely watched by many observers. His final testimony lasted several hours, covering questions offered by presiding vice chairman Thomas Phillips; Rep. John Gardner (R-N.J.) from the House Labor Committee; overall commission chairman Albert Clarke, and public members John Kennedy, Michael Ratchford, and John Farquhar. The thousand-page final report, issued in 1902, appeared as one of nineteen Commission volumes.[53]

Most of White's extremely detailed testimony dealt with specific questions posed by commissioners on economic conditions facing southern black laborers that were decidedly noncontroversial. But on several important issues, including internal emigration of blacks from the South, which he saw as a sort of a practical "safety valve" economically and a possible solution to the "race problem," his thoughts were both realistic and unconventional. He opposed wholesale colonization of black Americans, either in designated sections of the United States or abroad, as supported by Bishop Henry Turner ("whom I know to be a very able man" with "an underlying purpose to accomplish"); he instead favored "a gradual thinning out" of southern black populations and their careful, gradual assimilation elsewhere:

> If there must be migration, I do not think it is wise for either the white or black that the migration be in bulk either within the United States or without. But I do believe that the stress of the great mass of colored people ought to be relieved by a gradual thinning out. . . . [I]f homes could be found for [the colored man] among the people East, West, and North, away from the South—not enough to depopulate the South, but to relieve the overcrowded agricultural communities . . . if these communities could be relieved by taking and distributing them here and there in one State and another, I believe it would be the best way to solve what is now regarded as the race problem.[54]

But even controlled emigration posed an economic danger to southern states dependent on cheap manual labor and hostile to recruiters. Physical intimidation from fretful whites was likely: "I do not know whether you live North or South, but if you go, say, to Wilmington, where all that murder and carnage was, or any other Southern city, and undertake to induce the colored man to pack up and leave any particular community, it will not be healthy for you there 24 hours, and not from the colored man, either."[55]

White strongly opposed the prevailing use of convict labor across the South to "work on farms, on the public roads, on canals, and all classes of labor" to the "exclusion of free labor," especially in Georgia. It was a "terrible system" in White's mind, not just because it was inhuman, but because it gave undeserved bargains to large farmers—especially turpentine farmers, who barely reimbursed state costs of imprisoning workers—while simultaneously punishing the free economy by reducing free blacks' employment. "It takes the bread and butter out of their mouths, and they are left without a livelihood," White charged.[56]

This was a personal crusade by White, acting for the NAAC, which had established the abolition of convict labor as a high-priority agenda item. Convict labor was not an issue in North Carolina—where "the best feeling that I have known anywhere in the Southland existed between the whites and colored in our State"—but overall conditions for the state's blacks had gone downhill steadily since 1898:

> Up to a year or two ago our condition was decidedly on the upper trend. Politics, though, has made things a little bad for us.... The colored man has adhered quite rightly . . . to one political party, and that party has been recently overthrown.... [I]n my opinion the most vicious element of the white race is now in possession of the State.
>
> A large majority of the whites are kindly disposed to the colored man . . . but unfortunately politicians have not only dragged the race into politics, but even on the farms and in domestic affairs. In the city of Wilmington, in the latter part of 1898 and the first of last year, domestic servants were discharged and driven hither and thither.... [T]he bad feeling has died down somewhat, but we have a bad state of affairs and the way looks dark for the future.[57]

But White was remarkably pessimistic about whether blacks and whites could ever hope to coexist as equals in the South. In a new prophecy, contradicting allegations that he demanded social equality of the races, he responded to one question on that issue: "Perfect equality of the two races, either in education, industry, or politics, is next to the impossible. . . . [T]he white man's superior civilization from long years in advance of him, and his supremacy, wealth, and superior education, would tend to keep the colored man his inferior."[58]

This rebutted perennial charges by Josephus Daniels and other white supremacists that White was hell-bent on achieving social equality, even as Jim Crow segregation took hold across the South. Still, he continued whenever possible to insist that as citizens, blacks deserved equal political rights, equal treatment at the polls, and equal protection by the Constitution. Just two weeks after testifying at the Industrial Commission, he took to the floor of the House to fire the next volley in his personal war with white supremacists: a detailed portrait of recent American lynchings, both statistically and graphically, in the longest speech of his House career thus far, nearly the equal of his better-known farewell speech in January 1901.[59]

Whether this battle between Daniels and White—and how much of White's push on the antilynching bill—was being watched closely by the White House is not clear. Biographer Robert Merry characterizes McKinley at this point in his presidency as willing to push the envelope on some issues, such as recruiting black soldiers and black officers for use in the Philippines, but not on others. Merry believes McKinley was content to select domestic battles carefully: "Generally he was comfortable accepting the state of racial politics that he had inherited."[60] Avoiding unnecessary battles with southern Democrats over hot-button racial issues was an unspoken necessity.

Preoccupied with urgent issues on the international front—a growing revolution in the Philippines, the first stirrings of the Boxer Rebellion in China, opposition to the president's plan for free trade with Puerto Rico, and in Central America, where reactions to a complicated revision of the old Clayton-Bulwer Treaty threatened Nicaraguan canal plans—the president had little time to devote to mediating the dispute or examining prospects for White's antilynching bill. Deprived of his most trusted and able ally in the Senate by Hobart's death, McKinley was increasingly drawn into personal negotiations with political adversaries and compromises he preferred to avoid.

The president badly needed a solid ally, someone very much in Hobart's mold, to share the burden. Finding someone with such skill and experience was virtually impossible, but as the nationwide campaign for reelection drew ever nearer, choosing a successor was ever more imperative. Some observers and party leaders were already booming New York's rambunctious and unpredictable Theodore Roosevelt, the popular and often brash war hero whose political star was rising quickly. But Governor Roosevelt, no team player, was seemingly impervious to political correctness. For African Americans—still McKinley's most faithful voting bloc—Roosevelt's record on racial matters contained a large blemish: perplexingly critical comments about the performance of black soldiers in Cuba.

In April 1899, Roosevelt had publicly declared in *Scribner's Magazine* that black soldiers served well only when commanded by white officers.[61] He claimed to have averted a full-scale retreat by black soldiers under his command only by drawing his own pistol and threatening to shoot anyone who retreated, a charge refuted by eyewitnesses; the soldiers whom Colonel Roosevelt mistakenly assumed were retreating had simply obeyed orders from their own officers to bring supplies back to the rear of their convoy. Roosevelt later admitted his mistake and effectively apologized to those troops, according to a *New York Age* account by Sgt. Presley Holliday of the Tenth Cavalry, but neglected to explain his error in his article, one of many written for *Scribner's*.[62]

Roosevelt was not critical of the overall behavior of black servicemen at Santiago, writing at one point that "no troops could have behaved better than the colored soldiers had behaved so far," but he described black soldiers as "peculiarly dependent upon their white officers. Occasionally they produce non-commissioned officers who can take the initiative and accept responsibility precisely like the best class of whites; but this cannot be expected normally, nor is it fair to expect it."[63] Threats to shoot retreating soldiers were vintage Roosevelt bravado, and he claimed they worked. Even so, his *Scribner's* article offended African American leaders and generated strong negative, sometimes angry reactions in black newspapers. McKinley pointedly praised black soldiers for heroism at San Juan Hill and El Caney in speeches in 1898 and 1899, and more recently emphatically endorsed using black officers to command black troops in the Philippines. After the war ended, five black soldiers from Holliday's Tenth received the Medal of Honor for bravery at San Juan Hill, and eleven more, the Certificate of Merit; Holliday and three others received retroactive Silver Stars in 1922.[64]

But Roosevelt's clear disagreement with the use of black officers put him squarely and publicly at odds with McKinley on that issue. Even a year later, when few Republicans showed a clear preference for a Hobart successor as the convention approached, remarkably thin enthusiasm emerged among African Americans for Roosevelt's vice-presidential hopes—and McKinley risked jeopardizing once-solid support among black voters by choosing him. In February 1900, the Philadelphia convention was still four months away, and there was still no urgency on McKinley's part for a decision, at least none perceived by the *Washington Evening Star.*

McKinley concentrated instead on another issue—postwar unity of the nation, as he described it in spring speeches—and put forth the most positive spin he could, as he neared his second campaign. The America of McKinley's vision was no longer the North and South of old, he told the Ohio Society of New York in March. "Party lines have loosened and the ties of union have been strengthened," he declared. "Sectionalism has disappeared and fraternity and union have been rooted in the hearts of the American people. Political passion has subsided. . . . [T]he flag—our flag—has been sustained on distant seas and islands by the men of all parties and sections and creeds and races."[65]

It was ironic that McKinley spoke in the nation's largest city, in the state governed by the man so many expected to be his next running mate. But McKinley was not ready for the political battles of the summer and fall, nor was he yet convinced Roosevelt was the best choice. Many Republicans were interested in pushing Roosevelt forward in early 1900—for various reasons, not all favorable to the governor—but neither the president nor Mark Hanna were yet public fans.[66] Pushed to choose a successor to Garret Hobart, black Republicans could not agree on any candidate to be enthusiastic about, but Roosevelt was generally in last place.

White possibly had a more charitable opinion of Roosevelt than many black colleagues, but if so, he was keeping his own counsel—and for once, telling no one what he thought.

10

TAKING THE BATTLE TO THE NEXT LEVEL

Our constitutional rights have been trodden under foot; our right of franchise in most
every one of the original slave States has been virtually taken away from us, and ...
fully 50,000 of my race have been ignominiously murdered by mobs.
—**George H. White**, U.S. House, February 23, 1900

George White harbored few illusions in 1900 about the importance of his mission to outlaw lynching—or of his obstacles. As single-minded as Don Quixote, he knew he had powerful opponents and probably fewer friends than enemies in his native South. Whatever the costs, political or otherwise—and however unlikely his success—he had no choice. So he plunged forward, marshaling arguments with precision and a prosecutor's fearless determination as he brought his battle to the floor of the House.

In his first major speech since introducing H.R. 6963, White confronted both his chief tormentor—journalist Josephus Daniels—and the intransigence of those who had perverted the proud tradition of states' rights under the Constitution as a bar to national calls for action. But because his remarks arose during debate nominally confined to discussing a specific issue—promulgating new rules regarding tariffs and trade with Puerto Rico—White was forced to preface his remarks with a broader, related question. If the United States planned to extend its rules and democratic processes to lands and peoples gained through war, was it not proper first to examine such rules as currently practiced within the states?

He offered a ringing call to action against "a growing, and as I regard it, one of the most dangerous evils in our country"—increasing numbers of U.S. citizens lynched by armed mobs: "Should not a nation be just to all of her citizens, protect them alike in all their rights, on every foot of her soil!—in a word, show herself capable of governing all within her domain before she undertakes to exercise sovereign authority over those of a foreign land?—with foreign notions and habits not at all in harmony with our American system of government? Or, to be more explicit, should not charity first begin at home?"[1]

Of course, he said, the answer should be yes. But the guarantees of democracy, equal rights, and equal protection could not be said to be yet enjoyed by all Americans—specifically, not by African Americans:

> Unfortunately for us, what should have been done has not been done . . . during the past thirty-five years. We have struggled on as best we could with the odds against us at every turn. Our constitutional rights have been trodden under foot; our right of franchise in most every one of the original slave States has been virtually taken away from us, and during the time of our freedom fully 50,000 of my race have been ignominiously murdered by mobs, not less than 1 per cent of whom have been made to answer for their crimes.[2]

While no one, including the onetime prosecutor, would dismiss the gravity of the crimes with which some victims were charged, the right to trial by jury was guaranteed by the U.S. Constitution to all, even to those confessing guilt:

> I deprecate as much as any man can the fiend who commits an outrage upon any woman, and do not hesitate to say that he should be speedily tried and punished by the courts, yet I place little credence in the statement [of] a victim [who] confessed with a rope perhaps around his neck. . . . No court of justice anywhere . . . would allow testimony under duress of this kind to be introduced against a defendant. A shoe track, a confession while being burned at the stake with the hope that life may be spared thereby, are very poor excuses for taking of a human life.[3]

Even now, he noted with sad emphasis, among his fellow congressmen were those who excused and sometimes rationalized such behavior, for their own political reasons. Fellow House members from Mississippi and Georgia had described grisly mob executions in some detail, like the controversial lynching of Sam Hose, who had reportedly killed his employer in self-defense but was falsely accused of raping his wife, a sordid tale that electrified the nation in 1899.

This requirement for rape—"the race crime," often as not called up by mobs "in order to fasten public crime against the negro race" that permeated their accounts—offered irrefutable justification for hanging, or burning, or mutilation, or all three, of the perpetrators. Yet mobs such as Wilmington's in late 1898, whose members had not bothered to manufacture any crime at all, killed innocent blacks for no discernible reason. It was no surprise that such "miserable butchery" by an enraged band of marauders might not have seemed quite so authentic to his Georgia colleague, who "might have depicted also, if he been so inclined, the miserable butchery of men, women, and children in Wilmington, N.C., in November, 1898, who had committed no crime, nor were they even charged with crime. He might have taken the minds of his auditors to the horrible scene of the aged and infirm, male and female, women in bed from childbirth, driven from their homes to the woods, with no shelter . . . where many died from exposure, privation, and disease contracted while exposed to the merciless weather."[4]

But doing so, White pointed out, would have defeated the Georgian's true purpose, "riveting public sentiment upon every colored man of the South as a rapist from whose brutal assaults every white woman must be protected." Lending factual perspective to a discussion plagued by sensational exaggeration, White then reported his independent investigation of lynching cases: In just one sixteen-month period in 1898–99, "there were lynched in the United States 166 persons, and of this number 155 occurred in the South. Of the whole number lynched, there were 10 white and 156 colored. The thin disguise usually employed as an excuse for these inhuman outrages is the protection of the virtue among white women," White added. But that was far from the truth. Among the 166 lynching victims he listed, 32 were charged with murder, 17 with assault, 10 with arson—all serious crimes in their own right, just not related to sexual attacks.[5] Astoundingly, 40 percent of victims (72 of 166) were lynched "without any specific charge being preferred against them whatever."

An even more detailed listing of causes for another 63 lynchings—counted between April and October 1899—included such nonviolent offenses as two victims who "talked too much," three who "defended a colored man," seven who "wanted to work," and almost surreally, two victims who merely "spoke against lynching." No causes were listed for three lynchings. Two more victims were described as "innocent"; one victim was simply related to an alleged murderer. Most victims, though not all, were black; one Italian, one Cuban, and four white men were also lynched.[6]

White next incorporated journalistic articles on lynching from the nation's press. One recent editorial, "How 'Usual' Is the 'Crime,' " from a New York newspaper detailed other statistics on lynching in cases of alleged rape: only 12 of 103 lynchings in 1900 were for rape, but "Southern politicians and Southern writers and speakers proceed, as they invariably do, to justify the practice of lynching on the ground that its terrors are necessary to restrain the brute instincts of the black . . . as serious a libel as was ever perpetrated by one race on another."[7] Having observed tendencies among southern Democrats to defend lynching, the newspaper declared that "the few remaining Southern Republican members [of Congress] cannot do a greater national service than by reiterating these facts to Congress and the country, as did Messrs. Linney and White in the recent debate."[8]

"The Terrors of Mob Law," from Virginia's *Roanoke Times,* involved a case of false testimony, against a black man by a white woman, which a grand jury, remarkably, resolved in the defendant's favor. Still waiting for mention was the *News and Observer,* which "together with other lesser lights in the State, pounded upon me as a slanderer of white men in the South and especially in North Carolina" after brief remarks during January's Linney-Burke debate. Yet even Josephus Daniels's newspaper could occasionally report news more fairly, having chronicled a white state magistrate's indictment for criminal assault upon a young black woman, days after presiding over the trial and ordering the (legal) execution of a black man for raping a white woman.[9]

As a former prosecutor who had never opposed the death penalty, this issue of extralegal execution had become a cause célèbre for White. Such mob violence, he warned, ate at the very root of American jurisprudence, as "a flagrant defiance of all law, morals, the State, and nation," yet "the actors are dubbed as the best citizens of the community. Only the banning of lynching and punishment by the severest penalty of all—execution—could right the wrong." Not to act was unthinkable, sickening. "I tremble with horror for the future of our nation when I think what must be the inevitable result if mob violence is not stamped out of existence and law once [again] permitted to reign supreme," he said.[10] State laws could not accomplish this, only a truly national law—his proposed bill, whose text he read into the public record for the first time.

His bill was imperfect, he admitted, but Congress could and should enact it. After citing a series of legal precedents, he now read at length from a letter from Albert Pillsbury, among his advisers in drafting the bill. The ex–attorney general called the subject "difficult to deal with, but not to be dismissed offhand. The precise question is whether the United States has any power, under the Four-teenth Amendment or otherwise, to protect the lives of its own citizens against mob violence within the state which the states do not . . . prevent or punish."

Pillsbury noted compelling arguments for the constitutional right of the federal government to protect its own citizens' lives against armed violence by mobs; political considerations might well prevent Congress from acting on a bill such as White proposed, but any notion that it was unconstitutional to do so was simply wrong. Allowing individual states to claim superiority over the federal government's authority on this issue, Pillsbury asserted, "is to admit, if I mistake not, the soundness of the late contested platform of secession"[11]—a provocative statement certain to annoy southerners still sensitive to the Civil War's outcome.

White ended his hour-long speech on a personal note provoking loud and prolonged applause. He had no wish to stir "any friction between the races or the sections of this country" with his bill. As the only African American in Congress, he spoke out of necessity on behalf of "a people who have no one to speak for them from a racial point of view . . . a patient and, in the main, inoffensive race, a race which has often been wronged but seldom retaliated."[12]

He had accomplished an important goal on the nonpartisan NAAC's high-priority list of action items, a task only he could have performed, as the nation's highest elected black official. If he could persuade the House to pass his bill—with the public support, he hoped, of McKinley and backing by other Republican leaders—White knew the momentum might well carry him into important new positions either in or out of Congress, perhaps even to leader-ship of the Council.

Bishop Walters was understandably weary of the job he had held since 1898. After two grueling years of fundraising, organizing, and keeping the peace in his often-fractious new organization, he seemed to be contemplating retirement. White, as a ranking NAAC vice president, was almost a perfect choice to succeed him, but there were logistical and temperamental draw-backs. Walters served without salary, balancing unpaid part-time Council duties with a full-time position in his denomination; even a part-time salary would require new resources for the cash-poor Council. It was just as import-ant to find the right personality to mediate inevitable squabbles and maintain its nonpartisan nature.

That election still lay months in the future; much groundwork remained.

With few close party allies on the House Judiciary Committee—and at least five southern Democrats almost certain to oppose its language—White had few illusions about his bill's future.[13] More immediate hurdles remained: his own decision over seeking another term in Congress, the party's nominating convention in Philadelphia, and North Carolina's crucial August referendum.

❧

Little escaped McKinley's eye on legislative matters of party importance. He tended to listen quietly to advisers and visitors without commitments or public announcements of private views on a subject, and he was often criticized for keeping silent on controversial issues such as lynching, despite his solid record as governor of Ohio and occasional public references. Whether he discussed the lynching bill with White or other party leaders is not known, although he did meet with White a month after his major speech, regarding the nomination of North Carolina Republican leader Charles Cook for a federal patronage position. Their March 24 chat might easily have veered over into White's latest legislative venture—but if so, no public statement came from the White House on the antilynching bill.[14]

Perhaps with a trace of historical irony, the two most significant public statements made by the president since December had dealt with two of his illustrious predecessors—one a slaveholder, the father of his country, the other McKinley's commander in chief in the war to free those same slaves. McKinley's tributes artfully interwove the legacies of two great American presidents, perhaps with an unconscious eye toward his own legacy in a reelection year.

At Washington's Mount Vernon estate on December 14, McKinley marked the hundredth anniversary of the first president's death with a moving tribute to his unparalleled leadership and legacy:[15] "After a lapse of a century he is better appreciated, more perfectly understood, more thoroughly venerated and loved than when he lived. He remains an ever-increasing influence for good in every part and sphere of action of the republic. He is recognized as not only the most far-sighted statesman of his generation, but as having had almost prophetic vision."[16]

Just ten weeks later, on Washington's birthday, McKinley delivered a shorter but singularly impassioned speech invoking Lincoln's Gettysburg Address, while recalling his own olive branch offered to descendants of Confederate soldiers on his southern tour. "There has been within the past two years a reunion of all the people around the holy altar of country, newly sanctified by common sacrifice. The followers of Grant and of Lee have fought under the same colors and have fallen for the same cause," he said, in the war with Spain: "Let us . . . on this, the anniversary of the birth of the Father of his Country, resolve, in the language of Lincoln, to dedicate ourselves anew to the imperishable cause which he advanced so far upon its way; and as Lincoln said at Gettysburg, let us firmly resolve that those who gave their lives shall not have died in vain; that the nation for which they shed their blood shall not have died in vain."[17]

That "imperishable cause" Lincoln had once espoused and "advanced so far upon its way" had persisted, even succeeded, but had cost hundreds of thousands of lives. Decades later, armed hostilities were long past, but their tragic consequences still played out upon the national body politic. The war to save the Union had succeeded, with a reconstructed Union, if not as Lincoln might have hoped; the resurgence of a monolithic South thirty-odd years later would have confounded the sixteenth president. And his second, simultaneous war to free the slaves—the one he undertook in a desperate, last-ditch effort to accomplish the first goal—still awaited its own resolution, with millions of former slaves trapped in limbo, thwarting advancement.

McKinley was an unlikely inheritor of both of Lincoln's wars. He was determined to win back the South, if possible—but if unable to win the South over to his own Republican cause, then to establish a new era of political peace with its ruling Democrats. He was still equally determined to preserve hard-won freedoms of the nation's African Americans, which defied the new logic of the Jim Crow South, and to continue inspiring new generations of black Americans to become productive citizens. Whether he could accomplish either task remained to be seen. But whether he could accomplish both—accomplishing a feat Lincoln had attempted, at the cost of his life, in a cruel twist of fate—remained a mystery.

☙

Other matters important to African Americans were at the forefront of the president's spring agenda. On April 5, McKinley met briefly with prominent black educators Booker T. Washington and Richard Wright, both of whose campuses he had visited sixteen months earlier. No record of their discussion exists; neither educator would likely raise lynching with McKinley unless prompted. But a more sensational local battle with racial overtones was raging outside, after derogatory comments about blacks and other city minorities, made by the president of the District of Columbia commission to a congressional subcommittee, were widely reported by local newspapers.

Businessman John Wight was up for reappointment to another three-year term on the commission, which he had served since 1898 as president, the equivalent of mayor at the time. Until a deluge of circulars recounting his comments flooded the city in March, reappointment seemed certain. During testimony before the House Appropriations Committee on February 20, however, Wight made unflattering comments about Italian, Irish, and especially African American District residents, including one widely reprinted statement: "The 90,000 colored people here are equal to the criminal conditions in any city; they regard life as of no value whatever."

Wight later insisted to the *Washington Evening Star* that his comments were taken completely out of context during a discussion over increasing the size of the city's police force. "I had only in mind and supposed at the time that I was fully understood to refer only to the criminal class of our colored population, and not to the race as a whole," Wight said. "Any other construction of the statement made by me is wholly unwarranted," as well as its extension to the Irish and Italian populations.[18] But black leaders, led by journalist Calvin Chase, were busily poring over Wight's complete record during his tenure and finding evidence of his distaste for the city's black population: only one black fireman had been hired during his three years as commissioner, for instance. "Mr. Wight has made an unwarranted attack upon the 90,000 colored people in this District," Chase told the *Evening Star*. "He has never had any fair estimate of the colored race."[19]

Furor over his remarks continued unabated, soon reaching the White House, as Chase mobilized black leaders to demand Wight's immediate removal, the *Evening Star* reported.[20] The source of Wight's leaked comments—perhaps Chase or another black journalist—was never revealed. But it was certainly not White, brand-new member of the House Committee on the District of Columbia, who would never have risked embarrassing the White House and endangering his own relationship with the president by engineering the public campaign.

The three-member District board of commissioners served three-year staggered terms as the city's only governing body. Wight, a Republican and former supervisor of Gallaudet College for the hearing impaired, had been appointed by McKinley in 1897; other current members included Democrat John Ross, former city postmaster, appointed in 1890 and reappointed by McKinley in 1897, and Republican Lansing Beach, a military engineer appointed by McKinley in 1898. Both Ross and Wight were widely expected to return to the board before the scandal broke. In the end, only Ross was renominated after Wight's candidacy collapsed. Journalist Henry MacFarland, a reliable and presumably more discreet Republican, replaced Wight as commissioner and mayor-president. McKinley nominated both MacFarland and Ross to terms on the commission April 27, weeks after the scandal broke.[21]

With no clear signal or public word from McKinley on the antilynching bill, White and his NAAC comrades now turned their energies toward a second course: persuading the GOP to include strong antilynching language in the party's 1900 platform—as well as strong language on disfranchisement—when the nominating convention convened in Philadelphia in June. White himself was selected in April as a delegate from his Second District to the convention but delayed any decision on seeking renomination for Congress until after the August referendum. Meanwhile, North Carolina's political atmosphere was confusing and troubling. By the time the state party held its own annual convention in May, it was clear that black Republicans were fast losing influence in the state party.

For the first time since 1868, no black delegate-at-large represented North Carolina; Cheatham declined his election, reportedly in favor of a white Republican. Now only three black delegates represented the state in Philadelphia—White and Henry Hagans of Goldsboro, representing the Second District, and Maxton newspaper editor Robert Russell, of the Sixth District— or half as many as North Carolina sent in 1896. During his May 5 visit to the White House regarding McKinley's tentative plans to visit North Carolina that month, Pritchard brought up the matter; some black Republicans were "offended" at the absence of blacks from the state's at-large list, but most were simply unaware of Cheatham's election or withdrawal.[22]

The national convention subcommittee on resolutions and platform language was slated to hold hearings in mid-June, and many black leaders pinned their hopes on the eloquence of subcommittee member John Roy Lynch, ex-congressman and army paymaster. Accordingly, the NAAC selected

White to chair its delegation, perhaps as a prelude to his candidacy for Council presidency. As White later recalled, Walters had approached him "some time ago" about taking the job, but he "did not want it," at least not initially; he later agreed to accept only after Walters complained about his clerical duties suffering from Council responsibilities.[23] Walters made no secret of his plans, although he perhaps floated White's candidacy to gauge reactions among other black leaders, or to deflect campaigning by other vice presidents—among them T. Thomas Fortune and five bishops, including Benjamin Arnett.

In May, black editors were already publicly discussing Walters's rumored desire to step down, with no consensus on a successor. Calvin Chase of the *Washington Bee* half-playfully suggested Booker T. Washington's name in March, while the *Colored American* eagerly pushed White's name forward in early May. But the *Cleveland Gazette* thought White "too deeply imbedded in politics for such a position" and said Walters needed to be followed by "a man who is above political interference."[24] All the bishops save Arnett, too closely identified with McKinley, were sound nonpartisan choices, perhaps even willing to assume the unsalaried post. Fortune, a logical choice to some, had refused it years earlier; his *New York Age* was well respected, but he was perennially broke and would demand a substantial salary—and worse, suffered from a weakness for alcohol.

White himself was likely to demand a salary, particularly if he should choose not to seek reelection to Congress. His demanding lifestyle and his wife's medical expenses would not permit him to donate services; such a demanding post might interfere with a full-time patronage appointment or legal practice. Perhaps with an eye to such a future, he had been licensed to practice law in the District of Columbia since 1899, and on March 13, 1900, he was formally admitted to the Bar of the U.S. Supreme Court.[25]

White was content to campaign quietly against the forthcoming referendum on North Carolina's constitutional amendment to disfranchise illiterate voters. In mid-May he told the *Colored American* he fully expected a resounding victory for amendment opponents—"more than 40,000 majority"—on August 1, and early consideration afterward by the House Judiciary Committee of his antilynching bill. Having just visited his hometown of Tarboro, he saw no evidence of "the bitterness and strife presented through the Democratic newspapers." On the contrary, white citizens of Tarboro cordially crossed the street to shake his hand and discuss current events.[26]

But the *News and Observer* was about to dispel his optimism and make his life more complicated, by resuming personal attacks on him. An unusual cast of characters figured in Daniels's summertime strategy, including a commercial artist with a penchant for racist cartoons, an unexpectedly candid federal judge with little sympathy for defendants, a disgraced postmaster, and a railroad conductor's arbitrary enforcement of Jim Crow–era segregation. It began with a blatantly offensive front-page cartoon that summed up the "new normality" of race relations in the Old North State.

Wayne County native Norman Jennett was a gifted young artist who became a staff cartoonist for the *Raleigh News and Observer* in 1895 and gained early fame in the 1896 political campaign before pursuing formal education in art in New York. At Daniels's personal request, Jennett returned home in 1898 to provide front-page political cartoons during that year's campaign. Even after leaving North Carolina in 1899, he continued to contribute cartoons from his perch at the *New York Herald,* and Daniels again made good use of his remarkable talents during the 1900 campaign. Jennett's drawings ranged from humorous to savage and fairly dripped journalistic acid on favorite targets, particularly when depicting black Republican politicians as comically dressed, squired about by befuddled-looking white party leaders.

Jennett worked closely with Daniels to perfect each cartoon. "He and I would confer daily on the character of the cartoons," Daniels later recalled. "He eagerly devoured the editorial page to see what I was writing about. . . . We would decide together what particular Republican or Populist deserved to be hit over the head that day."[27] For the May 26 *News and Observer,* the Jennett-Daniels team returned to a favorite subject of scorn: George White as an elephant whose back was labeled "G.O.P." topped by a human head, seated on a milking stool, sucking sustenance through his trunk from a money-jug labeled "Term in Congress worth $5,000 a year."[28]

"He doesn't like to let go," read the caption's first line, printed atop the cartoon and continuing beneath: "But most people think our only negro Congressman has had it about long enough." The cartoon's timeliness was unmistakable. One day earlier, Democrats had nominated their 1900 aspirant for Congress in the Second District: Claude Kitchin, son of a former one-term congressman in the "Black Second" and brother to current Rep. William Kitchin, Democrat of the Fifth District. Over the next few months, increasingly partisan cartoons flooded the front pages of the *News and Observer*, but few achieved the level of nastiness of the so-called "elephant man" cartoon, arguably the low point of the white-supremacy campaigns, for which Jennett—later a successful commercial artist for New York newspapers and magazines—remained best known.

As the referendum approached, White found himself under frequent attack, both directly and indirectly, for his record in Congress and alleged commitment to social equality for blacks under Jim Crow. A week after its notorious cartoon, the *News and Observer* publicly linked him, Jeter Pritchard, and McKinley as responsible for a trio of black postmasters removed from office and imprisoned for misappropriating postal funds, all described as "Jeter's Jail Birds." In the astounding words of the federal judge hearing the case—a McKinley appointee!—"the postmasters of the Second District are becoming a stench in the nostrils of the people. This is the third one that has recently been sent to jail," and part of a disturbing new pattern; he promised all future defendants would be sentenced to the penitentiary instead.[29]

Judge Thomas Purnell was no novice, but a reliable Republican lawyer, Trinity College graduate, and ex-legislator appointed in April 1897 by McKinley, after a decade as a federal commissioner. His caustic comments came at the sentencing of Israel Hargett, onetime Rocky Mount postmaster, who drew a term of one year in the Wake County jail; Hargett's conviction followed similar outcomes for Tillery's James Pittman and Clinton Battle of Battleboro, now serving sentences in Halifax County's jail. Purnell may well have been frustrated by "the pleadings and solicitations of public officials" on Hargett's behalf; "I can't understand why it is that officers of the government continue chaffering with criminals and scheming to get them off light," he told the *News and Observer*.[30] But the judge's language still seemed disturbingly inappropriate.

Purnell did not refer to McKinley, Pritchard, or White in quoted remarks. But as the correspondent helpfully added, all three postmasters—Hargett, Pittman, and Battle—had "been appointed by President McKinley, with the consent of Jeter C. Pritchard, and upon the recommendation of George H. White."[31] White had nominated both Hargett and Pittman in 1897, but not Battle, whose post office lay inside Nash County, part of the adjacent Fourth District. Responsibility for nominating Battle that year had fallen to Populist William Strowd of Chapel Hill, who may well have queried White for advice.

Hargett's sentencing was exquisitely painful for White, who had first proposed the schoolmaster for Rocky Mount during a summer recess in the Fifty-Fifth Congress. Hargett operated under a temporary commission until the Senate reconvened, before being formally nominated by McKinley on January 5, 1898; his nomination, reported out favorably April 20, was eventually approved by the Senate after several delays. But his tenure was poorly received by Rocky Mount's white residents, who complained about dealings with black staff; frustrated, he offered to resign, according to a late 1898 report, but was rebuffed.[32] By February 1899, he was removed from office and charged with misappropriating postal funds. As in most such cases, poor bookkeeping was probably as much a culprit as criminal intent, but for Hargett, that offered little consolation.

Less than a week later, White visited the White House, intending to propose appointing local educator George Cook to the District's new Board of Charities, and perhaps he mentioned Hargett's conviction to McKinley during their June 9 meeting.[33] Depending on their conversation's length, it seems more likely that the president inquired only about news of the state's referendum on disfranchising illiterate voters, not Hargett. What is known is that the president took Cook's name under favorable advisement, and six months later, appointed the Howard University professor as that board's first black member.[34]

McKinley gained more information the following week from Sen. Marion Butler, according to the *Evening Star*, when they discussed "the situation in North Carolina and the threatened disfranchisement of the blacks. The future consideration of this question by the administration promises to be as careful and deliberate as the seriousness of it demands."[35] Butler doubtless provided a comprehensive readout on political developments; although unlikely to be re-elected by the Democratic General Assembly when his term expired in 1901, he had every reason to hope for the constitutional amendment's defeat. Ratifying the amendment would effectively doom the state's Populist Party by forcing fusionists to return to the Democratic fold or face selective disfranchisement in much the same fashion as black Republicans.

By this time, White had all but decided to retire, even if the amendment failed. His summer campaign speeches were conciliatory and conservative, yet even such uncharacteristic restraint did not free him from misleading reports about his views on social equality. A July 23 business trip by train from Goldsboro to New Bern provoked a minor sensation when the *Kinston Free Press* reported that White and his personal secretary had nearly been ejected from the train, after allegedly refusing to honor railroad policy of segregating passengers in different compartments by race. The *Free Press* compared this incident to an 1898 story, late in that year's campaign, when White and his party were evicted from a circus for refusing to sit in the black patrons' section.[36]

For once, White had enough of unfair bad publicity, and he wrote the *Free Press* demanding a correction. "I do not know who your informant was but beg to state that your editorial does, inadvertently, perhaps, a grave injustice. The facts in the case can be proven by at least a dozen white men and colored men," he wrote a week later, naming only one other person: the train's conductor.[37] Said White, he and his secretary had traveled to New Bern and points east, riding in the compartment "partitioned off and set aside for colored people, where there were several other colored persons including two ministers."

At New Bern, they left their car briefly for the platform to converse with visitors in the station, leaving luggage and umbrellas behind; they returned to discover the section earlier set aside for black travelers had disappeared, with all seats occupied by white travelers. It was a scenario soon familiar to black travelers across the South, best exemplified by Rosa Parks's experience a half century later on a Birmingham bus. "The conductor, Mr. Chas. K. Hancock, came along and suggested we would find comfortable seats in the rear car," White wrote.[38]

"I thereupon remonstrated upon the humiliation of going through several crowded cars when I was already riding in the compartment provided by law for colored people. The captain made some remark to the effect that he disliked to ask the people to remove, and without any further words we gathered our satchels, etc., and went back to a car in the rear." But he was never accosted by travelers of either race, and no incident occurred.[39]

"I have never had, have not now, nor do I ever expect to have any hankering to push myself among any class of people where I am not wanted," White said, clearly exasperated at the image the *Free Press* conjured. "The circus incident to which you allude was started in much the same way as the incident now under discussion and had no foundation in truth. I beg that you will do me the justice to reproduce this statement in your columns and correct the error which you have made, unwittingly, no doubt."[40]

With only days left before the referendum, White made no further comment. But with unexpected deference, the *Free Press* took him at his word, adding this postscript: "We do not wish to misrepresent anyone. If White states the matter truly we have done him an injustice and take pleasure in correcting the same."[41] It was an unusual attitude for any North Carolina newspaper, much less one previously owned and still influenced from afar by the *News and Observer*, which, uncharacteristically, withheld comment. Josephus Daniels preferred, perhaps, to avoid giving White even the faintest favorable publicity as voters prepared their verdict on the constitutional amendment.

11

EYE OF THE STORM

The Republican party was dedicated to freedom forty-four years ago. It has been the party of liberty and emancipation from that hour.... It broke the shackles of 4,000,000 slaves and made them free.
—**William McKinley**, Canton, July 12, 1900

The Republicans' national gathering in mid-June of 1900 was a congratulatory event for a popular incumbent president about to be nominated for a second term after leading the nation to victory over Spain. William McKinley's certain opponent was William Jennings Bryan, the same Democrat he had defeated handily four years earlier. Much of the Saint Louis convention environment would be re-created in Philadelphia, if with perhaps half the black delegates who had helped nominate McKinley and Hobart. This time, of course, a new vice president would succeed Hobart; the only element of mystery was whether Theodore Roosevelt would accept second spot, after a spring of up-and-down speculation.

The mood of white party delegates was nearly euphoric as the convention opened June 19. But the week's proceedings were not without disappointments for some, including a smaller contingent of African Americans, and the nation's only black congressman, George White. The delegate from North Carolina—one of just three African Americans from his state—had a score fewer black colleagues to help him push for issues of interest to the race: fewer than fifty delegates in Philadelphia, compared to more than seventy in Saint Louis. And after White, few were true movers and shakers on a national level; black Republicans of national stature included ex-congressmen John Roy Lynch of Mississippi and Robert Smalls of South Carolina, each at their fifth national conventions, and Judson Lyons of Georgia, joined by Mississippi's James Hill and Joseph Lee, chairing Florida's delegation, plus a few federal appointees from Georgia and South Carolina.

Gone were giants of yesteryear: Bruce, Langston, and Cuney. All had died since the last convention, and with their passing, much of their race's collective influence dissipated. Gone, too, was the relentless guidance of Ohio's Mark Hanna, whose organizational skills and patronage offers had been crucial to McKinley's nomination in 1896. As chairman of the Republican National Committee, Senator Hanna still played an influential role in GOP national strategy, but courting the dwindling number of black delegates was no longer necessary; for them, and indeed for almost all delegates, there was no alternative but McKinley.

African American delegates were perhaps the least enthusiastic of any group for Roosevelt's surging vice-presidential candidacy—easily the favorite among most convention delegates but still distrusted by black leaders for unflattering comments about black soldiers in 1899. District of Columbia delegate Chase, for instance, preferred New York lieutenant governor Tim Woodruff—Roosevelt's second-in-command—while other delegates briefly supported Iowa representative Jonathan Dolliver, soon to become U.S. senator, or McKinley's navy secretary, John Long.

But there was little else for prominent black delegates to do in Philadelphia. North Carolina's Robert Russell, a black journalist, was appointed to the convention's committee on rules and business, the same post held by White in 1896; four black delegates—including Chase and Lee—were appointed to the convention committee to notify McKinley of his renomination, journeying as a group to Canton after the convention; two black delegates joined Roosevelt's committee.[1] White made only one recorded comment during the convention, during consideration by the convention of its rules.[2]

Perhaps nowhere else did the waning influence of black delegates stand out so visibly as in the platform's final language, a notable disappointment to black Republicans.[3] White and his NAAC colleagues counted on the presence of John Roy Lynch and two other blacks on the resolution committee to ensure passage of strongly phrased planks on lynching and disfranchisement, but even Lynch was unable to force the issue. Gone was the assertive antilynching language of the 1896 platform, replaced with a watered-down appeal to "protect the person and property of every citizen wherever they are wrongfully violated or placed in peril."[4]

The platform's disfranchisement plank was equally vague, citing the purpose of the Fifteenth Amendment "to prevent discrimination on account of race or color in regulating the elective franchise" but offering no solution to disfranchisement of southern black voters. It merely condemned as "revolutionary" any "devices of state governments, whether by statutory or constitutional amendment to avoid the purpose of this amendment."[5] The resolutions committee declined to approve the NAAC language submitted on either issue. To his credit, Lynch later attempted to insert disfranchisement language similar to that rejected by his committee into convention rules governing the representation of states at future party gatherings.

Essentially a symbolic effort with no effect on reducing representation in Congress by southern states disfranchising black voters, the prospect of having it in the convention's official record would still have put the party on record as acknowledging the concept of Crumpacker's amendment in the House: "In any state wherein the right to vote is denied is denied to any of the male inhabitants thereof on account of race, color, or previous condition of servitude, or wherein said right is in any way abridged for the same reason, representation in Congress should be reduced in the proportion which the whole number of male inhabitants so deprived of the right to vote shall bear to the whole number of male inhabitants twenty-one years of age in such State."[6]

But Lynch was unsuccessful; his amendment to Rules 1 and 12 of the convention rules was objected to as out of order ("not germane to the matter before the Convention"), delayed for consideration, and then never voted on, with Lynch outmaneuvered by ex-representative Lemuel Quigg of New York. For all his efforts, however, Lynch drew editorial fire from Ohio's Harry Smith, who excoriated Lynch as "wholly responsible for the mutilation and practically the ruination of the Afro-American Council's resolution" and quoted Quigg as saying that the committee, including Lynch, had voted unanimously to approve the final platform.[7] Smith, of course, was notoriously quick to condemn, far slower to analyze or reflect; given the committee's initial unwillingness to approve his language, what else Lynch or any other black leader might have done was never specified.

Nearly forty years later, Lynch recalled the events in his autobiography, devoting a full chapter ("Controversial Convention Procedures") to the 1900 convention difficulties and the complicated procedures dooming his disfranchisement language. Senator Foraker had submitted a draft platform, said Lynch, "that . . . was not at all satisfactory to a majority of the committee," especially to Quigg, who rewrote the draft platform to his specifications, and whose report was accepted and adopted with minor changes by the full committee. But even in his nineties, Lynch still believed his party missed a historic opportunity to offer satisfaction to "Southern Republicans . . . denied access to the ballot box through an evasion of the Constitution" by allowing them to "know . . . that if they cannot vote themselves, others cannot vote for them." Failing to enact the proposed change was, in effect, "sending of a message of sympathy and encouragement to the Democrats of North Carolina who [were] now engaged in an effort to disfranchise the colored Republicans of that state."[8] (Lynch never delivered the remarks shown in his autobiography, because his amendment was never voted on.)

On its last day, the 1900 convention voted unanimously to renominate McKinley, then selected Roosevelt as his running mate. Three weeks later, the notification committee—including black members Joseph Lee, Calvin Chase, William Pledger, and Edmund Deas—made its trek to Canton to advise the president of his formal renomination. A separate committee with just two black members—John Cooke of Louisiana and Charles Ferguson of Texas— extended the same courtesy to Roosevelt in New York.[9]

The platform on which McKinley and Roosevelt ran was accepted as a roundly congratulatory one, detailing the accomplishments of McKinley's first term. It made no mention of the struggle still facing southern black citizens or possible solutions to their political difficulties. For White, the handwriting on the wall was now clear. With his career in Congress set to end in March 1901, his once-high hopes of satisfying NAAC goals on either lynching or disfranchisement during the Fifty-Sixth Congress, reconvening for a short final session after the election, were disappearing.

Without a stronger platform statement on lynching than the anodyne language finally approved, his antilynching bill had no new impetus; even repeating the 1896 platform's language would have been more helpful. And without clear endorsement by the party platform of penalties for states disfranchising black voters, the Crumpacker amendment faced an uphill battle in the House and a questionable future in the Senate—unless a miracle occurred.

The dejected congressman still held lingering hope for one last major victory as the curtain fell on his national career. He still believed the voters of North Carolina, given a fair election, would defeat the proposed disfranchisement amendment to their state's constitution. His energies during June and July were concentrated on this hope with a calm, conservative strategy for black Republicans: register to vote, show up at the polls, and do not create a disturbance. He told the party faithful at Edgecombe County's nominating convention June 30 that he was "out of politics as far as wanting office" and advised listeners "to register and to vote, but to create no disturbance and to strive to create harmony and good feeling between the races." Perhaps hoping to reinforce its newly cooperative image with ruling Democrats, the county party for the first time in three decades offered no local slate.[10]

But even as he exhorted black voters to follow his strategy, the split between White and party white leadership—epitomized by Jeter Pritchard—grew into a chasm. Pritchard's statements at the spring state convention had not reassured White of his continuing support for black party members. The opposite was true. Competing versions emerged of what Pritchard had said and done at that convention, including involvement in Cheatham's withdrawal as at-large delegate. For the first time since 1892, White was not allowed to address the convention at all—perhaps by choice or out of fear among party leaders over his lightning-rod status. His last address to the convention in 1898, which sparked extremely negative coverage by the *Raleigh News and Observer*, was still being reprinted two years later.

Pritchard had apparently also made statements that White and other black leaders interpreted as knuckling under to Democratic demands: language suggesting the General Assembly should once again abolish home rule in black-majority counties, as during and after Reconstruction, to prevent elections of black county commissioners and officials. White saw such actions as political heresy, evidence that Republican leaders were edging closer to alignment with "lily-white" strategy in other southern states. Yet tactics implemented by Pritchard and Butler involving a larger issue—the constitutional amendment—were actually shrewder and more complicated than black leaders imagined.

Pritchard, for instance, had already told the Senate that the proposed North Carolina amendment was unconstitutional on its face, by contradicting the Fourteenth and Fifteenth Amendments to the U.S. Constitution; in effect, North Carolina forfeited its status as a state with "a republican form of government."

Resolved, That an enactment, by constitution or otherwise, by any State which confers the right to vote upon any of its citizens because of their descent from certain persons or classes of persons, and excludes other citizens because they are not descended from such persons or classes of persons having all other qualifications prescribed by law, in the opinion of the Senate, is in violation of the Fourteenth and Fifteenth amendments to the Constitution of the United States and of a fundamental principle of our republican form of government.[11]

To Pritchard's mind, North Carolina's proposed amendment was "the most important question we have been called upon to deal with since the war." It would overturn the state's 1868 constitutional provision guaranteeing "free suffrage to the rich, the poor, the illiterate and the educated alike," in short, to all male voters. For more than thirty years, state Democrats had schemed and sought for purely partisan reasons to amend that Republican-passed constitution "so as to restrict the right of suffrage and, if possible, prevent the poor and illiterate white people of that state from exercising that privilege." Now Democrats sought to disqualify the very people to whom the Fourteenth and Fifteenth Amendments had expressly provided eternal suffrage protection: freed slaves.[12]

Butler then added a subtler, more intriguing argument: if passed, the amendment's hated "grandfather clause"—found in Section 5—was most likely to be overturned by federal courts, leaving other provisions intact but preventing illiterate whites from being able to register by using its exemption.[13] The practical benefits of Pritchard's overall strategy were lost on White, who still believed the amendment would be defeated and questioned Pritchard's loyalty to black voters and potential officeholders. But the pragmatic carrot-and-stick strategy employed by Republican leaders in the last months before the referendum was born of sheer desperation.

By appearing to concede publicly the issue of future black officeholders to Democrats and concentrate instead on challenging the amendment's constitutionality, either in part or totally, Pritchard and Butler were maximizing losing hands in a high-stakes poker game. They doubtless expected the amendment to pass and become law. There was no upside for Republicans in opposing inevitable changes in state law, since the Democratic General Assembly needed no Republican votes to change election rules; the 1899 legislature had already radically revised fusionists' reforms of 1895 and 1897, revamping structures of county election boards and eliminating bipartisan membership.

But the sudden prospect of winning the battle against "negro domination" while losing the war in the process—permanently disfranchising thousands of illiterate white voters, not just targeted black voters—alarmed many Democratic leaders, who could ill afford to lose so many Democratic votes. Worried Democrats called the General Assembly into special session in June 1900 to amend the referendum's wording with a "poison pill" provision: if the "grandfather clause" were declared unconstitutional, the whole amendment would be invalid.

The widening break between White and Pritchard—indeed, a break with the state GOP's white leadership—was perhaps inevitable. Pritchard, ever practical, may well have tried to explain the situation to White, but if so, he failed badly. Their alliance after 1896, one born of political expediency, had served them both well since then; if never close personal friends, the two were well acquainted from service together in the General Assembly, a decade before either entered Congress.[14] White now saw himself as leader of a faithful group of voters being victimized by Pritchard's whims and could not forgive what he saw as party betrayal of its base—first by not fighting the amendment publicly and, second, by projecting a smaller future party without half its previous members.

As the summer entered its final, fateful phase, White prepared for the annual session of the NAAC in Indianapolis, where he still expected to become its new head. If the amendment were defeated, he could hold his head high, despite failure so far to accomplish either of the Council's legislative goals in Congress or to convince Republicans to endorse either goal in the party platform. He might no longer be in Congress, but he still envisioned himself on a national stage from which to help lead America's black citizens forward in battles for fairness and political justice.

McKinley entered his reelection campaign season with a novel plan of his own: no campaigning at all. His acceptance speech in Canton in mid-July had outlined his positions on the campaign issues—most dealing with foreign issues, particularly the Philippines and China—included an endorsement of the party's platform, and ended with a plea to history:

> The Republican party was dedicated to freedom forty-four years ago.
> It has been the party of liberty and emancipation from that hour; not
> of profession, but of performance. It broke the shackles of 4,000,000
> slaves and made them free, and to the party of Lincoln has come another

supreme opportunity, which it has met in the liberation of 10,000,000 of
the human family from the yoke of imperialism.

In the solution of great problems, in the performance of high duties,
it has had the support of the members of all parties in the past and confidently invokes their cooperation in the future.[15]

The president waited until September to announce that he planned no campaign speeches or tours, nor even to conduct a "front-porch" campaign as in
1896; he planned instead to campaign "simply by doing his job," in the words
of biographer Merry.[16] McKinley drew appreciative crowds whenever he
traveled and enjoyed meeting the public. His response to one Pennsylvania
fan's question—"Major, what are you going to plan to do with us the next four
years?"—provided a humorously humble turn of phrase: "It is more important just now to know what you are going to do with me the next four years."[17]
Not to be outdone, the admirer shouted back, "We are going to stand by you."

The real campaign stars, however, were the president's high-energy running mate, Theodore Roosevelt—traveling more than twenty thousand miles in
eight weeks, delivering an astounding 673 speeches in twenty-four states—and
the president's stand-in, Sen. Mark Hanna. Hanna drew even larger crowds
on an unauthorized mission in Nebraska and elsewhere, despite presidential
wishes otherwise. "I have taken South Dakota out of the doubtful column,"
Hanna told the *New York Times* in October, clearly relishing his enthusiastic
reception and correctly predicting that "Nebraska will go for McKinley."[18]

Other surrogates were summoned to campaign for the ticket by Sen. Nathan
Scott of West Virginia, chairman of the GOP national speakers committee.
White, ever faithful to his mentor, later recalled canvassing "seven different
states" for McKinley in the fall, visiting the president's home state of Ohio for
several speeches in September, probably with ex-senator John Green.[19] But he
did so with a heavy heart, after back-to-back losses at home and in Indiana, and
following a pair of public outbursts that frayed his once-strong relationship
with his party and its leadership.

❧

The first setback was the significant victory on August 1 of North Carolina's
constitutional amendment; White and other black leaders were astounded

by the sheer ease of its ratification, even if tainted by obvious miscounting. Disappointingly, nearly 60 percent of North Carolina voters approved the amendment's language, by a vote of 182,217 to 128,285. It would not take effect until 1902, however, and many Republicans—Pritchard included—still hoped a successful court battle would prevent it from taking effect at all.

Voters in sixty-six of the state's ninety-seven counties ratified the amendment. But all thirty-one counties voting against it were white-majority counties in the western and central regions; not a single black-majority county in the east voted against it. Butler, energetic organizer of the anti-amendment fusion forces, had for months pleaded with both Populist and Republican voters to turn out, but to little avail; Hertford County Populists reportedly "surrendered" to pressure in the last weeks and were afraid to go to the polls.[20]

Elections for governor and the General Assembly took place the same day, returning to the pre-1880 schedule of August over November. Outspoken white-supremacist Democrat Charles Aycock, now governor-elect, won an equally demoralizing victory that same day over lackluster fusion candidate Spencer Adams. Aycock's tally outran the amendment by four thousand votes. Meanwhile, Republican representation in the General Assembly dropped to its lowest level in decades, 30 of 170 seats—a mirror image of the 1896 outcome, when Democrats had been similarly decimated. For the first time since 1868, when blacks regained the vote in North Carolina, not a single black legislator was elected to either house.

Democratic Party strategists indeed pulled out all the stops to ensure a victory; accordingly, much of the vote counting took place out of public view. The reappearance of 1898's "Red Shirts" at rallies and on Election Day intimidated many black voters into staying away from polls entirely, although ballots cast by those blacks who did turn out took on an unmistakably fraudulent tinge in their counting—with heavily black precincts and counties joining the Democratic sweep, sometimes exceeding the total registration levels of both races. So despite widespread suspicions of ballot-box stuffing, even black-majority counties produced seemingly healthy majorities in favor of disfranchisement. Heavily Republican and majority-black New Hanover County, still healing its wounds from 1898 violence, produced just two votes against the amendment.

Stunned by the outcome, White brooded for weeks before publicly announcing his retirement from politics, a statement immediately published by mainstream dailies in New York and Washington, D.C. Convinced no Republican could now be elected in his district, he announced plans to step down when his term ended. His family's welfare was a major reason; his wife's health "has been wrecked on account of the maliciousness of the political attacks made on me," and he could not earn enough to care for her or his children as a private citizen in North Carolina. "I cannot live in North Carolina and be a man, and be treated as a man," he told the *Washington Evening Star*. "I expect to practice law in New York, and if not there, then I will locate in some state up this way."[21]

"I am afraid it will be a long time before there is another colored man in Congress," he added, "and I think it is a shameful condition that one-eighth of our population should be denied a representation in the person of some member of their race." Still, he planned to keep his home in North Carolina "until the constitutionality of the election law has been tested in the courts. The new law does not go into effect until 1902, but it is a duplicate in most respects of the Louisiana law, and I have been retained as counsel to test that law, and after the coming elections a case will be made out, and it will be carried through the courts."[22]

But he made a startling new prediction—that others would follow his lead in moving away from North Carolina. The new constitutional amendment, if allowed to stand, would cause the state to "lose 50,000 colored people in the next eight or ten years. You must remember this restrictive measure against the negro is not really political," he said. "The political part of it is a mere subterfuge, and is a means for the general degradation of the negro." He envisioned and encouraged "the immigration of the negroes of North Carolina to the west and north, but especially to the west," adding:

> I do not want to see them colonized anywhere, for that would result in a repetition of what has taken place in North Carolina and the south generally. I think they should lose themselves among the people of the country. A few families should settle here and a few there. Then their children will be better educated.
>
> But the bulk of the colored people must of necessity remain in the south. . . . [T]his plan of immigration will not only benefit those who leave the south, but those who remain there as well. This immigration should be systematic. . . . There should be no wholesale removal.[23]

White was discouraged about the political status of black voters, who should no longer expect "relief" from "any political party. He must paddle his own canoe and act for himself. Legislation will not help him." Expounding on this, he began what would become a flood of ever-sharper attacks on North Carolina's Republican leaders, specifically Pritchard, for betraying and abandoning black members: "The fact is, the white republicans of North Carolina are republicans in order to get the negro vote to maintain them in office, but they do not want the negroes to hold office."[24]

Pritchard had made that perfectly clear in May, telling the state convention "that the white people pretended not to want the negro in office." Furthermore, as he had explained, "the supreme court of the state has said that the legislature has power to pass legislation for local government, giving to certain classes the right to hold office, and Senator Pritchard . . . said that if the democrats meant what they said about preventing negroes from holding office, he would join them in passing through the joint assembly legislation placing those counties in which colored people are in the majority under white control."[25]

In other words, North Carolina's black voters could no longer trust their state's Republican leaders to represent their best interests and no longer owed any allegiance to Pritchard or party elders. White still believed the national party had the best interests of black Americans at heart, but he argued that North Carolina's Republican leadership had essentially forfeited any right to black loyalty—once the great majority of the party, soon to be a tiny minority once disfranchisement became official. It was by far the longest public statement White had given to the press since his political career began twenty years earlier, and his candor must have startled party leaders, whom he neither consulted nor warned.

Once he read the interview, the ever-practical Jeter Pritchard may have attempted to reason with White, but without luck. White, on his way to Indianapolis for the annual NAAC meeting, was keeping a low profile. If national Republican leaders expected him to return to the party fold now that his anger and frustration were vented, they were in for disappointment. Less than a week later, as White prepared to address the NAAC before his expected election as its president, his attacks on the party and Pritchard entered a new, sharper phase, as the two men's paths crossed again, unexpectedly, in the Midwest.

12

REELECTING A PRESIDENT

If that man is allowed to speak at this convention, it will be over my persistent protest. I am no pet of Senator Pritchard's. . . . I have quietly borne enough from him already without being forced to sit patiently and hear him.
—**George H. White**, Indianapolis, August 30, 1900

What George White did not know until it actually happened—and what few others except Bishop Walters seemed to know as the Council's meeting convened—was that Walters had intentionally invited Senator Pritchard to address the Indianapolis conclave. The Executive Committee authorized him to invite any speaker he wished, and he wanted "fair and impartial discussion" of one topic in particular: disfranchisement of black southern voters. To that end, Walters extended confidential invitations to "two prominent men of both parties . . . to express their views."

Their subject was "Why the Negro Should Not Be Disfranchised."[1] Former West Virginia governor William MacCorkle, a Democrat, never appeared, but Pritchard did so eagerly. White exploded at the mention of Pritchard's name, according to the *Indianapolis Sentinel*'s account: "In scathing terms he denounced Senator Pritchard . . . [who had] no right to come before the Afro-American Council" after publicly allying himself with Democratic control of predominantly black counties in North Carolina, "and for him now to express opposition to the disfranchisement of the negro in the southern states would amount to little more than dry rot."[2]

Pritchard was due at any moment, so some delegates quickly demanded a committee meet him at the railroad station to ask whether he had made such statements—and presumably cancel his invitation to speak if he said yes. Register Lyons pleaded, diplomatically, with White to withdraw charges against Pritchard and allow him to speak, but White refused. "No sir," he told Lyons. "If that man is allowed to speak at this convention, it will be over my persistent protest. I am no pet of Senator Pritchard's, and in no manner under his domination. I have quietly borne enough from him already without being forced to sit patiently and hear him exploit his opinions upon negro disfranchisement, when he contributed to bringing about the present existing conditions of the race in North Carolina."[3]

White seemed not to care how personally dangerous such a course might be. But by disregarding the president's clear affection for Pritchard—a close adviser, once described by the *Washington Evening Star* as "one of the President's closest friends"—the nation's only African American congressman risked a larger break than simply with his own party in his home state. Whatever else happened, Pritchard's term continued until 1903, and the pragmatic senator—once considered for a cabinet post—was not the kind of political ally an ex-congressman needed to alienate. There were always possible consequences to weigh—yet White rashly plunged ahead, ignoring all warning signals.[4]

Only the noon recess prevented the Council session from descending into complete pandemonium. During the afternoon, Pritchard addressed the Council without major incident, with remarks generally well received, except by White, who did not attend, and by Democratic Council members, including former U.S. minister Milton Turner, who questioned the appropriateness of partisan speeches at a nonpartisan venue.

Pritchard's speech dealt with disfranchisement primarily by attacking Democrats. "It is amusing to hear our Democratic friends talk about the 'consent of the governed,' in view of their performance in North Carolina, South Carolina, Louisiana, Mississippi and other Southern States, wherein . . . they have denied the colored men the rights that are guaranteed him by the fifteenth amendment," he was quoted in the *Indianapolis Journal*. "If we have so much solicitude for [Cubans and Filipinos], who are so remote from us, in the name of common sense, isn't it proper that we should care for those who were born and reared among us? Can we consistently deprive them of the liberty which they have enjoyed for thirty years?"[5]

In the *Indianapolis Sentinel*'s competing summary, Pritchard added, "The white people of the country needed the black people," and that "the Democrats of the South, who were the only political class that has disfranchised the negroes, were flying in the face of their best good." Democratic fear of so-called "Negro domination" was "a shadowy thing," in Pritchard's words, for Republicans had never opposed black officeholding or political equality: "The blessings the black man enjoys came from the Republican party."[6]

He did not explicitly address White's grounds for objecting to his speech—alleged cooperation with Democrats to block black officeholding—but approached the issue indirectly, by declaring that "Negro domination could not prevail in North Carolina, for under the organic laws of that state, legislation could be had in any election district in the state that would prevent the negro from holding office."[7] The state's supreme court had upheld past legislative actions allowing the appointment of local officials, leaving no legal basis on which to challenge it; politically speaking, Republican legislators were powerless to block such a law. But it was a double-edged sword, as Pritchard knew, depending on who controlled the legislature; the supreme court's ruling had actually upheld an 1897 Republican act empowering the governor to appoint additional members of Wilmington's city council and secure a Republican majority.[8]

Not all of Pritchard's remarks were cordially received, such as his suggestion that "negroes ought to rid themselves of the members of their race who commit outrageous crimes," reported the *Journal.* He was nonetheless warmly applauded and congratulated after his speech, yet almost immediately "made haste to leave the hall," taking no questions—doubtless wishing to avoid sitting through Democratic responses.[9]

Ex-minister Milton Turner replaced MacCorkle, railing against the strong partisanship of Pritchard's address and questioning why Pritchard had been invited to speak on the subject at all, when White, a Council member, had equal expertise on the disfranchisement issue. Turner gleefully pointed out an inconvenient historical truth: that Congress had authorized the first disfranchisement of black voters. In the early 1870s, Republicans voted to end home rule in the District of Columbia by creating an appointed commission—named by presidents, still governing decades later—to prevent black voters from electing blacks to its city council.[10]

With that, the Pritchard episode was over, for now. White's vigorous protest drew unexpected national attention, perhaps less helpful than desired. His hopes to be elected NAAC president ended when the Executive Committee's list of official nominees was released, with Walters the only nominee for president. Confusion reigned as an attempt was made to substitute White's name for that of Walters; White addressed the delegates, withdrew his name from consideration, and now publicly accused Walters of duplicity.

Walters had approached him months ago, saying he wanted White to replace him as Council head "at a time when I did not want it," the *Indianapolis*

Journal reported. He had agreed, reluctantly, "to the use of my name for the place. But I dislike duplicity, whether practiced by a ward politician or by a bishop," wrote the *Indianapolis Sentinel*. Walters followed White onto the podium, explaining his change of heart: his brother bishops had recently reconsidered previous objections to his devoting so much time to unpaid Council duties and explicitly asked him to run again.[11]

In the end, Walters was reelected, and White left the Executive Committee, indignantly discarding his ranking vice presidency. He would remain active in the NAAC, continuing as a legal adviser in the lawsuit against Louisiana's "grandfather clause" clause and serving as president of the District of Columbia chapter, the largest in the nation. But the rift between White and Walters and the NAAC's leadership, much like that between White and Pritchard, widened as the national election drew nearer. What effect it might have on McKinley's campaign—and enthusiasm among black Republican voters for a second endorsement—remained to be seen.

Despite a growing number of African American Democrats in large northeastern and midwestern cities, the vast majority of black voters remained aligned with the GOP. And despite vocal dissatisfaction with Roosevelt's vice-presidential candidacy, the issue of endorsing the Republican ticket was a question of when, not if. Among the few nonpartisan black groups, the NAAC had steadfastly declined so far to endorse McKinley's reelection, wishing not to alienate its minority of valuable Democratic members, including Fred McGhee and Turner. The National Afro-American Press Association (NAAPA), meeting in Indianapolis that same week, pleaded its own nonpartisan nature in refusing to adopt a resolution favorable to McKinley, construed as "bringing politics into the organization."[12] Individuals in either group remained free to endorse any candidate, so long as they did not claim to speak for all.

By the end of September, McKinley's campaign gained two key endorsements from African American leaders, including twenty-three NAAPA members—80 percent of those at the meeting—who endorsed McKinley on August 27, one day after the group officially distanced itself from the administration. "The undersigned members . . . unreservedly indorse the foreign and domestic policy of the National Republican administration and believe that the best interests of the country at large, and the Afro-American people in particular, will be served by a consistent support of McKinley and Roosevelt in the coming election," read the statement.[13]

Signers included full-time journalists from public newspapers and religious journals, as well as correspondents and "stringers"—patronage appointees and one college president. Among signers were T. Thomas Fortune (*New York Age*), Cyrus Adams (*Chicago Appeal*), Indianapolis editors George Knox (*Freeman*) and George Stewart (*Recorder*), John Wheeler (*Saint Louis Palladium*), and John Adams (*Saint Paul [MN] Appeal*).[14] College president Richard Wright of Savannah represented his *College Journal*, flanked by religious editors Isaiah Scott (*South-West Christian Advocate*), Hightower Kealing (*AME Church Review*), and William Steward (*American Baptist*).[15]

Not surprisingly, many signers were also active NAAC members, in Indianapolis primarily for that meeting; White, representing the *True Reformer* of Littleton, North Carolina, was last on the list. The two groups, already nearly indistinguishable in the public mind, had pledged to remain officially nonpartisan but struggled at times to maintain separateness and neutrality. Past Council officers, like Fortune and White, joined seven other newcomers: Adams, Pledger (*Atlanta [GA] Age*), Scott, Steward, Wheeler, Lillian Fox (*Kosciusko [MS] Preacher-Safeguard*), and John Marshall (*Paducah [KY] Bee*).[16]

In mid-October, fifty Council members signed an almost identically worded endorsement of McKinley, one now led by Bishop Walters and eleven other officers, including some from the Press Association endorsement. Published by the *Saint Paul Appeal*, the statement added one sentence to that the journalists had signed six weeks earlier, noting, "This is not action of the Council per se." First among signers was Walters, followed by four vice presidents—Pledger, Mrs. Fox, Ernest Lyon, and Bishop George Clinton—and other leaders.[17]

White no longer represented the NAAC, having relinquished his office, although his dedication to the campaign was duly noted by the *Washington Bee* and *Colored American*. His feud with Pritchard and party leaders in North Carolina intensifying, he now made a complete break with what he described as "the 'Lily White Republicans' in the late State Convention at Raleigh, where the Negro was almost entirely ignored."[18]

In an open letter to the party's Executive Committee and Second District voters, reprinted by newspapers in October, White called himself "a Republican of the Grant and Lincoln stripe, and shall do all I can for the reelection of President McKinley, but I have lost all faith in the 'Office Deep and Dollar Wide' so-called Republicans that we have at the head of affairs in our State at this time." Disavowing such leadership, he cited lack of "hearty cooperation from many of the white Republicans in North Carolina" as a major reason for retiring from Congress.[19]

His break with the state party came as a turbulent year ended for White, who blamed Pritchard for one major patronage betrayal: failure to help White appoint enumerators for the 1900 census: "My recommendations for appointment of Enumerators were ignored by the advice and direction of Senator Pritchard; and Democrats and a few Republicans appointed instead. So far as I know, there was not a single colored Enumerator appointed in my District ... [or] anywhere in the State of North Carolina." But for complicity, White singled out State Chairman Alfred Holton, Wiley Shook, Hiram Grant, and "others of their stripe [who] would vote with the Democrats to pass legislation which would eliminate and entirely disfranchises the Negro from holding office in any county in the State where our race is in the majority."[20]

Just weeks before the election, White essentially abandoned his state's Republican Party, including the ill-fated congressional candidacy of Tarboro postmaster Joseph Martin, whose appointment White had once recommended to McKinley. The ex-congressman, a respected and popular figure, was the first white Republican nominated by the Second District in two decades.[21] Named September 14 by district leaders, Martin was "probably the best man in the party," said the *Tarboro Southerner*, but a weak campaigner, with no chance of defeating Democrat Claude Kitchin, brother of one congressman and son of another.[22]

The general election outcome was foreordained. Kitchin swamped Martin by almost two to one, carrying every district county, even Martin's Edgecombe home. In 1896, White polled 19,000 votes in a three-way race, winning by 52 percent; four years later, Martin polled fewer than 13,000 votes, to Kitchin's 22,000-plus. Martin trailed McKinley across the district, but even the president's statewide total—roughly 46 percent of a smaller turnout—declined from 1896. In New Hanover, once the bastion of statewide Republican strength, just 60 Republican ballots were counted for McKinley—compared to more than 3,000 four years earlier.

Losing North Carolina—and the rest of the South—was disappointing for the McKinley-Roosevelt ticket, but nationwide results were more gratifying. In his rematch with Bryan, McKinley increased both his popular and electoral votes convincingly over 1896, as the first president reelected since 1872. His party, meanwhile, increased majorities in both houses of Congress. With a new, energetic vice president and a more agreeable Congress to deal with, McKinley's second-term future seemed limitless.

For black Americans, however, the McKinley-Roosevelt victory was bittersweet. In North Carolina, 1900 was the last statewide election for decades in which black voters played an important role. In 1896, about 87 percent of registered black voters had turned out to elect Republican candidates: White, Governor Russell, and a Republican-Populist fusionist legislature with a dozen black members. In 1900, there were no victories to celebrate. How many black voters braved "Red Shirt" intimidation to turn out is not clear—perhaps half as many as in 1896—but almost-implausible totals won by Kitchin and Democratic candidates in predominantly black counties like Warren and Halifax showed a discounted value to even those votes cast.

Martin was stoic about his loss, though not pessimistic, and rapidly began planning to challenge Second District results when the Fifty-Seventh Congress convened in 1901, basing his case on fraudulent counting of ballots in reliably Republican Halifax, where Kitchin received more votes than any victorious Republican, even White, ever tallied; and Warren, where Martin received 43 percent in a county that had not elected a Democrat to Congress in twenty years. But Martin's congressional contest never occurred.

Just a month later, with the final session of the Fifty-Sixth Congress barely under way, the candidate died unexpectedly on December 18.[23] As a thoughtful leader and trusted party man, Martin was widely mourned, and sorely missed, across the Second District. As a political ally and mentor, Martin would also be missed by White, who returned to Washington for the final session of his congressional career amid sober reflection.

The outgoing congressman had burned almost all his political bridges already. His once-strong alliance with Pritchard lay in ruins, his relationship with the state party was shredded, and plans for a court test of the constitutional amendment uncertain. His hope to use the NAAC as a springboard to prominence as a spokesman for disfranchisement and lynching had vanished.

Another mentor whose advice he would miss was Rep. Alfred Harmer of Pennsylvania, who died the previous March. On December 8, 1900, White offered a heartfelt eulogy to Harmer on the House floor, extolling "one of [the nation's] oldest and wisest counselors and lawmakers" as "grand, useful, noble, in every instance, and in every purpose, strictly honest."[24] White had a strong relationship with the older Republican, a veteran with whom he had recently served on the House District of Columbia Committee.

What was next for the crusading congressman? Accustomed to his steady salary in Congress of five thousand dollars per year, he hoped to establish a reasonably lucrative law practice in Washington, but the city was already saturated with black attorneys. So only a secure federal job with a steady income could allow his family to live comfortably in their expensive new home. Determined to salvage his languishing relationship with McKinley, he sent the president a hopeful, congratulatory message after the election, to which the president responded briefly November 12, thanking him for his "kindly comments and good wishes" without encouragement.[25]

Hoping to build a new future on that foundation—perhaps an important patronage appointment—White struggled to keep his name in the president's mind. But he had competitors. McKinley, ever mindful of patronage for black applicants, held general meetings with adviser Bishop Arnett on December 20, and with Bishop Walters. According to the *Evening Star* account of Arnett's meeting ("Positions for Colored Men"), no high-level vacancies were anticipated; "it is generally understood that there will be no changes among the prominent colored men in office," specifically Henry Cheatham and Judson Lyons.[26]

The president also spent time with his longtime friend John Roy Lynch, now an U.S. Army paymaster, now stationed in Cuba, as Major Lynch passed through Washington on his way home to Illinois for a brief December vacation. He reported primarily on Cuban conditions, including impressions of popular sentiments toward the United States, although McKinley surely welcomed his take on domestic issues.[27]

After his extended absence from the White House, White paid two visits to McKinley in the last week of December alone: once for a private meeting on Christmas Eve, and again on New Year's Eve, on official business: choosing a successor to Martin as Tarboro's postmaster. His choice? None other than the late candidate's widow.

McKinley, gracious as ever, agreed to Victoria Martin's appointment and took action on White's final postal recommendation of 1900 just after the New Year dawned.[28] Mrs. Martin held that post for nearly a decade, in a silent courtesy extended by White's Democratic successor, long after White left Congress and North Carolina behind.[29]

1901

13

LEAVING THE NATIONAL STAGE

> I want to submit a brief recipe for the solution of the so-called American Negro
> problem. He asks no special favors, but simply demands that he be given the
> same chance for existence, for earning a livelihood.... Treat him as a man.
> —**George H. White**, U.S. House, January 29, 1901

The political winter of 1900–1901 was not satisfying politically for George White. His antilynching bill was trapped in the House Judiciary Committee, and he was frustrated by technical circumstances blocking him from addressing the House on disfranchisement and proposed reduction of southern representation. Republican leaders limited debate on the Crumpacker amendment to reapportionment bills and related resolutions to selected speakers, denying White an opportunity to address the issue at length. But some observers interpreted his silence as proof of poor performance.

Not everyone in his own race understood the reasons for White's tangible frustration, although observers like George Knox praised him for tenaciousness. Others, like the *Cleveland Gazette,* assumed he had failed to act decisively. In early January, the *Gazette* sarcastically ridiculed White's silence: "Our 'great' and only Congressman ... was conspicuously absent from all debate on the resolution and bills. It was a grand opportunity for him to show that he is really true and loyal to himself and his race. With the exception of Mr. Crumpacker, there seemed to be none to plead for justice."[1]

Harry Smith did not represent the mainstream view and drew a sharp response from the *Colored American,* a perennial sparring partner. Edward Cooper called the former Ohio state legislator "grossly ignorant of parliamentary usage" and obviously misinformed about White, who had repeatedly sought permission to speak but "was pushed aside" by party leaders afraid of alienating southern Democrats if White spoke.[2] In fact, White *had* spoken—just not specifically to this point: recognized by the Speaker for his brief statement January 8 under one condition, that he not refer to the bill. He circumvented that pledge with a backdoor ploy: he had "sought diligently on both sides of this House to get an opportunity to be heard during general debate on this measure" and "thought it rather strange that the gentlemen managing the two sides of this question . . . might have accorded me an opportunity to defend [my people]. God bless Judge Crumpacker, who . . . has said in a word in defense of those people who have . . . since their emancipation served their country faithfully."[3]

Uncharacteristically sheepish, Smith soon retracted his errors by blaming "imperfect reports sent local daily newspapers" by others. "We owe Mr. White an apology and take pleasure in making it," Smith editorialized January 19. "He is a man of exceptional ability and we believe a loyal Afro-American. It should be a matter of regret . . . that he is not to be a member of the next congress. The great need of his presence there will make us miss him all the more."[4] White, busy preparing his final speech to the House, said nothing.

A fortnight later, White confounded his critics with the most stirring speech of his career, returning to the House floor for his "farewell address," as it has since been labeled. His hour-long speech on January 29 featured a stirring defense of his race and their patient efforts to show themselves as deserving full rights of citizenship. "I want to enter a plea for the colored man, the colored woman, the colored boy and the colored girl of this country," he said. "The new man, the slave who has grown out of the ashes of thirty-five years ago, is inducted into the political and social system, cast into the arena of manhood where he . . . is put upon trial to test his ability to be counted worthy of freedom, worthy of the elective franchise." Now, "under conditions but little removed from slavery, he asks a fair and just judgment . . . that he might demonstrate the truth of 'the fatherhood of God and the brotherhood of man.'"[5]

But his speech had more than one purpose: he vented frustration at failing to accomplish all he had hoped before leaving Congress. His attempt to protect his race from lynching had been blocked, even though "the arena of the lyncher no longer is confined to Southern climes, but is stretching its hydra head over all parts of the Union." Still, he had hope. "I want to submit a brief recipe for the solution of the so-called American Negro problem. He asks no special favors, but simply demands that he be given the same chance for existence, for earning a livelihood, for raising himself in the scales of manhood and womanhood that are accorded to kindred nationalities. Treat him as a man," White begged the House.[6]

Much of his hour-long speech detailed the chronicle of black Americans' many advancements since emancipation. He described two bills he had introduced in this Congress—the antilynching bill and another reimbursing depositors in the failed Freedmen's Savings and Trust Company—not brought up for votes. Congress should be especially ashamed of inaction on lynching. "It is needless to ask what the harvest will be. You may dodge this question now; you may defer it to a more seasonable day . . . [but] This evil, peculiar to America, yes, to the United States, must be met somehow, someday."[7]

"Obliterate race hatred, party prejudice, and help us to achieve nobler ends, greater results, and become more satisfactory citizens to our brothers in white," White asked. "These parting words are in behalf of an outraged, heart-broken, bruised, and bleeding, but God-fearing people, faithful, industrial, loyal people—rising people, full of potential force." He might not live to see his now-famous prophecy fulfilled—that black Americans would one day return to Congress—but he was certain of its truth. "This, Mr. Chairman, is perhaps the Negroes' temporary farewell to the American Congress; but let me say, Phoenix-like he will rise up some day and come again."[8]

White realized his passion and earnestness might be ridiculed, but he offered only one explanation and apology for it: "I am pleading for the life, the liberty, the future happiness, and manhood suffrage for one-eighth of the entire population of the United States."[9] The prophet's lengthy farewell speech was widely reprinted in both mainstream and black newspapers, enthusiastically applauded by almost all who heard it, and even "electrified the country," or so Knox's *Freeman* claimed. If consensus was less than universal, his eloquence had in fact moved many, including Republican Knox. "We hope that able members of Congress and their voices have been lifted up in elective appeal to the conscience of the nation," the *Freeman* wrote. "Mr. White has made himself heard, and he has compelled respect."[10]

What McKinley and GOP leaders thought of White's speech is not known; whether White even discussed his farewell speech with the president during their next few visits is unclear. But ten days after delivering his speech, White did return to the White House with one last postal patronage request: reappointing North Carolina's longest-serving postmistress on February 9. Mrs. Mary Green, a seventy-nine-year-old white widow, had run Warrenton's post office for three decades, first appointed by Johnson in April 1866 and reappointed periodically by every subsequent president from Grant to McKinley.[11]

On this issue, at least, the president agreed with White, and two weeks later, her nomination went to the Senate.[12]

Pleading Mrs. Green's case would mark White's final nomination during his congressional career, if not his final visit to the White House. Despite his increasingly strained relationship with Pritchard, he joined the senator and North Carolina office-seeker Oliver Dockery there two weeks later. On February 26, a week before the president's second inauguration, this meeting was described in a vivid gambling metaphor by the *Evening Star:*

"Mr. White, as already stated in The Star, is seeking some good appointment in the government service. Mr. Dockery, who has long been prominent in republican politics in North Carolina, wants to be a minister of this country," the correspondent wrote. Despite frequent presidential cautions that few new positions could be expected—at least "in the important and well-paying offices"—Dockery and White were both convinced "that there may be a shuffling of the political cards in the near future and, in the language of poker players, they hope to be drawn when the discard takes place."[13]

White's turn in the national spotlight was ending, with occasional omens of how life might be about to change for the nation's most famous black office-holder, after office. A case in point was a minor controversy associated with his service on the House District of Columbia Committee. A curious incident involving a private dinner honoring the District's three commissioners, hosted by another member of the District committee, was periodically reported by many black newspapers over the next few months. Some committee members allegedly refused to attend because White appeared on the guest list. First reported by the *Cleveland Gazette* in mid-February, the dinner was planned, postponed, rescheduled, and then canceled by retiring Representative Sprague of Massachusetts. Its title was "Color-Liners Not Invited": "Representative C. F. Sprague . . . will give a dinner on the 26th in place of the one for which invitations were recently withdrawn because of an unseemly wrangle over the impending presence of Representative George H. White, of North Carolina, the only Negro member of the House. The dinner was originally arranged in honor of the commissioners of the District of Columbia, and to meet them Mr. Sprague invited, with others, his colleagues on the district committee, among whom was Mr. White."[14]

At least one of the members—presumably a southern Democrat—must have informed Republican Sprague of the reason for refusal, leading him to

reschedule the dinner and revise the guest list: "To avoid a possible unpleasant experience Mr. Sprague recalled his invitations for that function, and now
the commissioners of the district will meet at dinner on the 26th inst., not the
members of the district committee in a body, but a number of members of the
House, which will include a portion of the committee membership, but not
those who failed to accept Mr. Sprague's first invitation."[15]

Reputedly the wealthiest single member of the House, Sprague had declined a third term in 1900; the Harvard Law graduate had served in the Massachusetts legislature before winning election to Congress in 1896. His dinner
would have been his farewell to Congress. But there is no indication as to who
attended the rescheduled dinner, or whether it was even held; a March *Colored
American* report indicates not. Overshadowing the scandal was a delicate com-
plication involving Sprague's health, declining rapidly; less than a year later, he
would die of a brain tumor or other related disorder, at a Rhode Island hospital.
His *New York Times* obituary cited "symptoms of brain trouble . . . before the
close of his term in the House of Representatives" but noted how he had been
"able to discharge his duties until his term expired."[16]

If the *Colored American* were aware of his condition, its editor gave no sign,
instead ridiculing the unfortunate Sprague for not holding the dinner even "if
only the commissioners, Mr. White and himself had been present. Mr. Sprague
has given the other members of the committee an opportunity of explaining it off and to make him look like thirteen cents."[17] Not well publicized in
mainstream newspapers, the incident was still an open secret and must have
dominated conversations in drawing rooms of the increasingly segregated city.
Regardless of circumstance, cancellation of Sprague's dinner was an embar-
rassment for all concerned, especially the very proud and very private White.

Almost lost in the swirl of events during the months of January was a singu-
lar victory for White: passage of his prized H.R. 10305, which established a
"home for aged and infirm colored people" by using funds long held in limbo
by the U.S. Treasury. The funds included unclaimed "moneys, arrears of pay,
and bounty which are due the estates of deceased colored soldiers who served
in the late civil war," once held by the Freedmen's Bureau but repaid into the
Treasury. White introduced that bill in December 1899, after the Fifty-Sixth

Congress convened, and the Committee on Military Affairs reported it out favorably.[18] The vote taken January 21, 1901, produced a margin of 135 to 59, authorizing $100,000 of the funds for constructing the home in the District of Columbia.[19]

It was White's most lasting legacy. As he noted in his farewell address a week later, the other bills he had hoped to pass in his second term had not been reported out of committee, a disappointing outcome for two worthy causes. But perhaps the most demoralizing political development at the end of the Fifty-Sixth Congress for White—and many Republicans determined to punish disfranchising southern states—was the Crumpacker amendment's defeat.

Despite Crumpacker's heroic efforts, aided by a core of outspoken comrades—including North Carolina's Romulus Linney—the amendment was never voted on by the full House. A related roll call only concerned whether to send the Hopkins bill—the census committee's proposal to retain the House size at 357, named for Illinois chairman Albert Hopkins—back to the committee and take up Crumpacker's controversial proposal to reduce congressional representation in Louisiana, Mississippi, North Carolina, and South Carolina, which had enacted constitutional provisions effectively disfranchising large numbers of voters.[20]

The debate was lengthy and tense. Democrats argued that the proposal was an unjust overreaction. One Alabama Democrat argued, remarkably, that the South could resolve the issue on its own, given another ten years and another census. In the end, although White and nearly one hundred Republican members of the House voted in favor of Crumpacker's plan, the Hopkins proposal prevailed, 136 to 94. Richmond Pearson, North Carolina Republican, actually voted against Crumpacker, declaring that reducing North Carolina's overall representation would damage Republican chances of winning any future House seats. Race prejudice in the South "is a concrete, an obdurate, and inexorable fact," he argued, and "will take a long time to disappear."[21]

Ironically, the Hopkins bill was then dropped, replaced by a more generous proposal from Maine's Edwin Burleigh, to expand the House to 386 members. Burleigh's plan increased the South's House contingent by eight new members, including one more for North Carolina; adding insult to Crumpacker's injury, the House rewarded disfranchisement instead of punishing it. Crumpacker found the southern situation intolerable, he told the *Baltimore Sun* in late January: "I believe that at present the average number of persons constitutionally entitled to the ballot in the South is reduced one-half. Yet the representation of those States in Congress is not reduced. In other words, with half the votes they have the same influence in the House and Electoral College as if they had the proper number of votes. That is not right."[22]

But the former judge understood his era's realpolitik, and his own losing battle: "Of course everyone knows that the Administration and the majority in Congress are favorably disposed toward the South," and this had always prevented efforts "to reduce southern representation." Lately, opponents of reduction "have become emboldened, because we have made no effort to enforce the Fourteenth and Fifteenth Amendments and believe they can carry on this work with impunity throughout other States." Only if Republican-dominated Maryland followed the examples of other disfranchising states, he warned, would Republicans unite to pass a reduction bill: "We may be driven to such a course as a matter of self-preservation."[23]

Just reelected to Congress in 1900, Crumpacker would serve another dozen years, and in 1903, became chairman of the census committee. His efforts to punish disfranchising states would continue, unsuccessfully, until he retired from Congress. In Maryland, disfranchisement efforts failed, perhaps in fear of the kind of political Armageddon Crumpacker predicted, although Georgia and Texas joined the group by denying votes to blacks before the 1910 census.

In February 1901, both White and Marion Butler were winding down their days in Congress. But just ahead of retirement, Butler joined Republican colleague Jeter Pritchard, with two years to go, in taking an almost unprecedented action: asking the Senate to block Butler's replacement, ex-congressman Furnifold Simmons, from being seated in the Fifty-Seventh Congress.[24] Their intervention had no chance of succeeding—the Fifty-Sixth Congress had no authority over its successor, and no real decision could be reached until that Congress convened in December, long after Butler was gone—but the formal request underscored the political animosity between victorious Democrats, controlling North Carolina almost completely, and demoralized opponents: the dying Populist party and their decimated Republican allies.

Senator-elect Simmons was anointed by the new Democratic-majority legislature in early January 1901. The new General Assembly was almost a mirror image of the 1895 legislature that had selected Butler and Pritchard, when Democrats formed only a quarrelsome minority. Unable to block that Fusion coalition from replacing Democratic senators Matt Ransom and Thomas Jarvis with a Populist and a Republican, Democrats regrouped in 1898 and 1900 to reclaim historical dominance in the General Assembly. Democrats now held a three-to-one advantage, with no black members in either house amid only a few powerless Republicans.

In 1895, Butler took the seat long held by Ransom, a four-term veteran first elected in 1872, and Senate president pro tempore during the Fifty-Third Congress. Pritchard won the seat held briefly by Jarvis, succeeding the late Zebulon Vance in 1894; in 1897, Pritchard was reelected for a full six-year term. The legislature elected in 1900 was overwhelmingly, exuberantly Democratic. Both Butler and Pritchard believed Simmons—a one-term congressman who helped direct white-supremacist victories in 1898 and 1900—was tainted by the legislature's all-white nature, underscoring the looming disfranchisement of black Republicans.

In North Carolina, the retirements from Congress on March 4 of White and Butler had been announced, with a rather unchivalrous sneer, from the floor of the state's General Assembly, by a Simmons ally, whose remarks were recorded for posterity by the *News and Observer*:

> Mr. Speaker, I rise to a question of the highest privilege. At this moment, Marion Butler, the renegade, is no longer Senator from North Carolina. Geo. H. White, the insolent Negro who has so long misrepresented the proud people of North Carolina in the Congress of the United States, has retired from office forever.
>
> We have a white man's government in every part of the old State, and from this good hour no negro will again disgrace the old State in the council chambers of the nation. For these mercies, thank God.[25]

According to the *News and Observer* columnist, "the people of the State have waited impatiently and watched anxiously for this to come to pass, and now that it has they are rejoicing with exceeding great joy. Even the Legislature, now in session, took a sort of semi-official notice of the passing of these two 'statesmen.'"[26]

Ignoring such indignities, White seemed unperturbed, announcing the establishment in the *Colored American* of his new law practice in the Capital Savings Bank Building on F Street, Northwest, just after leaving Congress. The ex-congressman "has entered upon the active practice of law ... and is making an excellent impression upon all the courts in which he appears. He invariably wins his cases by his tactful and finished methods, and is equal to the best counselors now before the District bar."[27] In addition, he maintained a busy speaking schedule. During February, he paid tribute to alma mater, Howard University, in a paper before the Bethel Literary and Historical Association. In the third week of March, the city's black leaders held his well-attended testimonial dinner at the Metropolitan AME Church, and he gave speeches to the Odd Fellows Lyceum, one of his own fraternal organizations, and the Pen and Pencil Club.[28]

Following the president's second inauguration in early March, White returned to the White House, this time as a private citizen, to meet with McKinley in mid-April, probably to discuss a possible appointment. But despite his best efforts to present a positive and confident image—especially to the White House—of a prospective appointee worthy of a high post, White soon touched off unfavorable publicity. His legendary temper again provoked him into public statements that resolved nothing and worked only to his disadvantage.

On March 4, 1901, McKinley was sworn into office for his second term before a crowd of forty thousand onlookers at the U.S. Capitol, again taking the oath from Chief Justice Fuller, and using a Bible provided by the Supreme Court's clerk. Two verses from the Old Testament book of Proverbs were noted: "The wise in heart shall be called prudent; and the sweetness of lips increases learning. Understanding is a wellspring of life unto him that hath it."[29]

For African Americans, the ceremony was impressive but failed to call attention to the president's African American supporters or issues important to them. Two events disappointed the race, one minor, one more substantive: McKinley did not use the same Bible as in 1897, so memorably provided him by Benjamin Arnett and fellow bishops. More significantly, his brief inaugural address dwelt almost entirely on international issues and did not refer, even indirectly, to civil rights issues of lynching or disfranchisement, as black leaders had hoped.

Still, within days of his inauguration, McKinley attempted to remedy any perceived oversights by meeting with high-ranking NAAC leaders, seeking to persuade him to increase opportunities for black soldiers in the reorganized U.S. Army—and to seek his assistance "to check the outrages perpetrated against black men and the disfranchisement of them in the south on account of their color."[30]

The delegation, led by NAAC president Bishop Walters, included a cross-section of formal and informal leadership, as well as Bishop Arnett and McKinley's best-known political appointees, Cheatham and Lyons, who had gone to Indianapolis. But for the first time since formation, the delegation did not include White, despite his announced inclusion; the former NAAC officer was absent March 6.[31] Half the members appointed by the Executive Committee, in fact, were absent. At least five out-of-staters—Fortune, Johnson, Lyon, Pledger, and Wells-Barnett, whose husband replaced her—had already returned home.[32]

Of more importance than numbers, however, was the gist of the formal address, reprinted in the *Evening Star*, highlighting both their purposes for existence and current goals:

> As representatives of the largest organization in existence which has for its objects the moral, industrial, financial and civil uplifting of the colored people of America, we come to pledge anew our loyalty to yourself and our grand old flag. . . .
>
> It is our cherished hope that the rights of the Afro-American citizens may not be allowed to suffer by reason of any indifference on your part, but that you will continue to use your potent influence to check the outrages perpetrated against black men and the disfranchisement of them in the south on account of their color. And since the colored seldom have made such a splendid record for bravery, discipline and loyalty in the revolutionary, civil, Spanish-American and Philippine wars we appeal to you, Mr. President, to give to Afro-American citizens in the reorganization of the army increase in representation and regular succession in the line of promotion of commissioned officers.[33]

NAAC officials ended their address by assuring McKinley "that everything within our power will be done to make our people good and capable citizens."

According to Walters's separate statement, "the President's response to their address was entirely satisfactory. . . . [H]e stated that he would appoint some colored officers in the new army."[34] Yet however encouraging the NAAC presence was to African Americans, an ominous cloud of racial antipathy was gathering over the White House that same day.

The possibility of future black appointees in the new McKinley administration was threatened by a Georgia congressman's "strong protest" over reappointing Monroe Morton, among that state's best-known African American officeholders, as Athens postmaster. Democratic Rep. William Howard reportedly told the president that "the opposition of the white people" to Morton's reappointment was now unanimous, unlike the situation four years earlier, when Morton assumed duty without incident.[35]

The wealthy black businessman and influential Republican leader had attended three national party conventions since 1884 and continued as a party delegate for years. But this public office would be his last; his expiring term as postmaster was not extended.

During the spring of 1901, McKinley continued meeting with influential black advisers, holding a lengthy conversation on April 13 with Judson Lyons and Henry Cheatham, each of whom was publicly announced for reappointment to a second term. Three days later, he held a meeting with now-ex-congressman White, whose name was described by the *Evening Star* as "still before the President for appointment as auditor or to some equally good position."[36]

Details of White's April 16 conversation with the president were never disclosed, but in a brief statement to the press afterward, he raised points doubtless already discussed with McKinley. "I have not decided yet what I shall do in the future," White told reporters. "Perhaps I may practice law in New York or Washington, as I have several offers. I shall not make up my mind, however, until after the constitutional amendment that disfranchises the Negro in North Carolina shall be finally passed upon by the courts. If it is decided to be constitutional I shall give up my residence in North Carolina."[37]

White said he could not "bring myself to live longer where I will be a man marked and persecuted for my color." He had just returned from Tarboro, once a Republican stronghold, where he now found "very few republicans left down there. Many of those who formerly voted the republican ticket have become democrats rather than suffer social ostracism or be shot down in their tracks." For the constitutional amendment, he had nothing but scorn; it was "not aimed alone at the illiterate and the vicious element of our race. It is framed to kill off the negroes who try to make something of themselves, those who try to enjoy the rights and privileges that our Constitution is supposed to guarantee to all law-abiding citizens, regardless of color."[38]

Circumstances now demanded he carry his continuing battle for civil rights and justice into a new arena, as a private citizen, although he still hoped for a federal patronage job. He held recommendations for a high-ranking job from almost every Republican member of the Fifty-Sixth Congress.[39] But others doubted that he deserved such a reward; the *Washington Post* openly scoffed editorially at his intention to stay in Washington, before predicting in a separate article that White would do almost anything to stay, including taking a low-ranking appointment.[40]

Famous for his thin skin and rash reactions, White unwisely took the bait. His sharply worded response to both articles in the *Post* was printed in full by that newspaper four days later.[41] He first noted the lack of context for his situation in either *Post* article. Having all but ignored him during four years in the House, the newspaper could hardly speak to changes in his situation or intentions. But the negative publicity he generated backfired, ending his chances of any quick appointment.

"Your editorial gives only one side of the question," he pointed out. If everything the editorial writer said might well have been true in 1897, when "I had not the remotest idea of changing my domicile from the State of my nativity," the current environment in North Carolina was "a very different state of affairs ... so far as the colored man is concerned." He offered the *Post* editorial staff a long-overdue academic lesson in what he called "moral philosophy," and for good measure, American race relations:

I have never seen where a people was called upon to commit a great national wrong that a small amount of good might follow to a certain class. I have also been taught that one of the cardinal principles for which our forefathers fought—I say "our," for the Negro was there—was that taxation and representation go hand in hand. ... I have been taught that of one flesh and blood God created all men, and endowed them with certain inalienable rights, among which are life, liberty, and the pursuit of happiness.[42]

In his mind, no one—not even the *Post*—could pretend basic principles were being "meted out to the Negro race in North Carolina, South Carolina, Mississippi, Louisiana, and other Southern States, under existing conditions." Current circumstances forced him to reside "where I can best care for my own household and do the most good for the race with which I am identified."[43]

Had he chosen to end his letter here, no one could fault White for resenting being told where he should or should not live. He had the right to choose that, and how he would earn his living after public office. But the remainder of his letter revealed his real reason for writing, in painfully explicit detail—inviting embarrassingly public discussion of expectations by ex-congressmen. The *Post* opened the can of worms by insisting that White should be "perfectly satisfied" to receive a salary of half his former income and should not expect to make more than that. But by discussing grubby details of income, he painted himself into a corner. The *Post* said White should lower his expectations and instead accept $2,500 a year as a deputy auditor. Why? "Just where your reporter got the information that I would be so easily contented with so small a position I am not advised. Why should I be 'satisfied' with a position of less dignity and salary than any other man situated as I am?"[44] His long record of unpaid service to the GOP and McKinley's campaigns since 1896 ("even at the cost of my own health in the canvass of seven different States last fall") proved he was as entitled as any former congressman to the auditor's slot.

And just in case the *Post* doubted it, he had "indorsements and recommendations from 189 Republican Members and Senators of the Fifty-sixth Congress, requesting that the President accord to me the recognition that I seek."[45] (That list, ironically, included Jeter Pritchard, White's former ally.) White offered to produce "strong letters from several chairmen of state Republican committees, including North Carolina, together with the national committeemen from that State, and from the chairman from the Second Congressional District, and other indorsements." Moreover,

I might be pardoned for here stating that in a letter to the President Senator Scott, chairman of the national speaker's committee in the last campaign (and he was in a better position to know than anyone else), stated that no speaker in that campaign did more to secure the election of Mr. McKinley than myself.[46] In concluding this statement, I will be pardoned for saying that I have the accord and good wishes of at least 90 percent of the 10,000,000 of Negroes in the United States, 90 percent of whom are Republicans, in the recognition that I seek.[47]

For all its facts and strong arguments, White's letter was easily subject to misinterpretation, for its undercurrents of wounded pride, personal vanity, and entitlement. What White had obviously *not* done was to consult party backers in preparing the letter, a classic case of hasty overreaction. A skilled attorney and experienced public servant, he was more qualified than most for the job he sought, but in an age when many politicians traded on influence to obtain well-salaried appointments, White now inadvertently emerged as the kind of person he most assuredly was not—a corrupt ex-official determined to stay on the public payroll—rather than the qualified man of unimpeachable integrity he most assuredly was.

Who might have encouraged White to write the letter? Several frequently unscrupulous journalists would gladly have goaded him into responding to the *Post's* impertinent jabs. Salary, after all, was of almost inestimable importance to African Americans as a measure of "manliness," according to frequent articles in the black press; how much a black man made at his government job was a favored yardstick of importance. At least six black weekly newspapers engaged in a lively discussion of the subject, including White's suitability for appointment, as the controversy neared its climax by early May.

In all likelihood, he acted purely on his own, consulting no one, for as was well known, White's impetuous statements needed little coaxing. His tendency to overreact to perceived slights—of major or minor importance—had in Indianapolis exploded in August 1900, when he attacked Pritchard for addressing the Council meeting, and Walters for inviting Pritchard and not stepping down. Had White sought counsel from wiser friends or party leaders—of either race—almost all would have advised him to ignore the *Post's* malicious slight. Those who knew him best might have begged him to step back and cool off.

Those who also knew McKinley reasonably well—particularly Henry Cheatham and Judson Lyons—were also aware of the president's weariness over relentless pressure for patronage appointments. He had already warned African American leaders to expect no changes at the highest levels in 1901, that the "top four" appointments of Cheatham, Lyons, and his ministers to Haiti and Liberia would remain in place, and the field would not expand.

Whether the president even saw the *Post* letter is not clear. Only days later, he and Mrs. McKinley left Washington for their long-planned trip to the western United States, not scheduled to return to the capital until late June. Despite at least one attempt by White, the two men never met again after the letter appeared—and despite White's admirable suitability and strong backing by party leaders, he never received any federal appointment.

Accustomed as he was to speaking his mind to friendly black audiences, White was less adept at grasping the possible repercussions of unfavorable publicity in the mainstream press. It was one thing to be attacked by hostile reactionaries and white-supremacist politicians for the color of his skin; in most cases, he stood to gain more sympathy by remaining an innocent victim, but he bristled at pity. Here, White intentionally pushed the envelope further than any black politician had ever done before—essentially by demanding equal pay and equal treatment by the president.

Now he found critics and defenders on both sides of the color line. Perennial letter-writer to the *Post* J. C. Cunningham openly ridiculed White's "manhood and common sense" for foolishly turning down the deputy auditorship. "Such positions don't come to a man of Mr. White's color every day," Cunningham scoffed. "It matters not what he did during the preceding national campaign. Some loyal white Republican will get the place that he thinks he is heir to," and blacks could expect only a poor consolation prize: "he will still remain with us and help us battle for our rights as American citizens."[48]

Chase chided White for refusing to go back to North Carolina, after musing snidely about both his personal wealth and motives. "Mr. White is the owner of 13 or 14 houses in North Carolina," sneered the *Bee.* "How did he accumulate so much property? Was he assisted by his people? If so, why does he want to leave them because he has some political misunderstanding with them. Is he looking out for himself?"[49]

Critics were countered by the *Colored American,* which defended White in a long editorial, "Mr. White is not a cheap man." He "cannot afford to accept any position that is not commensurate with his own dignity, and that of the people for whom he stands," Edward Cooper wrote April 27. "He is not in politics for a living, but with a good place as a leverage, he can be of more value to the race than in a purely private capacity." African Americans needed a leader "who is strong enough to decline the crumbs, and who insists on sitting at the first table or none." Days later, Cooper called White's letter "the statement of a man," which "went straight to the marrow of the situation." He "did not err in the exhibit of his political resources" but was "a man who knew his place . . . and knew that indorsements locked up in an official safe would grow cobwebs" and was "too valuable a man to be ignored when the honors are passed around."[50]

In Indianapolis, *Freeman* publisher George Knox reprinted much of White's letter with a carefully favorable comment: "Our last congressman should not put forward too much effort to secure an appointment. His services are known; he is known." Knox's crosstown rival, the Democratic *World,* took Knox to task for suggesting that White and others "remain humble at a certain kind of expense." Others gleefully joined in the journalistic fray, including the *Springfield (Ill.) State Capitol;* the *Charleston (S.C.) Messenger;* and, predictably, the *Cleveland Gazette,* always spoiling for a fight with Cooper.[51]

Almost lost in the free-for-all was the plight of White himself. Defenders and critics aside, and regardless of others' policy agendas, he had committed a faux pas with his rash letter. What White may not have known for sure—but should have guessed—was how intensely the president disliked unseemly publicity of this sort, and how easily such a public letter could be interpreted as a betrayal of their friendship and political relationship. Having met with McKinley on numerous occasions, he knew the president's view of politics well enough to understand that. In private conversations, perhaps such discussions could be tolerated and forgiven, but never on the printed public page.

So it was that White's quest for an audience with the president in May, after his return from his western tour, was politely rebuffed by McKinley's new secretary, George Cortelyou. Cortelyou acknowledged White's May 31 letter by return mail on June 1, calling the White House schedule so consumed by "the accumulation of public business during the President's absence from Washington" that no routine callers were being scheduled. "Under the circumstances I would suggest that you submit a written statement of the matter which you desire to bring to his notice," he wrote.

White's second letter, dated June 3, was a tacit admission of failure; he chose only to express personal sympathy for Mrs. McKinley's illness. "I have acquainted the President with your kindly message of sympathy which is very much appreciated," Cortelyou responded June 4.[52] McKinley and White shared a common domestic responsibility: helping care for beloved wives, and no one could have understood the sense of loving duty McKinley felt for Ida better than White, whose wife, Cora Lena, was recovering from the latest episode of a debilitating malady. The *Colored American* offered brief updates on her condition and improvements since early February; one, published the same week as White's letters to the White House, described her as "slowly improving from a long illness."[53]

Frustrated by his lack of success in reaching McKinley, White gamely resumed his own speaking schedule, leaving for a June 7 commencement address in Louisville, Kentucky. No text is available for his address at Eckstein Norton University, but a brief account in the *Louisville Courier-Journal* indicates characteristic optimism and a rousing response: "Ex-Congressman White's address covered the subject of the negro's development in a brilliant array of historical facts, entertaining stories, and striking opinions, all of which were punctuated by applause by the appreciative audience."[54]

White also continued to finish drafting the brief for what he hoped would prove to be his signature national case, soon to be filed in New Orleans. In *State ex rel. David J. Ryanes vs. Jerry M. Gleason, Registrar,* the five attorneys representing the NAAC planned to "test the validity of the Louisiana Constitution of 1898, made in violation of the Fourteenth and Fifteenth Amendments to the Constitution of the United States." The brief was filed July 12, 1901, in Civil District Court, Parish of Orleans, Division of Orleans, and in due course was heard by the Louisiana Supreme Court. Whether White joined fellow attorneys Albert Pillsbury, Arthur Birney, Armand Romain, and Fred McGhee for the actual filing in New Orleans is not known.[55]

White was increasingly involved in the planning process for what became a major land development scheme in southern New Jersey. Reported by both the *Washington Post* and *Colored American* in February, the Cape May County project involved establishing a "colony of Negroes who will live and work by themselves" on land purchased by the Afro-American Equitable Association, a consortium of citizens from nearby Cape May City led by the Rev. James

Fishburn. When George White became personally involved is not clear, but by August 1901, he was a major fundraiser behind final negotiations to purchase 1,400 acres of land on which the Association took its January option.[56]

There was more than enough on White's plate to keep him busy, if little that was regularly remunerative. His new law practice was not yet producing the revenue his family needed to live comfortably. Whether White might still salvage fading hopes for steady income from a federal appointment remained to be seen. Perhaps in the fall, when unfavorable publicity was forgotten, the president would revisit the issue. Only time would tell.

14

A PRESIDENT FOR ALL THE PEOPLE

What we want more than anything else, whether we be white or we be black—
what we want is to know how to do something well. If you will just learn
how to do one thing that is useful better than anybody else can
do that one thing, you will never be out of a job.
—**William McKinley,** Prairie View, Texas, May 10, 1901

Because both George White and William McKinley had major travels slated during the late spring and early summer of 1901, they were unlikely to meet again before the fall, the next time both were scheduled to be in Washington at the same time. White's hope for a more successful meeting regarding his appointment must therefore wait until September. By then, the president would return from his six-week train tour of southern and western states, culminating in Oregon, followed by a leisurely return swing along the northwestern and midwestern states to Buffalo ending in mid-June. After his major policy speech at the Pan-American Exposition—emphasizing hemispheric unity and outlining hopes for foreign policy achievements—McKinley would return to Washington only briefly, then spend the summer in Canton.

For the first time in five years, the now-former congressman would not spend his summer dealing with either campaign issues or legislative duties. Those months would instead be devoted to matters of more personal importance to White: planning for matters related to the NAAC annual meeting in Philadelphia in August and finalizing purchase of a large land parcel for his development in New Jersey. He would meet fellow lawyers in various locations, crafting the final version of the legal brief for the Council's planned lawsuit contesting legality of the new Louisiana constitution's disfranchisement provisions.[1] He would also spend time in New Jersey, near his company's development outside Cape May City. By September, he expected to reestablish himself as recognized leader of his race, this time as new president of the Council, with solid support for a lucrative federal appointment.

But both men's travels were altered by circumstances beyond either's control. By September, the president would still be in Canton, his Buffalo speech rescheduled by the nearly fatal illness of his wife, Ida, during their western trip. White's legal brief and business interests would go according to plan, but his hoped-for triumph in Philadelphia would be overshadowed by internal Council turbulence and negative publicity from two rivals for the NAAC presidency.

If and when the two men met again in the fall, what White had hoped for in the spring—a magnanimous gesture by the president to his loyal and patient supporter—was far less certain than he had once assumed. What had seemed a better than even bet in April, when his political reputation was fresh, was receding into the realm of barely even money as his political star dimmed.

The president's trip by special train to Texas and the West Coast was scheduled as his longest absence from Washington since 1897. The six-week trip included visits to Louisiana, Texas, and California, where he planned to launch the new battleship *Ohio* in San Francisco. Undertaken in a spirit of enthusiasm after his second inauguration, the trip was truncated by Mrs. McKinley's sudden illness.

The tour was to begin on April 29 and end in Buffalo on June 13, with a special celebration of President's Day at the Pan-American Exposition and a major policy address by McKinley. As envisioned by Cortelyou and other staff, the 10,500-mile trip crossed twenty-one states and two territories, easily the most ambitious tour ever planned for an American president.[2] The entourage aboard the specially equipped luxury train *Olympia* included forty-three officials, friends, staff, personal servants, and newspaper correspondents, along with McKinley's personal physician, Dr. Presley Rixey.[3]

McKinley wanted to take his entire cabinet with him, but only Postmaster General Charles Smith and Secretary of State John Hay were able to make the full trip; three other cabinet members joined the party at San Francisco.[4] If the president drew any criticism for the trip, it was over costs of the donated luxury train—some fifty thousand dollars—and use of funds donated by major businessmen. But surprisingly few observers quibbled about costs.

The first half of the trip was intended as a goodwill tour and vacation, not as a policy offensive or campaign-style tour; the president planned to speak at major stops but to give no important policy speeches until Buffalo. His attention focused largely on Republican core supporters in heavily Democratic states, particularly on African American voters who supported him enthusiastically in 1896 but dwindled by 1900 because of disfranchisement and Jim Crow–era oppression. So it was that during a two-day visit to New Orleans, the president greeted enthusiastic crowds and visited the campus of historically black Southern University, one of four local black colleges.

"The President desired to honor the colored people while here and so he visited the Southern University, where he was received with hearty demonstrations of good will by the colored officials, students, and people," wrote the *Washington Evening Star.* "He was touched by these evidences of the profound respect in which he is held by the negro race."[5] The huge crowd at Southern University, the city's only public college for black students, was indeed symbolic of black citizens' affection and admiration for McKinley. Black citizens and students affiliated with the city's three private black colleges also turned out to greet the president, in what resembled a public fair, full of energy and enthusiasm. The one ominous occurrence clouding his visit to the city was a possible assassination attempt, averted before McKinley's arrival by the temporary detention of a local pianist and songwriter, who was overheard predicting McKinley's death "by my hand" but was roundly dismissed as simply a crank.[6]

Next, his Texas itinerary featured major stops at Houston, Austin, San Antonio, El Paso, and an appearance at historically black Prairie View State Normal and Industrial College, northwest of Houston—a stop suggested by Judson Lyons and welcomed by school principal Edward Blackshear.[7] McKinley's Prairie View remarks were captured in print by the *Washington Bee,* after mentioning his visits to similar schools at Tuskegee, Savannah, and New Orleans: "It has given me great satisfaction to observe the advancement of your race since the immortal proclamation of liberty was made. The opportunity for learning is a great privilege. The possession of learning is an inestimable prize and I am glad to note that you are endeavoring wherever you live to enlighten your minds and prepare yourselves for the responsibility of citizenship under this free Government of yours."[8]

America's black citizens had always been "faithful to the Government of the United States. . . . true and patriotic and law-abiding," especially in the recent war, when black soldiers "displayed distinguished qualities of gallantry on more than one field. You were in the fight at El Caney and San Juan Hill, the brave black boys helping to emancipate the oppressed people of Cuba.... What we want more than anything else, whether we be white or we be black—what we want is to know how to do something well. If you will just learn how to do one thing that is useful better than anybody else can do that one thing, you will never be out of a job. And all employment is honorable employment. The race is moving on and has a promising future."[9]

During more recent service in the Philippines, black soldiers were "carrying the flag and they have carried it stainless in its honor and in its glory." In closing, he exhorted listeners to continue to be good citizens, true to the virtues he prized: "The last word I would leave with you is to be true to right, to home, to family, to yourselves, to your country and true to God."[10]

In Houston, thousands of black citizens cheered the president in a ceremonial parade, singing the national anthem and "Columbia, the Gem of the Ocean." Accompanied throughout Texas by Democratic Gov. Joseph Sayers and other dignitaries, the president also met the eighty-two-year-old widow of the last president of the Republic of Texas, Mrs. Anson Jones, who presented McKinley with a silk banner.[11]

The Texas tour abounded with pomp and circumstance, parades, and brief statements to the public at all stops. But it remained a low-key public relations tour, not a campaign swing—conceived as a vehicle for conveying the message that McKinley was truly "the president of the people," no longer just another politician. As a Republican president in Democratic territory, he hoped again to demonstrate that statement's truth by repeating the success of his 1898 tour of Old Confederate states, when he had visited two other black colleges.

McKinley's visit to El Paso was his last stop before departing for California, notable for two specific actions: one that he did not do, and one that he did. McKinley became the second U.S. president to approach the Mexican border. A decade earlier, then-president Benjamin Harrison had come close to entering Mexico on April 21, 1891, by viewing the bridge connecting the two countries.[12] But McKinley refused even to step onto the U.S. end of the bridge, instead meeting Mexican government representatives at Mexico's consulate in El Paso.

A hoped-for meeting with Mexican president Porfirio Diaz was replaced by one with his adviser General Juan Hernandez, and Chihuahua State governor Miguel Ahumada. McKinley pleaded a peculiar tradition that forbade presidents from leaving the country during their terms in office, but he expressed a wish to visit Mexico at a later date.[13] After explaining his caution, the president then offered a "powerful speech" to American citizens, with pointed references to the nation's political future.

As a self-styled "president of the people," McKinley exhorted listeners to transcend their political differences. He had explored this surprisingly bold, optimistic theme in his recent inaugural address—that sectionalism was an "old problem," one the nation's regions had moved beyond.[14] By acknowledging the diversity and unity of cosmopolitan El Paso, McKinley sought to "appeal to both the Democrats and the Republicans of Texas ... in a manner inoffensive to either party." Here "there are "men of all races, all nationalities, and all creeds ... united in their allegiance to their country." Their patriotism and willingness to sacrifice were unmistakable to the president, increasingly mindful of his legacy with his final campaign behind him. In New Orleans, Houston, and Prairie View, the president had appealed symbolically to his core base of Republicans—particularly black Republicans, still a significant portion of each state's party—but at El Paso, he carefully cultivated voters of both parties.[15]

He was joined at the speech by Mrs. McKinley, who did not accompany cabinet wives on their side trip into Juarez for breakfast with a distinguished Mexican banker. The precise state of her always-delicate health was not clear, but it was unraveling; by the time their train reached Los Angeles, she suffered from a near-fatal inflamed bone felon on her forefinger, which Dr. Rixey treated unsuccessfully. In Los Angeles, she developed a fever and complications, and in San Francisco, she collapsed from overexertion. There she was taken to a private residence, where her condition grew steadily worse and her heart began to fail.[16]

Only once the McKinleys were in San Francisco was the public alerted to the true nature of her dire condition; press announcements so far had been upbeat and low-key. But privately, plans were drawn up for her impending death and a funeral train to Washington, until a somewhat radical treatment—injecting salt intravenously, after other heart stimulants failed—revived her from a near-coma. The president was able to leave her bedside to view at least some of the official program. She grew stronger in the days ahead, but rather than risk a relapse, the president cut their trip short and returned to Washington in a near-record five days, arriving in the capital on May 30.

Due to uncertainty over Mrs. McKinley's condition, the president's trip to

Buffalo was canceled; Secretary of State Hay instead represented McKinley at the Pan-American Exposition in June, allowing the president to plan a longer vacation in Canton. Hay was reportedly among the prime proponents of a third term for McKinley; it was in Hay's absence, ironically, that the president publicly ended all speculation with a decisive, Sherman-esque refusal: "I not only am not and will not be a candidate for a third term, but would not accept a nomination for it if it were tendered me."[17]

Why he chose this moment can only be guessed at, but McKinley apparently longed to rise above partisan campaign demands and push, instead, new policy objectives as a statesman. McKinley was also well aware how close he had come to losing his wife in California and feared she would not recover completely by 1904. After her return, careful blood tests detected an acute case of endocarditis, or inflammation of the heart lining—perhaps exacerbated by treatment for her bone felon—requiring extended convalescence.[18] Perhaps the president himself was simply tired.

Or perhaps all three reasons coalesced. The trip to Canton began July 5, slated for three months, his longest absence ever from the White House. But one final holdover from the aborted western tour remained. According to Leech, McKinley "had never relinquished the idea of making his speech at the Pan-American Exposition," partly to support hopes for hemispheric unity and to further reciprocal trade agreements. After meeting in August with Buffalo representatives in Canton, the president decided to try once again. He already planned to attend the National Encampment of the Grand Army of the Republic in Cleveland in mid-September, and Buffalo could easily be added to that trip.

Pan-American President's Day was rescheduled for September 5, and the president readily agreed to attend. The speech in Buffalo—from which his wife's illness had spared him in June—received a second chance at life.

᠀

In Washington, White revisited his decision a year earlier to step down from the NAAC leadership. Embarrassing headlines and ill feelings spawned by his denunciation of Pritchard and Walters in Indianapolis, just before returning to Washington for the final session of the Fifty-Sixth Congress, had subsided. His subsequent retirement from Congress deprived him of any national platform for his own strategic agenda. Once again, Walters was rumored to be stepping down, and White's supporters, including George Knox, were urging him to run again; Knox vocally favored White's candidacy, describing him in the *Indianapolis Freeman* as "one of the most reliable and energetic leaders the race has today." Beyond Knox's endorsement, his impressive dedication to unpaid work on the *Ryanes* case on the Council's behalf also reinforced his image of committed service, useful if he did run again.[19]

"It doesn't matter half so much who is president," Knox said prudently, "as long as he is honest and capable," because the Council "is sound in principle, harmonious in action, and sincere in its efforts to live up to the standard marked out." That being said, Knox clearly preferred White, whom he envisioned as a "race pilot"—someone to "right about the Negro craft in America . . . a crying demand." Knox politely rejected Booker T. Washington, the man others might choose, because he was not a political leader but an educator; "if there is a leader at all, it is Mr. White," he wrote in March.[20]

White held useful credentials for the title; in July, he was reelected president of the District of Columbia NAAC chapter—the country's largest—and would represent the affiliated Second Baptist Lyceum in Philadelphia. His plans to develop New Jersey land into a utopian haven for southern blacks underscored commitments to social justice and fairness for African Americans plagued by segregation, reduced political influence, and lynch mobs.

Whether White could parlay such credentials into a leadership position in Philadelphia was uncertain and perhaps, in one respect, impractical. The question of salary for the NAAC presidency had never been resolved—Council revenues remained low—but White and the NAAC legislative bureau had raised sufficient funds for private attorney fees in the *Ryanes* case. White raised a small sum by speaking at Washington's Capital Pleasure Club in May and hoped to stimulate more donations.[21] Perhaps success in this project might inspire wealthy donors to stabilize a surging Council.

Others were actively recruiting Booker T. Washington as a *Ryanes* donor. Walters wrote Washington in late June at Fortune's insistence, explaining the urgency of more funding to pay Birney, who wanted five hundred dollars immediately, and seeking Washington's advice. Would Washington attend the Philadelphia meeting and help inspire others to donate funds? Pillsbury followed up in late July with a detailed update on the *Ryanes* case, just filed at the state level in New Orleans. He pointed out the likely need for a second, separate suit to challenge "the whole scheme of suffrage qualifications"—not just the grandfather clause itself but the inherent racial unfairness behind all such schemes—to avoid a Pyrrhic victory. If the court struck down the clause but did not allow illiterates to register, the large majority of black voters would be no better off.[22]

Striking down the grandfather clause was seen as the most likely outcome and "would be a 'sentimental victory, and may be all that is possible to accomplish," Pillsbury wrote. "Several of our most intelligent colored men here have said to me that they would be satisfied with this, as it would at least establish equality of right."[23] Washington supported the case but never responded and did not come to Philadelphia—in part because of his preoccupation with Alabama's complicated situation, where a new constitution was being drafted with ominous implications for black voters. Heading off the worst proposed changes required his diplomatic personal interventions, which might be weakened by identification with the Louisiana case.

As White headed to Philadelphia, he carefully maintained a low profile in the public press. But two more impetuous NAAC vice presidents—journalists and activists—were less mindful of the consequences of bold, widely reported pronouncements at a meeting preceding the NAAC conclave, and set the stage for a dramatic shift in its public image.

The NAAPA had long displayed a penchant for headlines, as in 1900, when Indianapolis delegates all but disavowed group support for McKinley and forced its members into public personal endorsements of the McKinley-Roosevelt ticket. William Pledger and T. Thomas Fortune, neither of whom had ever met a political issue that did not stimulate their contrarian instincts, both hit the speaker's podium with a vengeance in August.

The high-ranking NAAC officers made gleefully inflammatory statements before the press association calling for southern blacks to defend their families with rifles against lynch mobs and racial violence. Predictably, their comments were widely reprinted. Pledger said "the dollar and cold steel [are] the things the white man respects. Many of them are afraid to lynch us where they know the black man is standing behind the door with a Winchester," even when egged on by Sen. Benjamin Tillman and fire-eating white supremacists. Fortune carried the metaphor one step further. "We have cringed and crawled long enough," he told listeners. "I don't want any more 'good niggers.' I want 'bad niggers.' ... It is the bad nigger with a Winchester that can defend his home and children and wife."[24]

White declined to comment on or disavow either man's statements. With far less to lose, Henry Cheatham was less reticent, quickly telling the *Washington Post* he could not believe his ears; his colleagues must have been misquoted. Although no longer active in the Council, Cheatham wanted no part of such silliness; this advice was "dangerous and mischievous," and Cheatham roundly condemned it: "I cannot believe that such men as Pledger and Fortune, whom I know to be cool and considerate men, could in all seriousness give such dangerous and mischievous advice. I want to say emphatically that I want to have no part in the new doctrine of 'the bad nigger and the Winchester.'"[25]

Cheatham greatly deplored lynching, he told the *Post* August 7, but "inciting to crime to check one form of lawlessness" was no better than lawlessness itself. And more broadly, "the general arming of the negro" was counterproductive, "the very worst thing for the negro himself."[26] His sharp words fell on deaf ears, at least those of Fortune and Pledger, coming as they did from a McKinley appointee, out of step with the desired militancy of leaders ready to break ranks with the administration.

The annual session of the NAAC opened a day later, and the city's atmosphere crackled with tension as White arrived. Bishop Walters had assured him the previous week—during a meeting of religious leaders in New Jersey—that he would definitely not run again. This time, whatever happened, White would not back down from an open floor fight.

15

TWO CITIES, TWO PRESIDENCIES

Who can tell the new thoughts that have been awakened, the ambitions fired and the
high achievements that will be wrought through this exposition? . . . [L]et
us ever remember that our interest is in concord, not conflict.
—**William McKinley**, Buffalo, New York, September 5, 1901

As summer passed its midway point, the president and the prophet prepared
for respective turns in the limelight after a long vacation: confident, refreshed,
and full of energetic promise for the future. For George White, the NAAC
meeting would provide an opportunity to reclaim a major leadership role for
his race in his new postcongressional career, propelling him naturally into
a major appointment in the second McKinley administration. For William
McKinley, his triumphant appearance at the Pan-American Exposition in
Buffalo—a speech rescheduled from mid-June by his wife's near-fatal illness—
would afford historic opportunities to portray developing views on Western
Hemispheric unity and international economic policy and to emerge from
wartime leadership as a world statesman and guiding light for a brighter, more
peaceful future. Both could then return to Washington and the latest intersec-
tion of their political careers.

White had pinned all his hopes for a political future on winning the NAAC
presidency in Philadelphia. He clearly had felt betrayed a year earlier by
Bishop Walters, whose reelection in Indianapolis had upended NAAC equilibrium, but he had chosen not to force a floor fight he knew he would almost
certainly lose. His loss of that post in Indianapolis had disrupted long-term
plans, but it was not irretrievably damaging—although his impetuous outburst
in 1900 regarding his new nemesis, Jeter Pritchard, had done nothing to improve his image as a calm, strategic team player. It certainly had not strengthened his relationship with Walters, who had invited Pritchard to speak.

In Indianapolis, Walters had unexpectedly reneged on his promise to step
down, citing the unexpected reversal by his fellow AME Zion bishops of their

previous opposition to the amount of time he devoted to the NAAC's administration. This time, White believed—or strongly hoped—that Walters would keep his word. But this time he was taking no chances, having carefully nurtured support from a group of followers in case a floor fight materialized.

What forces were at work behind the scenes will never be completely explained. Journalistic coverage of Philadelphia's convention was minimal; local mainstream newspapers barely mentioned the gathering, and weekly black newspapers that did report on the outcome chose to play down turbulence during the August 9 plenary session. Only a handful of mainstream newspapers—the *Atlanta Constitution* and *Baltimore Sun*—and the *Philadelphia Record* paid significant attention to the session in a wire-service story, mostly highlighting a closing attack by AME Bishop Benjamin Tanner on the racist hypocrisy of U.S. Christian churches, and another screed by Chicago journalist Ferdinand Barnett against the federal government for denying promotions to black soldiers.

"The Church can strain her eyes to see anything but the equality of the negro," Bishop Tanner thundered in the account. "I lay at the door of the Christian churches every burden we have to bear. If it were in any way moved by Christian spirit all our battles and burdens would cease." Barnett vigorously denounced refusals by army officials to allow a mustered-out Spanish-American War volunteer from Illinois a chance at the entrance exam. The *Sun*'s provocative headline was barely accurate: "White Quits in a Huff: Ex-Congressman Doesn't Like Afro-American Methods." But the *Constitution*'s eye-catching headline—as long as the story over which it ran—relegated George White's latest angry outburst only to fine print: "Ex-Congressman White Attacks Bishop Walters."[1]

For maximum impact on the reader, the brief story opened with its most sensational news: "The closing session of the national Afro-American Council were held today and considerable excitement was occasioned by the resignation of ex-Congressman George H. White of North Carolina" as the Council's third vice president. White "did not want the position because of the methods pursued in the election, and arraigned Bishop Walters for accepting the presidency after his avowed intention not to be a candidate."[2]

Longer stories in the *Washington Bee,* among others, offered more colorful details, depicting White as telling horror-struck delegates after his defeat that "he could not sacrifice his manhood to longer remain in such an organization . . . as he took up his hat and was about to leave the convention." The ex-congressman relented only when "dozens of delegates got upon their knees and begged him not to go," citing two factors: "he had the interest of the race at heart and . . . he wanted to see the recent case that has been brought up from Louisiana pushed." Chase, who had longed feuded with NAAC leadership, offered a separate front-page article calling the convention "a farce" and predicting the Council's early demise.[3]

George Knox, loyal Republican editor of the *Indianapolis Freeman,* offered a more nuanced view of his friend's predicament: "If report is true the scene between Bishop Walters . . . and ex-Congressman White, which took place last year in Indianapolis, has been repeated at the Philadelphia meeting. . . . It seems that the presidential bee was not at all quiescent in the congressman's bonnet. The scene simply shifted; did not change." Knox was aware of White's "extreme provocation" at the developments, worrying aloud that White "has washed his hands of the whole business for all time" but hoping he would instead "act right along with the Council, in or out of office."[4] To Knox, White was too valuable a leader to lose.

The *Colored American* put its strongest spin on defeat, with Edward Cooper claiming that White "went out of the session a stronger man than at its opening. Some day [he] may yet, if he so desires, achieve his honorable ambition to be president of the Black congress," with as much support as Walters now held.[5] But not all onlookers agreed. From Cleveland, Harry Smith ridiculed White for his childish tantrum in resigning the third vice presidency. "We thought Cong. White too big a man to be so small over anything," Smith's *Gazette* sniped. "White has been carrying a 'sore spot' ever since a few weeks prior to the Indianapolis meeting of the Council over a year ago, because he could not get the presidency."[6]

Booker T. Washington probably agreed with his secretary, Emmett Scott, who summarized the convention news in a succinct letter from Houston, Texas: "Walters was re-elected. This brought on the only unpleasant feature of the convention. Geo. H. White was a candidate & was slaughtered, and I think for the best, as he only wanted to use it as a weapon to help him politically."[7] The situation was painfully clear to White; his options were dwindling. He could not afford to cut all ties with the NAAC and retain any credibility as a race leader; continuing to assist in the Louisiana disfranchisement case was an absolute necessity, if he played no other role. He remained president of his local Council chapter, reporting on the group's decisions and projects to the Second Baptist Lyceum in October. Though optimistic, his path forward was murky—as was how much support he retained among fellow blacks.

The Washington in which White regrouped was a city changed in his brief absence, at least in one respect. Republicans were abuzz over an astonishing prediction by incoming Republican freshman Rep. Spencer Blackburn of Winston for "a revolution in politics [that] is about to occur in North Carolina." After a Louisburg political meeting, Blackburn believed "the elimination of the negro question from politics in the north state will . . . result eventually in greatly added strength to the republican party there," primarily by drawing ex-Democrats across partisan divides. "Old-time prejudices must be laid aside and votes must be cast for party candidates standing upon platforms which conduce to the best interests of the community."

"It is certain," Blackburn declared, "that a great many men who have heretofore voted the democratic ticket will vote for the republican candidates" in 1902, perhaps giving his party control of the legislature. His optimistic assessment struck a responsive chord with Jeter Pritchard, whose reelection in 1903 would certainly require a seismic shift in the legislature but brought little joy to George White.[8]

Plans for President McKinley's speech at Buffalo were also being finalized that weekend by a delegation of city officials and Pan-American Exposition leaders, in Canton, Ohio, to meet with McKinley and advisers. "President's Day," postponed from June, would be a spectacular event, offering Americans the first chance to greet their elected leader since his appearance in California.[9]

McKinley had waited many months to deliver this speech. Its topic was of strong personal interest to him, intended to expound upon themes he hoped would guide his second term as president: hemispheric unity, befitting the chosen venue of the Pan-American Exposition, and his new cause of global free trade. In September, having nursed Ida McKinley back to health—as reasonable a state as seen in some time—the president and first lady set out from their Canton home aboard another special train for Buffalo.

Both the president and his wife were in rare form, with McKinley described by one Buffalo newspaper as "show[ing] the effect of his summer vacation at his old home in Canton and never looked better in his life. He is hale, hearty, and vigorous, has good color and appetite, and is in the full enjoyment of his strength." Mrs. McKinley appeared surprisingly energetic, and "her health is said to be better today than it has been in years," despite a mildly fatiguing train ride from Canton.[10] The exposition was billed as a grand celebration, essentially a world's fair to celebrate peacetime cultural and technological advancements. Originally scheduled years earlier, the exposition had been postponed by hostilities between the United States and Spain in 1898.

The president's speech to an enthusiastic crowd at Buffalo on September 5 offered an intriguing glimpse into the worldview of the world's newest "emperor," as McKinley had become—the world's first democratically elected overseer of a global empire, however paltry its physical possessions compared to its best-known recent Western predecessors, including the British, French, and Spanish, or the Ottoman Turks—or even to Romans, whose history every educated nineteenth-century schoolboy could recite. Yet McKinley had no desire to extend America's new empire beyond recently acquired Caribbean and Pacific isles—and may not even have wished to retain them beyond the short term.

Scattered over a half-mile-square island site just west of Buffalo, the fair's collection of popular displays featured such recent advancements as the X-ray machine and central "Electric Tower," drawing power from Niagara Falls twenty-five miles away. Citizens of Buffalo and fair promoters had smartly spared no expense to welcome the First Couple, including a 21-gun salute as McKinley's special train neared the fairgrounds on September 4. That artillery salute went slightly awry, its blasts shattering the train's windows and Mrs. McKinley's delicate nerves; not injured, she reportedly fainted, briefly, from shock of the concussion.[11] All shook off the odd omen quickly; the first lady continued with her husband to the events on their itinerary. They spent their first night at the closely guarded private residence of John Milburn, exposition president, under the watchful eyes of the Buffalo police and the Secret Service, as well as a small military unit from the Army Signal Corps assigned to him for fairground trips.

The crowd gathered to hear McKinley deliver his long-anticipated midmorning address on President's Day was huge—perhaps the largest of his career. No exact figures are available, but at least one newspaper account described overall attendance at the exposition that day as breaking all previous records—116,600, of whom 91,000 had entered by 3:00 p.m., at least 10,000 more than previous records. Almost all attendees on this date were from the

Buffalo area, according to the *Buffalo Courier,* and listeners hung on every word, cheering regularly and applauding vigorously.[12]

McKinley was well beloved in western New York, and the crowd awaiting his exposition appearance the next day was thrilled to hear him. His audience had every reason to cheer the message of peace and prosperity McKinley offered. The specter of war had long since faded from the public imagination, which now looked, instead, toward the unfolding of a new horizon unclouded by hostility or oppression. For it was not physical or political subjugation of any foreign peoples that McKinley envisioned, although he did believe, unlike some, that the United States was destined to play a continuing global role. For a moment, at least, the nation was committed to helping its new possessions become independent democratic successors to old colonial outposts.

This new world McKinley envisioned—with far more clarity than his comparatively provincial upbringing might have anticipated—was one in which the world's civilized nations worked in closer cooperation than ever before to benefit all mankind. It was no longer possible for Americans to live in isolation, with strictly nationalistic goals, for the world was suddenly shrinking, tangibly: "After all, how near one to the other is every part of the world. Modern inventions have brought into close relation widely separated peoples.... Geographic and political divisions will continue to exist, but distances have been effaced. Swift ships and swift trains are becoming cosmopolitan.... The world's products are exchanged as never before, and with increasing transportation facilities come increasing knowledge and larger trade.... We travel greater distances in a shorter space of time and with more ease than was ever dreamed of."[13]

McKinley was convinced the future demanded international cooperation between like-minded democracies. "No nation can any longer be indifferent to any other," he said. "And as we are brought more and more in touch with each other the less occasion there is for misunderstandings and the stronger the disposition, when we have differences, to adjust them in the court of arbitration ... the noblest forum for the settlement of international disputes."[14]

In the president's eyes, "Isolation is no longer possible or desirable. The same important news is read, though in different languages, the same day in all christendom. The telegraph keeps us advised of what is occurring everywhere, and the press foreshadows, with more or less accuracy, the plans and purposes of the nations."[15] Here McKinley might have foreseen Woodrow Wilson's futuristic League of Nations—with its own permanent Court of International

Justice—to resolve disputes before war could break out. But in McKinley's eyes, much of the promise of the future was not political but economic, blossoming from inexorable advances in recent technology—particularly transportation and communication—which had accomplished unimaginable changes in recent decades.

A century earlier, in 1801, there was not even "a mile of steam railroad on the globe. Now there are enough miles to make its circuit many times. Then there was not a line of electric telegraph; now we have a vast mileage traversing all lands and seas." In 1815, "It took a special messenger of the Government . . . nineteen days to go from the city of Washington to New Orleans with a message to General Jackson that the war with England had ceased and a treaty of peace had been signed. How different now!"[16]

Beneath this statesmanlike message lay the strong subtext of fervent religious beliefs, for McKinley asserted divine providence played at least as large a part as man: "God and man have linked the nations together," he said. But his message remained a tribute to man's ingenuity and his pride in mankind's achievements, particularly those by nations of the Western Hemisphere who "share with us in this undertaking . . . the Dominion of Canada and the British colonies, the French colonies, the republics of Mexico and Central and South America and the commissioners of Cuba and Puerto Rico," all helping celebrate "the triumphs of art, science, education and manufacture which the old has bequeathed to the new century." For, as he put it: "Expositions are the timekeepers of progress. They record the world's advancement. They stimulate the energy, enterprise and intellect of the people and quicken human genius. . . . They broaden and brighten the daily life of the people. They open mighty storehouses of information to the student. Every exposition, great or small, has helped to some onward step."[17] What McKinley saw as the "educational . . . comparison of ideas," one which "instructs[s] . . . the brain and hand of man," had another beneficial long-term effect: "friendly rivalry . . . which is the spur to industrial improvement, the inspiration to useful invention and to high endeavor in all departments of human activity." This catalyst for competitive trade provided "an incentive to men of business to devise, invent, improve and economize in the cost of production. Business life . . . is ever a sharp struggle for success." Recent events had verified this trend, which must continue and flourish, for "without competition we would be clinging to the clumsy antiquated processes of farming and manufacture and the methods of business of long ago, and the twentieth would be no further advanced than the eighteenth century."[18]

But there was a real caveat. Free trade—the concept McKinley had once opposed, to the detriment of his political career in 1890—meant that commercial competition must be encouraged, without rancor or hostility: "Though commercial competitors we are, commercial enemies we must not be." Telegraphic technology had advanced abilities of hostile armies to report losses and victories to respective governments, with almost unseemly haste: "We reached General Miles in Puerto Rico by cable, and he was able ... to stop his army on the firing line with the message that the United States and Spain had signed a protocol suspending hostilities."[19]

The "wonderful medium of telegraphy" had hidden side effects. For once accustomed to instantaneous news, both governments and public were at a loss when it ceased, even temporarily, as during China's Boxer Rebellion.[20] Boxer violence aside—as well as the more pressing Philippine insurrection, where U.S. troops of both races battled relentless rebels—McKinley saw a future of more productive interactions between nations, a world where "the expansion of our trade and commerce is the pressing problem ... [and] a policy of good will and friendly trade relations will prevent reprisals" in "unprofitable ... commercial wars." Military wars might well ensue as a discarded practice, if such spirits prevailed; as he saw it, "Reciprocity treaties are in harmony with the spirit of the times, measures of retaliation are not. If perchance some of our tariffs are no longer needed, for revenue or to encourage and protect our industries at home, why should they not be employed to extend and promote our markets abroad?"[21]

Indeed, McKinley's thinking had advanced since 1890, and even since 1897, when he had propelled the Dingley tariff—the most protective in U.S. history—to enactment. His concerns for the immediate future were to remedy "inadequate steamship service"—already nearing resolution, with "new lines of steamers hav[ing] already been put in commission between the Pacific coast ports of the United States and those on the western coasts of Mexico and Central and South America"—soon followed by "direct steamship lines between the eastern coast of the United States and South American ports" spurred by construction of a new Central American canal: "We must build the Isthmian canal, which will unite the two oceans and give a straight line of water communication with the western coasts of Central and South America and Mexico," followed immediately by construction of a Pacific cable.[22]

A canal would lead, inexorably, to a need for more and better ships to "direct commercial lines from our vast fields of production to the fields of consumption that we have but barely touched. . . . We must encourage our merchant marine. We must have more ships. They must be under the American flag, built and manned and owned by Americans" and "not only be profitable in a commercial sense; they will be messengers of peace and amity wherever they go." Such ships, and the trains increasingly interconnecting nations, were both "swift . . . and cosmopolitan. . . . The world's products are exchanged as never before, and with increasing transportation facilities come increasing knowledge and larger trade."[23]

His larger vision was of a U.S.-led century of peace and progress, continuing the fine example of exposition exhibits: "evidences of the highest skill and illustrating the progress of the human family in the western hemisphere." The Western Hemisphere "has simply done its best, and without vanity or boastfulness, and . . . invites the friendly rivalry of all the powers in the peaceful pursuits of trade and commerce, and will co-operate with all in advancing the highest and best interests of humanity." The "unexampled prosperity" McKinley saw surrounding Americans "show[s] that we are utilizing our fields and forests and mines and that we are furnishing profitable employment to the millions of workingmen throughout the United States, bringing comfort and happiness to their homes and making it possible to lay by savings for old age and disability." The president declared that "Our capacity to produce has developed so enormously and our products have so multiplied that the problem of more markets requires our urgent and immediate attention," including the creation of "sensible trade arrangements which will not interrupt our home production [which] shall extend the outlets for our increasing surplus."[24]

Such a system was critical to the success of McKinley's new world: "A system which provides a mutual exchange of commodities, a mutual exchange is manifestly essential to the continued and healthful growth of our export trade. . . . What we produce beyond our domestic consumption must have a vent abroad. . . . [W]e should sell everywhere we can, and buy wherever the buying will enlarge our sales and productions, and thereby make a greater demand for home labor."[25]

The Pan-American Exposition had another purpose, in McKinley's eyes— to extol and revere memories of James G. Blaine, "whose mind was ever alert and thought ever constant for a larger commerce and a truer fraternity of the republics of the new world." Blaine had championed the Pan-American movement itself—if more for political reasons than purely economic ones—but would surely have favored efforts to build an American-dominated hemisphere: "His broad American spirit is felt and manifested here.... The name of Blaine is inseparably associated with the pan-American movement . . . which we all hope will be firmly advanced by the pan-American congress that assembles this autumn in the capital of Mexico. The good work . . . cannot be stopped. These buildings will disappear; this creation of art and beauty and industry will perish from sight, but their influence will remain."[26]

McKinley closed with an appeal to his listeners—both those here and those listening hundreds or thousands of miles away—to "remember that our interest is in concord, not conflict, and that our real eminence rests in the victories of peace, not those of war. We hope that all who are represented here may be moved to higher and nobler effort for their own and the world's good, and that out of this city may come, not only greater commerce and trade, but more essential than these, relations of mutual respect, confidence and friendship which will deepen and endure."[27]

With his Buffalo speech, McKinley was clearly addressing an audience beyond immediate listeners, all but overlooking issues concerning the black contingent among the GOP faithful. His larger audiences lay at national and international levels. If by no means his longest speech on record, it was among his most significant, the clearest expression thus far of his earnest commitment to a new role as global statesman, following his declaration that he would retire after 1904. Having removed the shackles of partisan political campaigning, he was now free to push a broader global agenda than he might once have considered helpful to the goals of his party or his own personal aims.

Firmly established as capable of achieving military victory abroad—albeit in a brief war against a collapsing Old World empire unable to retain its last New World colonies—McKinley might well have capitalized on his new stature with a more aggressive tone. But such was against his grain. For one thing, he had never favored war with Spain, and he eschewed new international hostilities in his second term—once the Philippine insurrection was quelled and democracy cultivated in new American possessions abroad.

With characteristic caution and unfailing optimism, he sought instead to build a new international consensus with a core of like-minded nations, prodding them toward an era of cooperation—making war almost impossible, once more and more nations took initial steps toward self-perpetuating trade agreements. Gradually, he theorized, all nations would find it preferable to avoid disrupting increasingly intertwined economies, far less desirable to declare war over political or territorial issues resolvable without bloodshed.

McKinley did not say so, but he was seeking to spread the Founding Fathers' domestic gospel of "self-interest, properly understood"—enshrined in the *Federalist Papers,* concretized in the Constitution—across the globe, continent by continent. An idealist in many ways, McKinley remained a moderate pragmatist at heart. The goals he now preached were only theoretically possible among the world's slowly growing stable of democracies, not yet consistently achievable. Powerful autocratic empires still existed in McKinley's world—the Russians, Japanese, Germans, and Turks among them, all ruled by unelected monarchs—with Spain a fading reflection of centuries-old imperialism.

Not even America's more democratic allies—England, and to some extent, France, with powerful democratic parliaments—were in fact ready to shed their imperial natures and set former colonies free. Great Britain ruled a large swath of the globe with huge colonies in Asia and Africa, colonies exhibiting few of the democratic freedoms practiced at home. The Dominion of Canada, largely autonomous but technically still governed by the British Empire's foreign policy, was easily the best rare example of a practicing democracy among former colonies.

McKinley's speech was a trial balloon on many levels, directed at the new and emerging nations of the Western Hemisphere. Although he had yet to go abroad, he hoped to do so after his presidency, beginning with Mexico and Canada, and perhaps a host of independent southerly republics—at least eighteen so far. In fact, only a few European colonies remained in the Americas, mostly in the Caribbean Sea or along its coastline.[28]

In prefatory remarks, McKinley had singled out Pan-American commissioners to Buffalo from "the Dominion of Canada and the British colonies, the French colonies, the republics of Mexico and Central and South America," along with special commissioners from the newly acquired U.S. territories Cuba and Puerto Rico. Of those, only Canada offered the stable parliamentary democracy likely for prominence in McKinley's plans; the more turbulent American republics—Mexico, Hispaniola, and South American nations—were not yet the calm allies McKinley would need as stable trading partners.

Still, many diplomats from those nations named by McKinley did appear at his side—envoys from Mexico, Colombia, Costa Rica, Peru, and Venezuela—and were gratified at the president's ambitious, optimistic vision of a bright hemispheric future. The president visited impressive buildings erected by Canada, Honduras, and the Dominican Republic, along with large Agricultural Building exhibits by Puerto Rico, Mexico, Argentina, Guatemala, Bolivia, and Central American states.[29]

The next stage would be the Pan-American Union's upcoming meeting, set for October in Mexico City—the second such meeting of a group founded in 1890 by Blaine's tireless efforts. McKinley would not attend the meeting, declining to leave the country, but would send a high-level delegation, including two former U.S. ministers.[30] Eighteen nations had attended that 1890 conference in Washington, D.C., most as major players represented by high-level ministers: Argentina, Bolivia, Brazil, Chile, Colombia, Ecuador, Guatemala, Honduras, Mexico, Nicaragua, Peru, Venezuela, and the United States. (Costa Rica, Haiti, Paraguay, San Salvador, and Uruguay sent lower-level delegates; only Santo Domingo had not attended.)

If that conference had not produced the concrete results hoped for by Blaine and Harrison, it had established the hemisphere's first method of arbitration to settle territorial disputes, facilitating regular consultations and continuing discussions between the nations on such items as customs unions.[31] In the decade since, much had changed in the line-up: Spain was out of the picture completely, divested of its last colonies as a result of war, and its former colony Cuba was being groomed for autonomy and independence. Mexico, after a passive role in 1890, was now hosting the group—renamed the Pan-American Union—as a sign of growing commitment to hemispheric unity. Only the war between Colombia and Venezuela, now in an uneasy truce, clouded the hemisphere.

Of one thing McKinley was sure: the future looked bright, and the possibilities unlimited. A new era for foreign and economic policy was dawning in the Western Hemisphere, once the president returned to Washington. All that remained was to tour the Pan-American Exposition, visit Niagara Falls, and greet the public at a Temple of Music reception, after which the president and first lady would board their special train for home.

16

END OF A DREAM

*The race therefore feels the loss as the rest of their fellow citizens cannot.
In his death, they also recognized the loss of a friend and sympathizer.*
— The *Colored American*, September 21, 1901

As President McKinley surveyed his audience from a special pylon at the end of the Triumphal Bridge, he might well have mused upon the faces of many thousands in his audience. Unlike his mixed crowds at speaking tours in the South, very few faces were black. Buffalo boasted only a tiny percentage of black residents—fewer than two thousand of its more than four hundred thousand population—although many menial fair employees were doubtless of color, including transients drawn by steady employment.

Many national organizations held their annual conventions in Buffalo during the exposition, hoping to improve their attendance. African Americans held two significant local conventions of leaders—the National Association of Colored Women and the National Council of Educators of Colored Youth—in July alone, drawing large groups of influential black dignitaries to Buffalo and side excursions to the exposition. Booker T. Washington and his wife, incoming vice president of the women's group, had attended, along with national figures Mary Terrell of Washington, D.C., and NAAC president Alexander Walters.[1]

But by September, those lucky enough to hear McKinley's speech were most likely to be a mixture of Buffalo citizens, fair workers granted time off by supervisors, visitors from New York and nearby Canada, and vacationers drawn by the fair's appeal and clear, mild weather. In one respect, the large audience for this speech—some estimates topped fifty thousand—probably differed from most of the president's campaign speeches and partisan appearances, to which local organizers recruited as many African Americans—among his most fervent admirers—as possible. In his recent southern swing, McKinley had attracted large, enthusiastic crowds of African Americans in Louisiana and Texas, far less likely in Buffalo, with its largely white, mostly immigrant population from Germany, Poland, Italy, and Ireland.

The city's 1900 population was less than 1 percent nonwhite, compared to New York State's 1900 population of about 2 percent African American. Most black citizens lived in the southeastern tip of the state, around New York City, nearly four hundred miles away. Still, many fair service workers were African Americans, if primarily itinerants drawn, like Georgia's James Benjamin Parker, by promises of decent short-term wages. A literate southern journalist, postal worker, and former constable, Parker was awaiting another job, he later explained, by working temporarily as a waiter for a fairground caterer.

Parker later told local journalists that he had come to the Temple of Music—the president's destination the following day—specifically to hear speeches that did not take place. Had Parker attended the president's major speech the day before, he would have been hard to miss—a towering figure, six and a half feet tall, weighing 250 pounds. A less distinguishable attendee—a boyish-looking, innocent-faced man named Leon Czolgosz, blond-haired, of Polish-Russian extraction and medium height—was reportedly among McKinley's earlier listeners, but Czolgosz would have blended more easily into the crowd.[2]

All the president would probably see and hear from his perch was a vast, appreciative crowd, thrilling at a chance to see their recently reelected leader in person; newspaper accounts indicate enthusiastic cheers from the crowd before, during, and after the speech, and large throngs at every fairground stop.

McKinley did visit many exhibits, including those at the U.S. government building and New York State's building, where he, his cabinet, and Supreme Court justices enjoyed a special lunch. But the president's tight schedule precluded visits to every building or exhibit. Disappointingly, among those not on his itinerary was one he specifically helped create for another world's fair: the so-called *American Negro Exhibit,* created by McKinley appointee Thomas Calloway and W. E. B. Du Bois for the 1900 Paris exposition.

That the Paris exhibit of photographs and other materials even opened in Buffalo was flukish. Calloway planned to take the exhibit to Charleston, South Carolina, in 1902 as its next site, but he apparently lost control of it after Paris. The chief of the Liberal Arts Division at the Pan-American Exposition, Dr. Selim Peabody, had served as editor and statistician of the larger U.S. exhibit in Paris. Without informing Calloway, Peabody decided arbitrarily to bring the *Negro Exhibit* to Buffalo after local African American leaders spearheaded efforts for its appearance.[3]

The ex-president of the University of Illinois was accustomed to acting on his own volition and had been involved with world's fairs since 1893's Chicago Columbian Exposition. Calloway complained bitterly in the spring of 1901 about Peabody's decision, without success.[4] In January, the *Buffalo Express* quoted Peabody as planning to place the exhibit "under the supervision of some person, not yet designated by the Exposition Company, of the Negro race," but no such curator was ever identified, certainly not Calloway or Du Bois. There is no evidence that Calloway visited the exposition in Buffalo, perhaps out of displeasure with Peabody's actions, which violated what Calloway described to Booker T. Washington as "the plan I had arranged for . . . in Paris."[5]

With neither man available to help arrange and explain the complex perspective the exhibit had once so grandly displayed, "the exhibit gradually became less oppositional and lost the power that it demonstrated in Paris," writes historian Miles Travis.[6] Peabody shepherded the exhibit to Charleston without Calloway's assistance, and it eventually entered storage at the Library of Congress. Meanwhile, its exact location at the exposition is not certain— probably in the U.S. government building, which McKinley did visit briefly on September 5, after his speech and luncheon in the New York State building.

While at the U.S. building, McKinley spent much time shaking hands with an astounding 1,500 guests[7]—perhaps even Dr. Peabody, in his larger capacity as chief of the Liberal Arts Division. But Calloway—who would have most appreciated the rare opportunity to visit once again with his 1899 benefactor— was not there.[8] Another familiar figure missing from McKinley's itinerary was ex-congressman George White, who had once helped facilitate the exhibit's development and helped Calloway obtain the Paris position. Despite his interest in its various exhibits and the president's message on Pan-American unity, White does not appear to have visited the exposition at all. He remained in Washington, D.C., awaiting McKinley's return—and strategizing for his own federal appointment.

⁂

The crowd awaiting McKinley's arrival at the Temple of Music was enormous. After a momentous trip to Niagara Falls, the nation's leader was clearly energized and at his best, always good with quick handshakes and warm platitudes. There is no record of any remarks that day; at least one person hoping to hear McKinley and others speak, James Parker, was disappointed. He was trying to leave the crowded receiving line as he neared McKinley but could not fight the crush. Perverse fate had other plans for him.

One of the Secret Service agents beside the president remembered having to gently push along one overly enamored hand-shaker, a man of Mediterranean appearance with a "short cropped heavy black moustache" who lingered moments longer than anyone wished, to allow the next person in line—an innocent-looking young man with a heavily bandaged hand—to reach McKinley. Parker was next in line.

According to one detailed account, published weeks later: "There was an immense, sonorous pipe organ in the Temple—one of the largest and one of the best ever built. An organist was playing, and at the moment he had opened the lower diapason for a Bach sonata—a negative invocation, charged with all the tremendous emotional and subtle aesthetic power that that master possesses. Its tremulous pulsation caused by the magnificent acoustics of the building surcharged the mellow air with intense unfelt weight—not oppressive, but formidable, like the deep displacement of a man-of-war."[9]

As the organist's shattering crescendo thrilled the crowd, two muffled gunshots rang out.[10] Leon Czolgosz's bandaged hand concealed a revolver purchased in Buffalo, and his makeshift bandages were literally smoking. The president seemed puzzled by the shots but unflappable as ever, giving Czolgosz "the most scornful and contemptuous look possible to imagine," said Secret Service agent Sam Ireland.[11]

According to Ireland's initial account in the *Buffalo Courier*, "the big negro standing just back of him, and who would have been next to take the president's hand, struck the young man in the neck with one hand and with the other reached for the revolver." The *Los Angeles Times* said James Parker immediately "struck the assassin in the neck with one hand and with the other reached for the revolver." A dozen bystanders wrestled Czolgosz to the floor, gun in hand, as he desperately tried to fire a third shot. But Parker "knocked it from his hand. As it went across the floor, an artilleryman picked it up." One eyewitness said Parker "spun the man around like a top and . . . broke Czolgosz's nose . . . split the assassin's lip and knocked out several teeth."[12]

Secret Service agent George Foster did not identify Parker by name but described action by "a colored man by Czolgosz's side [who] struck the latter's arm, sending it up and probably preventing the firing of a third shot." Foster's initial report to Chief Wilkie of the U.S. Secret Service added that he, Foster, then leaped forward and knocked the assassin and the unnamed black man to the floor.[13] Foster's account all but contradicted the description given by his fellow agent Sam Ireland and many eyewitnesses of intervention by "a big colored man" behind Czolgosz in line, but Foster never changed his account, even at the trial.

Another onlooker said Parker seemed "infuriated. . . . I believe he would have killed Czolgosz" had he not been physically restrained, the man said. As chronicler Richard Barry described the scene, a dozen men went for Czolgosz at the same time, but "a big negro, James Parker, burst through the crowd and elbowed his herculean way to an assistance which was too late."[14] Parker himself remembered it differently: "I did what every citizen of this country should have done. I am told that I broke his nose—I wish it had been his neck. I am sorry I did not see him four seconds before. I don't say that I would have thrown myself before the bullets. But I do say that the life of the head of this country is worth more than that of an ordinary citizen and I should have caught the bullets in my body rather than the President should get them."[15]

"I can't tell you what I would have done and I don't like to have it understood that I want to talk of the matter. I tried to do my duty," he said. "That's all any man can do." Parker said he had gone to the Temple only "to hear what speeches might be made. I got in line and saw the President. I turned to go away as soon as I learned that there was to be only a handshaking. The crowd was so thick that I could not leave. I was startled by the shots." Parker made two surprising observations: First, the assassin was "very strong. I am glad that I am a strong man also, or perhaps the result might not have been what it was." Furthermore, his race deserved the credit—not him: "I am a Negro, and am glad that the Ethiopian race has whatever credit comes with what I did. If I did anything, the colored people should get the credit."[16]

A much longer statement Parker supposedly gave to the *New York Journal*—reprinted later in the *Colored American Magazine*—was more dramatic, almost theatrical: "'You scoundrel!' I cried, 'you've shot the President.' . . . I closed upon him, my right hand clawing at his throat. . . . I tore at him like a wild beast . . . down we went in a death struggle for he was as strong as an ox and had I been a smaller man he would have overpowered me." His mind went blank for a moment, he said. Then he looked up at the wounded president—"his face was like a sheet . . . I thought he was dying." [17]

Parker believed that he "saved President McKinley's life in preventing the third shot. . . . I do not make this statement for glory, but because I believe it is best for the public to know." At the time of his interview, he fully expected to be called to testify, adding, "The truth will come out on the witness stand." [18] Even as he spoke, the man he had helped was recovering after emergency surgery, and Parker roundly hailed as a hero. But as days drew on, McKinley suddenly began to decline and, in final moments, accepted his fate with a stoic dignity.

"It is useless, gentlemen, I think I ought to have prayer," the president told his doctors, after asking for his wife to be brought. "Good-bye—good-bye, all. It is God's way. His will, not ours, be done," he whispered to Ida, lapsing back into a final stupor, whispering the words of a favorite hymn: "Nearer, My God, to Thee." [19] The twenty-fifth president died of his wounds and a raging gangrenous infection early on September 14, in the Milburn residence, where he had lain since the shooting.

Had the prototype X-ray machine on display at the exposition been used instead of a manual examination of the president's wounds, which had almost certainly helped spark infection, it is conceivable that he might have survived longer—although his ravaged pancreas may never have recovered—and Parker might have become a household name, likely with a medal and personal commendations from the president. Inventor Thomas Edison had offered the machine for use at the makeshift hospital, but it was refused.

The autopsy confirmed the sad truth: surgery to repair abdominal wounds had worked as well as could be expected. But gangrene had invaded tissue around each set of sutures, extending to the pancreas. According to the autopsy, "death resulted from the gangrene, which affected the stomach around the bullet wounds as well as the tissues around the further course of the bullet. Death was unavoidable by any surgical or medical treatment, and was the direct result of the bullet wound." Without modern antibiotics, there was simply no way to save him. [20]

But in the frantic, charged atmosphere surrounding McKinley's unexpected death, Parker's helpful role in preventing a third shot was now suddenly discredited, thanks to an aggressive disinformation campaign by Buffalo attorney James Quackenbush, a member of the exposition's committee on ceremonies escorting McKinley. He had stood just six feet from Czolgosz—and Parker—when the shooting occurred. Yet even before McKinley's death, Quackenbush began to deny publicly that Parker had any part in stopping or disarming the assassin. His minutely detailed account contradicted Ireland's description of intervention by "a big colored man" behind Czolgosz in line, but Quackenbush was emphatic: "I do not recall seeing anyone seize upon Czolgosz except the secret service men, Messrs. Ireland, Foster, and Gallagher, Artilleryman O'Brien and the other artillerymen," he told the *Buffalo Express* on September 13.[21]

Quackenbush was not alone. According to historian Roger Pickenpaugh, the Secret Service itself "would later launch a monumental campaign to discredit Parker and diminish his role," despite "overwhelming eyewitness testimony" to the contrary.[22] Pickenpaugh's exhaustive reexamination of the campaign to marginalize Parker builds a strong case for this "grave disservice," if no decisive explanation as to why; the implication remains that the Secret Service felt its own performance and credibility were threatened if Parker or anyone else was credited with saving McKinley from a third shot.[23]

Parker would not even be called to testify at Czolgosz's trial, a fact that puzzled him and almost everyone who saw him save the president's life—however temporarily—at the Temple of Music. Ironically, another eyewitness, Agent Foster, most discredited Parker's claims of intervention moments after the assassination by testifying that Parker was much farther away when the shooting occurred and not involved "in the fracas" of the assassin's apprehension. Asked by Prosecutor Thomas Penny whether he saw Parker in the line, Foster answered that he "noticed a colored man in the line, but it seems to me he was in front of this man . . . instead of behind him. I never saw no colored man in the whole fracas."[24]

*

The mood among America's black population in the weeks after McKinley's death was somber, mirroring that of the broader population. Many African Americans realized the distinct enormity of their loss only gradually. But one black editor quickly translated their grief into clearer perspective, noting that black citizens had "for a generation suffered at the hands of the same spirit of anarchy that struck down our beloved president. The race therefore feels the loss as the rest of their fellow citizens cannot. In his death, they also recognized the loss of a friend and sympathizer."[25]

Booker T. Washington, soon to become the next president's trusted adviser, penned a remarkable public note to an Alabama newspaper a week after McKinley's death, one in which he blamed the assassination on the same nationwide obsession with violence, particularly violence directed against black citizens: "With united voice we condemn the individual who was the direct cause of removing, the perhaps, most tenderly and universally loved President the nation has ever had. But in all sincerity, I want to ask, is Czolgosz alone guilty?," Washington asked. "Has not the entire nation had a part in this greatest crime of the century? What is anarchy but a defiance of the law and has not the nation reaped what it has been sowing?"[26]

Washington's detailed accounting of instances of lynching and his condemnation of such violence—along with a less specific call for concerted nationwide efforts to "create such a public sentiment as will make crime disappear"—echoed the words of George White and the sentiments of civil rights leaders and antilynching activists in the NAAC and beyond. It was a rare public foray into a controversial political issue for the Alabama educator, who had long condemned lynching but rarely so openly or directly.

African American clergy minced few words in their analysis. McKinley, said bishops of the AME denomination—Arnett's fellow clerics—in the week after his death, "was deeply concerned about the American Negro and wanted him to attain his full status as a man and a citizen under the American flag." The slain president had become a revered symbol of racial hopes for justice during his four years in Washington, and "their greatest friend since Lincoln." During the first McKinley administration, "the Negro race in the country received the highest political preferment in its history."[27]

Perhaps the poetic sentiments of writer Cleveland Suarez best summed up feelings of most black Americans toward the slain president's memory in the *Colored American Magazine*'s October issue:

> The silent air is musical with thought—
> I hear the beating of the nation's heart;
> It cannot hush the aching tears of grief
> Since one has passed into the perfect night.
> The people bow their heads in the belief

He was a benefactor, faithful from the start.
O hero, martyr, and the nation's chief,
The fragrant breathing of the silver chimes
Is but the adieu;
We see no more the placid face
That stood to greet the benediction of a RACE.[28]

As for Roosevelt, many African Americans viewed the man who had suddenly replaced McKinley with curiously mixed feelings. Roosevelt, of course, still carried the burden of 1899 statements criticizing the bravery of black soldiers in Cuba, and many skeptical of him then had yet to change their minds. Despite many positive attributes in the man and his past, the jury was still out on certain issues—those regarding "anarchy of lynching and their citizenship rights in general"—as black citizens awaited his public statements.

As civil service commissioner, Roosevelt had ensured "that the colored competitor for admission to the government service was treated with absolute fairness in the examination, in the certification and in the appointments," the bishops wrote. "We express belief that the colored man has in Mr. Roosevelt a discriminating friend and that in so far as in him lies he will see the colored man treated with fairness."[29]

But perhaps no one was more symbolic of changing American attitudes toward black citizens in the post-McKinley era than "Big Jim" Parker, who had gone rapidly from hero to unworthy glory-seeker in the tumultuous weeks after McKinley's shooting and death. The former journalist and Pullman car attendant quickly gave up plans to work as a traveling agent for James Ross's *Gazetteer and Guide,* a Buffalo magazine for African Americans catering to railroad porters and hotel workers. Ross, a practicing attorney who also published the *Globe and Freeman,* quickly took up Parker's cause, as did Buffalo's small but vocal African American community. Despite their untiring efforts, his role as McKinley's near-savior was quickly obscured in the six-week rush to try, convict, and execute Czolgosz.

But Parker was not forgotten by all. On October 8, he was at the White House "to pay his respects to President Roosevelt," according to the *Evening Star,* just before making a public address at the Metropolitan AME Church, where he was introduced by George White.[30] Parker would persist in telling his version of events to paying audiences for years to come. But his story had begun evolving along slightly revised lines.

The *Evening Star* briefly noted his appearance before two thousand listeners: "Ex-representative George H. White introduced Parker, whose narrative was a recital of the incidents with which the public is already familiar."[31] A longer and more revealing synopsis of Parker's speech appeared days later in the local *Colored American:*

> When the assassin dealt his blow, I felt it was time to act. . . . President McKinley was looking right at me; in fact, his eyes were riveted upon me when I felled the assassin to the floor. [He] was in front of me, and as the President went to shake his hand he looked hard at one hand the fellow held across his breast bandaged. I looked over the man's shoulder to see what the President was looking at. . . .
>
> Just then there were two flashes and a report, and I saw the flame leap from the supposed bandage. I seized the man by the shoulder and dealt him a blow. I tried to catch hold of the gun but he had lowered that arm. Quick as a flash I grasped his throat and choked him as hard as I could. As this happened he raised the hand with the gun in it again as if to fire, the burning handkerchief hanging to the weapon. I helped carry the assassin into a side room and helped to search him."[32]

Parker had clearly grown weary of hearing himself described as a glory-seeker. "It is no great honor I am trying to get but simply what the American people think I am entitled to," he said. "If Mr. McKinley had lived, there would have been no question as to this matter." But he was also puzzled as to why he could not testify against Czolgosz. "I don't know why I wasn't summoned to the trial," he declared; one female supporter yelled, "cause you're black, dat's de reason." Prosecuting attorney Penny took his deposition but did not introduce it, he said. "I was not at the trial. I don't say this was done with any intent to defraud me, but it looks mighty funny, that's all. Because I was a waiter, Mr. Penny thought I had no sense. At the proper time I am going to show him better than I can tell him that he is fooling with the wrong man," Parker declared, ominously.[33]

Parker spurned lucrative opportunities to sell his story, and the only significant payment he apparently received was directed to his mother. He had not sought the limelight and seemed wary of it. He did accept contributions in lieu of speaker's fees, and at least one organized effort—the J. B. Parker Fund, established in Washington, D.C., by Mary Terrell and like-minded friends—solicited contributions on his behalf "as a public testimonial of appreciation of his patriotic conduct."[34]

What he and his supporters did not understand was why so few of those who had seen his heroic actions were willing to defend him against a shrill campaign to discredit him. Whether any eyewitnesses were as puzzled about his lack of recognition as Parker was has never been documented. But the *Buffalo Courier*, which printed attorney Quackenbush's long interview, defended its accuracy in a post-trial editorial, claiming the transcript verified Quackenbush's account. "Not a scintilla of evidence had been developed to show that Mr. Parker grappled with Czolgosz," the newspaper declared.[35] Quackenbush never changed his account, and if prosecutor Penny regretted not calling Parker to corroborate Czolgosz's actions, there is no evidence of it in the public record.

Penny may have feared that describing Parker's actions might confuse the jury and introduce real doubts as to Czolgosz's sanity. Perhaps, as Parker speculated, Penny assumed his account was not credible enough to convince a Buffalo jury. Only the judge himself seemed curious as to the accuracy of reports of Parker's involvement, asking Agent Foster that question directly. Yet Parker's testimony would hardly have changed the outcome, for Czolgosz had cited only his newly acquired anarchist beliefs—however muddled—and claimed he shot McKinley "as an enemy of the people," not out of dislike.

The trial began less than two weeks after McKinley's death, ending on its second day with a guilty verdict. The jury rejected a plea of insanity, and the assassin was executed just three weeks after Parker spoke in Washington. By then, of course, the horror of the assassination had faded slightly, as the nation rallied behind Roosevelt. Still, the net effect of Parker's excision from the trial and further accounts of the assassination was regrettable, from both a personal and historical perspective. It symbolized, in a very real way, how far the fortunes of black Americans fell with the death of the man so many had so recently and so long supported, both in Ohio and the nation.

Nearly mirroring Parker's decline in influence, White's complicated relationship with power—and more specifically, with GOP leaders—suffered badly in the months after McKinley's death. Had a healthy McKinley returned to the White House in September 1901, there is reason to believe that he might quietly have found some suitable federal sinecure for the ex-congressman whose friendship and support he had long enjoyed. But as White discovered in the weeks after Roosevelt's accession, no such hopes existed in the radically new environment of Rough Rider politics. The passing of William McKinley was the death knell for his own hope of a further public career on the national stage—and an end to the dream he and McKinley had once shared.

EPILOGUE

A Long Fall from Grace

After the President had been informed, he drew from his vest pocket a
small pad and, writing a few words addressed to the Departmental
official, signed the name of William McKinley and handed it
to Mr. White. The appointment was made that day.
—*Philadelphia Tribune,* January 5, 1919

With his mentor McKinley lost, George White was forced to make other plans
to revitalize his failed campaign for an appointment from the previous spring.
In early October, he made his first trek to President Theodore Roosevelt's office at the White House, only to be disappointed—told, essentially, that he must
first approach Booker T. Washington for a recommendation. His star was in
decline, just as Washington's star was rapidly rising, but their tenuous relationship was a poor substitute for the more direct ones that White had enjoyed
while in Congress.

White's letter to Washington that week underscores his frustration and
waning hopes for financial security as he struggled to build up his law practice in the fiercely competitive atmosphere of the nation's capital. The two
men were reasonably well acquainted, but White's directness and occasional
naïveté were no match for the wiles of the ever-cagey Washington, always several steps ahead of supplicants and loath to push the wrong buttons too early
in the Roosevelt era.

"I have just returned from a visit to the White House, where it was intimated to me that in my fight for an Auditorship under the Treas. Dept. here, a
letter from you would greatly strengthen my chances," White said in a handwritten note beseeching Washington to "please help me in this instance by
writing a personal letter to Pres. Roosevelt, giving him the estimate you have
of me from my public life and your personal knowledge of me."[1] Washington

was already aware of White's predicament, for Emmett Scott had witnessed the embarrassing episode during his more successful visit to the Executive Mansion on October 4. According to Scott, at least three other black visitors were turned away that day—White, Henry Arnett, and Paul Dunbar—once guaranteed audiences with McKinley, "all were waiting to see the President but failed."[2]

No immediate reply appears in Washington's meticulous archive, indicating personal delivery of the bad news to White, probably after Washington's infamous White House dinner in mid-October. Only a plaintive letter months later from White's wife—written without her husband's knowledge, certainly against his better judgment—kept the issue alive. "Mr. White does not know that I am writing you. . . . Please, Mr. Washington, do what you can for him. . . . Do you think the President would give Mr. White Mr. Lyons's place & Mr. Lyons Mr. Rucker's in Atlanta which pays quite as much?," Cora Lena wrote Washington in January 1902.[3]

Her earnest but unrealistic hopes were soon gently dashed. Washington's response to her is described only fleetingly in her husband's stilted letter but must have laid the blame squarely—and neatly—at the feet of Jeter Pritchard, whose onetime alliance with White collapsed in 1900. Now cultivating Roosevelt himself—in anticipation of the federal judgeship he received in 1903—Pritchard could easily metamorphose into Iago, in White's mind at least, discreetly whispering anti-White propaganda in Roosevelt's ear.[4]

This ruse perhaps concealed the real reason from a distressed invalid, forced to dictate her letter to a trusted servant or friend. But the truth was more complicated. White certainly knew that Pritchard's negative opinion would not have swayed Roosevelt, if he had ever been inclined to appoint White. The hidden issue was Washington's unwillingness to waste rare political capital without positive advance indications of White's chances, and no such indication ever came.

Pritchard, in fact, was more closely allied with White's brother-in-law, Henry Cheatham, who expected imminent reappointment to another four-year term as recorder of deeds. The scandal that dragged Cheatham down and prevented reappointment—surprising Pritchard and most others—was still brewing quietly. McKinley's influential adviser Bishop Arnett was preparing to duel Cheatham over the forced resignation of Arnett's son Henry, among Cheatham's chief clerks, in a botched power play that left almost no one standing.

By taking the duel directly and publicly to Roosevelt, Bishop Arnett very nearly forced Cheatham's indictment on murky charges of violating federal law—a matter resolved quietly by resignation. (What Cheatham or a staff member had actually done was never specified, although Attorney General Philander Knox hinted at a serious technical infraction of federal law.)[5] Washington had no hand in Cheatham's fall from grace, but he and Pritchard were both careful to back only the best replacement: John Dancy, whose spotless record as a high-ranking customs official since 1897 made him an ideal choice.

There is no evidence of anyone except Dancy being proposed, although White may have been considered briefly. The corridors of influence for almost everyone else were effectively narrowing to one lane, running to the White House only through Tuskegee. After a disastrous unrelated appointment of a newcomer as U.S. minister to Liberia—an ambitious, reportedly randy Republican physician who circumvented Tuskegee, then embarrassed the administration with a major sex-and-gunfire scandal in Monrovia—Washington became the only gatekeeper for black appointments.[6]

The collective effect of such intrigue was to confirm Roosevelt's innate discomfort with—perhaps, long-term distrust of—most African American politicians. It solidified Roosevelt's long-term dependence on Washington's prudence in future appointments of African Americans, at least to offices requiring Senate confirmation. Sadly, that short list would not include the outspoken White, despite his solid credentials, strong record of honesty and integrity, and much support in party ranks.[7]

If White envisioned his own return in delivering his farewell speech to the U.S. House in January 1901, his prediction was never realized. Instead, his role in national politics was vastly diminished; even as an elder statesman, he had little influence in his own party outside Pennsylvania, where he moved in 1906. White's dream was officially interred with the remains of the man he had so long admired; with the end of the McKinley era went the last African American congressman's hopes for continued recognition of his talents and achievements.

Less than a year after McKinley's death, White himself ruefully recounted his sudden fall from grace in a June 1902 letter to the *Colored American*. He had recently visited the director-elect of the new U.S. Census Bureau, William Merriam, following the termination of his daughter Della, a temporary census clerk. Merriam, a former Minnesota governor and McKinley appointee in 1899, had spoken kindly of his daughter's "efficient and faithful" services in his termination letter, leading White to hope for her rehiring as the temporary agency transitioned into a permanent bureau.

"I told him that I understood" the likely requirements for permanent hiring and that "each member of Congress would be entitled to at least one clerk and that I was anxious for Miss White to remain," her father went on.[8] Because White had met with Merriam as census director at least once to review enumerator appointments for the 1900 census, he assumed such a small request might be granted him as a personal courtesy and saw no harm in trying.

To his shock, however, his reception echoed the White House playbook of the previous fall—with fewer niceties. White was briskly advised "that I was out of Congress and was entitled to nothing. When I told him that my successor was a Democrat and had no appointee in the office, the Director stated with some feeling that if my Democratic successor had no clerk there he was entitled to one, and that I was unnecessarily taking up his time in talking about the matter."[9] White was flabbergasted and humiliated. "I meekly took my hat and left the census office to remain away from there for a season," White wrote the *Colored American.* "I cannot speak for others, but I do not like the treatment I received from Mr. Merriam. I have no redress now."

White's Democratic successor was unlikely to help him, especially when it meant giving a civil service job to a Republican. And if White might not be able to prevent Merriam's appointment as the first permanent director, he still hoped to "reach some of those who are instrumental in securing his retention in office."[10] His hopes for Merriam's departure were realized a year later—if with no discernible help from White—when Merriam voluntarily stepped down, succeeded by the chief 1900 census statistician, Simon North.[11]

Della White soon married and moved away. Only a handful of McKinley's appointees remained in office during the Roosevelt administration as holdovers; John Dancy until 1910, while Judson Lyons was replaced in 1906.[12] Few new black appointees emerged during either Roosevelt term, most notably Rev. Ernest Lyon of Maryland, the next minister to Liberia, and in 1905, Dr. Henry Furniss as U.S. minister to Haiti, although Roosevelt did name black consuls in the Americas and Africa, including James Johnson, in Venezuela and Nicaragua after 1906; Christopher Payne, in the Danish West Indies; and John Terres, in Port-Au-Prince, Haiti.[13]

After 1900, presidential campaigns were no longer on White's agenda; Roosevelt neither sought nor encouraged speaking campaigns by African American officeholders and party elders once orchestrated by McKinley's campaign strategists. Having no real affection for the man who effectively sealed his fate after McKinley's death, White played no visible role in Roosevelt's 1904 re-election campaign. The death of Mark Hanna that same year removed White's strongest remaining link to McKinley, and the only candidate for whom White might have campaigned as Republican nominee.

In 1906, while acting as staff attorney for the Constitution League, White helped challenge Roosevelt's stinging dismissal of nearly two hundred black soldiers after Brownsville, at the behest of Ohio senator Joseph Foraker, Roosevelt's rival in 1904 and occasional critic. As lines in the sand deepened into a trench, White withdrew into his own new world in Philadelphia, refusing to participate enthusiastically in the 1908 campaign of William Howard Taft, Roosevelt's secretary of war; Taft's significant role during the Brownsville incident was blamed by many black leaders for Roosevelt's hard-line approach and ongoing refusal to reconsider it.

Then, in 1912, White witnessed Roosevelt's astounding reentry into national politics, in a turbulent three-way campaign elevating Democrat Woodrow Wilson to the White House by ousting Taft. Yet until the end of his life, White remained steadfastly active in local and state Republican politics, though as a cheerleader, not a candidate—always boosting his beloved party and urging black voters to remain faithful to it, even as the inexorable slide toward the Democratic Party gained momentum in the North. He watched the emergence of a new generation of local and state candidates in Philadelphia from the sidelines. His only party office was as alternate delegate from Pennsylvania to another Republican nominating convention in 1916, in Chicago, with an unfamiliar nominee, Charles Evans Hughes.

But in that turbulent spring of 1912, George White mounted one last attempt at major political office—seeking the Republican nomination to succeed the late Rep. Henry Bingham, a longtime congressman with whom he had once served—but he could gain no traction. His open letter to the black-owned *Philadelphia Tribune* called on "the great state of brotherly love" to return him to Congress, hoping that "a 'square deal' can afford to give my race this one national position."[14] Black voters held the balance of power in several Pennsylvania districts, White believed, but he ran behind the field of prospective candidates in the April 1912 primary, won easily by the redoubtable William Vare.[15]

A boomlet by backers in 1913 unsuccessfully sought White's appointment by Pennsylvania governor John Tener to one of five newly created judgeships in Philadelphia County's Court of Common Pleas. But he sought no elective office after 1912. His last appointment, made in 1917, was as assistant city solicitor for Philadelphia, succeeding former state legislator Harry Bass in that position—the last public office either man ever held.

White held no brief for Woodrow Wilson, a man he did not know and of whom he surely disapproved, with whom he had far less in common than either Taft or Roosevelt. Many of his own and younger generations of black voters were already edging toward a full break with the GOP, although Wilson's ardently segregationist views made becoming a Democrat unthinkable for many thoughtful, progressive blacks. Some, like Bishop Walters, had long made no secret of their disenchantment with empty Republican promises, and the northern wing of the Democratic Party was making strong, steady inroads in urban centers of northern and midwestern states. Meanwhile, intellectuals such as W. E. B. Du Bois were gaining more and followers with calls for independent action.

Caught in the philosophical middle between extremes of Tuskegee's accommodationism and Du Bois's radical activism, White remained resolutely practical, urging blacks who would listen to be pragmatic and leverage their position by forcing both parties to bid for their participation. In a 1902 article written for a national collection of essays—a contribution aptly titled "What Should Be the Negro's Attitude in Politics?"—White all but endorsed independent action by blacks who could still vote, almost all in the Northeast, Midwest, and West.[16]

In North Carolina—once home of the South's proudest, most resilient black Republicans—only a handful of the state's black voters, perhaps five thousand, could register under stringent new literacy requirements taking effect in 1902, after court challenges ended. Their future votes doubtless remained Republican but had no real value in a state completely dominated by the Democratic Party's segregationist wing.

In his most lasting signal contribution to racial betterment, White's small utopian settlement in southern New Jersey took hold and briefly flourished. The all-black community known as Whitesboro attracted a sturdy core of North Carolina economic pioneers and remains in existence a century after his death. If never quite the industrial success or tourist mecca he had hoped for, it nonetheless produced generations of successful businessmen and professionals, as home to distinguished sons: author Stedman Graham, comedian "Flip" Wilson, and Pennsylvania's first African American state superior court judge, Theodore Spaulding.

White himself lived to see the armistice ending World War I, in which his nephew Henry Cheatham Jr. served with distinction in France before studying law in Philadelphia. And White also lived to mark the loss of many younger colleagues and friends from his political days, outliving his sometime friend Booker T. Washington, who died in 1915; Council adversary Bishop Walters (d. 1916); and many Second District predecessors in the U.S. House, including two-term Reps. James O'Hara (d. 1905) and Frederick Woodard (d. 1915), the man he defeated in 1896.

In 1907, White marked the sad passing of former first lady Ida McKinley, who had serenely survived her husband's assassination. In 1908, he lost the energetic services of Edward Cooper, the Washington journalist and unofficial public-relations agent who had once boosted his career. On a more personal note, White outlived three women instrumental in shaping his adult life. All died in Washington, D.C.: his third wife, Cora Lena; his stepmother, Mary Anna White; and his oldest daughter, Della Garrett. Cora Lena died in January 1905, at age forty, of chronic neurasthenia.[17] Mary Anna White moved to Washington after 1900, dying there of natural causes in 1912. Three months after her father's remarriage, Della died in early 1916 at her home, victim of a scarlet fever epidemic.

In 1908, White quietly mourned the loss of another younger man he had once introduced on a Washington stage as McKinley's savior, "Big Jim" Parker—the last living link to his martyred mentor. Though they both now lived in Philadelphia, how much White knew of Parker's final years and declining circumstances is unclear; that the two were only blocks apart from each other at Parker's death is another of history's small ironies.[18] Ill and despondent, Parker had sought assistance in early 1906 from Ida McKinley, who referred the request to a sympathetic George Cortelyou, once her husband's personal secretary, now U.S.

postmaster general.[19] The plaintive appeal, handwritten on the stationery of a Washington, D.C., physician, clearly shows a despondent, desperate man:

> Kind Madam, I wish to ask a favor of you. I have been sick in the hospital for some time and am sick yet. I want you to help me. I done all I could for your husband in trying to save his life and if I had of been successful, I know he would of place[d] me for my efforts. A word from you to Mr. Cortelyou is all I need. Will you for God sake say that word—you dont know the hearts you will make glad—I don't ask for a clerkship but anything he will give me there are hundreds of places he can give me if he chooses from driving a wagon to a place in the U.S. capital if you will do this for me in remembrance of your dear husband I will always pray to our heavenly father to spare your life and have mercy on you.
>
> In great distress I am your humble servant, J. B. Parker[20]

According to some reports, Cortelyou arranged for Parker's hiring as a federal messenger, but whatever action was taken soon failed; within a year, Parker was destitute on the resort streets of Atlantic City, New Jersey, after being a performer for various hotels and saloons.[21] An emaciated panhandler there in early 1907, he was arrested for vagrancy and judged by a benevolent judge to be unable to care for himself; rather than jail him, the judge ordered him confined to an asylum for the insane in West Philadelphia.[22]

Parker's health and huge frame had been ravaged by disease and apparent alcoholism, according to one friendly witness: "Prosperity and too much glory proved the undoing of Jim." Parker's final demise occurred a year later under sad circumstances, with his body dissected in the spring of 1908 by medical students at the city's Jefferson Medical College, in a near-ghoulish denouement to the fate of the assassin he had once tackled.[23]

White also outlived many white Republican politicians with whom he had once shared the political limelight, including Senators Mark Hanna and Joseph Foraker of Ohio, and many onetime House GOP colleagues, especially former Speaker David Henderson of Iowa (d. 1906), Charles Sprague of Massachusetts (d. 1902), and George Southwick of New York (d. 1912), all counted as personal friends. But White would not live to see Republicans regain the White House in 1920. Nor would he live to see his famous prophecy of a return by African Americans to the U.S. House fulfilled.

Nearly three decades would pass before the next African American won a seat in the House: Chicago's Oscar De Priest, elected in 1928 from Illinois's First District. By then, White had been dead for ten years, yet he was survived almost miraculously by three former House comrades-in-arms—each a leader of the same "black phalanx" White once boasted of representing: former brother-in-law Henry Cheatham; John Roy Lynch of Mississippi; and Thomas Miller of South Carolina. (George Murray, his escort to McKinley's inauguration in 1897, died in 1926.)

Two of those three survivors—Lynch and Miller, energetic octogenarians, both living in Chicago—stood by De Priest's side on a wintry day in February 1930 to be introduced to the U.S. House once again, shortly after the Seventy-First Congress convened.[24] Lynch had last served in Congress nearly fifty years earlier, before becoming McKinley's paymaster in the U.S. Army during the Spanish-American War. Miller left the U.S. House in 1891, after overlapping for one term with Cheatham, the youngest survivor at seventy-three, who did not attend.

Still, it is not hard to visualize the proud faces of Cheatham, White, and all the rest of their nineteenth-century predecessors in the aisles that day, offering spiritual support and giving new flesh to the skeletal remains of a once-proud tradition—fulfilling the prediction George White had made nearly three decades earlier. And with almost surrealistic whimsy, black congressmen soon became permanent fixtures on the House floor—just not as Republicans. De Priest, the only black congressman for three terms, would become the last black Republican in the House for half a century.

In 1934, De Priest was defeated by the nation's first Democratic black congressman, Arthur Mitchell, a former Republican who switched parties in 1932. Never again would the House be without its "black phalanx" leader— even though newer congressmen, unlike their nineteenth-century predecessors, would hail from the North and Midwest until the 1970s. The South's next black congressmen—Democrats Andrew Young of Georgia and Barbara Jordan of Texas—were elected in 1972. North Carolina's next black members of Congress, Democrats Eva Clayton and Mel Watt, entered the Capitol in 1993. The next black House Republican, Oklahoma's J. C. Watts Jr., won election only in 1994.

❧

In another of history's small ironies, White died only a week before former president Theodore Roosevelt. The Rough Rider's death in early January 1919 predictably overshadowed almost everything else of note, just as he had once overshadowed his martyred predecessor. Roosevelt's death, along with the Versailles peace negotiations, prevented many newspapers from giving more than cursory notice to the man Roosevelt had once passed over for appointment.

Ten days after his sixty-sixth birthday, George White passed away in his sleep in Philadelphia, on December 28, 1918, of natural causes. His long life and sudden death were widely noted, if only briefly, in newspaper articles across the eastern and southern United States, although the *New York Times,* which had once cited his speeches on its front page, used the incorrect middle initial in its two-line obituary, almost as a sloppy afterthought.[25]

In another ironic twist, the *Raleigh News and Observer,* still published by White's longtime adversary Josephus Daniels, paused to reflect on White's passing with a front-page version of the Associated Press story, despite Daniels's animosity toward White.[26] A less personalized yet full-page article, complete with photograph, appeared months later in the *Crisis,* the quarterly journal of the National Association for the Advancement of Colored People (NAACP), penned by W. E. B. Du Bois. With only minor errors, the article re-traced White's illustrious career, mentioning a little-known instance of civil rights activism: "When 'The Clansman' was offered in the theatres of Philadelphia, ex-Congressman White voiced a protest against it to Mayor Weaver and it was barred."[27]

That incident had occurred a decade earlier, just after White's move to Philadelphia. White had served in North Carolina's General Assembly decades earlier with *The Clansman*'s Democratic author, Thomas Dixon Jr., whom he derided; White had also served with a Republican legislator with a similar name and may have confused the two.[28] Author Dixon, a bestselling proponent of racial segregation, had moved to New York in 1889, writing *The Clansman* in 1905 to discredit Harriet Beecher Stowe's *Uncle Tom's Cabin.*

Du Bois and White had never been close, philosophically or personally, yet each respected the other's talents and substance from working together in organizational affiliations. After noting his many offices, including final service as assistant city solicitor, assigned to cases in Philadelphia's Municipal Court, Du Bois paid the ultimate closing tribute to his fallen comrade—and fellow leader in the NAAC and NAACP. Often an acid-tongued critic of politicians in general, and an independent thinker—radically so, as years wore on—he was not given to praising many black Republican colleagues, whom he regarded as incapable of true racial leadership. But George White was uniquely different, and Du Bois did not expect him to be equaled, or even replaced.

"This man was elected to Congress in the era following Reconstruction," Du Bois noted respectfully. "Since that time, the 'Grandfather Clauses' have operated to make Mr. White 'the last of the Negro congressmen.'"[29] But the longest and most flattering account of White's life came in a personal tribute by his longtime friend T. Thomas Fortune for Philadelphia's black-owned *Tribune.*

As fellow students at Howard in the mid-1870s—Fortune in college preparatory courses, White in the last year of teacher training—the two men had known each other for more than forty years. They had once served together as officers in the NAAC's early days. In the decades since their first meeting, Fortune had continued to follow his career closely; in his own memory, one anecdote in particular stood out to epitomize White's great contributions:

> He [White] was much in favor with national leaders during his incumbency in Congress and this included President McKinley. On the occasion of one of the visits to the White House, the writer was present during a conversation between President McKinley and Mr. White. They discussed several matters, but just before leaving Mr. White said, "By the way, Mr. President, I don't seem to be able to get the ear of a Department Chief in appointing a constituent of mine."
>
> After the President had been informed, he drew from his vest pocket a small pad and, writing a few words addressed to the Departmental official, signed the name of William McKinley and handed it to Mr. White. The appointment was made that day.[30]

He and White had differed on a host of public issues over the years, particularly over White's fervent support for McKinley in Congress. Fortune had not been an admirer of McKinley, and he and White had crossed intellectual swords on occasion, yet the two had remained respectful friends in spite of it all. "To have known Mr. White didn't necessarily mean that you would share his views," Fortune concluded, "but it is safe to say that on account of his strong personality and ability, coupled with his stately and gentlemanly bearing, you were compelled to respect him."[31]

To those who had known George White well, no more revealing words were ever spoken of him than those of Fortune's epitaph. And perhaps no more apt description could ever be offered of the statesman and prophet now following William McKinley to his own final reward.

NOTES

INTRODUCTION

1. Margaret Leech, *In The Days of McKinley* (New York: Harper and Brothers, 1959).

2. Kevin Phillips, "Surprisingly Modern McKinley," in *William McKinley* (New York: Times Books; Henry Holt, 2003), 28–53.

3. Ibid., 149.

4. Robert W. Merry, *William McKinley: Architect of the Twentieth Century* (New York: Simon and Schuster, 2017), 47.

5. Mary M. Fisher, "Benjamin W. Arnett," in *DANB*, ed. Rayford W. Logan and Michael R. Winston (New York: Norton, 1982), 17–18.

6. John R. Lynch, *Reminiscences of an Active Life: The Autobiography of John Roy Lynch*, ed. John Hope Franklin (Chicago: University of Chicago Press, 1970). Lynch outlived the president by thirty-eight years, completing his memoirs just before his death at age ninety-two. Friends with McKinley from 1884—when Lynch chaired the convention—until 1901, he was appointed as wartime U.S. Army paymaster in 1898, remaining in the army until 1906.

7. Louis R. Harlan, *Booker T. Washington: The Making of a Black Leader, 1856–1901* (New York: Oxford University Press, 1972), 286.

8. Rayford W. Logan, *The Betrayal of the Negro, from Rutherford B. Hayes to Woodrow Wilson* (repr., New York: Da Capo, 1997), 84, 88.

9. "Ohio's African American Origins and History," accessed April 7, 2016, www.blackdemographics.com/states/ohio .

10. Logan, *Betrayal of the Negro,* 29–32.

11. "The Character of the Man," *WCA,* September 28, 1901. After McKinley's death, John Green recalled an 1891 incident when McKinley declined to check into a segregated Cincinnati hotel because it refused to serve Green and sought another hotel serving both races.

12. The three were William Clifford and Harry Smith of Cuyahoga County and Samuel Hill of Hamilton County, all elected to Ohio's legislature in 1893.

13. Lynch, *Reminiscences,* 282–83, 371–80.

14. Ibid., 283.

15. "McKinley in the South," *AJ,* March 21, 1895.

16. Herbert Croly, *Marcus Alonzo Hanna: His Life and Work* (New York: Macmillan, 1912), 175.

17. Eric Rauchway, *Murdering McKinley: The Making of Theodore Roosevelt's America* (New York: Hill and Wang, 2003), 67–68.

18. Clarence A. Bacote, "Negro Officeholders in Georgia under President McKinley," *Journal of Negro History* 44, no. 3 (July 1959): 217; "No Color Line for 'Mack,'" *AJ,* March 28, 1895.

19. Lynch, *Reminiscences,* 373.

20. "McKinley in the South."

21. The race of delegates is not listed in the *Official Proceedings of the Eleventh Republican National Convention,* although one locally prepared version—*History of the Republican Party Together with the Proceedings of the Republican National Convention at St. Louis, June 16th–18th, 1896* (Chas. M. Harvey, ed.)—gave racial designations for most "colored" delegates from Florida, Mississippi, South Carolina, and Texas. Many 1896 delegates returned in 1900, when a commemorative book displayed photographs of most black delegates (*An Art Souvenir of the Republican National Convention Held at Philadelphia, June 19–22, 1900* [Philadelphia: Gatchell and Manning, 1900]).

22. The author compared names of delegates listed in Harvey's *History* and *Official Proceedings* against period newspaper articles, previous state delegations to conventions, U.S. census listings, the 1900 Gatchell and Manning's *Art Souvenir,* and other references to determine race of southern delegates and from other states, identifying at least seventy-four black voting delegates

in 1896. In addition to those named in the text, other voting delegates were: *Alabama*—John Harmon, Andrew N. Johnson; *Arkansas*—Elias Morris; *District of Columbia*—Perry Carson; *Florida*—Isaac Purcell, Lemuel Livingston; *Georgia*—Thomas Dent, John Deveaux, Henry Johnson, Judson Lyons, William Matthews, Luther Price, J. C. Styles, Frank Wimberly, Christopher Wimbish, Isaac Wood; *Louisiana*—J. B. Brooks, Thomas Cage, S. W. Green, William Harper, W. W. Johnson, Richard Simms; *Maryland*—William Tilghman; *Mississippi*—George Bowles, Wesley Crayton, George Granberry, E. H. Lampton, Richard Littlejohn, Eugene Pettibone, R. A. Simmons, William Simmons; *Nebraska*—Lloyd Lindsey; *North Carolina*—James Butler, Jonathan Hannon, Edward Johnson, Abraham Middleton; *South Carolina*—William Boykin, R. C. Brown, Wesley Dixson, John Fordham, Zacharias Walker, Charles Wilder, Joshua Wilson; *Tennessee*—John Bosley; *Texas*—David Abner, Richard Allen, Edward Anderson, Robert Armstrong, Charles Ferguson, Hugh Hancock, M. W. Lawson, Mack Rodgers, David Taylor, B. F. Wallace; *Virginia*—John Asbury, Alfred Harris, Thomas Walker.

23. Ibid. At least sixty alternate delegates in 1896 were African Americans; how many went to Saint Louis is uncertain. Black alternates came from the District of Columbia and eleven of twelve southern states sending black delegates, plus Illinois, Indiana, Kentucky, Massachusetts, Michigan, Minnesota, Missouri, New York, Ohio, Pennsylvania, West Virginia, and Arizona Territory.

24. *Official Proceedings of Eleventh Republican National Convention,* 35.

25. "Sambo for Fat Tom," *St. Louis Post-Dispatch,* June 15, 1896.

26. "Negroes' Demands," *St. Louis Post-Dispatch,* June 16, 1896.

27. Ibid.

28. "Under the Dome," *RNO,* June 21, 1896.

29. Maurine Christopher, *America's Black Congressmen* (New York: Thomas Y. Crowell, 1971), 120–22.

30. North Carolina elected a dozen black legislators in 1896, joining other winners from South Carolina, Tennessee, Texas, and West Virginia. Blacks no longer served in most southern legislatures, although Georgia elected four black legislators in 1900 and 1901. At least ten non-southern states periodically elected black legislators, beginning with Vermont in 1836, including postwar legislatures in Colorado, Illinois, Indiana, Kansas, Massachusetts, Michigan, Nebraska, Ohio, and Wyoming.

31. George H. White, letter to the editor, *WP,* April 23, 1901; "John Patterson Green," in *Who's Who in Colored America,* ed. Thomas Yenser (New York: Who's Who in Colored America Corp., 1941), 214–17; Lynch, *Reminiscences,* 393.

CHAPTER ONE

1. Leech, *In the Days of McKinley,* 118.

2. "The White House," *WES,* March 10, 1897. The Bible was formally presented to McKinley on March 10 by Bishop Arnett and other black clergymen and leaders.

3. Swearing-in ceremony for President William McKinley, accessed April 5, 2016, www.inaugural.senate.gov/swearing-in/event/william-mckinley-1897.

4. Ibid., italics added.

5. Ibid.

6. Republican Party Platform of 1896, June 16, 1896, www.presidency.ucsb.edu/ws/?pid=29629.

7. www.inaugural.senate.gov/swearing-in/address/address-by-william-mckinley-1897.

8. "Louisiana Republicans Angry," *NYT,* July 20, 1898.

9. Judson W. Lyons, *Appointments Which Afro-Americans Have Received from President McKinley* (Washington, D.C.: n.p., 1898), 7–9. Among 1896 convention delegates identified as African American, dozens were either nominated for or held postmasterships or other federal jobs after 1897: William Boykin, Herschel Cashin, Walter Cohen, Edmund Deas, Henry Demas, Thomas Dent, John Deveaux, Charles Ferguson, Mifflin Gibbs, John Fordham, Jonathan Hannon, Alfred Harris, Ferdinand Havis, James Hill, Edward Johnson, Henry Johnson, Joseph Lee, Lemuel Livingston, Judson Lyons, William Matthews, Abraham Middleton, Monroe Morton, Mack Rodgers, Henry Rucker, Robert Smalls, Thomas Walker, Charles Wilder, Joshua Wilson, Frank Wimberly, and Christopher Wimbish. Alternates John Green, Thomas Keys, James Lewis, and Richard Wright received federal jobs under McKinley.

10. Leech, *In the Days of McKinley,* 122.

11. "At the White House: Great Demand for an Elevator," *WES,* May 6, 1897. The building's only elevator, installed by James Garfield near the dining room, used hydraulic pressure with water pumped from a roof reservoir and was reserved for family use. Official users in 1897 included Secretary of State Sherman and "occasionally some prominent man who doesn't feel able to climb the steps."

12. Leech, *In the Days of McKinley,* 133.

13. By mid-April, the *Evening Star* began to retitle the column periodically as "At the White House." Its position varied from front page to an inside page.

14. "The White House," *WES,* March 8, 1897.

15. *AJ,* April 21, 1897, cited in Bacote, "Negro Officeholders in Georgia under President McKinley," 217–39.

16. "The White House," *WES,* April 17, 1897.

17. Ibid.

18. "The White House," *WES,* March 31, 1897; "From Washington," *Alexandria (Va.) Gazette,* April 19, 1897. The applicant, Capt. John Leach, wished to become U.S. consul at Victoria, British Columbia, Canada; White represented Pritchard with this application, while Populist congressman Skinner favored another candidate, former state senator John Respess of Washington, North Carolina. Person, elected to the North Carolina Senate in 1896, served as Rocky Mount postmaster for three years under Harrison.

19. *CR,* 55th Cong., 1st Sess., 30, 1:550–51.

20. Ibid.

21. Ibid.

22. Ibid.

23. Rep. William Kitchin of Roxboro was the state's lone Democrat. Four years earlier, Democrats had held an eight-to-one edge. In the Fifty-Fourth Congress, the state's delegation had

originally consisted of three from each party, until Populist Rep. Charles Martin won his contest against Democrat James Lockhart, changing the makeup to two Democrats, four Populists, and three Republicans.

24. "The White House: First Formal Meeting of the Cabinet Today: The Rush of Callers on the President Continues," *WES,* March 9, 1897. According to the column, Pritchard was seen entering or leaving the White House at least five times that month: March 15, 17, 18, 20, and 25.

25. "The White House," *WES,* June 16, 1898; Joe L. Morgan, "Jeter Conley Pritchard," in *DNCB,* ed. William S. Powell (Chapel Hill: University of North Carolina Press, 1979–1997), 5:139. In mid-1898, the *Evening Star* described Pritchard as "one of the President's closest friends." Morgan does not specify which cabinet post Pritchard declined.

26. Benjamin R. Justesen, *George Henry White: An Even Chance in the Race of Life* (Baton Rouge: Louisiana State University Press, 2001), 206–8.

27. "Objection Made to Minister Taylor," *NYT,* December 21, 1893. Cleveland nominated Taylor as minister to Bolivia in September 1893, but withdrew the nomination in 1894 in the face of certain rejection, after the outgoing minister called Taylor "unacceptable to Bolivia." Black nominee Herbert Astwood was rejected by the Senate in 1893 as consul to Calais, France.

28. "Gossip on Offices: Positions That Will Be Given to Colored Men," *WES,* April 9, 1897.

29. Ibid.

30. Redistricting—shifting black-majority counties into adjacent districts and replacing them with Democratic-majority counties—and other changes in voting rules engineered by North Carolina's Democratic legislative majority after 1890 had depressed Republican votes in the "Black Second." Cheatham lost a three-way race in 1892 to Democrat Frederick Woodard by two thousand votes. Cheatham's total declined significantly in 1894, carrying only one county; even a united Republican Party would have lost that election. For a thorough discussion of the 1892 and 1894 elections, see Eric Anderson, *Race and Politics in North Carolina, 1872–1901: The Black Second* (Chapel Hill: University of North Carolina Press, 1981), 200–220.

31. "Cheatham Is Named: Ex-Congressman from North Carolina to Be Recorder of Deeds," *WES,* May 11, 1897.

32. "Mr. Taylor's Place: His Resignation in the Hands of the President, Said to Have Been Called For: Ex-Representative Cheatham Slated for Recordership," *WES,* May 7, 1897.

33. *Journal of the Executive Proceedings of the Senate of the United States of America,* February 8, 1898.

34. "Eastern Snapshots," *RG,* 24 April 1897. Strong support from Pritchard and lukewarm support from Butler strengthened White's hand; no other black congressman had ever enjoyed such an advantage.

35. "About People You Know," *RG,* July 31, 1897, and August 14, 1897; Anderson, *Race and Politics in North Carolina,* 243–46, including table 6. "Congressman White left for Wilmington Sunday last; he has made about 39 appointments up to the present—about 23 Negro postmasters. He's moving on," wrote the *Gazette,* soon trimming numbers to 36 and 20, respectively.

36. *Post Office Department Records of Appointment of Postmasters,* microfilm, National Archives; Twelfth Census of the United States, Bertie and Halifax Counties, N.C., 1900, microfilm, National Archives. Of these seven, five remained active as postmasters in June 1900, when the

census was taken. Baker left office in early 1899 to return to school teaching; Pittman, also Tillery's postmaster from 1890 to 1893, was removed by October 1898. Cheek's youngest son, born in April 1900, was named Jeter C. Cheek.

37. *Post Office Department Records of Appointment,* microfilm, National Archives; Twelfth Census of the United States, Edgecombe, Northampton, Warren, and Wayne Counties, N.C, 1900, microfilm, National Archives. Three of the five remained active postmasters in June 1900. Hargett was removed from office by February 1899; Langford was replaced in January 1898.

38. *Official Register of the United States, 1897* (Washington, D.C.: U.S. Government Printing Office, 1897). Most postmasters received salaries of less than $500 annually. In July 1897, Bertie County figures ranged from $190 at Powellsville to $642 at Windsor; in Halifax, the highest salaries were at Littleton ($998.40) and Scotland Neck ($1,100). The highest Second District salaries that year: Kinston ($1,300), Rocky Mount and Tarboro (both $1,600), and Wilson ($1,700). Not shown in 1897, Weldon's salary in 1899 was $1,100.

39. "Eastern Snapshots," *RG,* November 6, 1897.

40. Phillips, *William McKinley,* 18–19, 48, 148–49; Leech, *In the Days of McKinley,* 23–24. Phillips posits that McKinley had felt this way since his Civil War experiences. Leech barely mentions the issue but concedes a philosophical commitment to the issues of racial justice, based on Civil War service and black suffrage.

41. "Negroes in Federal Offices," *NYT,* April 16, 1903. After eighteen months in office, Roosevelt had appointed or reappointed just fifteen African Americans, according to the *Times,* whereas "President McKinley made a record on colored men, his appointments extending to almost every department of the government." Roosevelt had recently defended his record of black appointments in a well-publicized letter to *Atlanta Constitution* editor Clark Howell.

42. The William F. Powell Elementary School, Camden, N.J., accessed May 21, 2018, www.dvrbs.com/camden-school/CamdenNJ-School-WiiliamFPowell.htm. The school was named for Powell in 1926. Its website says Powell's political activities led Senator Sewell "to encourage President McKinley to appoint Powell U.S. chargé d'affaires to Santo Domingo (February 18, 1898 to July 12, 1904) and U.S. Minister (his actual title was Envoy Extraordinary and Minister Plenipotentiary) to Haiti (June 17, 1897 to November 1905)."

43. "At the White House: Field Day for Office-Seekers at the Executive Mansion," *WES,* June 26, 1897. Dahomey was a popular topic in the black press, the French having reduced the kingdom to colony status in 1894. Cook's *In Dahomey,* the first modern African American musical comedy, opened on Broadway in 1903.

44. "Self-Constituted Leader: He Is to Pass upon All Colored Presidential Appointments," *WB,* June 5, 1897.

CHAPTER TWO

1. The phrase and similar ones recurred in White's speeches on the House floor, beginning in 1898 and for the rest of his congressional career: "An even chance in the race of life is all we ask; and then if we cannot reach the goal, let the devil take the hindmost one!" (*CR,* 55th Cong., 2d Sess., 31, 1:2556, March 7, 1898).

2. "Normal Graduates," *WES,* June 2, 1897; "Eastern Snapshots," *RG,* September 18, 1897.

3. *Report of the Industrial Commission on Agriculture and Agricultural Labor, Including Testimony, with Review and Topical Digest Thereof,* vol. 10 (Washington, D.C.: U.S. Government Printing Office, 1901), 427.

4. Ibid.

5. Ibid., 428.

6. Ibid., 426.

7. "Negroes at Ridgewood: Issuing of the Emancipation Proclamation Suitably Celebrated: Congressman White Makes a Speech," *Brooklyn Daily Eagle,* September 22, 1897.

8. "To Afro-Americans: Plain Talk by Colored Congressman White of North Carolina," *Brooklyn Daily Eagle,* September 24, 1897.

9. Ibid.

10. "At the White House: A North Carolina Office," *WES,* October 9, 1897.

11. American Historical Society, *A Standard History of Oklahoma,* vol. 3 (Chicago: American Historical Society, 1916), 1159–61. Cook was elected to the Oklahoma state house in 1908 and ran unsuccessfully for Congress in 1914.

12. White also appointed Emma Roberts, twenty-nine, at Jackson; Elenora Newsome at Margarettsville; Willie Coats, thirty-four, at Seaboard; and Ada Dickens, twenty-two, at Lawrence. Cora Davis, appointed by Cheatham, served for less than two years at Halifax (1889–90) before removal; he appointed Mrs. Baker in 1891. Another Rocky Mount nominee, Sylvia Drake, failed to secure bond in 1890 and was replaced by Lee Person.

13. Other men were Winfrey Roberts, forty-one, at Rich Square; Henry Watson, twenty-five, at Macon; former legislator Hilliard Hewlin, fifty-five, at Brinkleyville; and two reappointed postmasters, Norman Keen, thirty-eight, at Essex, and William Baker, forty-four, at South Gaston.

14. Benjamin R. Justesen, "Black Tip, White Iceberg: Black Postmasters and the Rise of White Supremacy in North Carolina, 1897–1901," *North Carolina Historical Review* 82, no. 2 (April 2005): 193–227.

15. Benjamin R. Justesen, "African American Postmasters in North Carolina, 1874–1909," *North Carolina Postal Historian* 25, no. 2 (Spring 2006): 3–11. Representative Strowd appointed at least three black postmasters in predominantly black Vance: John Thorpe at Kittrell, Brutus Young at Middleborough, and Robert Field at Williamsboro. Long-serving black postmasters at Wake County's Method (Berry O'Kelly) and Craven's James City (Washington Spivey) continued to serve by reappointment.

16. "At the White House," *WES,* September 17, 1897.

17. Ibid.; *AJ,* September 14, 1897, cited in Bacote, "Negro Officeholders in Georgia under President McKinley." Bacote discusses the Lyons controversy at length.

18. "Office for a Colored Man: Ex-Senator Blanche K. Bruce Appointed Register of the Treasury," *NYT,* December 3, 1897.

19. "Georgia Post Office Boycott," *NYT,* February 5, 1898. John Clopton, Troup County farmer-businessman, held the post briefly under Harrison.

20. "Negro Postmaster Shot: Isaac H. Loftin of Hogansville, Georgia, Dying of His Wounds," *WES,* September 16, 1897; "White Citizens of Hogansville, Georgia, Oppose the Appointment of

a Negro Postmaster with Rifle Bullets," *CT,* September 26, 1897; "War on Negro Officials: The Attempt to Assassinate the Postmaster at Hogansville, Ga., a Carefully Planned Crime," *NYT,* September 18, 1897. Isaiah Loftin's first name was sometimes misspelled as "Isaac."

21. "The Administration Halts: No Appointments of Negro Postmasters in the South since One Was Shot in Georgia," *NYT,* October 2, 1897. Any moratorium was short-lived; temporary commissions were issued by McKinley during the Senate recess (July 24–December 15) for two appointees requiring Senate confirmation: Samuel Bampfield of Beaufort, South Carolina, son-in-law of ex-representative Robert Smalls, and Colin Anthony at Scotland Neck, North Carolina.

22. "White Citizens of Hogansville, Georgia," *CT,* September 26, 1897.

23. Ibid.

24. "The Hogansville Incident Closed," *NYT,* September 29, 1897.

25. "At the White House," *WES,* October 4, 1897.

26. "Postmaster Loftin to Stick," *NYT,* October 4, 1897.

27. Justesen, "Black Tip, White Iceberg," 213.

28. The sawmill operator Cicero Harris Jr., thirty-one, was the son of the Panacea Springs postmaster under Harrison. The farmers were Edward Clarke, twenty-five, at Kelford; William Bennett, thirty, at Powellsville; and York Whitehead, forty-nine, at Aurelian Springs. and merchant-grocers Matthew Martin, thirty-two, at Kitchin, and Edmond Hart, thirty-six, at Princeville.

29. "Colored Office Holders," *NYT,* October 27, 1897.

30. Ibid. This total reflected only national departmental positions, not the two dozen–plus black local postmasters named since March 4.

31. "Colored Office Holders," *NYT,* October 27, 1897.

32. Mary Fisher, "Benjamin W. Arnett," in *DANB,* ed. Logan and Winston, 18. Elected in 1885 to a single term in the Ohio State House, Arnett (1838–1906) was its first black Republican.

33. Cheatham soon hired Arnett's son Henry as an assistant; Benjamin Jr., a minister, became an army chaplain in mid-1898. According to the *Washington Post* (April 24, 1897), Green was a strong candidate for the District recorder's post, having enlisted powerful assistance from John D. Rockefeller and "nearly every millionaire in the Mississippi Valley states," plus Sen. Mark Hanna and Republican leaders in fifteen states.

34. Benjamin R. Justesen, "African American Consuls Abroad, 1897–1909," *Foreign Service Journal* (September 2004): 72–76.

35. "At the White House. Rev. Owen L. W. Smith to be Minister to Liberia," *WES,* December 23, 1897.

36. *Who's Who in America, 1901–1902,* s.v. "Owen Lun West Smith," 1053; *The National Cyclopedia,* s.v. "Owen Lun West Smith," 14 (1906): 206.

37. "Rev. Owen L. W. Smith to be Minister."

38. "William McKinley: First Annual Message to Congress, December 6, 1897," The American Presidency Project, Miller Center, University of Virginia, Charlottesville, www.presidency.ucsb.edu/ws/index.php?pid=29538. The new U.S. minister to Spain was Gen. Stewart Woodford, confirmed in June 1897.

39. "William McKinley: First Annual Message to Congress."

40. Benjamin R. Justesen, *George Henry White: An Even Chance in the Race of Life* (Baton Rouge: Louisiana State University Press, 2001), 179–200.

41. "North Carolina's Colored Congressman May Appoint a Negro," *RNO,* April 23, 1897. Only two black candidates had been appointed to West Point since 1880: "If Mr. White does this, without leaving the selection to competition, many men say it will defeat him in his district, as white Republicans would rebel against such action."

CHAPTER THREE

1. "Excitement at the Zoo," *WES,* February 2, 1898 ("Last night was the coldest night of the year").

2. Leech, *In the Days of McKinley,* 138–39.

3. *CR,* 55th Cong. 1st Sess., 31, 1:541–42, January 11, 1898.

4. Ibid.

5. Ibid., 1:542.

6. William Fitzhugh Lee to William R. Day, January 26, 1898, Dispatches from Havana, RG 59, National Archives, Washington, D.C.

7. "Harry Gratwick, "Remembering Mainers on Board the USS *Maine,*" accessed May 2, 2019, www.WorkingWaterfront.com; Rebecca Livingston, "Sailors, Soldiers, and Marines of the Spanish-American War: The Legacy of USS *Maine,*" *Prologue* 30, no. 1 (Spring 1998), U.S. National Archives & Records Administration, Washington, D.C. The unnamed teammate was probably John Bloomer of Portland, Maine, the only team member to survive the *Maine* disaster.

8. Gratwick, "Remembering Mainers on Board the USS *Maine.*"

9. Gerald Astor, *The Right to Fight: A History of African Americans in the Military* (Novato, Calif.: Presidio, 1998), 56–57.

10. Jose M. Hernandez, "Cuba in 1898," in "The World of 1898: The Spanish-American War," accessed May 2, 2019, Hispanic Division, Library of Congress, www.loc.gov/rr/hispanic/1898/hernandez.html.

11. "No Longer Minister: Senor de Lome's Resignation Accepted by His Government," *WES,* February 10, 1898.

12. "Will Also Go to Cuba," *WES,* February 2, 1898.

13. "The Destruction of USS Maine," U.S. Department of the Navy, Naval Historical Center, accessed May 2, 2019, www.history.navy.mil/browse-by-topic/disasters-and-phenomena/destruction-of-uss-maine.html. Eyewitness reports from shore did not see the characteristic "plume" of water associated with mine explosions. Technical experts also argued that a far more likely cause of the explosion was spontaneous combustion of coal in the hold, which ignited five tons of explosives adjacent to it.

14. The *Cleveland Gazette,* for instance, published a full list—including names of four uninjured black sailors—in its "Doings of the Race" column on April 9, 1898.

15. Known as the Sampson Board for its president, Rear Admiral William Sampson, the Naval Court published its findings quickly under congressional pressure. Available at www.spanamwar.com/mainerpt.htm, accessed May 2, 2019.

16. *CR,* 55th Cong., 2d Sess., 31, 1:2556.

17. "Baker's Character," *New York Independent,* April 2, 1898. The magazine obtained details by interviewing a "reliable" Lake City source.

18. *List of South Carolina Postmasters,* U.S. Post Office Department Records, National Archives.

19. "The Cause of the Tragedy," *CNC,* February 23, 1898.

20. Ibid.

21. "The Lake City Case," *CNC,* April 14, 1899. Inspector Moye's detailed testimony came at the 1899 trial of Baker's accused killers.

22. "The Cause of the Tragedy."

23. Ibid.

24. "All Is Very Quiet down in Lake City," *Columbia (S.C.) State,* February 25, 1898.

25. "The Lake City Case."

26. Ibid.

27. Details are taken from Mrs. Baker's testimony, given in federal court in April 1899 and recounted in "Story of a Terrible Crime," *CNC,* April 12, 1899.

28. "Story of a Terrible Crime"; "The Story of Baker's Wife," *CNC,* February 23, 1898; "More Divers Wanted: Consul General Lee Wires the State Department," *WES,* February 21, 1898. The Charleston newspaper's special correspondent cited a dubious interview with Mrs. Baker at Duke Burgess's house on February 22.

29. "All Is Very Quiet down in Lake City."

30. Terence Finnegan, *A Deed So Accursed: Lynching in Mississippi and South Carolina, 1881–1940* (Charlottesville: University Press of Virginia, 2013), 81–95.

31. Ibid.

32. "President Directs Investigation," *WES,* February 24, 1898.

33. "Murder in South Carolina: Negro Postmaster and Baby Killed, and the Bodies Burned," *NYT,* February 23, 1898; "The Outrage at Lake City: Post Office to Be Discontinued and a Reward Offered for Murderers," *NYT,* February 24, 1898.

34. "What Is Said in Washington," *CNC,* February 23, 1898; "The Outrage in Washington," *CNC,* February 25, 1898.

35. "What Is Said in Washington," *CNC,* February 23, 1898; "The Outrage in Washington," *CNC,* February 25, 1898.

36. *AJ,* September 27, 1897, cited in Bacote, "Negro Officeholders in Georgia under President McKinley."

37. "William H. Ellerbe Dead," *NYT,* June 3, 1899. Ellerbe died of tuberculosis at age thirty-six.

38. "The Outrage in Washington"; "Lake City Citizens under Arms," *Charleston (S.C.) Sunday News,* February 27, 1898.

39. "President Directs Investigation"; "Official Report on Lake City Case," *Columbia (S.C.) State,* March 5, 1898.

40. "Objectionable Postmasters," *CNC,* March 2, 1898. The murder of J. R. Freeman, a "well recommended" recent appointee not yet bonded or serving, did not seem related to his appointment.

41. "Efforts to Avenge Murder, Cabinet Offers Heavy Rewards for the Slayers of Postmaster Baker of South Carolina," *CNC,* March 5, 1898.

42. "The Lake City Tragedy," editorial, *Baltimore Sun,* February 24, 1898. This was Gary's last public office, but his declining health did not prevent him from living to the age of eighty-seven (dying in late 1920) or, indeed, from outliving McKinley, all but two onetime cabinet colleagues, and even the new postmaster general, Charles Smith.

43. H.R. Res. 171, *CR,* 55th Cong., 2d Sess., p. 2427; Senate Con. Res. No. 29, *CR,* 55th Cong., 2d Sess.

44. H.R. Res. 171, *CR,* 55th Cong., 2d Sess., p. 2427; Senate Con. Res. No. 29, *CR,* 55th Cong., 2d Sess.

45. H.R. Rep. No. 1379, *CR,* 55th Cong., 2d Sess., p. 5058.

46. Alfreda M. Duster, ed., *Crusade for Justice: The Autobiography of Ida B. Wells* (Chicago: University of Chicago Press, 1970), 253.

47. Ibid., 252–53.

48. As reprinted in *CG,* April 6, 1898.

49. Duster, *Crusade for Justice,* 253; "To Punish the Lynchers: Mrs. Ida B. Wells Barnett Makes an Appeal to the President," *Indianapolis (Ind.) News,* March 21, 1898. See also Trichita Chestnut, "Lynching: Ida B. Wells-Barnett and the Outrage over the Frazier Baker Murder," *Prologue* 40 (Fall 2008): 20–29

50. Duster, *Crusade for Justice,* 253.

51. *Congressional Directory, Fifty-fifth Congress, March 4, 1897, to March 3, 1899.* Once all contests were settled, a total of twenty-three southern and Border State Republicans sat in the Fifty-Fifth Congress: five from Maryland, four each from Kentucky and Virginia, three each from North Carolina and Missouri, two from Tennessee, and one each from Alabama and Texas. The old southern Republican caucus may have become dormant; unlike Cheatham, White was not an active member of any regional group.

CHAPTER FOUR

1. "Register Bruce Dead: Eminent Representative of Colored Race Expires This Morning," *WES,* March 17, 1898.

2. "His Worth Attested," *WES,* March 21, 1898.

3. Ibid.

4. Ibid.

5. Ibid. Other honorary pallbearers: James Lewis of Louisiana; M. M. Holland and Rev. William Waring of Ohio; and Robert Church of Tennessee.

6. "Judson Lyons for Register," *NYT,* March 23, 1898.

7. Bacote, "Negro Officeholders in Georgia under President McKinley," 222.

8. Ibid., 223; *AJ,* May 10, 1897, and September 14, 1897, cited by Bacote, "Negro Officeholders in Georgia under President McKinley," 223.

9. Historian, U.S. Postal Service, 2017, *List of Known African American Postmasters, 1800s,* pdf file, accessed June 26, 2019, https://about.usps.com/who-we-are/postal-history/african-american-postmasters-19thc.pdf. The most comprehensive official list available of black

postmasters between 1866 and 1900, this list includes appointment and completion dates for all terms served by each postmaster. McKinley appointed or reappointed at least one black postmaster in eleven states and territories: Florida, Georgia, Indiana, Kansas, Maryland, Mississippi, North Carolina, Oklahoma, Pennsylvania, South Carolina, and Virginia, between inauguration and the end of his first term in March 1901.

10. Ibid. Only six black postmasters had served in Arkansas since 1867, the most recent being William A. Sloan at Ripley, whose three-year term ended in April 1894.

11. One state senator, George Bell of Desha County, had served in the 1893Arkansas legislature, along with four House members: Peter Booth and Howard McKay (Jefferson), John Carr (Phillips), and Nathan Edwards (Chicot). A total of eighty-five black men served in the Arkansas legislature after 1868.

12. "Ferdinand Havis," in *Arkansas Biography: A Collection of Notable Lives* (Fayetteville: University of Arkansas Press, 2000), 134–35.

13. "Havis Turned Down, Will Not Be Postmaster at Pine Bluff," *Pine Bluff (Ark.) Daily Graphic,* March 31, 1898. The *Graphic* story incorporated the *Daily Gazette* report into its own version.

14. *Journal of the Executive Proceedings of the Senate,* 55th Cong., March 30, 1898. Another nominee, the successful Tucson lawyer Thomas Hughes, was a respected Civil War general but fell victim to a whispering campaign involving unfounded charges of shady business dealings.

15. Joel Williamson, *The Crucible of Race: Black-White Relations in the American South since Emancipation* (New York: Oxford University Press, 1984), 192.

16. Edward T. Clark to Marion Butler, April 4, 1898, Marion Butler Papers, Southern Historical Collection, Wilson Library, University of North Carolina at Chapel Hill.

17. USPS Publication 119: *Sources of Historical Information on Post Offices, Postal Employees, Mail Routes, and Mail Contractors, October 2006.* That salary cutoff, set in 1836, applied to all postmasters appointed by the president for first-, second-, and third-class post offices.

18. Justesen, "Black Tip, White Iceberg," 201; Anderson, *Race and Politics,* 242.

19. W. A. Dunn to Marion Butler, March 16, 1898, Marion Butler Papers, Southern Historical Collection, Wilson Library, University of North Carolina at Chapel Hill.

20. Robert Kenzer, *Enterprising Southerners: Black Economic Success in North Carolina, 1865–1915* (Charlottesville: University Press of Virginia, 1997), 105; Anderson, *Race and Politics,* 243. Former sheriff R. J. Lewis of Littleton had never "heard one word, or intimation, that would in the least reflect upon his [Anthony]'s good name."

21. *Executive Journal of the U.S. Senate,* 55th Cong., 2d Sess., 818, May 23, 1898.

22. Ibid.

23. Vernon L. Stroupe, ed., *Post Offices and Postmasters of North Carolina, Colonial to USPS,* vol. 2: *Edgecombe through Northampton* (Newell: North Carolina Postal History Society, 1996), 2:121; Kenzer, *Enterprising Southerners,* 105; U.S. Census for Halifax County, N.C., 1900, microfilm. Anthony's occupation that year was listed as "assistant postmaster." Despite half-hearted attempts to remove them, the team served until May1901.

24. "Around the Lyons Banner," *WCA,* May 21, 1898; "City Paragraphs," *WCA,* June 11, 1898; "Negro Congressman Here," *AJ,* May 28, 1898.

25. *CR,* 55th Cong., 2d Sess., 31, 1:4194, April 22, 1898.

26. Ibid.

27. Ibid.

28. Ibid.

29. Ibid.

30. Ibid.

31. Ibid.

32. *CR,* 55th Cong., 2d Sess., 31, 1:4086, April 19, 1898.

33. "Letter from Congressman White," *TS,* April 14, 1898. White's letter, dated April 11, barely made the *Southerner*'s Thursday edition.

34. "J. H. Howard, Postmaster," *Roanoke News* (Plymouth, N.C.), January 13, 1898.

35. Stroupe, ed., *Post Offices and Postmasters of North Carolina,* 3:390; *Executive Journal of the U.S. Senate,* 54th Cong., 2d Sess., 375, January 28, 1897. Vick remained in office until his successor, Edwin Barnes, was confirmed by the Senate in February 1894; after Barnes died in 1897, his four-year term was completed by William Harriss, nominated by President Cleveland in January and confirmed on March 1, days before McKinley's inauguration.

36. *Executive Journal of the U.S. Senate,* 55th Cong., 2d Sess., 838, May 28, 1898; 846, May 31, 1898.

37. *CR,* 55th Cong., 2d Sess., 31, 1:4265, April 25, 1898.

38. "Race Representatives Tender the Services of 9,000,000 Loyal Colored Americans," *WCA,* April 30, 1898.

39. Other signers included ex-congressmen George Washington Murray and Robert Smalls of South Carolina; John Lynch of Mississippi, and Lynch's law partner, Robert Terrell; P. B. S. Pinchback; Lewis Douglass; Republican leaders James Lewis of Louisiana and Charles Ferguson of Texas; *Colored American* editor Edward Cooper; AME Bishops Wesley Gaines of Georgia and Moses Salter of South Carolina; a few southern state party leaders; and thirteen ministers, mostly AME, led by the Rev. W. A. J. Phillips of Little Rock, Arkansas.

40. "North Carolina," *WB,* May 28, 1898.

41. Phillips, *William McKinley,* 149; Marvin Fletcher, "The Black Volunteers in the Spanish-American War," *Military Affairs* 38, no. 2 (April 1974): 48. The *Colored American* (May 14, 1898) dated the meeting "the day following the savage attack by the *Washington Post* upon Negro leaders and organs, and its contemptuous references to the colored soldier."

42. *WCA,* May 14, 1898.

43. "Roosevelt's Resignation," *WES,* May 11, 1898; "A Colored Cavalry Regiment," *WES,* May 11, 1898; "Five Die in Action: Ensign Bagley and Four Men Killed at Cardenas, Cuba," *WES,* May 12, 1898.

44. John F. Marszalek, "Henry O[ssian] Flipper," in *DANB,* ed. Logan and Winston, 227–28.

45. West Point's second black graduate (1887), Lt. John Alexander, died of natural causes in 1894. Its third black graduate, Lt. Charles Young, now thirty-four, completed studies in 1889; assigned as a professor of military science at Wilberforce University, he was seconded temporarily from the U.S. Army's Ninth Cavalry regiment. From May 1898 to January 1899, he served as major (wartime rank) of the Ninth Ohio Volunteer Infantry, stationed in Virginia, Pennsylvania,

and South Carolina (Nancy Gordon Heine, "Charles Young," in *DANB*, ed. Logan and Winston, 677–79).

46. *CR*, 55th Cong., 2d Sess., 31, 1:2556, March 7, 1898.

47. Ibid., italics added.

48. Fletcher, "The Black Volunteers," 48–52.

49. Astor, *The Right to Fight*, 58; Willard B. Gatewood Jr., *"Smoked Yankees" and the Struggle for Empire: Letters from Negro Soldiers, 1898–1902* (Fayetteville: University of Arkansas Reprint Series, 1987), 4–5.

50. Marvin Fletcher, *The Black Soldier and Officer in the United States Army, 1891–1917* (Columbia: University of Missouri Press, 1974), 32.

51. Fletcher, "The Black Volunteers," 49; Astor, *The Right to Fight*, 60–61; Gatewood, *"Smoked Yankees,"* 22.

52. Editorial, *WCA*, May 14, 1898.

53. George Prioleau, letter to the editor, *CG*, May 13, 1898, cited in Gatewood, *"Smoked Yankees,"* 28; ibid., 24.

54. Gatewood, *"Smoked Yankees,"* 9–10; "Colored Men in the Army," *NYT*, June 25, 1898.

55. Theophilus G. Steward, letter to the editor, *Christian Recorder*, ca. May 1, 1998, reprinted in *CG*, May 28, 1898.

56. Gatewood, *"Smoked Yankees,"* 28.

57. Ibid.

58. John E. Lewis, letter to the editor, *Illinois Record* (Springfield), June 11, 1898.

59. But as Lewis himself noted in a later letter, the situation in Lakeland, Florida, tested that bond more severely (*Illinois Record*, June 25, 1898).

60. "Colored Men in the Army."

61. Ibid.

62. Fletcher, "The Black Volunteers," 49.

63. Ibid. Although scientific and medical communities remained undecided about yellow fever's cause, the theory that surviving one bout guaranteed lifetime immunity was true, according to the *Encyclopedia Britannica* (vol. 10:810, 1974 ed., s.v. "Yellow fever"). In 1898, survival was the only real vaccine for the disease, which ravaged coastal areas across the South, killing twenty thousand in 1878 alone.

64. *WB*, May 21, 1898. George White had departed for his speaking tour in Georgia and Alabama.

65. Ibid.; *NYT*, March 4, 1898.

66. Willard B. Gatewood Jr., "Alabama's 'Negro Soldier Experiment,' 1898–1899," *Journal of Negro History* 57 (October 1972): 333–34; Fletcher, "The Black Volunteers," 50.

67. Young, a prominent newspaper editor and ex-legislator, was the highest-ranking black state official and openly despised by Democrats as the apotheosis of "Negro domination." Yet even detractors grudgingly admitted his capable service as regimental colonel. Democrats took back the General Assembly after the November election (see Willard B. Gatewood Jr., "North Carolina's Negro Regiment in the Spanish-American War," *North Carolina Historical Review* 48 [October 1971]; and Gatewood, "James Hunter Young," in *DNCB*, ed. Powell, 296–98).

68. Gatewood, "North Carolina's Negro Regiment," 334–35; see also Gatewood, "Kansas Negroes and the Spanish-American War," *Kansas Historical Quarterly* 38 (Autumn 1971): 307–8. The 1900 U.S. Census shows Illinois, with nearly 5 million residents and just over 85,000 black residents, about 1.8 percent. Kansas, with 1.4 million residents, had 52,000 black residents, about 3.6 percent.

69. Gatewood, "North Carolina's Negro Regiment," 334–35; *NYT,* April 12, 1898; Edward A. Johnson, *History of Negro Soldiers in the Spanish-American War and Other Items of Interest* (Raleigh, N.C.: Capital Printing Company, 1899), 136–37. Russell, Leedy, and Tanner were elected in November 1896. Leedy was defeated in November 1898; Russell and Tanner left office in 1901.

70. Gatewood, "North Carolina's Negro Regiment," 335. Democrat Tyler served from 1898 to 1902.

71. Ibid., 336–38.

72. Ibid., 339.

73. Letter to the editor from "Ham," *RP,* October 13, 1898. His regiment, the Sixth Virginia, was not involved.

74. Young's report was cited in Gatewood, "North Carolina's Negro Regiment," 339.

75. Letters from "Ham," *RP,* 1898 and 1899.

76. Letter from "Ham" dated December 13, 1898, *RP,* December 17, 1898.

77. "Macon News" column, *Atlanta (Ga.) Constitution,* 21 December 1898; "Negro Soldier Killed in Macon," December 23, 1898; "Two Negroes are Killed in Macon," *Atlanta Constitution,* December 27, 1898; letter from "Ham" dated December 29, 1898, *RP,* January 7, 1899.

78. Gatewood, "North Carolina's Negro Regiment," 343. Black noncommissioned officers sent out across Alabama also reported occasional "harassment from local police officials," according to Gatewood, citing press reports from the *Mobile (Ala.) Daily Register* in July and August 1898.

79. Gatewood, *"Smoked Yankees,"* 9.

80. Fletcher, "The Black Volunteers," 51.

81. Astor, *The Right to Fight,* 70.

CHAPTER FIVE

1. "The Convention Very Harmonious," *RMP,* July 21, 1898.

2. "The Negro White Speaks," *RNO,* July 21, 1898.

3. Ibid.

4. Ibid.

5. "There Will Be More," editorial, *WMS,* July 23, 1898, italics added.

6. Justesen, *George Henry White,* 242. The three newspapers reacted to White's remarks after the Northampton County Republican convention, qtd. by the *Rich Square Patron and Gleaner* and *RMP.*

7. "Southwick Praises White, Letter to J. E. Bruce," letter reprinted in *WCA,* June 11, 1898.

8. "Vice Presidents and Committee Men," *Omaha Daily Bee,* July 14, 1898.

9. Willard B. Gatewood, "Washington: Capital of the Colored Aristocracy," in *Aristocrats of Color: The Black Elite, 1880–1920* (Bloomington: Indiana University Press, 1990), 39–68.

10. Mary Church Terrell, "Society among the Colored People of Washington," *Voice of the Negro* 1 (March 1904): 150–56.

11. Paul Laurence Dunbar, "Negro Life in Washington," *Harper's Weekly* 44 (January 13, 1900): 32; see also Dunbar, "Negro Society in Washington," *Saturday Evening Post* 174 (December 14, 1901): 9, 18. Dunbar recounted verbal abuse by white onlookers who saw him with Mrs. Terrell.

12. Richard W. Thompson, "Phases of Washington Life," *IF,* June 8, 15, 1895. Thompson moved to Washington in 1894, becoming managing editor of Edward E. Cooper's *Colored American;* he ran the National Negro Press Bureau, distributing syndicated articles to black newspapers.

13. Gatewood, *Aristocrats of Color,* 65. His discussion of the changing atmosphere at the turn of the twentieth century quotes a January 1907 article in the *Independent* ("What It Means to Be Colored in the Capital of the United States").

14. "Political Pointers," *WCA,* July 23, 1898.

15. Ibid.

16. The legislators' race was not typically listed in state documents; no official state directory appeared for the 1897 General Assembly. Newspaper accounts and other records confirm two state senators—Lee Person and William Henderson—and at least nine House members in 1897 were black, representing Edgecombe (2), Granville (1), Halifax (2), New Hanover (1), Northampton (1), Vance (1), and Wake (1) Counties.

17. Howe's fellow legislators were Democrats: David Sutton of Wilmington in the House and George Cannon of Brunswick County, representing the Senate's Tenth District.

18. William M. Reaves, *Strength through Struggle: The Chronological History of the African-American Community in Wilmington, North Carolina, 1865–1950* (Wilmington, N.C.: New Hanover County Public Library, 1998), 4.

19. Ibid., 310; *WMS,* January 2, 1891; *RG,* November 21, November 28, and December 5, 1896.

20. Wilmington, N.C., *Messenger,* March 26, 30, 1897.

21. Jeffrey J. Crow and Robert F. Durden, *Maverick Republican in the Old North State: A Political Biography of Daniel L. Russell* (Baton Rouge: Louisiana State University Press, 1977), 92. See *Private Laws of North Carolina,* 1897, chap. 149, pp. 280–89, and chap. 150, p. 282. The General Assembly made similar provisions for the charter of New Bern, which elected six members and to which Russell could appoint five more.

22. Ibid., 98.

23. "Rebecca Latimer Felton: American political activist," accessed November 1, 2018, https://www.britannica.com/biography/Rebecca-n-Felton. Her husband, Dr. William Harrell Felton, represented Georgia in Congress from 1875 to 1881, and more recently served in the Georgia legislature. At eighty-seven, Mrs. Felton became the first woman seated in the U.S. Senate, appointed by Georgia's governor in 1922; she served for two days after a special election, until the new senator was sworn in.

24. "Mrs. Felton Speaks: She Makes a Sensational Speech before Agricultural Society: Believes Lynching Should Prevail as Long as Defenseless Woman Is Not Better Protected," *AJ,*

August 13, 1897, reprinted in *WMS,* August 18, 1898. This text appeared in LeRae Sikes Umfleet, *A Day of Blood: The 1898 Wilmington Race Riot* (Raleigh: North Carolina Office of Archives and History, 2009), 62.

25. Editorial, *Wilmington (N.C.) Daily Record,* August 18, 1898. This text appeared in Umfleet, *A Day of Blood,* 63.

26. Umfleet, *A Day of Blood,* 215n2; Reaves, *Strength through Struggle,* 255–56. Assistant editor William Jeffries later claimed authorship; Jeffries was in Chambersburg, Pennsylvania, in December 1898, said the *Wilmington Weekly Star,* telling an acquaintance there that "I wrote the article while Manly was fifty miles away . . . without consulting Manly. . . . They may burn and kill him if he returns to Wilmington, but they will get the wrong man."

27. Umfleet, *A Day of Blood,* 64.

28. Ibid., 65. Tillman's speeches were reported in the *Wilmington (N.C.) Messenger* (October 22, 1898) and *RNO* (November 5, 1898).

29. Umfleet, *A Day of Blood,* 41–43.

30. Frank E. Saffold to Booker T. Washington, August 30, 1898, in *The Booker T. Washington Papers,* ed. Louis R. Harlan and Raymond W. Smock (Urbana: University of Illinois Press, 1975), 4:459–60. Saffold, formerly Washington's private secretary, now served as Tuskegee's business agent for boarding students.

31. Ibid.

32. *WMS,* September 6, 1898.

33. "At the White House," *WES,* September 12, 1898; "White on the Color Line," *RMP,* September 13, 1898.

34. "White on the Color Line."

35. *St. Paul (Minn.) Appeal,* September 23, 1898; *Rochester (N.Y.) Union and Advertiser,* September 15, 16, 1898. There were two competing lists of signers, one with 112 names (in Walters's posthumous memoir, *My Life and Times,* 1918) and a longer list by T. Thomas Fortune, including White and another three dozen signers not in Walters's book.

36. "Leaders Clash on Race Theories," *Rochester (N.Y.) Union and Advertiser,* September 16, 1898. Smythe's controversial views on segregated schools were anathema to many black leaders, who found his opposition to interracial marriage personally insulting to Douglass's white widow. Fortune reportedly stormed out of the meeting after Smythe won membership, returning only after that decision was reversed.

37. "A Great Campaign Is On," *WCA,* October 1, 1898. Other black nominees listed were W. P. Threatt (Alabama), Cornelius Jones (Mississippi), D. W. Scott (Missouri), George Murray (South Carolina), James Napier (Tennessee), and Thomas Jones and Daniel Butler (Virginia). The *Congressional Directory of the Fifty-Sixth Congress* listed vote totals for the following candidates: Jones, Mississippi's Third District; Scott, Missouri's Twelfth District; Murray, South Carolina's Sixth; Napier, Tennessee's Sixth; and Butler, in Virginia's Sixth. Other unsuccessful black GOP candidates included Thomas Jones in Virginia's Fourth District; two in Alabama's Sixth District (William Turner) and Ninth District (L. F. Schwartz); and Pratt Suber in South Carolina's Fourth District.

38. "Here's Result of Russellism, The Negro Congressman Demands to Sit with White People at Circus," *Greenville (N.C.) Reflector,* October 11, 1898, reprinted in *RNO,* October 12, 1898; *Wilmington (N.C.) Messenger* qtd. in *Kinston Free Press,* October 25, 1898.

39. *RMP,* October 7, 1898. The *Post* accepted his version, grudgingly admitting surprise at original reports of his "incendiary language" at Rich Square: "for he is a man of more than ordinary intelligence, and must know that . . . results naturally consequent upon [such] language falls most heavily upon his own race."

40. "Negro Women Active: Congressman White's Wife Gets Rifles and His Daughter Asks Negro Women Not to Work for White People," *RNO,* November 1, 1898.

41. Ibid.

42. "Speech at Springfield, Illinois, October 15, 1898," in William McKinley, *Speeches and Addresses of William McKinley, March 1, 1897, to May 30, 1900* (New York: Doubleday and McClure, 1900), 126–28; "At Lincoln's Old Home," *NYT,* October 16, 1898. "The crowd at Springfield was the record-breaker for the day," reported the *Times.*

43. Ibid.

44. "Color Line in Virginia: Appointment of a Colored Postmaster Used as an Argument," *WES,* October 17, 1898.

45. Historian, U.S. Postal Service, *List of Known African American Postmasters, 1800s.* McKinley also appointed Cauthorn at Dunnsville (Essex County) in 1897, while John Jackson had served since 1891 at Alanthus (Culpeper County). William Johnson, named by Cleveland in 1893, served Baynesville (Westmoreland County).

46. "Color Line in Virginia." After resigning, Twyman eventually moved to West Virginia, where he died in 1942.

47. "Thousands at Service of Thanks: Choice of the Negro," *CT,* October 17, 1898; "Chicago's Peace Jubilee Is Metaphorically and Literally Launched: The Enthusiasm Was Waterproof," Associated Press, *Los Angeles Herald,* October 19, 1898. Estimates of the size of the audience ran as high as sixteen thousand.

48. *An Address by Booker T. Washington, Principal, Tuskegee Normal and Industrial Institute, Tuskegee, Alabama, at the Thanksgiving Peace Jubilee Exercises at the Auditorium, Chicago, Illinois, October 16, 1898* (n.p., ca. 1898), 7. Washington's prepared text ran verbatim elsewhere ("Thousands at Service of Thanks," *CT*).

49. Ibid. See William Rainey Harper to Booker T. Washington, September 21, 1898, in *The Booker T. Washington Papers,* ed. Harlan and Smock, 4:472–73.

50. Anderson, *Race and Politics in North Carolina,* 1872–1901, table 20, p. 350.

51. *Congressional Directory of the Fifty-Sixth Congress,* 376. Republican Richmond Pearson, initially reported as defeated by Democrat William T. Crawford, was seated by the House in May 1900.

52. Three more southern Republicans were added in Alabama, North Carolina, and Virginia, after contests decided by the House in 1900; eleven more Republicans also represented the Border States of Kentucky, Maryland, Missouri, and West Virginia, bringing the total to nineteen. Twenty-four Republicans represented southern and Border States in the Fifty-Fifth Congress.

53. "Assembly of 1899–1900," in *North Carolina Government, 1585–1979: A Narrative and Statistical History* (Raleigh: North Carolina Department of the Secretary of State, 1981), 476–78.

CHAPTER SIX

1. Accounts of the violence often differ in detail and numbers, but at least seven blacks were killed on November 10 and 11, according to most reports. Comprehensive accounts appear in H. Leon Prather Sr., *We Have Taken a City: Wilmington Racial Massacre and Coup of 1898* (Cranbury, N.J.: Associated University Presses, 1984); and Umfleet, *Day of Blood.*

2. "The Wilmington Refugees," *WES,* November 14, 1898.

3. *Fayetteville (N.C.) Observer,* November 12, 1898.

4. Thomas Settle and R. D. Douglas to President William McKinley, telegram, November 10, 1898, and Thomas Settle to President William McKinley, telegram, November 10, 1898, both in WMcKP. Settle, a two-term Republican congressman defeated for reelection in 1896, practiced law in Asheville.

5. Crow and Durden, *A Maverick Republican,* 130. Two of Chadbourn's public letters to Pritchard were printed in the *Hickory (N.C.) Press* before the election.

6. *Wilmington (N.C.) Messenger,* October 25, 1898. Waddell spoke at Wilmington's Thalian Hall on October 24, 1898.

7. "In Wilmington: Light Negro Vote But No Intimidation Reported," *WES,* November 8, 1898. Waddell also lost to a black Republican a decade earlier for the North Carolina House of Representatives.

8. Crow and Durden, *A Maverick Republican,* 134.

9. *NYT,* October 25, 1898.

10. "To Stop Violence: If Disorder Is Renewed at Wilmington, President May Take Action," *WES,* November 11, 1898. The unnamed cabinet member was not Attorney General John Griggs, who was absent; Griggs was asked to review the situation and report back to McKinley.

11. John Q. Adams to President William McKinley, telegram, reprinted in *St. Paul (Minn.) Appeal,* November 12, 1898.

12. Ibid.

13. *Fayetteville (N.C.) Observer,* November 12, 1898.

14. Crow and Durden, *A Maverick Republican,* 135.

15. Ibid.

16. "Aims to Help Negro, Opening Sessions of the Afro-American Congress," *WP,* December 30, 1898. Green first told the audience that "it was upon the advice of some of the prominent men of the colored race that President McKinley had said nothing about the protection of the negroes in his message to Congress" but admitted later that he could name no one.

17. George H. White to President William McKinley, December 12, 1898, WMcKP. The Greensboro school is known today as North Carolina Agricultural and Technical State University.

18. James B. Dudley to President William McKinley, November 21, 1898, and John Addison

Porter to Dudley, November 26, 1898, both in WMcKP. Dudley, a Wilmington native, became president of the college in 1896.

19. James B. Dudley to Booker T. Washington, August 28, 1903, in *The Booker T. Washington Papers*, ed. Harlan and Smock, 4:521.

20. "Simple Justice," *Boston Globe,* December 2, 1898.

21. Ibid.

22. Ibid.

23. "Our 'Subject Race' at Home," *Boston Transcript,* December 15, 1898; Emmett J. Scott to Booker T. Washington, January 3, 1899, in *The Booker T. Washington Papers,* ed. Harlan and Smock, 4:549.

24. "Congressman White Lectures," *WCA,* December 17, 1898. White spoke on December 4, 1898, at the Halifax Academy of Music; his audience included both the mayor and provincial lieutenant governor. Robinson, a Virginia native and pastor of Cornwallis Street Baptist Church, had served African American pastorates in New York and Texas and soon moved on to Connecticut.

25. Judson W. Lyons, "Black Side of the Race Issue," *WP,* December 4, 1898.

26. McLaurin resigned from the Fifty-Fifth Congress on May 31, 1897, and was elected to the Senate to succeed the late Eli Stackhouse (D-S.C.) (*Biographical Directory of the United States Congress*). McLaurin served with Sen. Benjamin Tillman (D-SC), known as "Pitchfork Ben" for his fiery rhetoric, in the Senate since 1894.

27. John L. McLaurin, "The Race Problem," *WP,* November 27, 1898. McLaurin's column recounted South Carolina's Reconstruction-era experience with black legislators and applauded North Carolina efforts to end "negro domination."

28. "Answers Senator McLaurin: Representative White, of North Carolina, on the Race Troubles," *WP,* November 30, 1898. The *Post* letter was reprinted in *WB,* December 10, 1898.

29. Ibid.

30. McLaurin and Tillman were both censured by the Senate in 1902 for engaging in a fistfight on the Senate floor (*Biographical Directory of the United States Congress,* s.v. "John Lowndes McLaurin"). McLaurin stepped down at the end of his term; Tillman served until his death in 1918.

31. "To Keep Up the Fight: Senator Pritchard Not in Favor of Lily White Party," *WP,* November 30, 1898.

32. "President Visits Alabama: His Speech in the Old Confederate Capitol at Montgomery," *NYT,* December 17, 1898.

33. "Speech at Tuskegee Normal and Industrial Institute, Tuskegee, Alabama, December 16, 1898," in McKinley, *Speeches and Addresses of William McKinley,* 166–70; "Mr. McKinley at Tuskegee," *NYT,* December 17, 1898.

34. "Speech at Georgia Agricultural and Mechanical College, Savannah, Georgia, December 18, 1898," in McKinley, *Speeches and Addresses of William McKinley,* 176–77; "Address by the President: He Talks to Colored People in a Savannah Institution," *NYT,* December 19, 1898.

35. "Speech at Georgia Agricultural and Mechanical College, Savannah, Georgia, December 18, 1898," in McKinley, *Speeches and Addresses of William McKinley,* 176–77; "Address by the President: He Talks to Colored People in a Savannah Institution," *NYT,* December 19, 1898.

36. "Speech before the Legislature in Joint Assembly at the State Capitol, Atlanta, Georgia, December 14, 1898," in McKinley, *Speeches and Addresses of William McKinley,* 158–59; "The Atlanta Peace Jubilee," *Sacramento (Calif.) Record-Union,* December 15, 1898; Leech, *In the Days of McKinley,* 455–56.

37. "Racial Troubles," *WES,* December 20, 1898. Fortune addressed the National Racial Protective Association, convened by Calvin Chase, editor of the *Washington Bee.* Some believed that Chase had gotten Fortune drunk and fed him the words, hoping to discredit and embarrass him.

38. *WCA,* December 24, 1898.

39. "What Must We Do to Be Saved?," *WB,* December 24, 1898.

40. J. M. Holland to Booker T. Washington, December 20, December 21, 1898, in *The Booker T. Washington Papers,* ed. Harlan and Smock, 4:642–44; T. T. Fortune to Booker T. Washington, December 27, 1898, ibid., 4:549–50.

41. "Aims to Help Negro." Walters spoke to the Council on December 29, 1898.

42. Ibid. Green, a former Ohio state senator, was superintendent of postage at the Post Office Department, the highest-ranking black staff member there.

43. "Aims to Help Negro." Cheatham addressed the Council as last speaker on December 29, 1898.

44. Henry P. Cheatham to President William McKinley, telegram, December 15, 1898, WMcKP.

45. "Aims to Help Negro"; "A Great Uproar, Pandemonium Reigned," *WP,* December 30, 1898.

46. "Memorial to President," *WES,* December 30, 1898.

47. "Memorial on Race Troubles," *RNO,* January 1, 1899.

48. "An Influential Delegation," *WCA,* January 7, 1899.

49. "The Negroes Appeal," *RNO,* January 1, 1899; "An Influential Delegation"; "Will Not Be Suppressed," *WP,* January 3, 1899. The *RNO* account—probably gleaned from wire service reports—listed Fortune, but the *WCA* list was probably more accurate. Other members on both lists included Bishop George Clinton, Robert Pelham (Michigan), John Mitchell Jr. (Virginia), C. S. Morris (Massachusetts), Jesse Lawson, Frank Blagburn (Iowa), James Lewis (Louisiana), Richard Thompson (Indiana), F. J. Sanford (Iowa), J. A. Bray (Georgia), Daniel Murray, Alfred Cosey (New Jersey), and I. F. Bradley (Kansas). Listed on one but not both were Cooper, Cyrus Field Adams, Theophile Allain, William Ferris, and William Pledger.

50. "An Influential Delegation."

CHAPTER SEVEN

1. "Convention Called to Memorialize the Legislature," *RNO,* January 18, 1899.

2. Ibid. Estimates of the number of attendees varied widely.

3. "Booker Pays the Penalty," *Charlotte (N.C.) Daily Observer,* January 19, 1899.

4. "Memorial of Negroes Presented by Sen. Fuller on Behalf of Council," *RNO,* January 20, 1899.

5. Isaac H. Smith, "The Other Side Looked Into," letter to the editor, *RNO,* January 5, 1899.

6. Ibid.

7. *New Bern Weekly Journal,* March 3, 1899.

8. "The Negroes Appeal," *RNO,* January 19, 1899.

9. Ibid. Peace and Wright served in the 1895 General Assembly; Wright, initially elected to the 1893 General Assembly over incumbent Democrat W. W. Long, was unseated after Long's election challenge.

10. Johnson, dean of Shaw University's law department, became Claude Bernard's clerk in 1899; he held the post until 1907, when he moved to New York and became the New York State Assembly's first black member in 1918. His 1891 children's textbook, *A School History of the Negro Race in America from 1619 to 1890,* was long used in Virginia and North Carolina black schools.

11. Other officers included Charles Lane and Rev. C. S. Brown, vice presidents; Rev. James Dean, treasurer; and Rev. W. A. Byrd, chaplain.

12. "Booker Pays the Penalty."

13. *CR,* 55th Cong., 3d Sess., 32, 1:1124, January 26, 1899.

14. Ibid.1:1125–26.

15. Ibid.

16. Ibid.

17. Ibid.

18. Ibid.

19. "Not Up to Expectations," *WCA,* March 25, 1899.

20. Ibid.

21. Ibid.

22. "Council's Plan of Work," *WCA,* May 13, 1899.

23. Ibid. Reform Rabbi Silverman (1860–1930) was the first American-born rabbi to serve New York City's influential Temple Emanu-El. Colonel Ingersoll (1833–1899) was a controversial orator and former attorney general of Illinois.

24. Ibid.

25. "Cong. George H. White speaks," *WCA,* March 18, 1899.

26. Ibid.

27. Ibid.

28. *CR,* 56th Cong., 1st Sess., 33, 1:2151.

29. Willard B. Gatewood, *Black Americans and the White Man's Burden: 1898–1903* (Urbana: University of Illinois Press, 1975), 198.

30. "The Lake City Lynching, Thirteen Men Indicted in a Federal Court for the Alleged Murder of the Negro Postmaster," *NYT,* April 8, 1899.

31. Finnegan, *A Deed So Accursed,* 81–95.

32. Ibid., 88. Lathrop wrote Griggs in April 1898 that Lake City citizens were "terrorized to such an extent that it is difficult to get anyone to speak" about the crimes.

33. John William Griggs to Booker T. Washington, April 13, 1899, in *The Booker T. Washington Papers,* ed. Harlan and Smock, 5:80. Griggs responded on behalf of McKinley, to whom Washington had written earlier regarding the trial.

34. "Lake City Lynching Case: The Jury Disagrees and Judge Brawley Weeps Again," *NYT,* April 23, 1899.

35. Others on trial: Martin Ward, William Webster, Ezra McKnight, Henry Stokes, Henry Godwin (alias Toby Godwin), Moultrie Epps, Charles Joyner, Oscar Kelly, Alonzo Rogers, and Edwin Rodgers.

36. *CNC*, April 8, 1899.

37. Ibid.

38. Ibid.

39. Ibid.

40. Ibid.

41. Three African American jurors were rejected after defense objections: C. M. Mills, Edward DuReef, and W. T. Alexander.

42. *CNC*, April 13, 1899.

43. "Story of a Terrible Crime," *CNC*, April 12, 1899.

44. "Lake City Lynching Case: The Jury Disagrees."

45. *Charleston (S.C.) Sunday News*, April 23, 1899.

46. Ibid.

47. Ibid.

48. Finnegan, *A Deed So Accursed*, 91.

49. The case was first postponed to the fall term of 1899, then officially closed by the Department of Justice in 1909.

50. Roger K. Hux, "Lillian Clayton Jewett and the Rescue of the Baker Family, 1899–1900," *Historical Journal of Massachusetts* 19, no. 1 (Winter 1991): 13–23. After her last surviving child, Rosa, died in 1942, Lavinia Baker returned to Florence County, South Carolina; Rosa's siblings all died of tuberculosis. Lavinia Baker died in South Carolina in 1947, forty-nine years after her husband's murder.

51. "To Aid the Baker Family," *NYT*, September 21, 1899; David C. Carter, "The Lynching of Postmaster Frazier Baker and His Infant Daughter Julia in Lake City, South Carolina, in 1898 and Its Aftermath," Auburn University, accessed July 26, 2005, www.usca.edu/aasc/lakecity.html.

52. Twelfth Census of the United States, Williamsburg County, S.C., 1900, microfilm, National Archives; Thirteenth and Fourteenth Censuses of the United States, Florence County, S.C., 1910, 1920, microfilm, National Archives. Mrs. Carter was listed as postmaster in June 1900 and in 1910; in 1920, she still lived in Lake City.

53. P. Butler Thompkins, letter to the editor, *NYT*, May 24, 1899.

54. "Attack on the President," *NYT*, May 11, 1899.

55. Lyons, *Appointments Which Afro-Americans Have Received*. The Lyons pamphlet and list used language similar to that of *The Colored American Republican Text Book*, ca. 1899 (during the off-year Ohio state campaign).

56. Ibid.

57. Gatewood, *"Smoked Yankees,"* 232.

58. Ibid., 233–35.

59. Ibid., 240.

60. "Fair Treatment Wanted," *WES*, October 2, 1899.

61. Leech, *In the Days of McKinley*, 459; William McKinley to John Barber, April 13, 1899, WMcKP.

62. Leech, *In the Days of McKinley,* 459; William McKinley to John Barber, April 13, 1899, WMcKP.

63. Justesen, *George Henry White,* 257. In her letter to Washington, Mrs. White said she had been an invalid for "over three years," dating as far back as the 1898 campaign (Cora L. White to Booker T. Washington, January 3, 1902, BTWP).

64. "Southern Negro's Plaint," *NYT,* August 26, 1900.

65. "The Dream of Whitesboro," in Justesen, *George Henry White,* 357–84.

66. "Given Back to Earth, Death of Mrs. Henry P. Cheatham," *WCA,* September 30, 1899.

67. Leech, *In the Days of McKinley,* 366–78.

68. "Congressman White Talks on Conditions as They Exist across the Canadian Border," *WCA,* August 12, 1899.

69. *Negro Population, 1790–1915* (Washington: U.S. Bureau of Census, Department of Commerce, 1918), table 13: "Population by States: Negro and White," p. 43. In 1900, nearly 3.5 million blacks lived in four southern states: Alabama, Georgia, Mississippi, and South Carolina.

70. Bacote, "Negro Officeholders in Georgia under President McKinley," 234.

71. Ibid. Rucker remained Georgia's collector of internal revenue until 1910. Deveaux was collector of customs at Savannah until 1909; McHenry and Wimbish were customs collectors in Atlanta.

72. Ibid., 236.

73. Ibid., 234. Here Bacote cites a February 25, 1899, article in the *Savannah Tribune.*

74. John E. Lewis, letter dated December 30, 1899, to the (Milwaukee) *Wisconsin Weekly Advocate,* January 18, 1900, cited in Gatewood, *"Smoked Yankees,"* 233–35.

75. Ibid., 235.

76. John E. Lewis, June 5, 1898, letter to the *Illinois Record* (Springfield), published June 11, 1898, cited in Gatewood, *"Smoked Yankees,"* 31–33.

CHAPTER EIGHT

1. "A Law to Stop Lynching: Afro-American Council Wants to Make It a Crime against the United States Government," *NYT,* August 18, 1899.

2. "Text of the Resolution," *CT,* August 20, 1899.

3. Théophile T. Allain to Booker T. Washington, August 20, 1899, in *The Booker T. Washington Papers,* ed. Harlan and Smock, 5:176.

4. Editorial, *CT,* August 19, 1899.

5. White's fellow vice presidents included journalists Fortune and Chris Perry, along with Rev. Reverdy Ransom of Chicago and four denominational bishops: George Clinton and Cicero Harris (AME Zion, North Carolina); Lucius Holsey (CME, Georgia), and Benjamin Arnett (AME, Ohio).

6. Third Annual Message to Congress by President Benjamin Harrison, December 9, 1891, accessed May 29, 2018, text recorded at https://millercenter.org/the-presidency/presidential-speeches/december-9-1891-third-annual-message.

7. Ibid.

8. Alan Gauthreaux, "An Inhospitable Land: Anti-Italian Sentiment and Violence in Louisiana, 1891–1924" (University of New Orleans Theses and Dissertations, 2007), 515, https://scholarworks.uno.edu/td/515; Benjamin Harrison's Fourth Annual Message to Congress, December 6, 1892, in Messages and Papers of the Presidents, 1789–1897, Benjamin Harrison, accessed June 1, 2018, www.gutenberg.org/files/13617/13617.txt.

9. Rory K. Little, "The Federal Death Penalty: History and Some Thoughts about the Department of Justice's Role," *Fordham Urban Law Journal* 26 (1999): 367–68, https://ir.lawnet.fordham.edu/ulj/vo126/iss3/1. "An Act To Reduce the Cases in Which the Death Penalty May Be Inflicted" was sponsored in 1897 by Rep. Newton Curtis (R-N.Y.), onetime Civil War general turned ardent opponent of the death penalty.

10. Ibid., 368. The 1897 act removed the possibility of mandatory federal death sentences by empowering federal or military juries in most murder or rape cases to impose lesser penalties; in treason trials, federal judges were also authorized to impose lesser sentences. The Supreme Court ruling came in *Winston v. United States,* 172 U.S. 303 (1899), combining cases from the District of Columbia.

11. Republican Party Platform of 1896, June 18, 1896; text from the American Presidency Project, accessed May 30, 2018, www.presidency.ucsb.edu/ws/index.php?pid=29629.

12. Kathy Bennett, "Lynching," in *Tennessee Encyclopedia,* https://tennesseeencyclopedia.net/entries/lynching/, Accessed May 30, 2018.

13. Johnson, *History of Negro Soldiers,* 94–95; "Colored Regiments: The War Department Has Ordered Two to Be Formed. Company Officers to Be of the Same Race as the Men," *WES,* September 9, 1899; "Order for Two Negro Regiments," *New York Sun,* September 10, 1899.

14. Johnson, *History of Negro Soldiers,* 94–95. The seventy-one new officers had served in the Ninth and Tenth Cavalry regiments; Twenty-Third and Twenty-Fourth Infantry regiments; Seventh, Eighth, Ninth, and Tenth United States Volunteer Infantry regiments; black state volunteer regiments from Alabama, Illinois, Kansas, North Carolina, Ohio, and Virginia; and black companies from Indiana and Massachusetts.

15. "Political Leaders Call," *WES,* October 2, 1899.

16. "Fair Treatment Wanted: Delegation of Colored Men Call upon the President," *WES,* October 2, 1899. Cheatham's wife had died a week earlier; he had just returned from her burial in North Carolina. Other delegates: Jonathan Hannon, H. C. Bruce, Reuben Smith, Samuel Lacy, Julius Chilcott, and J. T. Schell.

17. "The National Council, Resolutions," *Saint Paul (Minn.) Appeal,* August 26, 1899.

18. "Fair Treatment Wanted."

19. Alexander, Shawn Leigh, *An Army of Lions: The Civil Rights Struggle before the NAACP* (Philadelphia: University of Pennsylvania Press, 2012), 128.

20. "Fair Treatment Wanted."

21. Alexander, *An Army of Lions,* 129.

22. John L. Love, *The Disfranchisement of the Negro,* pamphlet, Occasional Paper No. 6, American Negro Academy (Washington, D.C., 1899), 18. Love served on the Executive Committee of the Academy, founded by Rev. Alexander Crummell.

23. Ibid., 30, 33.

24. Leech, *In the Days of McKinley*, 424.

25. "Remarks at Quinn Chapel, Chicago, October 8, 1899," in McKinley, *Speeches and Addresses of William McKinley*, 241.

26. "President at Three Services: He Addresses Colored People at Quinn Chapel," *CT*, October 9, 1899.

27. "Vice President Hobart Dead: Surrounded by His Family as He Passes Away," *NYT*, November 22, 1899.

28. Leech, *In the Days of McKinley*, 434, 435, 438.

29. "Vice President's Funeral: Among Those Present," *NYT*, November 26, 1899. White was among at least forty-three congressmen and fifty-four senators, including North Carolina's Pritchard and Butler, who walked to the church behind the casket "through a throng such as has never crowded the streets of [Paterson]." Perhaps two hundred thousand persons lined the funeral route.

30. The most recent to die had been Vice President Thomas Hendricks, shortly after his inauguration with Grover Cleveland in 1885; Henry Wilson died in 1875, midway through Ulysses Grant's second term.

31. Michael J. Connolly, "'I Make Politics My Recreation': Vice President Garret A. Hobart and Nineteenth-Century Republican Business Politics," *New Jersey History* 125, no. 1 (2010): 20–39.

32. "Vice President's Funeral: Among Those Present."

33. Jennie Hobart's recollection is cited in *Vice Presidents of the United States, 1789–1993* (Washington, D.C.: U.S. Government Printing Office, 1997), 289–93. See also Jennie Tuttle Hobart, *Memories* (Paterson, N.J.: n.p., 1930).

34. "Mr. White's Bill," *WCA*, December 9, 1899.

35. "When M'Kinley Doth Speak," *WCA*, December 16, 1899.

36. "Now for Mr. White's Bill," *WCA*, January 6, 1900.

37. Third Annual Message to Congress by President William McKinley, italics added.

38. Ibid.

39. "Speaker Henderson: The Afro-American Has a Friend in the Chair of the National House of Representatives," *WCA*, December 16, 1899.

40. Leech, *In the Days of McKinley*, 464–65.

41. *Official Proceedings of Eleventh Republican Convention*. At least thirty black delegates from eleven southern states in 1896 were again selected as delegates in 1900, more than half from Georgia and South Carolina alone.

42. "Politics and Politicians," *Ohio State Journal* (Columbus), October 17, 1899.

CHAPTER NINE

1. "The Political Horoscope," *WCA*, January 13, 1900.

2. Ibid. Other members attending: John Bruce, H. T. Johnson, Jesse Lawson, and Richard Thompson.

3. "Gentlemen of the Pulpit, Press and Bar Participate in a Feast, Intellectual and Gastro-

nomic," *WCA,* January 13, 1900. The article, apparently penned by "Grit" Bruce, included the meal's menu, attendance list, and guests' remarks.

4. "City Paragraphs: Mr. White as a Host," *WCA,* December 9, 1899.

5. Ibid. Other guests: White's private secretary, William Hagans, and two of Cheatham's clerks, Jonathan Hannon and Henry Arnett.

6. "The Negro in Politics," *WCA,* January 6, 1900.

7. The *Independent,* a Congregationalist weekly magazine once edited by Henry Ward Beecher, published in New York from 1848 to 1928, supported abolitionism and women's suffrage. Under the editorship (1896–1913) of the minister and journalist William Hayes Ward, the magazine devoted increasing coverage to political affairs and invited outsiders' contributions.

8. George H. White, "The Injustice to the Colored Voter," *Independent,* January 18, 1900, 176–77. White's article was solicited by Ward.

9. Hernando D. Money, "Shall Illiteracy Rule?," *Independent,* January 18, 1900, 175.

10. Ibid.

11. White, "The Injustice to the Colored Voter," 176.

12. Ibid., 177.

13. "Address Adopted for Presentation to President McKinley," *WES,* December 31, 1898.

14. White, "The Injustice to the Colored Voter," 177.

15. In the Fifty-Sixth Congress, after all contests were settled, Republicans held three House seats in North Carolina, two in Tennessee, and one each in Alabama, Texas, and Virginia.

16. Benjamin R. Justesen, *Broken Brotherhood: The Rise and Fall of the National Afro-American Council* (Carbondale: Southern Illinois University Press, 2008), 51–54. *Ryanes v. Gleason* was brought by Ryanes, a longtime Louisiana voter, after he attempted unsuccessfully to reregister to vote under Louisiana's new law in July 1901.

17. "The Colored Member," *RNO,* February 2, 1900.

18. "Happy New Year: The Annual Function at the White House, Thousands Greet the President," *WES,* January 1, 1900.

19. "At the White House," *WES,* January 2, 1900.

20. Merry, *President McKinley,* 349, 380, 398.

21. "In the Sunny South," *WCA,* January 6, 1900. Commissioner-General Ferdinand Peck selected Calloway at McKinley's suggestion.

22. "The Negro Exhibit," in *Report of the Commissioner-General for the United States to the International Universal Exposition, Paris, 1900* (Washington, D.C.: U.S. Government Printing Office, 1901), 408–9, 463–67.

23. Thomas J. Calloway, "The American Negro Exhibit at the Paris Exposition," *WCA,* November 3, 1900. The article reprinted Calloway's original letter and favorable replies from Kelly Miller and Mary Terrell; college president William Councill of Alabama A&M College; Isaiah Scott, ex-president of Wiley College in Texas; and NAAC officers Fortune, Bishop Arnett, and Bishop Lucius Holsey.

24. Ibid.

25. Ibid.

26. *CR,* 56th Cong., 1st Sess., 33, 1:594, December 19, 1899.

27. John Addison Porter to George H. White, January 20, 1900, WMcKP.

28. *CR*, 56th Cong., 1st Sess., 33, 1:1021, 1022, January 20, 1900. Similar petitions signed by hundreds of Americans were introduced by White during the Fifty-Sixth Congress.

29. Pillsbury, a Harvard graduate and strong advocate for civil rights, later helped found the NAACP.

30. *CR*, 56th Cong., 1st Sess., 33, 1:1017, January 20, 1900.

31. *CR*, 56th Cong., 1st Sess., 33, 1:2153, February 23, 1900; "Mr. White's Bill," *WCA*, December 2, 1899. White and Murray had "several conferences with Attorney General Griggs and other gentlemen high in authority."

32. "Mr. White's Bill" ("The President has promised his aid to Mr. White's measure").

33. *CR*, 56th Cong., 1st Sess., 33, 1:1017, January 20, 1900.

34. "The Colored Member."

35. *CR*, 56th Cong., 1st Sess., 33, 1:1365, January 31, 1900.

36. "The Colored Member."

37. "What the Negro Really Said, and How He Afterward Tried to Get out of It," *RNO*, February 10, 1900.

38. *CR*, 56th Cong., 1st Sess., 33, 1:1507, February 5, 1900.

39. Ibid.

40. Ibid.

41. *CR*, 56th Cong., 1st Sess., 33, 1:1037, January 22, 1900, 1034.

42. Ibid. Pritchard's entire speech and debate with other senators covered eleven pages in the *Record*.

43. "Pritchard's Speech: His Reply to Senator Morgan's Argument," *WES*, January 22, 1900; "Negro's Rights Defended. Senator Pritchard Protests against Disfranchisement," *NYT*, January 23, 1900.

44. "At the White House," *WES*, February 1, 1900; "Mr. Butler on Southern Suffrage," *WES*, February 6, 1900.

45. "Congressional Campaign," *WES*, February 5, 1900.

46. "At the White House: Death Struggle in North Carolina," *WES*, February 20, 1900.

47. Ibid.; Michael J. Fawcett, "Oliver Hart Dockery," in *DNCB*, ed. Powell, 1:88. Dockery died six years later.

48. "At the White House: Personnel of the Philippine Commission Practically Complete," *WES*, February 24, 1900.

49. "The House," *WES*, February 5, 1900.

50. Simon N. D. North, "The Industrial Commission," *North American Review* 168, no. 511 (June 1899): 708–19. North resigned on July 1, 1899.

51. Ibid., 714.

52. Alabama educator Rev. Pitt Dillingham and Tennessee farmers Albert Mason and Peter Edmondson also testified.

53. *Report of the Industrial Commission*, 10:20. Witnesses listed included farmers, businessmen, state officials, academics, and representatives of federal agencies and regional and national organizations.

54. "Hearings before the Industrial Commission," in *Report of the Industrial Commission,* 10:428.

55. Ibid.

56. Ibid., 10:430.

57. Ibid., 10:426.

58. Ibid., 10:428.

59. *CR,* 56th Cong., 1st Sess., 33, 1:2151–54, February 23, 1900.

60. Merry, *President McKinley,* 392.

61. Theodore Roosevelt, "The Rough Riders: The Cavalry at Santiago," *Scribner's Magazine,* April 1899.

62. Presley Holliday, letter to the editor, dated April 22, 1899, *New York Age,* May 11, 1899. Sergeant Holliday's detailed account of the events was no attack on Roosevelt but his attempt to set the record straight; he was not unsympathetic to Roosevelt, who "thought he spoke the exact truth," and added "I cannot believe that he made that statement maliciously."

63. Roosevelt, "The Rough Riders."

64. Anthony L. Powell, "An Overview: Black Participation in the Spanish-American War," accessed July 19, 2018, www.spanamwar.com/AfroAmericans.htm. The retroactive Silver Star awards came in 1922, after a systematic review of battle records and officers' reports by the Department of the Army.

65. "Speech at Banquet of the Ohio Society of New York, New York, March 3, 1900," in McKinley, *Speeches and Addresses of William McKinley,* 361–66.

66. "The Vice Presidency," *WES,* February 13, 1900.

CHAPTER TEN

1. *CR,* 56th Cong., 1st Sess., 33, 1:2151.

2. Ibid.

3. Ibid.

4. Ibid.

5. Ibid., 1:2152. White's figures reportedly covered the period from January 1, 1898, to April 24, 1899.

6. Ibid.

7. Ibid. Statistics cited by the *New York Press* were compiled separately by *CT* and by Booker T. Washington's magazine article.

8. Ibid.

9. Ibid., 1:2153. The case of Reuben Ross, a black ex-convict hanged two weeks earlier in Robeson County after being convicted of raping a white woman, had been widely reported in the state press.

10. Ibid.

11. Ibid., 1:2153–54. Pillsbury had written the letter "to a friend of his in this city"; the unnamed friend had presumably provided the letter's contents to White for use in this presentation.

12. Ibid.

13. *CR,* 56th Cong., 1st Sess., 33, 1:573. Despite a nine-member GOP majority on the Judiciary Committee, the eight Democrats included southerners from Alabama, Arkansas, Georgia, Mississippi, Texas, and South Carolina. William Elliott's First District included Lake City, home of murdered postmaster Frazier Baker.

14. "At the White House," *WES,* March 24, 1900. C. A. Cook was proposed for a federal position; other North Carolinians that day were former Populist Rep. Harry Skinner, soon to become a Republican, and Republican James Boyd, the state's assistant attorney general.

15. "Address at the Washington Memorial Services, Mount Vernon, December 14, 1899," in McKinley, *Speeches and Addresses of William McKinley,* 355–59.

16. Ibid., 358.

17. "Speech at Banquet of the Loyal Legion, Washington, February 22, 1900," in McKinley, *Speeches and Addresses of William McKinley,* 360–61.

18. "Aroused a Storm: Commissioner Wight's Statement before a Congressional Committee," *WES,* March 31, 1900.

19. Ibid.

20. Ibid.; "At the White House: Commissioner Wight's Remarks Have Attracted Attention," *WES,* April 4, 1900.

21. *Journal of the Executive Proceedings of the Senate, 56th Congress,* April 27, 1900, 472.

22. "At the White House: President May Not Visit Charlotte," *WES,* May 5, 1900. The president was invited to attend the 125th anniversary of the Mecklenburg Declaration of Independence in Charlotte but declined because of travel conflicts.

23. "Friction between Delegates," *IS,* August 31, 1900.

24. Editorial, *WCA,* May 12, 1900; editorial, *CG,* May 26, 1900.

25. Justesen, *George Henry White,* 288. Rumors already touted White's plans to remain in Washington, D.C., or practice in the North or Midwest after Congress.

26. Editorial, *WCA,* May 26, 1900.

27. Josephus Daniels, *Editor in Politics* (Chapel Hill: University of North Carolina Press, 1941), 225.

28. Front-page cartoon, *RNO,* May 26, 1900.

29. "Jeter's Jail Birds: Three of His 'Cullud Gemmen' Come to Grief," *RNO,* June 3, 1900.

30. Ibid.

31. Ibid.

32. "Negro Week in Edgecombe: Incompetency in the Post Office at Rocky Mount," *Charlotte (N.C.) Daily Observer,* September 20, 1898.

33. "At the White House," *WES,* June 9, 1900.

34. "George William Cook," in *DANB,* ed. Logan and Winston, 124–25.

35. "At the White House," *WES,* June 14, 1900.

36. Editorial, *Kinston (N.C.) Free Press,* July 24, 1900.

37. "Negro Congressman Geo. White Writes Saying He Was Not Trying to Force Himself among Whites on the Train," *Kinston (N.C.) Free Press,* July 30, 1900.

38. Ibid.

39. Ibid.

40. Ibid.

41. Ibid. The *Free Press* noted that the Tarboro circus incident "occurred several years ago, and we have never heard before that [White] denied it in any particular."

CHAPTER ELEVEN

1. Russell published the *Maxton Blade*. Each state had one member of the notification committee; other black state delegates were William Pledger of Georgia and Edmund Deas of South Carolina.

2. *Official Proceedings of the Twelfth Republican National Convention, held in the City of Philadelphia, June 19, 20, and 21, 1900* (Philadelphia: Press of Dunlap Printing Co., 1900), 101. "Mr. Chairman, I desire to have Rules 1 and 12 re-read," White asked, "so that we might thoroughly understand the distinction."

3. Ibid., 40. Black delegates Henry Rucker of Georgia and Edward Dickerson of South Carolina were also on the resolutions committee, which held preconvention hearings and recommended platform language.

4. Ibid., 106; "The Republican Platform," *WES,* June 20, 1900.

5. Ibid.

6. *Proceedings of Twelfth Republican Convention,* 101.

7. "Is Lynch to Blame?," editorial, *CG,* June 30, 1900.

8. Lynch, *Reminiscences,* 421–36.

9. *Proceedings of Twelfth Republican Convention,* 141–42. By contrast, just two black delegates—Edmund Deas of South Carolina and Georgia's Monroe Morton—served on McKinley's 1896 notification committee; North Carolina's Hannon was the only black delegate on Hobart's committee (*Proceedings of Eleventh Republican Convention,* 212).

10. "The Republican Convention," *TS,* July 5, 1900.

11. *CR,* 56th Cong., 1st Sess., 33, 1:670–71, January 8, 1900. Pritchard here offered a new, shorter version of Senate Resolution 68, introduced weeks earlier.

12. *CR,* 56th Cong., 1st Sess., 33, 1:1028, January 22, 1900. Senate debate covered eleven pages in the *Record,* including remarks by Jeter Pritchard, South Carolina's Benjamin Tillman, and other southerners.

13. *CR,* 56th Cong., 1st Sess., 33, 1:1544; Michael Perman, *Struggle for Mastery: Disfranchisement in the South, 1888–1908* (Chapel Hill: University of North Carolina Press, 2001), 166.

14. *North Carolina Government, 1585–1979,* 464–65. Pritchard represented Madison County in the state House for three terms, beginning in 1885, when White represented Craven in the Senate.

15. "Mr. M'Kinley Is Notified," *NYT,* July 13, 1900.

16. "No Speeches by M'Kinley," *WP,* September 22, 1900.

17. "President Returns to Canton," *WP,* September 14, 1900.

18. "Hanna Back in Chicago," *NYT,* October 22, 1900. According to Merry, the president had tried, through a surrogate—Postmaster General Charles Emory Smith—to talk Hanna out of the tour (*President McKinley,* 447–48).

19. *WB,* September 15, 1900; "Ex-Representative White," *WP,* April 23, 1901.

20. J. S. Mitchell to Marion Butler, July 25, 1900, Butler Papers, Southern Historical Collection, Wilson Library, University of North Carolina at Chapel Hill. Mitchell's correspondence with Butler regarding Populist efforts in Hertford County is discussed at length in Perman, *Struggle for Mastery*, 170–71.

21. "Driven from Home, Representative White Cannot Remain in Congress," *WES*, August 25, 1900. A similar account appeared in the *NYT* the following day ("Southern Negro's Plaint," *NYT*, August 26, 1900).

22. Ibid.

23. Ibid.

24. Ibid.

25. Ibid.

CHAPTER TWELVE

1. "Senator Pritchard Denounced," *IS*, August 30, 1900.

2. Ibid.

3. Ibid.

4. "The White House," *WES*, June 16, 1898; Morgan, "Jeter Conley Pritchard." The *Evening Star* described Pritchard, a frequent visitor to the White House, as "one of the President's closest friends." Morgan does not specify which cabinet post Pritchard declined.

5. "The Afternoon Session," *IJ*, August 31, 1900.

6. "Bitter Republican Speech," *IS*, August 31, 1900.

7. Ibid.

8. Ibid. The Supreme Court's ruling helped galvanize armed overthrow of that city's Republican-dominated government in 1898.

9. Ibid.; "The Afternoon Session."

10. "Congressman White Ignored," *IS*, August 31, 1900.

11. "Two Lively Sessions," *IJ*, August 31, 1900; "Friction between Delegates," *IS*, August 31, 1900.

12. "Afro-American Press," *Indianapolis (Ind.) Recorder*, September 1, 1900.

13. "Indorsed McKinley," *Indianapolis (Ind.) Recorder*, September 1, 1900.

14. Ibid. Patronage appointees included Dancy for the *A. M. E. Zion Review*, Deveaux of the *Savannah Tribune*, and Green, representing the *Washington Bee*.

15. Ibid.

16. "Election of Officers," *IJ*, August 31, 1900.

17. "Afro-American Council: Members Endorse McKinley Administration," *Saint Paul (Minn.) Appeal*, October 13, 1900. Other Council officers signing included Cyrus Adams, Silas Harris, John Wheeler, J. S. Caldwell, O. M. Wood, John Thompson, and Frank Blagburn. Pledger, Mrs. Fox, Woods, Dancy, and Wheeler signed both.

18. "Congressman Geo. H. White Renounces the North Carolina Republican Leadership," *Windsor (N.C.) Ledger*, October 25, 1900. The open letter appeared in the *Scotland Neck Commonwealth* on October 11, 1900.

19. "Congressman Geo. H. White Renounces."

20. "Congressman Geo. H. White Renounces."

21. *Biographical Directory of the American Congress, 1774–1961* (Washington, D.C.: U.S. Government Printing Office, 1961), 1430. Martin represented the First District in the Forty-Sixth Congress (1879–81). The Martin County native also served as solicitor for the Second Judicial District—White's former office—from 1868 to 1878.

22. Editorial, *TS,* September 20, 1900.

23. Obituary, J. J. Martin, *TS,* December 20, 1900.

24. *CR,* 56th Cong., 3d Sess., 34, 1:192. The Philadelphia congressman was serving his fourteenth term at the time of his death; his vacant seat had recently been filled in a special election.

25. William McKinley to George H. White, November 12, 1900, WMcKP. The full message was boilerplate: "Please accept my cordial thanks for your message of congratulations. Assuring you that your kindly comments and good wishes are appreciated, I am very sincerely yours, William McKinley." No copy of White's message appears in the McKinley Papers.

26. "At the White House: Positions for Colored Men," *WES,* December 20, 1900.

27. "At the White House: How the Cubans Like Us," *WES,* December 29, 1900.

28. "At the White House," *WES,* December 24, 1900; "At the White House: A North Carolina Postmaster," *WES,* December 31, 1900. Victoria Martin was formally nominated by McKinley in January 1901 and confirmed by the Senate on February 7, 1901.

29. Stroupe, *Post Offices and Postmasters of North Carolina,* 2:210. Mrs. Martin was postmaster until her death in 1910 and was succeeded by Democrat Frank Liles.

CHAPTER THIRTEEN

1. Editorial, *CG,* January 12, 1901.

2. Editorial, *WCA,* January 19, 1901.

3. *CR,* 56th Cong., 2d Sess., 34, 1:737, January 8, 1901.

4. Editorial, *CG,* January 19, 1901.

5. *CR,* 56th Cong., 2d Sess., 34, 1:1635.

6. Ibid., 1:1638.

7. Ibid., 1:1637.

8. Ibid., 1:1638. Excerpts appeared the next day in many national newspapers (examples: "Mr. White's Speech. The Negro's Temporary Farewell to Congress," *WES;* "Negro Congressman Speaks," *NYT;* "Defends the Negro in House," *CT,* all January 30, 1901).

9. *CR,* 56th Cong., 2d Sess., 34, 1:1638.

10. "Valedictory of the Negro," *IF,* February 16, 1901.

11. "At the White House," *WES,* February 9, 1901.

12. "At the White House: Presidential Nominations," *WES,* February 22, 1901. After her death in 1906, Mrs. Green's son became postmaster.

13. "At the White House," *WES,* February 26, 1901.

14. "Color-Liners Not Invited: Mr. Sprague to Give a Dinner in Place of the One That Was Called Off," *CG,* February 23, 1901.

15. Ibid. Committee Democrats included Louisiana's Adolph Meyer, South Carolina's Asbury Latimer, Virginia's Peter Otey, and Tennessee's Thetus Sims, plus members from Missouri (William Cowherd), Ohio (James Norton), and New York (Bertram Clayton). See *CR*, 56th Cong., 1st Sess., 33: 574, December 18, 1899.

16. "Charles F. Sprague Dead," *NYT*, January 30, 1902.

17. Editorial, *WCA*, March 16, 1901.

18. *CR*, 56th Cong., 1st Sess., 33:188, December 12, 1899; *CR*, 56th Cong., 2d Sess., 34, 2:1268–71, January 21, 1901.

19. *CR*, 56th Cong., 2d Sess., 34, 2:1271, January 21, 1901.

20. Perman, *Struggle for Mastery*, 224–25. Perman's chapter "Exonerating the South: Congress, 1901–1906" carefully details Crumpacker's initiative and its defeat.

21. *CR*, 56th Cong., 2d Sess., 34, 2:665–66, January 7, 1901.

22. "Mr. Crumpacker's Opinion," *Baltimore Sun*, January 28, 1901.

23. Ibid.

24. *CR*, 56th Cong., 2d Sess., 34, 1:3275–78, March 1, 1901.

25. "Under the Dome," *RNO*, March 5, 1901. The speaker was freshman Rep. A. D. Watts of Iredell County, aide to future senator Furnifold Simmons.

26. Ibid.

27. "Here and There," *WCA*, March 9, 1901.

28. "Howard University in Public Life," *WCA*, March 2, 1901; "Condensed Locals," *WES*, March 22, 1901; "An Honored Guest," *IF*, April 2, 1901.

29. The verses were taken from the Bible's book of Proverbs 16, verses 20 and 21.

30. "At the White House: Prominent Negroes Call," *WES*, March 6, 1901.

31. Ibid. Others attending: vice president Harry Smith, secretary Cyrus Adams, and Frederick McGhee, legislative bureau director; and members A. T. Arnett, Ferdinand Barnett, John Crossland, Jesse Lawson, and Peter Smith.

32. "Washington: The Capital City and Its Happenings," *Saint Paul (Minn.) Appeal*, March 9, 1901.

33. "Prominent Negroes Call."

34. Ibid.

35. "At the White House: Protest against a Negro Postmaster," *WES*, March 6, 1901.

36. "At the White House," *WES*, April 13, 1901; "At the White House: May Not Go Back to His Home," *WES*, April 16, 1901.

37. "May Not Go Back to His Home."

38. Ibid.

39. Ibid.

40. "Mr. White's Dilemma," editorial, *WP*, April 18, 1901. "May Transfer Mr. Youngblood, Ex-Representative Aldrich Talked of for Position as Auditor," *WP*, April 20, 1901.

41. "Ex-Representative White," *WP*, April 24, 1901.

42. Ibid.

43. Ibid.

44. Ibid.

45. White's total was a slight exaggeration: Just 177 of 185 signatures appended to the peti-

tion for White's appointment belonged to congressmen (171 present or former Republican House members, one Republican territorial delegate, one Democratic House member, and four Republican senators). The remaining eight were Republican politicians not in Congress (see Personnel records, U.S. Department of the Treasury, National Archives, College Park, Md.).

46. Sen. Nathan Scott (R-W.V.) chaired the Republican national speakers committee in 1900. There is no copy in White House files of the letter White mentions, nor does it accompany White's petition in Treasury Department records.

47. "Ex-Representative White."

48. "Question of Common Sense," *WP,* May 7, 1901.

49. "Why Leave?," *WB,* April 20, 1901.

50. "Mr. White Is Not a Cheap Man," *WCA,* April 27, 1901; Lead editorial, *WCA,* May 4, 1901.

51. "Hon. George H. White," editorial, *IF,* May 4, 1901; editorial, *IF,* May 25, 1901; untitled editorial, *CG,* May 25, 1901. See also editorials from the *Charleston (S.C.) Messenger* and *Springfield (Ill.) State Capitol,* reprinted on the *Washington Bee*'s front page of May 11, 1901.

52. George B. Cortelyou to George H. White, June 1, 1901, WMcKP; George B. Cortelyou to George H. White, June 4, 1901, WMcKP. No copy of either White letters appears in the McKinley Papers.

53. *WCA,* December 29, 1900, February 2, May 25, June 1, 1901.

54. "Graduates from Eckstein Norton University," *LCJ,* June 8, 1901; "African American Schools in Bullitt County, Kentucky," Notable Kentucky African Americans Database, accessed September 3, 2018, www.nkaa.uky.edu/nkaa/items/show/2725. Founded in 1890 by William Simmons and Charles Parrish, and named for the president of the Louisville and Nashville Railroad, the tiny black industrial school offered primary, elementary, and high school programs, plus baccalaureate degrees. Eckstein Norton granted 189 bachelor's degrees before merging with Lincoln Institute in 1911 and closing in 1912

55. Legal brief for *State ex rel. David J. Ryanes vs. Jerry M. Gleason, Registrar,* No. 65,432. Published under the Auspices of the Legal Bureau, National Afro-American Council, and issued from the offices of the Secretary of the Bureau, 2011 Vermont Avenue, Washington, D.C., in Daniel Murray Pamphlet Collection, Library of Congress.

56. "Negro Colonists to Work Together," *WCA,* February 9, 1901; *WCA,* February 23, 1901; *WP,* February 1, 1901. Whether the group acted independently or was a front for White's investors—to prevent sellers from raising their price once outside buyers were revealed—is unclear. The final price of $14,000 was clearly beyond the means of the Cape May City group. See "The Dream of Whitesboro," in Justesen, *George Henry White,* 356–59.

CHAPTER FOURTEEN

1. "Washington News," *Saint Paul (Minn.) Appeal,* May 25, 1901; "Graduates from Eckstein Norton University," *LCJ,* June 8, 1901. White was also commencement speaker at Greenville School, location unknown.

2. William Klaess, "The President of the Whole People: William McKinley's Visit to Texas in 1901" (Ph.D. diss., Texas Christian University, 2015), 3; "Trip of President," *Dallas Morning News,* April 14, 1901. The train passed through Virginia, Tennessee, Mississippi, Alabama, and

Louisiana en route to Texas, then through New Mexico and Arizona territories before reaching California.

3. Merry, *President McKinley*, 452. Dr. Rixey was head of the U.S. Navy's Bureau of Medicine and Surgery. The president sought Rixey's assistance in 1899 to "take medical charge" of Mrs. McKinley's health.

4. Leech, *In the Days of McKinley*, 575–77.

5. "Seeing New Orleans: Calls at the Southern University for Colored Students," *WES*, May 2, 1901. Southern University, chartered by Louisiana's legislature in 1880, relocated to Baton Rouge in 1913. Its Magazine Street campus was bought by Xavier University, a preparatory school-college founded by Mother Katharine Drexel in 1915.

6. "Seeing New Orleans"; "Aimed to Murder McKinley: Crank Arrested in New Orleans before President Arrived," *WES*, May 3, 1901. The three private black schools were Leland University (Baptist, 1870–1915) and Straight University (Congregational, 1869–1934), which later merged to form Dillard University, and New Orleans University, a Methodist Episcopal school (1870–1935). See "Southern University: From New Orleans to Scotlandville (1880–1914)," accessed September 5, 2018, www.creolegen.org.

7. "The Prairie View A&M Story," accessed September 3, 2018, www.pvamu.edu/about_pvamu/college-history. Established in 1876 as the Alta Vista Agricultural and Mechanical College of Texas for Colored Youth, the school was a normal training school in 1878, then became a federal land-grant college after the Hatch Act of 1887 and Morrill Act of 1890, and is known today as Prairie View A&M University.

8. "Defends the Negro: The President's Kind Word," *WB*, May 11, 1901.

9. Ibid.

10. Ibid.

11. Klaess, "The President of the Whole People," 6–7. Anson Jones's term as president of the Republic of Texas ended in 1846, when Texas joined the Union. After her husband's death in 1859, Mrs. Jones raised four children and pursued extensive business interests; in 1901, she was president of the Daughters of the Republic.

12. "On the Mexican Border: Welcomed by Representatives of Two Nations," *NYT*, April 22, 1891.

13. Klaess, "The President of the Whole People"; "Past Presidential Visits: William McKinley in 1901," *El Paso (Tex.) Times*, May 7, 1901; "At City of El Paso Thousands of People Greeted Presidential Party," *McKinney (Tex.) Democrat*, May 9, 1901.

14. Klaess, "The President of the Whole People," 16.

15. Ibid., 19–20.

16. Leech, *In the Days of McKinley*, 576–78.

17. Ibid., 580–81; "Is Warmly Praised, President's Renunciation of Third-Term Candidacy," *WES*, June 12, 1901.

18. Leech, *In the Days of McKinley*, 579–80.

19. "Washington, D.C.: A Dull Season in Summer, But Our Correspondent Finds Plenty of News Items," *IF*, July 27, 1901.

20. "A Pilot the Demand," editorial, *IF*, March 9, 1901.

21. Ibid.; "Washington, D.C.: A Dull Season in Summer"; "Up the Palisades," *WCA*, May 11,

1901. "The distinguished gentleman was never more witty and eloquent. The rafters shook with applause after his speech."

22. Alexander Walters to Booker T. Washington, June 27, 1901, in *The Booker T. Washington Papers,* 6:151; Albert E. Pillsbury to Booker T. Washington, July 30, 1901, ibid., 6:183.

23. Pillsbury to Washington, July 30, 1901.

24. "Bad Nigger with a Winchester: Colored Editors Declare for Armed Resistance to Lynch Law," *WP,* August 7, 1901.

25. "Bad for the Negro, Cheatham Claims," *WP,* August 8, 1901.

26. Ibid.

CHAPTER FIFTEEN

1. "Race Prejudice Law on Church, So Bishop Tanner Tells Afro-American Council: Government Is Attacked for Its Treatment of the Negro Soldiers in the Matter of Promotion: Ex-Congressman White Attacks Bishop Walters," *Atlanta Constitution,* August 10, 1901. Tanner edited the *Christian Recorder.* Barnett, a Chicago attorney, owned the *Chicago Conservator,* now edited by his wife, Ida Wells-Barnett.

2. "Ex-Congressman White Attacks Bishop Walters."

3. "Ex-Congressman White Indignant," *WB,* August 17, 1901; "The Afro-American Council: The Meeting a Farce," *WB,* August 17, 1901.

4. "At Philadelphia," editorial, *IF,* August 17, 1901.

5. "Echoes of the Afro-American Council," *WCA,* August 31, 1901.

6. Editorial, *CG,* August 24, 1901.

7. Emmett J. Scott to Booker T. Washington, August 13, 1901, in *The Booker T. Washington Papers,* ed. Harlan and Smock, 6:186.

8. "Splitting the Solid South," *WES,* August 9, 1901. Representative Blackburn's prediction would not come true; he himself would be defeated in 1902, although he would later win a second term.

9. "Buffalo Men at Canton: Pan-American Exposition Committee Arranges for President's Day," *NYT,* August 10, 1901; "President to Visit Buffalo," *WES,* August 10, 1901.

10. "President and His Wife Are in Excellent Health," *BC,* September 5, 1901.

11. "Artillery Salute," *BC,* September 5, 1901.

12. "Proudest Day in Buffalo's History"; "All Records at Gates Broken," *BC,* September 6, 1901.

13. William McKinley's speech in Buffalo, New York, September 5, 1901, text from https://millercenter.org/the-presidency/presidential-speeches/september-5-1901-speech-buffalo-new-york.

14. Ibid.

15. Ibid.

16. Ibid.

17. Ibid.

18. Ibid.

19. Ibid.

20. Ibid.

21. Ibid.

22. Ibid.

23. Ibid.

24. Ibid.

25. Ibid.

26. Ibid.

27. Ibid.

28. European colonies in the Western Hemisphere included the three Guianas, British Honduras, and Jamaica in the Caribbean, plus the Danish Virgin Islands.

29. "Trip through the Foreign Buildings," *BC*, September 6, 1901.

30. Aubrey Parkman, *David Jayne Hill and the Problem of World Peace* (Lewisburg, Pa.: Bucknell University Press, 1975), 87. Led by William Buchanan, exposition director-general and former U.S. minister to Argentina, the delegates included former U.S. minister to Siam John Barrett, industrialist Volney Foster, journalist Charles Pepper, and ex-senator Henry Davis of West Virginia, the only holdover from the 1890 conference.

31. M. Romero, "The Pan-American Conference," *North American Review* 151, no. 406 (September 1890): 354–66.

CHAPTER SIXTEEN

1. "Lynching: It Was Vigorously Condemned by the National Association of Colored Women," *Buffalo Commercial*, July 13, 1901; "Negro Educators: The Annual Convention of the National Association Is Being Held in Buffalo," *Buffalo Commercial*, July 16, 1901.

2. "The People of the State of New York against Leon F. Czolgosz," unpublished trial transcript, September 26, 1901, 23–24. Buffalo Police Superintendent William Bull quoted Czolgosz during his interrogation, saying "that he had been to the Pan American Grounds on several occasions prior to the President's visit to Buffalo; that he was on the Exposition Grounds the day the President delivered his speech, and stood near the speaker's stand; that he went there with the determination to kill the President."

3. "Negro Exhibit: Buffalo Negroes Think Their Race Should Be Recognized at the Pan-American Exposition," *Buffalo Commercial*, November 12, 1900.

4. Thomas J. Calloway to Booker T. Washington, March 1, 1901, BTWP.

5. *Buffalo Express*, January 6, 1901.

6. Miles Everett Travis, "Mixed Messages: Thomas Calloway and the 'American Negro Exhibit' of 1900" (master's thesis, University of Montana at Bozeman, 2004).

7. "Speedy Inspection," *BC*, September 6, 1901.

8. See William Loos, Ami Savigny, Robert Gurn, and Lillian Williams, *The Forgotten "Negro Exhibit": African American Involvement in Buffalo's Pan-American Exposition, 1901* (Buffalo, N.Y.: Buffalo/Erie County Public Library, 2001).

9. Richard H. Barry, *An Historic Memento of the Nation's Loss: The True Story of the Assassination of President McKinley at Buffalo* (Buffalo, N.Y.: Robert Allan Reid, 1901), 20.

10. Ibid., 21.

11. "Secret Service Guard Ireland Tells Story of Anarchist's Deed," *BC,* September 7, 1901.

12. *Los Angeles Times,* September 10, 1901.

13. "Parker Gets Little Credit from Foster," *BC,* September 10, 1901.

14. Barry, *True Story of the Assassination,* 21–22.

15. *Buffalo Times,* September 10, 1901.

16. Ibid.

17. "Our Uncrowned Hero," from *New York Journal,* reprinted in *Colored American Magazine,* October 1901, 448–51.

18. Ibid.

19. Merry, *President McKinley,* 481–82.

20. "Report of the Autopsy," Executive File, William McKinley, September 12–14, 1901, George Bruce Cortelyou Papers, Library of Congress. The autopsy report was signed by fourteen physicians, including Preston Rixey—personal physician to the president and first lady—and two U.S. Army surgeons, W. P. Kendall and Edward Munson. Dr. Rixey became surgeon general of the U.S. Navy in 1902.

21. "O'Brien or Gallagher? Who Saved the President from a Third Bullet? Quackenbush's Story," *Buffalo Express,* September 13, 1901.

22. Roger Pickenpaugh, *McKinley, Murder, and the Pan-American Exposition: A History of the Presidential Assassination, September 6, 1901* (Jefferson, N.C.: McFarland, 2016), 248.

23. Ibid., 303–9.

24. "The People against Leon F. Czolgosz."

25. "The Past and the Present," editorial, *WCA,* September 21, 1901.

26. Booker T. Washington, letter to the editor, dated September 23, 1901, *Montgomery (Ala.) Advertiser,* reprinted in *Colored American,* October 5, 1901.

27. "Negroes Mourn McKinley," *WCA,* September 21, 1901.

28. Cleveland Suarez, "William McKinley," *Colored American Magazine,* October 1901.

29. "The Past and the Present."

30. "Parker to Lecture," *WES,* October 8, 1901; *WCA,* October 12, 1901. According to the *Colored American* article, Parker was accompanied to the White House by editor Edward Cooper and Baltimore political leader Hiram Cummings.

31. "Assassination of President Described," *WES,* October 9, 1901; "Parker Tells His Story," *WCA,* October 12, 1901.

32. "Parker Tells His Story."

33. Ibid.

34. "The J. B. Parker Fund," *WCA,* September 28, 1901.

35. "The Case of J. B. Parker," *BC,* September 26, 1901.

EPILOGUE

1. George H. White to Booker T. Washington, October 7, 1901, BTWP. A handwritten notation atop the archived letter reads, "Not Answd, 10/9."

2. Emmett J. Scott to Booker T. Washington, October 4, 1901, in *The Booker T. Washington Papers,* ed. Harlan and Smock, 6:224.

3. Cora L. White to Booker T. Washington, January 3, 1902, BTWP.

4. George H. White to Booker T. Washington, January 22, 1902, BTWP. "Had I been advised of her intentions, I would have persuaded her not to have written you, when your position so well known to me . . . leads your efforts in an entirely different direction from that of politics. . . . Yes, an evil one in no less personage than Senator Jeter C. Pritchard . . . is the one who takes delight in misrepresenting and speaking disparagingly of me."

5. The scandal was duly recounted by the *WP* and *WES* throughout December 1901. See, for example, "Cheatham Must Vacate, President Decides Not to Reappoint Him as Recorder of Deeds," *WP,* December 18, 1901.

6. Dr. John Crossland of Saint Joseph, Missouri, an obscure Republican activist, was confirmed in 1902 to succeed Smith. He was forced to resign in disgrace in 1903, after a racy scandal involving the wife of another man and an unseemly physical struggle, including use of a firearm, inside the Monrovia embassy.

7. More than 180 Republican officials, including nearly every House Republican in late 1900, signed White's application for auditorship before the Fifty-Sixth Congress adjourned in March 1901. See "Geo. H. White Makes Application for Auditor: Brief," an undated list presumably compiled in December 1900, in U.S. Treasury personnel records found in the National Archives.

8. "Hon. George H. White Takes the Stand," *WCA,* June 7, 1902.

9. Ibid.

10. Ibid.

11. History, United States Census Bureau, accessed February 16, 2019, www.census.gov/history/www/census_then_now/director_biographies/directors_1893_-_1909.html.

12. Della White married Oscar Garrett, Knox College graduate and principal of the black public schools in Asheville, North Carolina. Garrett practiced law in Philadelphia and New York City; after 1910, Della Garrett returned—ironically, as a federal clerk—to Washington, D.C. Roosevelt's nominations of Dancy as recorder of deeds and Crossland as U.S. minister to Haiti were the most visible first-term black appointees.

13. Justesen, "African American Consuls Abroad." Other Roosevelt appointees: Dr. Jarvis Bowens (Guadeloupe), Jerome Peterson (Puerto Cabello), Herbert Wright (Utila), James Carter (Tamatave), and Dr. William Yerby (Freetown).

14. "Announces His Candidacy for Congress, Has Always Been a Stalwart Party Man," *Philadelphia Tribune,* March 30, 1912.

15. Vare served seven terms in Congress before his controversial 1926 election to the U.S. Senate by ousting the incumbent; the Senate refused to seat Vare in 1929, citing fraud in the primary (see Samuel J. Astorino, "The Contested Senate Election of William Scott Vare," *Pennsylvania History* 28, no. 2 [April 1961]: 187–201).

16. George H. White, "What Should Be the Negro's Attitude in Politics?," in *Twentieth Century Negro Literature, or a Cyclopedia of Thought on Vital Topics Relating to the American Negro,* ed. Daniel W. Culp (Napierville, Ill.: J. L. Nichols, 1902), 224–27.

17. The disease, identified by American neurologist George Beard in 1869, was often

called "nervous exhaustion." The U.S. Centers for Disease Control and Prevention renamed it as "chronic fatigue syndrome" in 1988 (see http://www.medlink.com/article/chronic_fatigue_syndrome).

18. "McKinley Protector Mad?," *NYT,* March 23, 1907.

19. Ida S. McKinley to George B. Cortelyou, February 6, 1906, George Bruce Cortelyou Papers. Mrs. McKinley wrote, "I am also enclosing a letter from J. B. Parker, the negro who evidently did his best to aid my precious husband when he was in such need and if you would advise me as to the best way in helping him I would be very much obliged." A year later, Cortelyou became Treasury secretary.

20. Undated enclosure in letter from Ida S. McKinley to George B. Cortelyou, February 6, 1906, George Bruce Cortelyou Papers. The stationery belonged to Dr. Francis Hagner, a genitourinary specialist who apparently treated Parker for an unspecified illness. Dr. Hagner later became attending physician to President William H. Taft.

21. Carl Sferazza Anthony, *Ida McKinley: The Turn-of-the-Century First Lady through War, Assassination, and Secret Disability* (Kent, Ohio: Kent State University Press, 2013), 291–92.

22. "Prosperity His Undoing," *WP,* March 23, 1907.

23. "Dissect Body of Hero: Medical Students at Work on McKinley's Defender," *WP,* March 27, 1908.

24. *CR,* 71st Cong., 2d Sess. (1930), 1:3382.

25. "George P. White," obituary, *NYT,* December 30, 1918.

26. "Geo. White, Last Negro Congressman, Dead," *RNO,* December 29, 1918. The AP story listed White's residence while in Congress as Craven County—no longer in the "Black Second" District—rather than Edgecombe County, to which White moved in 1894.

27. W. E. B. DuBois, "A Negro Congressman," *Crisis,* April 1919.

28. Joel Williamson, "Thomas Dixon, Jr.," in *DNCB,* ed. Powell, 2:79–80; "Weaver Closes 'Clansman' after Hearing Protest," *Philadelphia Inquirer,* October 24, 1906. Author Dixon (b. 1862), was a Johns Hopkins University graduate who served in the 1885 North Carolina House as a Democrat from Cleveland County, while White served in the state Senate. Dixon's first novel, *The Leopard's Spots* (1902), sold a million copies; it was the basis for *The Clansman.* "In 1881 I had the privilege—I will not say the pleasure—to sit in the South [*sic*] Carolina legislature with this man Dixon, who wrote the play," White told the *Inquirer.* "He was mistrusted and shunned by his fellow legislators." But he probably confused the younger Dixon with an older Republican legislator with whom he served in the 1881 House, Greene County's William Thomas Dixon.

29. Du Bois, "A Negro Congressman."

30. T. Thomas Fortune, "Sudden Death of George Henry White," *Philadelphia Tribune,* January 4, 1919.

31. Ibid.

BIBLIOGRAPHY

PRIMARY SOURCES

Manuscript Collections

Library of Congress, Washington, D.C.
   George Bruce Cortelyou. Papers.
   William McKinley. Papers.
   Daniel Murray. Pamphlet collection.
   Booker T. Washington. Papers.
   Carter G. Woodson. Papers.

Ohio Historical Society, Columbus
   George A. Myers. Papers.

Southern Historical Collection, Wilson Library, University of North Carolina at Chapel Hill
   Marion Butler. Papers.

Western Reserve Historical Society, Cleveland, Ohio
   John P. Green. Papers (microfilmed version, Library of Congress).

Newspapers, 1895–1919

Atlanta (Ga.) Constitution
Atlanta (Ga.) Journal
Baltimore (Md.) Sun
Boston Globe
Brooklyn (N.Y.) Daily Eagle
Buffalo (N.Y.) Commercial
Buffalo (N.Y.) Courier
Buffalo (N.Y.) Enquirer
Buffalo (N.Y.) Times
Charleston (S.C.) News & Courier
Charlotte (N.C.) Daily Observer
Chicago Defender

Chicago Inter-Ocean
Chicago Tribune
Cleveland (Ohio) Gazette
Dallas (Tex.) Morning News
El Paso (Tex.) Times
Indianapolis (Ind.) Freeman
Indianapolis (Ind.) Journal
Indianapolis (Ind.) Recorder
Indianapolis (Ind.) Sentinel
Kinston (N.C.) Free Press
Louisville (Ky.) Courier-Journal
McKinney (Tex.) Democrat
New York Age
New York Sun
New York Times
Ohio State Journal (Columbus)
Philadelphia Inquirer
Philadelphia Record
Philadelphia Tribune
Pine Bluff (Ark.) Daily Graphic
Raleigh (N.C.) Gazette
Raleigh (N.C.) Morning Post
Raleigh (N.C.) News and Observer
Richmond (Va.) Planet
Roanoke News (Plymouth, N.C.)
Saint Louis (Mo.) Daily Globe-Democrat
Saint Louis (Mo.) Palladium
Saint Paul (Minn.) Appeal
Saint Paul (Minn.) Daily Globe
Springfield (Ill.) State Capital
Tarboro (N.C.) Southerner
Washington (D.C.) Bee
Washington (D.C.) Colored American
Washington (D.C.) Evening Star
Washington (D.C.) Post
Wilmington (N.C.) Messenger
Wilmington (N.C.) Morning Star
Windsor (N.C.) Ledger

Magazines and Other Publications

Colored American Magazine
Crisis
Harper's Weekly
Independent
Prologue
Saturday Evening Post
Scribner's Magazine

Government Publications

Post Office Department Records of Appointment of Postmasters. National Archives, microfilm.
State of Louisiana. Records of the Louisiana Supreme Court, Baton Rouge. University of New Orleans Library.
State of North Carolina. *North Carolina Government, 1585–1979: A Narrative and Statistical History*. Raleigh: North Carolina Department of the Secretary of State, 1981.
U.S. Congress. *Congressional Directory of the Fifty-Sixth Congress, 1899.*
———. *Congressional Record*, 52nd–57th Congresses.
———. *Journal of the Executive Proceedings of the Senate, 55th Congress.*
———. *Journal of the Executive Proceedings of the Senate, 56th Congress.*
———. *Preliminary Report of Commission of the Constitution League of the United States on the Affray at Brownsville, Tex.*, 59th Cong., 2d Sess., S. Doc. No. 107.
U.S. Department of Commerce, Census Office. *Negro Population, 1790–1915*. Washington, D.C.: U.S. Government Printing Office, 1918.
———. Twelfth Census (1900).
U.S. Department of State. Dispatches from Havana, 1898. RG 59, National Archives, Washington, D.C.
U.S. Department of the Treasury. Personnel records, U.S. Department of the Treasury, National Archives, College Park, Md.
U.S. Government Printing Office. *Biographical Directory of the American Congress, 1774–1961*. Washington, D.C., 1961.
———. *Official Register of the United States, Containing a List of the Officers and Employees, Civil, Military, and Naval Service, together with a List of Vessels Belonging to the United States, July 1, 1897*. Washington, D.C., 1897.
———. *Official Register of the United States, July 1, 1899*. Washington, D.C., 1899.
———. *Official Register of the United States, July 1, 1901*. Washington, D.C., 1901.

——. *Report of the Commissioner-General for the United States to the International Universal Exposition, Paris, 1900.* Washington, D.C., 1901.

———. *Report of the Industrial Commission on Agriculture and Agricultural Labor, Including Testimony, with Review and Topical Digest Thereof, Volume X.* Washington, D.C., 1901.

——. *Vice Presidents of the United States, 1789–1993.* Washington, D.C., 1997.

SECONDARY SOURCES

Books, Pamphlets, Dissertations

Adams, Cyrus Field. *The National Afro-American Council, Organized 1898: A History of the Organization, Its Objects, Synopses of Proceedings, Constitution and By-Laws, Plan of Organization, Annual Topics, Etc.* Washington, D.C.: Cyrus F. Adams, Secretary, 1902.

Alexander, Shawn Leigh. *An Army of Lions: The Civil Rights Struggle before the NAACP.* Philadelphia: University of Pennsylvania Press, 2012.

American Historical Society. *A Standard History of Oklahoma,* Vol. 3. Chicago: American Historical Society, 1916.

American Presidency Project. Miller Center, University of Virginia, Charlottesville. www.presidency.ucsb.edu/ws/index.php?pid=29538.

Anderson, Eric. *Race and Politics in North Carolina, 1872–1901: The Black Second.* Baton Rouge: Louisiana State University Press, 1981.

Anthony, Carl Sferazza. *Ida McKinley: The Turn-of-the-Century First Lady through War, Assassination, and Secret Disability.* Kent, Ohio: Kent State University Press, 2013.

Art Souvenir of the Republican National Convention Held at Philadelphia, June 19–22, 1900, An. Philadelphia: Gatchell and Manning, 1900.

Astor, Gerald. *The Right to Fight: A History of African Americans in the U.S. Military.* Novato, Calif.: Presidio, 1998.

Bacote, Clarence A. "The Negro in Georgia Politics, 1880–1908." Ph.D. diss., University of Chicago, 1955.

Barry, Richard H. *An Historic Memento of the Nation's Loss: The True Story of the Assassination of President McKinley at Buffalo.* Buffalo, N.Y.: Robert Allan Reid, 1901.

Cecelski, David S., and Timothy B. Tyson, ed. *Democracy Betrayed: The Wilmington Race Riot of 1898 and Its Legacy.* Chapel Hill: University of North Carolina Press, 1998.

Christopher, Maurine. *America's Black Congressmen.* New York: Thomas Y. Crowell, 1971.

Croly, Herbert. *Marcus Alonzo Hanna: His Life and Work.* New York: Macmillan, 1912.

Crow, Jeffrey J., and Robert F. Durden. *Maverick Republican in the Old North State: A Political Biography of Daniel L. Russell.* Baton Rouge: Louisiana State University Press, 1977.

Culp, Daniel W., ed. *Twentieth Century Negro Literature: Or, A Cyclopedia of Thought on the Vital Topics Relating to the American Negro.* Napierville, Ill.: J. L. Nichols, 1902.

Daniels, Josephus. *Editor in Politics.* Chapel Hill: University of North Carolina Press, 1941.

———. *Tar Heel Editor.* 1939. Reprint, Westport, Conn.: Greenwood, 1974.

Duster, Alfreda M., ed. *Crusade for Justice: The Autobiography of Ida B. Wells.* Chicago: University of Chicago Press, 1970.

Edmonds, Helen G. *The Negro and Fusion Politics in North Carolina, 1894–1901.* Chapel Hill: University of North Carolina Press, 1951.

Finnegan, Terence. *A Deed So Accursed: Lynching in Mississippi and South Carolina, 1881– 1940.* Charlottesville: University Press of Virginia, 2013.

Fletcher, Marvin. *The Black Soldier and Officer in the United States Army, 1891–1917.* Columbia: University of Missouri Press, 1974.

Franklin, John Hope, and August Meier, eds. *Black Leaders of the Twentieth Century.* Urbana: University of Illinois Press, 1982.

Gatewood, Willard B., Jr. *Aristocrats of Color: The Black Elite, 1880–1920.* Bloomington: Indiana University Press, 1990.

———. *Black Americans and the White Man's Burden, 1898–1903.* Urbana: University of Illinois Press, 1975.

———. *"Smoked Yankees" and the Struggle for Empire: Letters from Negro Soldiers, 1898–1902.* Fayetteville: University of Arkansas Reprint Series, 1987.

Gauthreaux, Alan. "An Inhospitable Land: Anti-Italian Sentiment and Violence in Louisiana, 1891–1924." University of New Orleans Theses and Dissertations, 2007.

Green, John P. *Facts Stranger Than Fiction: Seventy-Five Years of a Busy Life with Reminiscences of Many Great Men and Women.* Cleveland, Ohio: n.p., 1920.

Harlan, Louis R. *Booker T. Washington: The Making of a Black Leader, 1856–1901.* New York: Oxford University Press, 1972.

———. *Booker T. Washington: The Wizard of Tuskegee, 1901–1915.* New York: Oxford University Press, 1983.

Harlan, Louis R., and Raymond Smock, eds. *The Booker T. Washington Papers.* Urbana: University of Illinois Press, 1972–89.

Harvey, Charles M., ed. *History of the Republican Party Together with the Proceedings of the Republican National Convention at St. Louis, June 16th–18th, 1896.* St. Louis, Mo.: I. Haas Publishing and Engraving, 1896.

Hobart, Jennie Tuttle. *Memories.* Paterson, N.J.: n.p., 1930.

Johnson, Donald, comp. *National Party Platforms.* Vol. 1, *1840–1956.* Urbana: University of Illinois Press, 1978.

Johnson, Edward A. *A History of Negro Soldiers in the Spanish-American War and Other Items of Interest.* Raleigh, N.C.: Capital Printing Company, 1899.

Justesen, Benjamin R. *Broken Brotherhood: The Rise and Fall of the National Afro-American Council.* Carbondale: Southern Illinois University Press, 2008.

———. *George Henry White: An Even Chance in the Race of Life.* Baton Rouge: Louisiana State University Press, 2001.

———, ed. *In His Own Words: The Writings, Speeches, and Letters of George Henry White.* Lincoln, Nebr.: iUniverse, 2004.

Kenzer, Robert C. *Enterprising Southerners: Black Economic Success in North Carolina, 1865–1915.* Charlottesville: University Press of Virginia, 1997.

Klaess, William. "The President of the Whole People: William McKinley's Visit to Texas in 1901." Ph.D. diss., Texas Christian University, 2015.

Leech, Margaret. *In the Days of McKinley.* New York: Harper and Brothers, 1959.

Logan, Rayford W. *The Betrayal of the Negro, from Rutherford B. Hayes to Woodrow Wilson.* Reprint, New York: Da Capo, 1997.

Logan, Rayford W., and Michael R. Winston, eds. *Dictionary of Negro Biography.* New York: Norton, 1982.

Loos, William, Ami Savigny, Robert Gurn, and Lillian Williams. *The Forgotten "Negro Exhibit": African American Involvement in Buffalo's Pan-American Exposition, 1901.* Buffalo, N.Y.: Buffalo/Erie County Public Library, 2001.

Lynch, John Roy. *Reminiscences of an Active Life.* Edited by John Hope Franklin. Chicago: University of Chicago Press, 1970.

Lyons, Judson W. *Appointments Which Afro-Americans Have Received from President McKinley.* Washington, D.C.: n.p., 1898.

McKinley, William. *Speeches and Addresses of William McKinley, March 7, 1897 to May 30, 1900.* New York: Doubleday and McClure, 1900.

Merry, Robert W. *President McKinley: Architect of the Twentieth Century.* New York: Simon and Schuster, 2017.

Official Proceedings of the Eleventh Republican National Convention, Held in the City of St. Louis, June 16, 17, and 18, 1896. St. Louis: n.p., 1896.

Official Proceedings of the Twelfth Republican National Convention, Held in the City of Philadelphia, June 19, 20, and 21, 1900. Philadelphia: Dunlap Printing, 1900.

Perman, Michael. *Struggle for Mastery: Disfranchisement in the South, 1888–1908.* Chapel Hill: University of North Carolina Press, 2001.

Phillips, Kevin. *William McKinley.* The American Presidents Series, edited by Arthur M. Schlesinger Jr. New York: Times Books; Henry Holt, 2003.

Pickenpaugh, Roger. *McKinley, Murder, and the Pan American Exposition: A History of the Presidential Assassination, September 6, 1901.* Jefferson, N.C.: McFarland, 2016.

Powell, William S., ed. *Dictionary of North Carolina Biography.* 6 vols. Chapel Hill: University of North Carolina Press, 1979–97.

Prather, H. Leon. *We Have Taken a City: Wilmington Racial Massacre and Coup of 1898.* Cranbury, N.J.: Associated University Presses, 1984.

Rauchway, Eric. *Murdering McKinley: The Making of Theodore Roosevelt's America.* New York: Hill and Wang, 2003.

Reaves, William M. *Strength through Struggle: The Chronological History of the African-American Community in Wilmington, North Carolina, 1865–1950.* Wilmington, N.C.: New Hanover County Public Library, 1998.

Sherman, Richard B. *The Republican Party and Black America: From McKinley to Hoover, 1896–1933.* Charlottesville: University Press of Virginia, 1973.

Stroupe, Vernon L., ed. *Post Offices and Postmasters of North Carolina, Colonial to USPS.* 4 vols. Newell: North Carolina Postal History Society, 1996.

Thornbrough, Emma Lou. *T. Thomas Fortune, Militant Journalist.* Chicago: University of Chicago Press, 1972.

Walters, Alexander. *My Life and Work.* New York: Revell, 1917.

Washington, Booker T. *My Larger Education: Being Chapters from My Experience.* New York: Doubleday, Page, 1909.

———. *Selected Speeches of Booker T. Washington.* Edited by Ernest Davidson Washington. Garden City, N.Y.: Doubleday, Doran, 1932.

———. *Up from Slavery.* New York: Doubleday, Page, 1901.

Articles and Essays

Adams, Cyrus Field. "The Afro-American Council, the Story of Its Organization—What It Stands For—Its Personnel." *Colored American Magazine,* March 1903.

Bacote, Clarence A. "Negro Officeholders in Georgia under President McKinley." *Journal of Negro History* 44, no. 3 (July 1959): 217–39.

Bennett, Kathy. "Lynching." In *Tennessee Encyclopedia.* https://tennesseeencyclopedia.net/entries/lynching/. Accessed May 30, 2018.

Calloway, Thomas J. "The American Negro Exhibit at the Paris Exposition." *Colored American,* November 3, 1900.

Chestnut, Trichita M. "Lynching: Ida B. Wells-Barnett and the Outrage over the Frazier Baker Murder." *Prologue* 40 (Fall 2008): 20–29. U.S. National Archives & Records Administration, Washington, D.C.

Connolly, Michael J. "'I Make Politics My Recreation': Vice President Garret A. Hobart and Nineteenth-Century Republican Business Politics." *New Jersey History* 125, no. 1 (2010): 20–39.

"The Destruction of USS Maine." U.S. Department of the Navy, Naval Historical Center. Accessed May 2, 2019. www.history.navy.mil/browse-by-topic/disasters-and-phenomena/destruction-of-uss-maine.html.

Du Bois, W. E. B. "A Negro Congressman." *Crisis* 9 (April 1919).

Dunbar, Paul Laurence. "Negro Life in Washington." *Harper's Weekly* 44 (January 13, 1900): 32.

——. "Negro Society in Washington." *Saturday Evening Post* 174 (December 14, 1901): 9, 18.

Fawcett, Michael J. "Oliver Hart Dockery." In *DNCB*, ed. Powell, 1:88.

Fisher, Mary M. "Benjamin W. Arnett." In *DANB*, ed. Logan and Winston, 17–18.

Fortune, T. Thomas. "Sudden Death of George H. White, Esq., Saturday Morning." *Philadelphia Tribune,* January 4, 1919.

Gatewood, Willard B. "Alabama's 'Negro Soldier Experiment,' 1898–1899." *Journal of Negro History* 57 (October 1972): 333–34.

——. "James Hunter Young." In *DNCB*, ed. Powell, 296–98.

——. "Kansas Negroes and the Spanish-American War." *Kansas Historical Quarterly* 38 (Autumn 1971): 307–8.

——. "North Carolina's Negro Regiment in the Spanish-American War." *North Carolina Historical Review* 48 (October 1971): 373–75.

Gratwick, Harry. "Remembering Mainers on Board the USS Maine." Accessed May 2, 2019. www.WorkingWaterfront.com.

Harlan, Louis R. "The Secret Life of Booker T. Washington." *Journal of Southern History* 37 (August 1971): 393–416.

Heine, Nancy Gordon Heine. "Charles Young." In *DANB*, edited by Logan and Winston, 677–79.

Hernandez, Jose M. "Cuba in 1898." In "The World of 1898: The Spanish-American War." Accessed May 2, 2019. Hispanic Division, Library of Congress. www.loc.gov/rr/hispanic/1898/hernandez.html.

Historian, U.S. Postal Service. *List of Known African American Postmasters, 1800s.* Accessed June 26, 2019. pdf file. https://about.usps.com/who-we-are/postal-history/african-american-postmasters- 19thc.pdf. 2017.

Hux, Roger K. "Lillian Clayton Jewett and the Rescue of the Baker Family, 1899–1900." *Historical Journal of Massachusetts* 19, no. 1 (Winter 1991): 13–23.

Justesen, Benjamin R. "African American Consuls Abroad, 1897–1909." *Foreign Service Journal* (September 2004): 72–76.

——. "African American Postmasters in North Carolina, 1874–1909." *North Carolina Postal Historian* 25, no. 2 (Spring 2006): 3–11.

——. "Black Tip, White Iceberg: Black Postmasters and the Rise of White Supremacy in North Carolina, 1897–1901." *North Carolina Historical Review* 82 (April 2005): 193–227.

——. "George Henry White and the End of an Era." *Washington History* 15, no. 2 (Fall/Winter 2003–4): 34–51.

———. "George Henry White, Josephus Daniels, and the Showdown over Disfranchisement, 1900." *North Carolina Historical Review* 77 (January 2000): 1–33.

Livingston, Rebecca. "Sailors, Soldiers, and Marines of the Spanish-American War: The Legacy of USS *Maine*." *Prologue* 30, no. 1 (Spring 1998). U.S. National Archives & Records Administration, Washington, D.C.

Love, John L. *The Disfranchisement of the Negro.* Pamphlet. Occasional Paper No. 6. Washington, D.C.: American Negro Academy, 1899.

Marszalek, John F. "Henry O[ssian] Flipper." In *DANB,* edited by Logan and Winston, 227–28.

McLaurin, John L. "The Race Problem." *Washington Post,* November 27, 1898.

Money, Hernando L. "Shall Illiteracy Rule?" *Independent,* January 18, 1900.

Morgan, Joe L. "Jeter Conley Pritchard." In *DNCB,* ed. Powell, 5:139.

North, Simon N. D. "The Industrial Commission." *North American Review* 168, no. 511 (June 1899): 708–19.

Powell, Anthony L. "An Overview: Black Participation in the Spanish-American War." Accessed July 19, 2018. www.spanamwar.com/AfroAmericans.htm.

"The Prairie View A&M Story." Accessed September 3, 2018. www.pvamu.edu/about_pvamu/college-history.

Roosevelt, Theodore. "The Rough Riders: The Cavalry at Santiago." *Scribner's Magazine,* April 1899.

Terrell, Mary Church. "Society among the Colored People of Washington." *Voice of the Negro* 1 (March 1904): 150–56.

Thompson, Richard W. "Phases of Washington Life." *Indianapolis (Ind.) Freeman,* June 8, 15, 1895.

White, George Henry. "Congressman White's Address." *Southern Workman and Hampton Institute Record* 38 (1899): 244–45.

———. "Injustice to the Colored Voter." *Independent* 52 (January 18, 1900): 176–77.

———. "What Should Be the Negro's Attitude in Politics?" In *Twentieth Century Negro Literature: Or, A Cyclopedia of Thought on the Vital Topics Relating to the American Negro,* edited by Daniel W. Culp (Napierville, Ill.: J. L. Nichols, 1902), 224–27.

The William F. Powell Elementary School, Camden, N.J. Accessed May 21, 2018. www.dvrbs.com/camden- school/CamdenNJ-School-WiiliamFPowell.htm.

Williamson, Joel. "Thomas Dixon, Jr." In *DNCB,* ed. Powell, 2:79–80.

Winston, Michael R. "George William Cook." In *DANB,* ed. Logan and Winston, 124–25.

INDEX

CPSIA information can be obtained
at www.ICGtesting.com
Printed in the USA
LVHW032017261120
672688LV00004B/95